Grammarway 4

Jenny Dooley-Virginia Evans

Express Publishing

Published in 1999 by Express Publishing

Liberty House Greenham Business Park, Newbury,
Berkshire RG19 6HW, United Kingdom
Tel.: (0044) 1635 817 363
Fax: (0044) 1635 817 463
email: inquiries@expresspublishing.co.uk.
www.expresspublishing.co.uk.

© Jenny Dooley – Virginia Evans

Design & Illustration © Express Publishing, 1999

Colour Illustrations: Evan

First published 1999
Fourteenth impression 2016

Made in EU

ISBN: 978-1-903128-97-8

Note: To download the Picture Flashcards visit:
  http://www.teachers-corner.co.uk/free-resources

Contents

Introduction

Grammarway 4 is the fourth book in a four-level grammar series presented in full colour. The book is designed for learners of the English language at upper-intermediate level, and can be used for self-study or in the classroom as a supplement to any course at this level.

The aim of the book is to help learners understand English grammar structures through comprehensive theory tables and functional examples, accompanied by a wealth of attractive photographs and illustrations.

The book consists of **12 units**, each focusing on a particular grammar topic.

A typical unit contains:

- presentation of the grammar structure by means of visual prompts
- simple, concise explanation of the grammar structure
- examples in everyday conversational English, together with a few expressions showing slightly more formal use
- exercises practising the new structures, to help learners use appropriate patterns in everyday situations
- speaking and writing activities to practise the new structures in oral and written form
- a revision box in each unit
- common mistakes section
- word-formation exercises

A **revision unit** follows every three units to consolidate material presented in previous units.

Six Progress Tests, each covering two consecutive units, are included at the end of the book. They may be used to assess students' progress before the main class test.

The **Picture Flashcards** which accompany the book can be used for lively, motivating presentation of the target grammar structures.

The book adheres to the principle that every structure should first be heard, then practised in oral, and finally, in written form. Based on the use of full-colour visual stimuli, the book encourages learners to speak before writing, and allows them to practise English structures through a variety of enjoyable and useful activities.

The Student's Book is accompanied by a **Teacher's Book** containing:

- guidance on presenting the theory of each unit, with or without
  Picture Flashcards
- a full key to the exercises in the Student's Book
- four tests with two different versions of each test

Thanks

The authors would like to thank Rania Dunn, Eva Mitchel, Laura Houston, Tamzin Thompson and Steven Davies for their help in producing this book. Many thanks to the Express Publishing design team E. Morrison, J. Malls and V. Winston. We would also like to thank those institutions and teachers who piloted the manuscript, and whose comments and feedback were invaluable in the production of the book.

Present Forms

Present Simple

We use the present simple:

a) **for permanent states, repeated actions and daily routines.**

*He **works** in a bank.*
(permanent state)
*He **takes** the train to work every morning.*
(daily routine/repeated actions)

b) **for general truths and laws of nature.**

*The sun **sets** in the west.*

c) **for timetables (planes, trains, etc.) and programmes.**

*The plane from Brussels **arrives** at 8:30.*

d) **for sports commentaries, reviews and narration.**

*a) Peterson **overtakes** Williams and **wins** the race. (sports commentary)*
*b) Mike Dalton **plays** the part of Macbeth. (review)*
*c) Then the prince **gets** on his horse and quickly **rides** away. (narration)*

e) **to give instructions or directions (instead of the imperative).**

*You **sprinkle** some cheese on the pizza and then you **bake** it. (Instead of: Sprinkle some cheese on the pizza ...)*

The present simple is used with the following time expressions: *usually, often, always, etc., every day/ week/month/year, in the morning/afternoon/ evening, at night, at the weekend, on Mondays, etc.*

Present Continuous

We use the present continuous:

a) **for actions taking place now, at the moment of speaking.**

*He **is giving** the baby a bath at the moment.*

b) **for temporary actions; that is actions that are going on around now, but not at the actual moment of speaking.**

I'm looking for a new job these days.

(He is not looking for a job at the moment of speaking.)

c) **with adverbs such as: always, constantly, continually, etc. for actions which happen very often, usually to express annoyance, irritation or anger.**

*a) I'm **always meeting** Sara when I go shopping. (action which happens very often)*
*b) You're **constantly interrupting** me when I'm talking. (expressing annoyance/irritation)*

d) **for actions that we have already arranged to do in the near future, especially when the time and place have been decided.**

*They're **moving** into their new house next week. (The time has been decided.)*

e) **for changing or developing situations.**

*More and more species **are becoming** extinct.*

The present continuous is used with the following time expressions: *now, at the moment, at present, these days, still, nowadays, today, tonight, etc.*

Present Perfect

We use the present perfect:

a) for an action which started in the past and continues up to the present, especially with state verbs such as *be, have, like, know,* etc. In this case, we often use *for* and *since.*

   Rachel has had the dog for three years. (She got the dog three years ago and she still has it.)

b) for an action which has recently finished and whose result is visible in the present.

   She has just washed her hair. (She has now wrapped her hair in a towel, so the action has finished.)

c) for an action which happened at an unstated time in the past. The exact time is not mentioned because it is either unknown or unimportant. The emphasis is placed on the action.

   The Taylors have bought a sailing boat. (The exact time is unknown or unimportant. What is important is the fact that they now own a sailing boat.)

d) for an action which has happened within a specific time period which is not over at the moment of speaking. We often use words and expressions such as *today,* this *morning/evening/week/month,* etc.

   She has taken fifteen pictures today. (The time period - today - is not over yet. She may take more pictures.)

   BUT: *She took twenty pictures yesterday. (The time period - yesterday - is over.)*

Note: We use the present perfect to announce a piece of news and the past simple or past continuous to give more details about it.

   The police have finally arrested Peter Duncan. He was trying to leave the country when they caught him.

The present perfect is used with the following time expressions: *for, since, already, yet, always, just, ever, never, so far, today, this week/month,* etc., *how long, lately, recently, still (in negations),* etc.

Present Perfect Continuous

We use the present perfect continuous:

a) to put emphasis on the duration of an action which started in the past and continues up to the present, especially with time expressions such as *for, since, all morning/day/ year,* etc.

   Sam has been talking on the phone for half an hour. (He began talking on the phone half an hour ago and he is still talking.)

b) for an action which started in the past and lasted for some time. The action may have finished or may still be going on. The result of the action is visible in the present.

   Her feet hurt. She has been walking all morning. (The result of the action is visible in the present - her feet hurt.)

c) to express anger, irritation or annoyance.

   *Somebody **has been giving away** our plans.*

   (The speaker is irritated.)

Note: With the verbs *live, work, teach* and *feel* (= have a particular emotion) we can use the present perfect or present perfect continuous with no difference in meaning.

   We have lived/have been living here for twenty years.

The present perfect continuous is used with the following time expressions: *for, since, how long, lately, recently.*

Note: We use the present perfect to put emphasis on number and the present perfect continuous to put emphasis on duration.

Compare the examples:
e.g. *I've typed* four reports so far.
I've been typing reports all morning.

Adverbs of Frequency

◆ Adverbs of frequency (*always, usually, often, sometimes, seldom/rarely, never*, etc.) come before the main verb (*read, work*, etc.) but after the verb *to be*, auxiliary verbs (*do, have*, etc.) or modal verbs (*can, should*, etc.). Adverbs of frequency go before the auxiliary verbs in short answers.
e.g. Susan *often goes* skiing at the weekend.
Kim *is sometimes* rude to other people.
You *can always* call me if you need help.
'Do you help your mother with the housework?'
'Yes, I *usually do*.'

◆ Expressions such as *every day, once/twice a week/month*, etc., *most mornings/evenings*, etc. go at the beginning or the end of a sentence. *Usually, often, sometimes, normally* and *occasionally* can go at the beginning or the end of a sentence for more emphasis.
e.g. We go on holiday *twice a year*.
Usually, I finish work at five.
I feel bored *sometimes*.

◆ The adverbs *never, seldom* and *rarely* have a negative meaning and are never used with the word *not*.
e.g. I *rarely* go to bed late. (NOT: ~~I rarely don't go ...~~)

 Underline the correct tense.

1 The plane *leaves*/*has left* at four o'clock. We must be at the airport by two o'clock.
2 It *gets*/*is getting* colder and colder every day.
3 Have you seen Linda? I *have been looking*/*am looking* for her for almost an hour.
4 Sam is a very interesting person. He *knows*/*has known* all kinds of unusual facts.
5 First, you *are heating*/*heat* the oven to a temperature of 180˚C.
6 Have you heard the news? They *have just elected*/*have been electing* a new club chairman!
7 Martha *is finding*/*has found* a new job. She is starting next week.

8 The teacher *has been correcting*/*has corrected* essays for three hours.
9 Michael's car broke down last week, so he *uses*/*is using* his father's for the time being.
10 It rarely *gets*/*is getting* very hot in Britain.

 Choose the correct answer.

1 'I met our new boss this morning.'
'I ...C... him, too. He's very nice.'
A am meeting   B have been meeting   C have met

2 '................. in a hotel?'
'No, but my parents did last summer in Rome.'
A Have you ever stayed   B Did you ever stay
C Are you ever staying

3 'Who is in that new film?'
'Well, a young actress .... the leading role.'
A has been playing   B plays   C has played

4 'Is David at home?'
'Yes, but he .... a shower at the moment.'
A is having   B has been having   C has

5 'Why are you so upset?'
'I .... my favourite ring.'
A lose   B have been losing   C have lost

6 'Have you found a house yet?'
'No. I .... with my aunt at the moment.'
A stay   B am staying   C have stayed

 Put the *adverbs of frequency* in the correct position.

1 A: Do you wear sunglasses in the winter?
B: No, I do. (never)
No, I never do.
2 A: Do you like fishing, Alan?
B: Yes, I go fishing at weekends. (sometimes)
3 A: Do you go to the gym very often?
B: Yes, I go. (once a week)
4 A: How often do you visit your parents?
B: I visit them. (every weekend)
5 A: Do you eat in restaurants very often?
B: No, I do. (rarely)
6 A: Do you like oysters?
B: I don't know. I have eaten oysters. (never)
7 A: How often do you go on holiday?
B: I go on holiday. (once a year)
8 A: When do you read your post?
B: I read it on the way to work. (usually)
9 A: Shall I lock the door?
B: Of course. You should lock the door when you go out. (always)
10 A: You are breaking things! (always)
B: I'm sorry. I don't mean to.

4 **Identify the tenses, then match them to the correct descriptions.**

1 The plane to Sydney **leaves** at eleven o'clock.
2 I **have written** two letters this morning.
3 They'**re going** on holiday on Saturday.
4 Graham **has known** Errol for five years.
5 You'**re always leaving** the door open.
6 We **are rehearsing** a new play at the moment.
7 George **has bought** a new car.
8 Lisa **has been cleaning** the house all morning.
9 Look! Alison **has dyed** her hair!
10 More and more people **are recycling** their rubbish.

a actions which started in the past and continue up to the present
b action which has recently finished and whose result is visible in the present
c to put emphasis on the duration of an action which started in the past and continues up to the present
d to express criticism or annoyance
e timetables and programmes
f actions that we have arranged to do in the near future
g action which has happened within a specific time period which is not over at the moment of speaking
h action which happened at an unstated time in the past
i changing or developing situations
j temporary actions

5 **Put the verbs in brackets into the correct *present form*.**

1 A: Tortoises ...*live*... (live) to be very old.
  B: I've heard of one which is over a hundred years old.
2 A: Are you still busy?
  B: Yes. I .... (read) this article for an hour and I still .... (not/finish).
3 A: More and more people .... (go) to university these days.
  B: Yes. I think it's a good thing.
4 A: I .... (have) a party tonight. Do you want to come?
  B: Yes. What time does it start?
5 A: Why are your shoes wet?
  B: I .... (wash) the car.
6 A: What's the matter?
  B: I .... (break) my ankle.
7 A: What do I need to do next?
  B: You .... (add) the sugar to the mixture and you .... (mix) it well.
8 A: Who .... (use) my car?
  B: I have.
9 A: Are you new here?
  B: No. Actually, I .... (live) here for almost ten years.
10 A: Pete is playing his music very loud.
  B: Again! He .... (always/do) that!
11 A: Have you made plans for Saturday yet?
  B: I .... (go) to the cinema with Jack.
12 A: Mr Collins is a very good teacher.
  B: Well, he .... (teach) Maths for twenty-five years, you know.
13 A: Are you going to the concert on Saturday night?
  B: Yes. Actually, I .... (already/buy) the tickets.
14 A: Hello, Simon.
  B: Oh! We .... (always/meet) each other in this supermarket.

6 **a) Put the verbs in brackets into the correct tense.**

Dear Kathleen,

    I **1)** ...*'m writing*... (write) to tell you my news. My school **2)** .... (choose) me to spend six weeks at a school in the USA. I'm very happy about it!
    At the moment, I **3)** .... (pack) things for my trip, because I **4)** .... (leave) next week. My mother **5)** .... (book) the ticket.
    I **6)** .... (wait) for this opportunity for ages, so I'm very excited. I **7)** .... (finish) reading two books about the USA and I **8)** .... (borrow) another one from the school library. I **9)** .... (become) more and more nervous every day!
    Well, I must go now. I've got a lot of things to do. I'll write to you from the USA.

                                            Love,
                                            Tracy

b) Which of the *present forms* in the text above are used to express:

1 actions which happened at an unstated time in the past ☐
2 actions which started in the past and continue up to the present with emphasis on duration ☐
3 actions happening at or around the moment of speaking ☐ ☐
4 changing and developing situations ☐
5 actions that we have arranged to do in the near future ☐

State Verbs

State Verbs are verbs which describe a state rather than an action and therefore do not normally have continuous tenses. These include:

a) **verbs which express likes and dislikes:** *like, love, dislike, hate, enjoy, prefer, adore,* etc. *e.g. I love chocolate ice cream.*

b) **verbs of the senses:** *see, hear, smell, taste, feel, look, sound.* We often use *can* or *could* with these verbs when we refer to what we see, hear, etc. at the moment of speaking. *e.g. Jim must be at home. I can see his car parked outside.*

c) **verbs of perception:** *know, believe, understand, realise, remember, forget, notice, recognise, think, seem, see (=understand), expect (=think),* etc. *e.g. I expect they will be late.*

d) **some other verbs such as** *be, contain, include, belong, fit, need, matter, cost, mean, own, want, owe, have (=possess), require, weigh, wish, keep (=continue),* etc. *e.g. My uncle owns a hotel.*

Some of the above verbs are used in continuous tenses when they describe actions and not states. Study the following examples:

1 I **think** he's lying. (= believe)
I'm **thinking** about the plan. (= am considering)
2 The food **tastes** delicious. (= has a delicious flavour)
He **is tasting** the food. (= is testing the flavour of)
3 I can **see** some people. (= perceive with my eyes)
I **see** what you mean. (= understand)
I'm **seeing** my doctor tomorrow. (= am meeting)
4 It **looks** as if they've finished the job. (= appears)
Mike **is looking** out of the window. (is directing his eyes.)

5 This perfume **smells** nice. (= has a nice smell)
He **is smelling** the milk. (= is sniffing)
6 The baby's hair **feels** like silk. (= has the texture of)
She **is feeling** the baby's forehead. (= is touching)
7 Bob **has** a Porsche. (= possesses)
He'**s having a shower** at the moment. (= is taking a shower)
8 The chicken **weighs** 2 kilos. (= has a weight of)
The butcher **is weighing** the meat. (= is measuring how heavy it is)
9 This dress **fits** you perfectly. (= it is the right size)
We **are fitting** new locks. (= are putting in)
10 He **appears** to be nervous. (= seems)
He **is appearing** in a new play. (= is taking part)
11 He **is** a rude person. (= character - permanent state)
He **is being** rude. (= behaviour - temporary situation, usually with adjectives such as *careful, silly, (im)polite, lazy,* etc.)

Note: a) The verb *enjoy* can be used in continuous tenses to express specific preference.
e.g. I'm enjoying this party a lot. (specific preference)
BUT: *I enjoy going to parties. (I enjoy parties in general.)*

b) The verbs *look* (when we refer to a person's appearance), *feel* (= experience a particular emotion), *hurt* and *ache* can be used in either the continuous or simple tenses with no difference in meaning.
e.g. You look/are looking great today.

---

 7 Put the verbs in brackets into the *present simple* or the *present continuous*.

1 A: Why ...*are you smelling*... (you/smell) the soap?
B: It .... (smell) lovely. It's like roses!
2 A: Why .... (you/taste) the soup?
B: To see if it .... (taste) good. I think it needs more salt.
3 A: I .... (feel) very tired.
B: You should go to bed early.
4 A: I .... (see) Andy this evening.
B: I .... (see). So, you don't want to come to the cinema with me, do you?
5 A: How much ....
.... (the bag of apples/weigh)?
B: I don't know yet. The man .... (weigh) the bag now.
6 A: I .... (think) about buying a new car soon.
B: Why? I .... (think) your car is fine. You don't need a new one.
7 A: What .... (you/look) at?
B: The sky. It .... (look) as if it's going to rain.

8 A: I really .... (enjoy) home-made food.
B: So do I, and I .... (enjoy) every bit of this meal.
9 A: Why .... (you/feel) the radiator?
B: It .... (feel) cold in here. Is the heating on?
10 A: That famous opera singer .... (appear) at the opera house tonight.
B: Yes. He .... (appear) to be feeling better after his operation.
11 A: Chris .... (be) a sensible person, isn't he?
B: Yes, but in this case he .... (be) rather foolish.
12 A: My dad .... (fit) the old blind from the living room in my bedroom today.
B: Really? .... (it/fit) that window?
13 A: My back .... (hurt).
B: Why don't you lie down for a while?

Have gone (to) / Have been (to)

◆ She **has gone to** the office. *(This means she has not come back yet. She is still at the office.)*

◆ He **has been to** Rome twice. *(This means that he has visited Rome twice; he is not there now. He has come back.)*

Note: In this case *been* **is used as the past participle of the verb** *to go.*

8 **Fill in the gaps with** *have / has been (to)* **or** *have / has gone (to).*

1 A: Hello, Jim! Have you seen Mum?
  B: Yes. She ...*has gone to*... the shops. She'll be back soon.
2 A: Where .... you .... today?
  B: I .... the cinema.
3 A: Shall we go on a picnic this weekend?
  B: Oh, yes! I .... not .... on a picnic for ages.
4 A: I'm going to India this year.
  B: I .... never .... India.
  A: Really? I .... there twice before.
5 A: Where are the children?
  B: They...............................the park to play football.
  A: .... Dad .... with them?
  B: Of course. Don't worry!

9 **Underline the correct word in bold.**

1 I **always/already** do the housework on Saturdays.
2 We haven't booked our summer holiday **just/yet**.
3 My brother has **just/ever** joined the football club.
4 Linda has **already/ever** bought a new dress for the party.
5 Have you **so far/ever** tasted Japanese food?
6 Joe has been in Paris **since/for** two weeks.
7 I have **never/just** seen this film before.
8 The secretary has typed twenty letters **yet/so far** this morning.
9 I have been working here **since/still** July.
10 The Taylors have moved house **recently/so far**.
11 They **still/already** haven't employed a new supervisor.

10 **Put the verbs in brackets into the correct** *present* **form.**

1 A: Linda ...*is learning*... (learn) to drive at the moment.
  B: I know. She told me last week.
2 A: Has Alan got a job?
  B: Oh yes. He .... (be) the manager of a leisure centre.
3 A: Do you want to have a break now?
  B: Not yet. I .... (write) a report for tomorrow's meeting.
4 A: It's ten o'clock. Have you given the manager his letters?
  B: Yes, and I .... (also/type) six reports so far this morning.
5 A: Is Jeff still in the garden?
  B: Yes. He .... (plant) flowers all afternoon.
6 A: That author is very well-known, isn't she?
  B: Yes. She .... (write) twenty novels so far.
7 A: You look very happy today.
  B: I am. I .... (just/hear) some good news.
8 A: What time .... (the play/ start) tonight?
  B: Seven o'clock, I think.
9 A: Are you new to this company?
  B: Not really. In fact, I .... (work) here for almost two years.
10 A: Are you ready for the concert?
  B: Yes. I .... (practise) for weeks.
11 A: Do you do any exercise at all?
  B: Yes. Actually, I .... (go) swimming three times a week.

11

Past Forms

Past Simple

We use the past simple:

a) for an action which happened at a definite time in the past. The time is stated, already known or implied.

*They **went** camping by the lake last month. (When did they go camping? Last month. The time is stated.)*

b) for actions which happened immediately one after the other in the past.

*First she **paid** the driver, then she **got out** of the taxi.*

c) for past habits or states which are now finished. In such cases we can also use the expression *used to*.

*Kitchens **were/used to be** very different a hundred years ago.*

The past simple is used with the following time expressions: *yesterday, then, when, How long ago ...?, last night/week/month/year/Tuesday,* etc., *three days/weeks,* etc. *ago, in 1997,* etc.

Past Continuous

We use the past continuous:

a) for an action which was in progress at a stated time in the past. We do not mention when the action started or finished.

*At seven o'clock yesterday evening they **were having** dinner. (We do not know when they started or finished their dinner.)*

b) for an action which was in progress when another action interrupted it. We use the past continuous for the action in progress (longer action) and the past simple for the action which interrupted it (shorter action).

*He **was walking** down the street when he **ran into** an old friend.*

c) for two or more simultaneous past actions.

*She **was talking** on her mobile phone while she **was driving** to work.*

d) to describe the atmosphere, setting, etc. in the introduction to a story before we describe the main events.

*One beautiful autumn afternoon, Ben **was strolling** down a quiet country lane. The birds **were singing** and the leaves **were rustling** in the breeze.*

The past continuous is used with the following time expressions: *while, when, as, all morning/evening/day/night,* etc.

Past Perfect

We use the past perfect:

a) for an action which happened before another past action or before a stated time in the past.

She had finished work when she met her friends for coffee. (She finished work first and then she met her friends.)

b) for an action which finished in the past and whose result was visible in the past.

He was happy. He had signed an important contract. (The action finished in the past and its result was visible in the past, too.)

Note: The past perfect is the past equivalent of the present perfect.

e.g. a) *He had fixed the old armchair. It looked brand new. (The action —had fixed— happened in the past. The result —looked brand new— was also visible in the past.)*

b) *He has fixed the old armchair. It looks brand new. (The action —has fixed— happened in the past. The result —looks brand new— is still visible in the present.)*

The past perfect is used with the following time expressions: *before, after, already, just, for, since, till/ until, when, by, by the time, never,* etc.

Note: We can use the past perfect or the past simple with *before* or *after* without any difference in meaning.
e.g. *They went out after it had stopped / stopped raining.*

Past Perfect Continuous

We use the past perfect continuous:

a) to put emphasis on the duration of an action which started and finished in the past before another past action or a stated time in the past, usually with *since* or *for*.

They had been looking for a house for six months before they found one they liked.

b) for an action which lasted for some time in the past and whose result was visible in the past.

Last Friday Ron had to fly to New York. His flight was delayed. *He was annoyed. He had been waiting at the airport for three hours. (He waited at the airport for three hours and the result of the action was visible in the past, too.)*

Note: The past perfect continuous is the past equivalent of the present perfect continuous.

e.g. a) *I had been driving for ten hours, so I felt exhausted. (The action —had been driving— lasted for some time in the past. The result —felt exhausted— was also visible in the past.)*

b) *I have been driving for ten hours, so I feel exhausted. (The action —have been driving— started in the past. The result —feel exhausted— is still visible in the present.)*

The past perfect continuous is used with the following time expressions: *for, since, how long, before, until,* etc.

11

A *Brian and Ruth went on a day trip yesterday. Look at the notes below and say what they did, using the linking words from the list.*

first, then, next, after that, later, finally

S1: First, they travelled to Brighton by train.

9:15 - 10:30:	travel to Brighton by train
10:30 - 11:30:	look around shops
11:30 - 12:30:	walk on beach
12:30 - 2:00:	eat lunch at seaside restaurant
2:00 - 4:30:	visit funfair
4:30 - 5:30:	have afternoon tea

B **Now, in pairs, ask and answer questions about what Brian and Ruth were doing at the times in the list below, as in the example.**

SA: What were Brian and Ruth doing at half past nine in the morning?

SB: They were travelling to Brighton by train.

9:30 am	11:45 am	2:30 pm
11:00 am	1:15 pm	5:00 pm

12 **Put the verbs in brackets into the *past simple* or the *past continuous*.**

A The sun **1)** ...*was shining*... (shine) and the birds **2)** .... (sing) as Mike **3)** .... (drive) down the country lane. He **4)** .... (smile), because he **5)** .... (look forward) to the journey ahead. Mike **6)** .... (enjoy) driving, especially when he **7)** .... (go) somewhere new. Then, suddenly, the engine **8)** .... (begin) to make a strange noise and the car **9)** .... (stop) dead in the middle of the road. Mike **10)** .... (try) to start it, but nothing **11)** .... (happen). He **12)** .... (sigh), then **13)** .... (get out) of the car. As he **14)** .... (push) the car to the side of the road, Mike **15)** .... (start) to wish he had stayed at home.

B John **1)** .... (enter) his flat and **2)** .... (close) the door. He **3)** .... (hang up) his coat when he **4)** .... (hear) a strange noise. A tap **5)** .... (run) in the kitchen. He **6)** .... (walk) into the kitchen and **7)** .... (turn) it off. Then, he **8)** .... (freeze). Someone **9)** .... (stand) behind him. He **10)** .... (take) a deep breath and **11)** .... (turn) around. His flatmate, Steve, **12)** .... (lean) in the doorway. 'You

13) .... (give) me a fright!' John exclaimed. Steve **14)** .... (laugh) at him. John **15)** ....(start) to laugh, too. 'I **16)** .... (think) you had gone to London today,' he said. 'No,' **17)** .... (reply) Steve. 'Unfortunately, I **18)** .... (miss) the train.'

13 **Choose the correct answer.**

1 'Were you expecting James and Paul to stay for dinner?'
'No, but I ...*A*... a lot of food, so it didn't matter.'
A had prepared **B** was preparing
C had been preparing

2 'Tony has been singing for years, hasn't he?'
'Yes. He .... his first record when he was sixteen.'
A made **B** was making **C** had made

3 'There was a power cut last night.'
'I know. I .... some paperwork when the lights went out.'
A had been doing **B** was doing
C had done

4 'Did you see Paul Simon in concert?'
'No. I was hoping to get tickets, but they ....'
A had sold out **B** sold out
C were selling out

5 'The restaurant was packed last night.'
'Yes. Luckily, I .... a table in advance.'
A was booking **B** had booked
C had been booking

6 'Did you watch the film yesterday?'
'No. It .... by the time we got home.'
A finished **B** was finishing
C had finished

7 'Did you stay up late last night?'
'No. I .... all day, so I went to bed early.'
A had been working **B** worked
C was working

8 'Did you enjoy your holiday?'
'Yes. We .... most of our time on the beach.'
A had spent **B** were spending **C** spent

9 'Kim looked tired this morning.'
'I know. She .... all night long.'
A studied **B** had studied
C had been studying

10 'So what happened?'
'We .... through the woods when we heard a gunshot.'
A had walked **B** walked **C** were walking

Used to/Be used to/ Get used to/Would

◆ We use **used to + infinitive** to refer to **past habits or states**. In such cases, *used to* can be replaced by the past simple with no difference in meaning.
e.g. They **used to travel**/*travelled* a lot when they were younger. *(They don't any more).*

◆ We use the **past simple**, and not *used to*, in the following cases:

a) to refer to an action which happened at a **definite time in the past**.
e.g. I **drove** to work yesterday. *(NOT: I used to drive to work yesterday.)*

b) to say how many times an action happened at a **definite time in the past**.
e.g. I **went** to the cinema four times last month. *(NOT: I used to go to the cinema four times last month.)*

◆ We use **would/used to** for repeated actions or routines in the past.
e.g. We **would**/*used to* eat out on Sundays.

We do not use *would* with state verbs.
e.g. a) They **used to live** in London.
(NOT: They would live in London. - state)
b) I **used to have** a pet dog.
(NOT: I would have a pet dog.)

◆ **Be used to + noun/pronoun/-ing form = be accustomed to, be in the habit of**
e.g. a) They **are used to the cold**. *(present)*
b) I don't mind walking. I'm **used to it**. *(present)*
c) She **wasn't used to living** in the country. *(past)*

◆ **Get used to + noun/pronoun/-ing form = become accustomed to**
e.g. a) I **am getting used to the weather**. *(present)*
b) He didn't like using the computer at first, but **he got used to it**. *(past)*
c) She **will** soon **get used to wearing** contact lenses. *(future)*

14 **Choose the correct answer.**

1 'Sharon looks different now, doesn't she?'
'Yes. She ...*B*... to have long dark hair, didn't she?'
A is used   B used   C would

2 'I have never driven an automatic car before.'
'You will soon .... to it.'
A get used   B be used   C used

3 'How is Sarah?'
'She's fine. She .... to life in the countryside.'
A got used   B used   C is getting used

4 'Have you always worked as a nurse?'
'No. I .... a childminder.'
A was used to being   B used to be
C am used to being

5 'Do you remember when we were little?'
'Yes. Dad .... always read us a bedtime story.'
A was used to   B would   C got used to

6 'Aren't you tired?'
'No. I .... to walking long distances.'
A am used   B got used   C used

7 'Jane had trouble with her job at first.'
'Yes. She .... to working on her own.'
A used   B got used   C wasn't used

8 'Did you find your degree course difficult?'
'Yes, but I soon .... to it.'
A used   B got used   C was used

9 'Do you remember Uncle Danny?'
'Yes. He .... always bring us presents.'
A would   B was used   C used

10 'Have you ever lived in a flat before?'
'No, but I will .... to it.'
A be used   B get used   C used

11 'Why are you so tired?'
'Because I .... to getting up early in the morning.'
A am used   B used   C am not used

12 'Do you know that man?'
'Yes. He .... to work for me.'
A was used   B used   C is used

15 *Mary had to move to Italy for her job. At first, she found living in a foreign country quite difficult, but she is slowly getting used to it.* **Use the prompts below to talk about how she is getting along, as in the example.**

S1: *She wasn't used to living by the sea, but she is used to it now.*

S2: *She still hasn't got used to living on her own.*

• live by the sea	✓	• use a new currency	✓
• live on her own	✗	• new customs	✓
• be away from her family and friends	✗	• drive on the other side of the road	✗
• speak Italian	✓	• hot weather	✓

Past Simple

The past simple is used for actions which happened in the past and are not related to the present.

We use the past simple:

- for an action which happened at a definite time in the past. The time is stated, already known or implied.

  Simon Cook **painted** his first picture in 1980. (When? In 1980. The time is stated.)

- for an action which began and finished in the past.

  Mr Clark **taught** Maths for thirty years. (He is no longer a teacher. He has retired.)

- for an action which happened in the past and cannot be repeated.

  e.g. a) Mike **won** more than twenty medals when he was an athlete. (He is no longer an athlete. He cannot win another medal.)
  b) I once **spoke** to Frank Sinatra. (He is no longer alive. I won't speak to him again.)

- for an action which happened within a specific time period which is over at the moment of speaking.

  e.g. I **wrote** three letters this morning. (The time period is over. It is evening or night now.)

Present Perfect

The present perfect is used for actions which happened in the past and are related to the present.

We use the present perfect:

- for an action which happened at an unstated time in the past. The exact time is either unknown or unimportant, and therefore it is not mentioned or implied.

  Simon Cook **has painted** a lot of pictures. (When? We do not know. The exact time is not mentioned or implied.)

- for an action which started in the past and continues up to the present.

  Mrs Nelson **has taught** French for twenty years. (She started teaching French twenty years ago and she is still teaching French today.)

- for an action which happened in the past and may be repeated.

  e.g. a) Ben is an athlete. He **has won** more than ten medals. (He is still an athlete. He may win some more medals.)
  b) I've **spoken** to Celine Dion. (She is still alive. I may speak to her again.)

- for an action which happened within a specific time period which is not over at the moment of speaking.

  e.g. I've **written** two letters this morning. (The time period is not over. It is still morning.)

Note: We use the past simple to talk about actions which were performed by people who are no longer alive, even if the time is not stated. e.g. Charles Dickens **wrote** 'Oliver Twist.'

16 Put the verbs in brackets into the *past simple* or the *present perfect*.

A A: I 1) ...'ve seen... (see) this film before.
B: Me too, but I love this actor. He 2) .... (play) a lot of good roles.
A: Tom Cruise? I 3) .... (meet) him, you know.
B: Really? When?
A: When I 4) .... (be) in Los Angeles on holiday.

B A: Who is that man?
B: He's an artist. He 1) .... (paint) a lot of beautiful pictures.
A: I think Van Gogh 2) .... (paint) the most beautiful pictures ever. But his life 3) .... (be) miserable.

C A: I 1) .... (just/hear from) an old friend of mine.
B: Oh, really?
A: Yes. Jim 2) .... (write) to me. I 3) .... (get) the letter this morning.
B: That's nice. When 4) .... (you/first/meet) him?
A: He 5) .... (live) next door to me for three years, but he 6) .... (move) away last June and I 7) .... (not/see) him since.

Past Simple – Past Continuous – Past Perfect

◆ The past simple is used for actions which happened immediately one after the other in the past.

When Jim came home, they **watched** *a film on TV. (Jim came home and then they watched a film together.)*

◆ The past continuous is used for a past action which was in progress when another action interrupted it.

When Jim came home, Mary **was watching** *a film on TV. (She was still watching the film when Jim came home.)*

◆ The past perfect is used for an action which happened before another past action or a specific time in the past.

When Jim came home, Mary **had already watched** *the film on TV. (She watched the film first. Jim came home afterwards.)*

◆ We can use the past simple, past continuous or past perfect without any difference in meaning with verbs such as *think, hope, mean, expect,* etc. for things we hoped or wished to do, but didn't.

e.g. I **expected/was expecting/had expected** him to call me, but he didn't.

 17 Put the verbs in brackets into the correct tense.

1 A: What ...*were you doing*... (you/do) at ten o'clock this morning?
   B: I .... (read) some important documents in my office.
2 A: Why are you so disappointed?
   B: Because I .... (hope) that I would pass the test, but I didn't.
3 A: Have you found your bag yet?
   B: No, but I .... (report) it stolen to the police yesterday.
4 A: Did you enjoy the play last night?
   B: No, even though I .... (read) good reviews of it before I bought the tickets.
5 A: Have you written your report yet?
   B: I .... (just/start) when you came in, actually.
6 A: Sorry I'm late.
   B: Where have you been? I .... (expect) you an hour ago.
7 A: We .... (go) to an antique market yesterday.
   B: .... (you/buy) anything?
8 A: Were you surprised that the factory closed down?
   B: Not really. In fact, I .... (know) it was going to happen.
9 A: Julia did well in the test, didn't she?
   B: Yes. She .... (study) very hard for it.

18 Put the verbs in brackets into the correct tense.

A When Simon 1) ...*arrived*... (arrive) at the cinema, dozens of people 2) .... (queue) outside. They 3) .... (wait) to see the same film as Simon. Simon, however, 4) .... (buy) a ticket in advance, so he 5) .... (walk) straight to the front of the queue and 6) .... (enter) the cinema. He 7) .... (feel) relieved that he didn't have to queue. He 8) .... (reach) his seat just as the lights 9) .... (go down) for the start of the film.

B Last weekend, Cathy 1) .... (hire) a car and 2) .... (drive) to the seaside. When she 3) .... (arrive) the wind 4) .... (blow) and the sky 5) .... (be) cloudy. She 6) .... (get out) of the car and 7) .... (take) a walk along the seafront. Then she 8) .... (decide) to go for fish and chips at a nearby restaurant that she 9) .... (see) earlier and liked the look of. By the time she 10) .... (leave) the restaurant, it 11) .... (already/grow) dark. As she 12) .... (walk) to her car it 13) .... (begin) to rain. However, Cathy 14) .... (not/mind) because she 15) .... (have) a wonderful day.

19 Identify the tenses, then match them to the correct descriptions.

1 People **used to have/had** very simple lives in those days.
2 She **was talking** on the phone when her boss came in.
3 Sam was in hospital because he **had crashed** his car.
4 They **had been studying** hard all morning, so they were tired.
5 I **was cooking** lunch while he **was pouring** the drinks.
6 We **had been living** in the house for a year before we decorated the kitchen.
7 Princess Diana **did** a lot of work for charity.
8 At two o'clock this afternoon they **were having** lunch at work.
9 First, she **knocked** on the door. Then, she **went** inside.
10 We **had bought** the tickets before we went to the theatre.

a to talk about actions of people who are no longer alive
b action which happened before another past action or before a stated time in the past
c actions which happened immediately one after the other in the past
d to put emphasis on the duration of an action which started and finished in the past before another past action
e action which was in progress at a stated time in the past
f two or more simultaneous actions
g action in progress when another action interrupted it
h action which lasted for some time in the past and whose result was visible in the past
i past habit or state which is now finished
j action which finished in the past and whose result was visible in the past

20 Underline the correct tense.

1 Lynne **was singing**/**had sung** as she was cleaning the windows.
2 Mr Todd **was teaching**/**had been teaching** for thirty years when he retired.
3 I phoned Jack because I **wanted**/**had wanted** to ask him a question.
4 They **had walked**/**had been walking** for hours when they stopped for a rest.
5 The shop **had been selling**/**had sold** the table by the time I got there.
6 Joe was happy. He **was winning**/**had won** first prize in the competition.
7 It **was raining**/**had rained** while they were playing the football match.
8 Rob **was opening**/**opened** the box and looked inside.
9 Eve was delighted to hear that she **was getting**/**had got** the job.
10 People **used to work**/**were working** very long hours in those days.
11 I was running when I **slipped**/**was slipping** on the ice.
12 They **were already buying**/**had already bought** the tickets when they went to the concert.
13 Carol **had broken**/**was breaking** her arm, so she couldn't write for six weeks.
14 We **had been staying**/**stayed** in a hotel by the sea last summer.
15 Elvis Presley **sang**/**had sung** lots of hit songs.
16 I **opened**/**was opening** the door and stepped outside.
17 They **had stood**/**were standing** outside when the results were announced.
18 Alexander Graham Bell **had invented**/**invented** the telephone.
19 She broke the glass while she **had washed**/**was washing** it.

21 Choose the correct answer.

1 He went to bed ...*B*... he had brushed his teeth.
   A before   B after   C while
2 I was watching television .... the doorbell rang.
   A when   B as soon as   C while
3 She .... hadn't finished the washing-up when the guests arrived.
   A yet   B just   C still
4 We had been walking for hours .... we reached the campsite.
   A since   B for   C before
5 John was repairing the car .... Steve was tidying the garage.
   A while   B before   C after
6 We went to Spain on holiday ....
   A tomorrow   B next year   C last year
7 I fell asleep .... I closed my eyes.
   A just   B as soon as   C already
8 .... did Jane and Ted get married?
   A How long   B How long ago   C While
9 She hasn't seen Jim .... she left school.
   A for   B just   C since
10 He won't go home .... he has finished his work.
   A how long   B until   C yet
11 I have lived in Kent .... ten years now.
   A since   B for   C before
12 We haven't finished work ....
   A yet   B until   C just
13 .... did Tina meet Steve?
   A How long   B How long ago   C While

22 a) **Fill in the gaps with an appropriate** *past* **form.**

One fine morning, a man **1)** ...*was fishing*... (fish) in a river. The sun **2)** .... (shine) and the man **3)** .... (sit) on the river bank. Everything was very quiet and peaceful. The man **4)** .... (wait) patiently for several hours when suddenly he **5)** .... (feel) something pulling on the fishing line. He **6)** .... (stand up) quickly and **7)** .... (begin) to take in the line. He **8)** .... (just/lift) the huge fish he had caught out of the water when there was a loud splash and it fell back into the river. At first, the man didn't know what **9)** .... (happen). Then, he **10)** .... (look) carefully at his fishing line. It **11)** .... (snap). The poor man was so disappointed that he **12)** .... (pack) away all his things and went home.

b) **Which of the** *past forms* **in the text above are used to express:**

1 emphasis on the duration of an action which started and finished in the past before another past action or a stated time in the past ....

2 action which happened at a definite time in the past time stated, known or implied ....

3 actions which happened immediately one after the other in the past ....

4 to describe the atmosphere, the setting, etc. in the introduction to a story ....

5 action which happened before another past action ....

23 **Complete the sentences using any appropriate** *past* **forms.**

1 While Joanne ...*was washing*... her hair, Carl was cleaning the house.
2 I have no idea where I .... my wallet.

3 He .... his leg when he fell off his skateboard.
4 We .... in the classroom for ten minutes before the teacher arrived.
5 She .... to the theatre last night.
6 My tooth .... for a week before I went to the dentist's.
7 She cried when she .... her driving test.
8 What .... when the alarm went off?
9 They got into the car and .... away.
10 I could tell she .... the competition because she couldn't stop smiling.
11 We .... along the beach when we heard a cry for help.
12 Tom .... the piano for years before he became famous.

24 **Put the verbs in brackets into the correct tense.**

A: Hello, Mark. You **1)** ...*took*... (take) a long time to answer the door.
B: Sorry. I **2)** .... (not/hear) the bell. Come in, Tony.
A: **3)** What .... (you/plan) to do today?
B: Well, I **4)** .... (think) of going for a picnic in the country, but the weather is awful so I **5)** .... (change) my mind.
A: Oh dear. Well, yesterday Mary **6)** .... (tell) me that she **7)** .... (buy) two tickets to see the Rocking Stars, but she couldn't go to the concert. So I **8)** .... (buy) the tickets from her, because I **9)** .... (think) you'd like to go.
B: Tony, that's brilliant! I **10)** .... (mean) to buy tickets for that concert, but they **11)** .... (sell out) by the time I **12)** .... (go) to the booking office.
A: Well, it's lucky I **13)** .... (see) Mary, then, isn't it?

25 **Put the verbs in brackets into the correct tense.**

1 A: Look at Steve! He is soaking wet.
  B: I know. He ...*has been washing*... (wash) the car.
2 A: Why .... (you/make) so much food?
  B: Well, I .... (expect) guests, but they phoned to say they couldn't come.
3 A: Julia performed well at the concert.
  B: Yes. She .... (practise) for months beforehand.
4 A: .... (you/ever/go) to Spain?
  B: Yes. I .... (go) last year.
5 A: I like your new coat.
  B: Thank you. I .... (wear) my old coat for years, so I decided to buy a new one.
6 A: Do you know this town well?
  B: Of course. I .... (live) here for six years.

Future Forms

Future Simple

We use the future simple:

a) in predictions about the future usually with the verbs *think*, *believe*, *expect*, etc., the expressions *be sure*, *be afraid*, etc., and the adverbs *probably*, *perhaps*, *certainly*, etc.

*I'm afraid we **won't be** on time for the meeting.*

b) for on-the-spot decisions.

I'll take this leg of lamb.

c) for promises (usually with the verbs *promise*, *swear*, *guarantee*, etc.), threats, warnings, requests, hopes (usually with the verb *hope*) and offers.

*I don't understand this exercise. **Will** you **help** me with it? (request)*

Of course! I'll explain it to you. (offer)

d) for actions/events/situations which will definitely happen in the future and which we cannot control.

*The temperature **will reach** 40˚C tomorrow.*

Be going to

We use be going to:

a) for plans, intentions or ambitions we have for the future.

I'm going to become a famous violinist one day. (ambition)

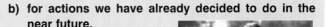

*Now that they've won the lottery, they **are going to buy** a big house. (intention/plan)*

b) for actions we have already decided to do in the near future.

*They **are going to get married** in three months. (They have already decided to do it.)*

*BUT: They're getting married next month. (They have decided **and** arranged to do it.)*

c) in predictions when there is evidence that something will happen in the near future.

Look at the clouds! It's going to rain.

Note: 1) We normally use *be going to* to talk about something we intend to do and *will* to give details or make comments.
e.g. A: *I'm going to have a party next week. I'll invite all my friends.*
B: *That'll be great.*

2) We normally use the *present continuous* rather than *be going to* with verbs which express movement, especially the verbs *go* and *come*.
e.g. Sam *is going to the market in a few minutes. Sheila is coming to my house for tea this afternoon.*

The future simple and be going to are used with the following time expressions: *tomorrow, the day after tomorrow, tonight, soon, next week/month/year, in a week/month/year, in two/three days/weeks,* etc.

Future Continuous

We use the future continuous:

a) for an action which will be in progress at a stated future time.

> This time next week, we'll **be cruising** round the islands.

b) for an action which will definitely happen in the future as the result of a routine or arrangement.

> Don't call Julie. I'll **be seeing** her later, so I'll pass the message on.

c) when we ask politely about someone's plans for the near future (what we want to know is if our wishes fit in with their plans.)

> Will you **be using** the photocopier for long?

> I need to make some photocopies.

> No. Why?

Future Perfect

We use the future perfect:

for an action which will be finished before a stated future time.

She **will have delivered** all the newspapers by 8 o'clock.

The future perfect is used with the following time expressions: **before, by, by then, by the time, until/till.**

Note: **Until/till** are only used in negative sentences.
a) She **will have finished** the report **by** tomorrow. (NOT: ... ~~until/till tomorrow.~~)
b) She **won't have completed** the report **until/till** 5 o'clock.

Future Perfect Continuous

We use the future perfect continuous:

to emphasise the duration of an action up to a certain time in the future.

By the end of next month, she **will have been teaching** for twenty years.

The future perfect continuous is used with: **by ... for.**

Note: After the time expressions **by the time, until, before,** we use the present simple because they introduce time clauses. The future perfect and the future perfect continuous may come either before or after the time clause.

Study the following examples:
a) I **won't have finished** cleaning the house **until** you **come back.**
b) **By the time** they **reach** York, they **will have been travelling** for four hours.

Note: We can use the future simple, future continuous or future perfect to make a prediction about the present or past, that is to say what we believe may be happening or have happened.
Study the following examples:
e.g. a) 'There's somebody on the phone for you.' 'That'**ll be** my mother.'
b) Don't call her now — she'**ll be sleeping.**
c) It's seven o'clock. Dad **will have left** the office by now.

Present Simple

We use the present simple for future actions when we refer to programmes, timetables, etc.
e.g. The bus **arrives** in Liverpool at 7:30.

Present Continuous

We use the present continuous for actions we have decided and arranged to do in the near future.
e.g. I'm **flying** to Lisbon tomorrow morning.

◆ We use the present simple or present perfect, and not future forms, after words and expressions such as *while, before, after, until/till, as, unless, when, whenever, if, suppose/supposing, once, as soon as, as long as, by the time, in case, on condition that*, etc.
e.g. Call me **as soon as** you **get** back.
(NOT: ...~~as soon as you will get back.~~)

◆ We use future forms:
a) with **when** when it is used as a question word. When it is used as a time word we use the present simple.
e.g. **When will** they **get** married?
I'm not sure **when** they **will visit** us.
BUT: I will let you know **when** I **decide**.

b) with **if** (= whether) when it is used after expressions which show ignorance, uncertainty, etc. such as **I don't know, I wonder, I doubt**, etc.
e.g. I don't know **if/whether** he'**ll move** house.
I doubt **if/whether** she'**ll pass** her exams.
BUT: **If** you **call** her, give her my regards.

26 Put the verbs in brackets into the correct *future* tense.

1 A: Your house is very small.
  B: I know. I ...*'m going to move*... (move) to a bigger house next year.
2 A: I have got a new job!
  B: Wonderful! I .... (call) Mum and tell her the good news.
3 A: How old is your daughter?
  B: She .... (be) fourteen next week.
4 A: I must phone Julia.
  B: Well, don't phone her now. She .... (sleep).
5 A: Have you been living here long?
  B: Yes. By next month, I .... (live) here for ten years.

6 A: Are you having a party next weekend?
  B: Yes. I hope I .... (finish) decorating the house by then.
7 A: What are your plans for tonight?
  B: Well, I .... (meet) Steve at eight o'clock.
8 A: I must buy some bread.
  B: You'd better hurry. The shops .... (close) in half an hour.
9 A: Shall I call you at ten o'clock tomorrow?
  B: No. I .... (leave) for work by then.
10 A: Are you coming to the disco on Friday night?
  B: I can't. I .... (study) for my exam then.
11 A: Are you excited about going to California?
  B: Yes! This time tomorrow I .... (fly) across the Atlantic.
12 A: It's seven o'clock.
  B: Yes. John .... (leave) the office by now.
13 A: There's somebody at the door.
  B: Oh. That .... (be) the postman.
14 A: I've left my jacket at home.
  B: I .... (go) back and get it for you.
15 A: Have you booked a taxi to take you to the airport?
  B: Yes. It .... (come) at eight o'clock in the morning.
16 A: Are you nervous about the interview?
  B: Yes. This time tomorrow, I .... (talk) to the managing director.

27 Fill in the *future simple*, the *present simple* or the *present perfect*.

A My car is being repaired and I don't know when it 1) ...*will be*... (be) ready. I doubt whether I 2) .... (be able to) collect it before the weekend. I wonder if John 3) .... (give) me a lift to the party on Saturday. I'll ask him when he 4) .... (come) home.

B I was calling to ask if you'd like to go out after we 1) .... (finish) work tomorrow or if you 2) .... (want) to watch a video instead. Call me back as soon as you 3) .... (get) in. I'll wait until I 4) .... (hear) from you.

C I will leave the hotel early in case there 1) .... (be) a lot of traffic. I don't know how long the journey 2) .... (take) or what time the plane 3) .... (land), but I 4) .... (call) you as soon as I 5) .... (arrive) at the airport. Then, I will wait until you 6) .... (come) to collect me.

D Paula is drinking tea as she is waiting for Charles. She wonders if he 1) .... (be) late as usual. She will wait until the clock 2) .... (strike) five and then she will call him in case he 3) .... (forget).

Future Simple versus Be going to

We use the future simple:

- when we make a prediction based on what we think, believe or imagine.

  *In the year 2020 people **will drive** electric cars.*

- for on-the-spot decisions.

I like this one better than the other. I'll take it.

We use be going to:

- when we make a prediction based on what we can see (evidence) or what we know.

  *She **is going to** cut the sunflowers.*

- for actions we have already decided to do in the future.

Do you like this

I'm going to give it to my daughter as a gift.

Yes. Why?

---

28 Fill in the *future simple* **or** *be going to*.

1 A: Have you finished your essay yet?
   B: No, but I'm sure I ...*'ll finish*... (finish) it on time.
2 A: I have decided what to wear for the party.
   B: Really? What .... (you/wear), then?
3 A: Why do you need hot soapy water?
   B: Because I .... (wash) the car.
4 A: Did you post those letters?
   B: No, I forgot. I .... (post) them this afternoon.
5 A: Did you book a table at the restaurant?
   B: Yes, but I don't expect it .... (be) busy.
6 A: I'm hungry.
   B: Me too. I .... (make) us something to eat.
7 A: What are you doing this weekend?
   B: Oh, I .... (probably/visit) my grandparents.
8 A: Look at that dog!
   B: Oh yes! It .... (swim) across the river.
9 A: Tony is nearly eighteen, isn't he?
   B: Yes. He .... (work) for his father when he leaves school.
10 A: Are you going into town today?
   B: Yes. I .... (give) you a lift if you like.
11 A: Your shirt is dirty.
   B: Oh dear! I .... (change) into another one.
12 A: I hope we .... (not/arrive) late for the meeting.
   B: Don't worry. There's plenty of time.

13 A: I'm really thirsty after all that hard work.
   B: I .... (make) some tea.
14 A: Did you give Steve his present?
   B: No. I .... (give) it to him tonight at dinner.
15 A: Watch out! You .... (bang) your head on the doorframe.
   B: Oh! I didn't realise it was so low.

---

29 Underline the correct tense.

A Next Saturday, Daisy **1)** *is flying*/*flies* to Paris for a business meeting. Her secretary has already booked the flight. The plane **2)** *will leave*/*leaves* at nine o'clock in the morning and one of her business clients **3)** *will have met*/*will be meeting* her at the airport when the plane lands. She doesn't know how long the meeting will last, but she **4)** *will have returned*/*will have been returning* home by Thursday evening.

B Florence **1)** *is going to become*/*will be becoming* a doctor when she finishes medical school. She thinks she **2)** *will probably work*/*will have probably worked* in a hospital for most of her career. This time next month, she **3)** *will have revised*/*will be revising* hard for her exams. By the time she gets her degree she **4)** *will have been studying*/*will have studied* medicine for five years. Florence hopes she **5)** *will have passed*/*will pass* all the exams with excellent grades.

Will/Won't - Shall

We use:

◆ **will you ...?** to give an order or make a request.
   e.g. **Will you** stop talking, please? (= Please stop talking.)

◆ **won't** to express unwillingness or an emphatic refusal, even when the subject is not a person.
   e.g. I've told him not to do that, but he **won't listen**.
   (= He refuses to listen.)
   The washing machine **won't work**.

   We use **wouldn't** to refer to the past.
   e.g. I asked him to help me, but he **wouldn't**.
   (= He was unwilling to help me.)

◆ **Shall I/we ... ?**
   a) to make an offer.
   e.g. **Shall I** do the washing-up for you? (= Do you want me to do the washing-up for you?)

   b) to make a suggestion.
   e.g. **Shall we** go out for dinner tonight?
   (= Why don't we go out for dinner tonight?)

   c) to ask for suggestions or instructions.
   e.g. 'Where **shall I** put the vase?' 'On the table.'
   'What **shall we** do tonight?' 'We could go out.'

Other ways of expressing the future

We can also express the future with:

◆ **be to + infinitive** (formal English).
   e.g. The President **is to visit** Poland next Monday.

◆ **be about to + infinitive/be on the point of + -ing form** (to refer to the near future).
   e.g. Look! The bus **is about to leave**.
   The company **is on the point of closing down**.

◆ **be due to + infinitive** (timetables).
   e.g. Their flight **is due to arrive** at 6:15.

◆ **verbs such as decide, plan, intend, arrange, mean + to -infinitive** (for plans or intentions).
   e.g. We **intend to buy** a bigger flat.

◆ **be sure to/be certain to/be bound to + infinitive** (to express certainty about the future).
   e.g. This plan **is sure to/is bound to succeed**.

   ### The future in the past

We use the following patterns to talk about things we intended to do or plans we had for the future.
a) **was going to/was to/was about to/ was due to + infinitive**
   e.g. Mr Simon **was going to resign**, but the manager offered him a better salary. (So he didn't resign.)
b) **was on the point of + -ing form**
   e.g. They **were on the point of leaving** the house when the phone rang. (So they didn't leave.)

30 Replace the words in bold with *will/won't* or *shall I/we*, as in the example.

1 **Can** you buy me some milk, please?
   ...*Will you buy me some milk, please?*...
2 What **do you want me to** do with this shopping?
   ....
3 I've asked Jane to tidy her room, but she **refuses to** do it.
   ....
4 **Can** you open the door for me, please?
   ....
5 **Do you want me to** walk the dog for you?
   ....
6 **Why don't we** go to the theatre tonight?
   ....
7 When **do you want me to** visit next?
   ....
8 **Please** be quiet!
   ....
9 Ann **is unwilling to** talk to me.
   ....

31 Complete each sentence with two to five words, including the word in bold.

1 The Queen will open the new sports centre next week.
   is The Queen ...*is to open*... the new sports centre next week.
2 We are planning to go to Spain next summer.
   intend We .... Spain next summer.
3 The guests should have arrived at nine, but they were late.
   due The guests .... at nine, but they were late.
4 Jane was thinking of looking for a new job, but she changed her mind.
   going Jane .... a new job, but she changed her mind.
5 The manager will be angry when he hears the news.
   bound The manager .... angry when he hears the news.
6 Hurry up! The bus is going to leave!
   about Hurry up! The bus .... leave!
7 Helen will love this present.
   sure Helen .... this present.

32 **Identify the tenses, then match them to the correct descriptions.**

1 I like these shoes. I'**ll buy** them.
2 They **will have eaten** lunch by two o'clock this afternoon.
3 I'**m going to open** my own business in the future.
4 This time tomorrow, I'**ll be taking** my driving test.
5 By the time Jack finishes the race, he **will have been running** for two hours.
6 Everyone believes he **will win** the competition.
7 I'll tell Paul about the party. I'**ll be seeing** him at work anyway.
8 **Will** you **be speaking** to Rob later? I've got a message for him.
9 Look at them! They **are going to catch** the thieves.
10 Since you're tired, I'**ll cook** dinner tonight.

a for offers, promises, threats, etc
b action which will definitely happen in the future as a result of a routine or arrangement
c for plans, intentions or ambitions we have for the future
d predictions about the future
e asking politely about someone's plans for the near future
f action which will be finished before a stated future time
g to emphasise the duration of an action up to a certain time in the future
h action which will be in progress at a stated future time
i on-the-spot decision
j predictions when there is evidence that something will happen in the near future

33 **A Fill in the gaps with an appropriate tense form.**

Next month, Maggie **1)** ...*is going*... (go) to Australia to visit her sister, who she hasn't seen for fifteen years. The plane **2)** .... (leave) early in the morning and **3)** .... (stop off) at Singapore before flying on to Sydney. It **4)** .... (be) a very long, tiring journey, but Maggie is very excited because this time next month, she **5)** .... (begin) her adventure on the other side of the world. She **6)** .... (stay) in Australia for one month. She has booked her flight, so she **7)** .... (fly) back to Britain on 31st May. She hopes that she **8)** .... (visit) lots of fascinating places and seen many interesting things by the time her holidays are over.

B Which of the tense forms in the text above are used to express:

1 timetables/programmes ⬜
2 actions which will have finished before a stated future time ⬜
3 plans or intentions ⬜
4 fixed arrangements in the near future ⬜
5 actions which will be in progress at a stated future time ⬜
6 predictions based on what we know ⬜

34 **Put the verbs in brackets into the correct *future form*.**

Dear Lionel,

I'm writing to tell you my exciting news. I have won a competition! I think my life **1)** ...*will change*... (change) a lot now! I **2)** .... (meet) the competition organisers next week to get my prize — a cheque for £50,000.

As soon as I **3)** .... (have) the money, I **4)** .... (buy) a new car, and I **5)** .... (also/redecorate) my house. Hopefully, I **6)** .... (finish) the whole house by the end of June. Then, on the fifth of July, I **7)** .... (fly) to Tahiti for an exotic holiday in the sun. I **8)** .... (return) by the end of July and then I **9)** .... (throw) a big party for all my friends. I hope you **10)** .... (come).

Well, it's almost lunchtime, so I **11)** .... (say) goodbye for now. I promise I **12)** .... (send) you a postcard from Tahiti.

Best wishes,
Emily

35 Fill in the correct *present* or *future forms*.

If you **1)** ...*like*... (like) watersports, you **2)** .... (love) Aquaworld. As soon as you **3)** .... (arrive) at this unique theme park, you **4)** .... (be greeted) by visitor hosts who **5)** .... (show) you to a luxury chalet. Once you **6)** .... (be) in your swimsuit, you **7)** .... (be able to) enjoy a wide variety of watersports, from swimming to water-skiing. You **8)** .... (find) plenty to do and you **9)** .... (have) the chance to try many exciting activities. Aquaworld **10)** .... (open) at 9 am every day and **11)** .... (close) at 8 pm. There **12)** .... (be) special facilities for children and lifeguards **13)** .... (supervise) all activities. Visit Aquaworld for an experience you **14)** .... (never/forget)!

36 Choose the correct answer.

1 'I ...*A*... about buying a new car recently.'
   'Really? What sort of car?'
   A have been thinking **B** have thought **C** thought

2 'I haven't seen Mark for weeks.'
   'Well, I .... him this afternoon. Why don't you come along?'
   A have met **B** am meeting **C** meet

3 'We'd better take a taxi to the station.'
   'Yes. The train .... in fifteen minutes.'
   A has left **B** will have left **C** leaves

4 'Where is the newspaper?'
   'I threw it away. I thought you .... reading it.'
   A have finished **B** finished **C** had finished

5 'I feel very tired.'
   'How can you be tired? You .... a thing all day.'
   A haven't been doing **B** aren't doing
   C haven't done

6 'Cathy doesn't study enough.'
   'I know. I'm afraid she .... her exam.'
   A won't pass **B** won't be passing
   C won't have passed

7 'It's bad news about Janet crashing her new car, isn't it?'
   'Yes. She .... for months to buy it.'
   A saved **B** is saving **C** had been saving

8 'There's someone here to see you.'
   'Oh, that .... my sister. Send her in.'
   A will have been **B** was **C** will be

9 'Whose is this earring?'
   'I don't know. I found it when I .... the house.'
   A was cleaning **B** had cleaned **C** am cleaning

10 'I .... to reach Jane on the phone all day.'
    'Don't you know? She's gone on holiday.'
    A tried **B** have been trying **C** have tried

11 'I want to visit Katie.'
    'Well, don't visit her before five o'clock. She ....'
    A is working **B** will be working
    C will have worked

12 'That .... like Dad's car.'
    'It is. He must have finished work early.'
    A sounds **B** had sounded **C** has sounded

13 'Is that a new jumper?'
    'No. I .... it from Laura yesterday.'
    A have borrowed **B** had borrowed **C** borrowed

14 '............. to the library today?'
    'Yes. Would you like me to return your books?'
    A Will you have gone **B** Will you have been going
    C Will you be going

15 'How is your grandfather?'
    'His condition .... day by day.'
    A improves **B** has improved **C** is improving

16 'When did you speak to Sue?'
    'I met her as I .... to work.'
    A had walked **B** was walking **C** am walking

17 'Shall we go shopping?'
    'I can't go until the babysitter ....'
    A arrives **B** will arrive **C** arrived

18 'I've invited Sam to my party.'
    'I doubt if he .... He's studying for an exam.'
    A comes **B** will come **C** is coming

19 'I'm sorry I'm late.'
    'I .... here for over an hour.'
    A have been waiting **B** have waited **C** was waiting

20 'I'm having trouble with the car.'
    'I'm sure John .... you fix it if you ask him.'
    A is going to help **B** helps **C** will help

21 'How long .... James?'
    'Since we were children.'
    A have you known **B** do you know
    C did you know

22 'You .... a good teacher one day.'
    'Do you really think so?'
    A were **B** will be **C** are being

IN OTHER WORDS

Study these examples. The second sentence has a similar meaning to the first sentence.

1 I've never heard such a sad story.
   ever   It's the **saddest story I have ever** heard.
2 He started painting fifteen years ago.
   been   He **has been painting for** fifteen years.
3 She hasn't finished decorating the flat yet.
   still   She **is still decorating** the flat.
4 I've never eaten Chinese food before.
   first   It's the **first time I have ever** eaten Chinese food.
5 When did they graduate from college?
   since   How long is it **since they graduated** from college?
   ago   How long **ago did they graduate** from college?
6 He didn't begin talking until everyone had sat down.
   before   He waited until everyone had sat down **before he began** talking.
7 We haven't been to the theatre for a year.
   time   The **last time we went** to the theatre was a year ago.
   last   We **last went to** the theatre a year ago.
8 It's two years since I went on holiday.
   have   I **have not been** on holiday for two years.
9 It was the first time they had travelled by boat.
   never   They **had never travelled** by boat before.
10 Jack was about to have dinner when his boss called.
   point   Jack was **on the point of having** dinner when his boss called.

37 **Complete each sentence with two to five words, including the word in bold.**

1 She began to play tennis when she was 10.
   since   She ...*has been playing tennis since*... she was 10.
2 I bought this coat three years ago.
   for   I .... three years.
3 I haven't finished writing the report yet.
   still   I .... the report.
4 We've never seen such a funny film.
   ever   It's the .... seen.
5 He's never played football before.
   time   It's the first .... football.
6 John hasn't played golf for years.
   time   The .... golf was years ago.

7 When did Mary move to Liverpool?
   since   How long is it .... to Liverpool?
8 It was the first time I had met a film star.
   never   I .... a film star before.
9 We didn't start tidying up until after the guests had left.
   before   We waited until the guests .... tidying up.
10 Kate was about to leave the house when the postman came.
   point   Kate was .... the house when the postman came.
11 It's four weeks since I spoke to Paul.
   have   I .... for four weeks.
12 When did they announce their engagement?
   ago   How long .... their engagement?
13 We haven't played squash for six months.
   last   We .... six months ago.
14 Kim was on the point of closing the shop when a customer walked in.
   about   Kim .... the shop when a customer walked in.
15 He is the kindest man I've ever met.
   never   I have .... man before.
16 They are still discussing the problem.
   finished   They .... the problem yet.
17 Mike started studying medicine four years ago.
   been   Mike .... four years.
18 The waiter didn't take our order until everyone had decided what they wanted.
   before   The waiter waited until everyone had decided what they wanted .... our order.

38 **Put the verbs in brackets into the correct tense.**

Kate Teale 1) ...*has decided*... (decide) to open her own restaurant. Yesterday, she 2) .... (have) a meeting with her bank manager and she 3) .... (ask) him for a loan. He agreed, so Kate 4) .... (be able) to start making plans. In fact, she 5) .... (already/find) a building for her restaurant and she 6) .... (look) at tables and chairs next week. By the end of the month, work on the restaurant 7) .... (begin) and by the summer, everything will be ready. Kate 8) .... (hope) that her business will be a success. At the moment, she 9) .... (interview) people to be chefs and waiters.

UNIT 1
Tenses

Common mistakes

- I'll call you **when I will finish**. ✗
  I'll call you **when I finish**. ✓

- I **have read** this book a month **ago**. ✗
  I **read** this book a month **ago**. ✓

- I **have met** him **two days before**. ✗
  I **have met** him **before**. ✓

- Take a map **in case you will get lost**. ✗
  Take a map **in case you get lost**. ✓

- When was **the last time you have been** to the cinema? ✗
  When was **the last time you went** to the cinema? ✓

- I haven't seen him **since I have finished** school. ✗
  I haven't seen him **since I finished** school. ✓

- I'm **learning** English **since 1996**. ✗
  I've **been learning** English **since 1996**. ✓

- He **stopped** smoking **a year before**. ✗
  He **stopped** smoking **a year ago**. ✓

- Sharon found a job last month. She **had left** school six months **ago**. ✗
  Sharon found a job last month. She **had left** school six months **before**. ✓

- They **still have** called us. ✗
  They **still haven't** called us. ✓

- He **hasn't still bought** a computer. ✗
  He **still hasn't bought** a computer. ✓
  She **still is** abroad. ✗
  She **is still** abroad. ✓

- They **haven't reached yet** a decision. ✗
  They **haven't reached** a decision **yet**. ✓

- They **will have returned until** noon. ✗
  They **will have returned by** noon. ✓

- I **used to go** to the cinema **twice last month**. ✗
  I **went** to the cinema **twice last month**. ✓

39 Correct the mistakes.

1 I'm playing chess since I was eight years old.
2 I used to eat at that restaurant three times last week.
3 They haven't still delivered my television.
4 We haven't read yet his letter.
5 I have met that man a week ago.
6 We moved to Glasgow a year before.
7 Mike and Kelly got married last week. They had met each other four years ago.
8 I'll make the dinner when I will get home.
9 Take some food in case you will get hungry.
10 The house will have been built until the end of May.
11 Peter still is at school.
12 When was the last time you have seen Tony?

13 I have seen this film three months before.
14 She hasn't been to a party since she has returned from her holiday.

40 Choose the correct answer.

1 The play had started ...C... we got to the theatre.
   A while B until C by the time
2 Tom has .... had some good news.
   A still B yet C just
3 Do you know .... she had been working there before she retired?
   A when B how long C how long ago
4 They will have had dinner .... eight.
   A before B until C by
5 I .... hadn't cleaned the house when the guests arrived.
   A still B yet C just
6 We have been training .... six months.
   A since B for C while
7 .... did you move to Essex?
   A How long ago B How long C While
8 She .... eats beans because they make her ill.
   A ever B never C always
9 I'm tired. I have been working very hard ....
   A so far B just C lately
10 .... Paul leaves, he will have typed ten letters.
   A By the time B By then C Before
11 James was washing the car .... Sue was cutting the grass.
   A as soon as B before C while
12 Colin has invited ten people to his party ....
   A yet B ever C so far.

41 Underline the correct preposition.

1 The advantage **of/in/over** computers is that they can process information quickly.
2 She accused him **for/of/about** stealing her bag.
3 The train arrived **at/to/in** Manchester at 5.30 pm.
4 Her parents did not approve **for/of/about** her outfit.
5 He was aware **about/for/of** being followed.
6 Mary agreed **to/with/on** help me arrange the party.
7 We were amazed **of/at/with** how many people attended the meeting.
8 Paul was angry with me **about/for/at** using his car.
9 Sarah is very bad **to/for/at** Mathematics.
10 I don't believe **in/on/at** ghosts.
11 According **with/to/by** the weather forecast, it will be sunny tomorrow.
12 She blamed me **on/for/from** the damage to the car.

28

Phrasal Verbs

be after:	(tr) 1) want, try to gain, 2) chase
be against:	(tr) oppose (opp: **be for**)
be in for:	(tr) expect sth (usu bad)
be off:	(tr) 1) not want/like any more, 2) be absent (from school, work, etc)
be on:	(tr) be shown (on TV, at the cinema, etc)
be out of:	(tr) not have sth; lack
be over:	(int) come to an end
be up:	(int) 1) be awake and out of bed, 2) stay awake at night, 3) be wrong or unusual
break down:	(int) 1) stop working, 2) lose control of feelings, 3) fail
break in (int)/ break into (tr):	1) enter by force, 2) interrupt
break out:	(int) 1) begin suddenly (of war, fire, etc) **BUT:** a storm breaks, 2) escape
break up:	(int) 1) stop for holidays (of schools, etc), 2) separate; split up

42 Fill in the correct particle.

1 War broke ...*out*... suddenly in the country.
2 My flat was broken .... while I was away.
3 The police are .... the bank robbers.
4 The washing machine has broken .... I'll call a repairman.
5 Many people are .... the new law.
6 The school will break .... for the holidays soon.
7 What's ....? Is something wrong?
8 The supermarket was .... bread, so I didn't get any.
9 Jack was .... school last week because he had the flu.
10 'Are you .... yet?' called Mum early this morning.
11 When she heard the bad news she broke .... and cried.
12 After three weeks, the exams are finally ....
13 Several prisoners broke .... of prison early this morning.
14 I was .... all night because of my bad cough.
15 Government negotiations broke .... last week.
16 James is .... a new bicycle for his birthday.
17 Look at the clouds. I think we're .... bad weather today.
18 I used to love pizza, but I'm .... it now.
19 The couple broke .... for a while, but then got back together.
20 There is a new play .... at the Empire theatre.
21 The secretary broke .... on the meeting to bring us coffee.

ORAL Activity

Life has changed a lot in the past century. Look at the information in the chart and make sentences, as in the example. You can add your own ideas.
e.g. S1: *100 years ago, people ate/used to eat simple, home-made food.*
S2: *Today, we eat tinned food and pre-packaged meals.*

WRITING Activity

Write an article about life in the future for a magazine called 'Millennium'. Write your predictions about food, transport, entertainment, settlements and shopping. Include words and expressions such as *be bound to*, *be on the point of*, *expect*, etc.

food pills - shuttle bus/electric cars - computers/virtual reality - space colonies/underwater cities - shopping via the Internet

LIFE · IN · THE · FUTURE

I believe that life will be very different in the future. Firstly, scientists are bound to invent food pills which will replace actual meals. Secondly,

....

On the whole, I think that life in the future will be very different from life today, as there will be many more changes which we cannot yet imagine.

The Infinitive/The -ing form

*Ken and Nancy **enjoy gardening**. They **could hire** a gardener, but they **prefer to do** the work themselves.*

Forms of the Infinitive		
	Active	**Passive**
Present	(to) lose	(to) be lost
Pres. Cont.	(to) be losing	————
Perfect	(to) have lost	(to) have been lost
Perf. Cont.	(to) have been losing	————

Active

◆ **present infinitive: refers to the present or future**
*e.g. He expects **to stay** here for a week.*

present cont. infinitive: (to) be + -ing
Refers to an action happening now.
*e.g. He seems **to be working** hard.*

perfect infinitive: (to) have + past participle
Refers to the past and shows that the action of the infinitive happened before the action of the verb.
*e.g. He claims **to have won** a lot of money. (First he won the money, then he claimed that he had won it.)*

perfect cont. infinitive: (to) have + been + -ing
Refers to the past and emphasises the duration of the action of the infinitive, which happened before the action of the verb.
*e.g. He's got a headache. He claims to **have been working** on the computer all morning. (We emphasise what he has been doing all morning.)*

The perfect infinitive is used with verbs such as *seem, appear, believe, know, claim, expect* and *modal verbs*.

Passive

◆ **present infinitive: (to) be + past participle**
*e.g. He hopes **to be offered** a promotion.*

◆ **perfect infinitive: (to) have been + past participle**
*e.g. She is believed **to have been kidnapped**.*

The verb tenses corresponding to the tenses of the infinitive are as follows:

Verb tenses	Infinitive
he works / will work	→ to work
he is working / will be working	→ to be working
he worked / has worked / had worked / will have worked	→ to have worked
he was working / has been working / had been working / will have been working	→ to have been working

Forms of the -ing form		
	Active	**Passive**
Simple	losing	being lost
Perfect	having lost	having been lost

The simple -ing form refers to the present or future.
*e.g. **Swimming** is an energetic form of exercise.* **The perfect -ing form shows that the action of the -ing form happened before the action of the verb.** *e.g. He denied **having lied** to his parents.* **We can use the simple -ing form instead of the perfect -ing form with no difference in meaning.**
*e.g. He admitted to **having stolen**/**stealing** the car.*

1 **In pairs, ask and answer questions using the prompts below, as in the example.**

SA: Has he lost his keys?
SB: Yes. He seems to have lost his keys.

1 Has he lost his keys? 2 Has he hurt his finger? 3 Has he been sleeping?

4 Is he building a house? 5 Have they been running? 6 Is she painting a picture?

Infinitive/The -ing form/Too-Enough/Participles

Use

The *to - infinitive* is used:

◆ **to express purpose**
e.g. *Sam went to the bank **to get** some money.*

◆ **after certain verbs (*agree, appear, decide, expect, hope, plan, promise, refuse*, etc.).**
e.g. *He **promised to help** us with the decorations.*

◆ **after adjectives which a) describe feelings/emotions (*happy, glad*, etc.), b) express willingness/ unwillingness (*willing, eager, reluctant, anxious, unwilling*, etc.), c) refer to a person's character (*mean, clever*, etc.) and also with the adjectives *lucky* and *fortunate*.**
e.g. *I was **annoyed to hear** that he had left.*
*He is **reluctant to help**.*
*You were **clever not to believe** them.*

Note: With adjectives which refer to character we can also use an impersonal construction.
It + be + adjective + of + noun/ pronoun.
e.g. *It was **clever of you** not to believe them.*

◆ **after certain nouns and pronouns such as *something, somewhere, anyone, nothing*, etc. usually to show that something is necessary or possible.**
e.g. *We've got a lot of **homework to do**.*
*Take **something to drink** on the bus.*

◆ **after *too/enough*.**
e.g. *She is **too young to stay** out so late.*

◆ **with *it + be + adjective/noun***
e.g. *It is **important to get** there on time.*
*It is her **ambition to open** her own shop.*

◆ **to talk about an unexpected event which can be unpleasant, usually with *only*.**
e.g. *She came home **to find** her sister waiting for her.*
*They rushed to the airport **(only) to be informed** that the flight had been cancelled.*

◆ **after: *be + the first/second*, etc./*next/last/best*, etc.**
e.g. *He **was the first to arrive**.*

◆ **after verbs and expressions such as *ask, learn, find out, wonder, want to know, decide, explain*, etc. when they are followed by question words (*who, what, where, how*, etc.). '*Why*' is followed by a subject + verb, not by an infinitive.**
e.g. *He **explained how to operate** the machine.*
*I don't know **why he left**.*

Note: If two to -infinitives are joined with 'and' or 'or', the 'to' of the second infinitive can be omitted.
e.g. *He agreed **to come** and **help** us.*

The *-ing form* is used:

◆ **as a noun.**
e.g. ***Cycling** is a popular form of exercise.*

◆ **after certain verbs (*admit, anticipate, appreciate, avoid, consider, continue, delay, deny, discuss, enjoy, escape, excuse, fancy, finish, forgive, go (for activities), imagine, involve, keep (= contInue), mention, mind, miss, postpone, practise, prevent, quit, recall, recollect, report, resent, resist, risk, save, stand, suggest, tolerate, understand*, etc.).**
e.g. *They **considered moving** abroad.*
*He **avoided answering** my question.*

◆ **after: *dislike, enjoy, hate, like, love, prefer* to express general preference.**
e.g. *She **likes painting**.*

BUT: *would like/would love/would prefer + to -inf* to express specific preference.
e.g. *I **would like to paint** your portrait.*

◆ **after expressions such as *be busy, it's no use, it's (no) good, it's (not) worth, what's the use of, can't help, there's no point (in), can't stand, have difficulty (in), have trouble, have a hard/difficult time*, etc.**
e.g. ***What's the use of waiting** for an answer?*
*She **is busy writing** the wedding invitations.*

◆ **after: *spend, waste, lose* (time, money, etc.).**
e.g. *We **wasted** a lot of time **trying** to find a parking space.*
*He **lost** £100,000 **investing** in unsuccessful companies.*

◆ **after prepositions.**
e.g. *He was found guilty **of lying** in court.*

◆ **after the preposition 'to' with verbs and expressions such as *look forward to, be used to, get round to, object to, in addition to, prefer (doing sth to doing sth else)*, etc.**
e.g. *She **objects to working** on Saturdays.*

◆ **after the verbs: *hear, listen to, notice, see, watch*, and *feel* to describe an incomplete action, that is to say that somebody saw, heard, etc. only a part of the action.**
e.g. *I **listened to** James **singing** a song. (I listened to part of the song. I didn't listen to the whole song.)*

BUT: *hear, listen to, notice, see, watch, feel + bare infinitive* to describe a complete action, something that somebody saw, heard, etc. from beginning to end.
e.g. *I **listened to** James **sing** a song. (I listened to the song from beginning to end.)*

The *bare infinitive* is used:

◆ after *modal verbs (can, should, must,* etc.).
e.g. He **should apologise** to his parents.
BUT: *Ought* is followed by to -infinitive.
e.g. She **ought to find** a job.

◆ after the verbs *let, make, see, hear* and *feel.*
e.g. They **saw** her **talk** to the manager.

BUT: *be made, be heard, be seen* + *to* -infinitive (passive).
e.g. She **was seen to talk** to the manager.

When *see, hear* and *watch* are followed by an -ing form, there is no change in the passive.
e.g. I **saw** her **getting** into a taxi.
She **was seen getting** into a taxi.

can/could + *see/hear* + -ing form.
e.g. We **could see** smoke **coming** out of the building.
(NOT: We could see smoke ~~come~~ ...)

◆ after *had better* and *would rather.*
e.g. You **had better see** a doctor.

◆ *Help* is followed by either the to -infinitive or the bare infinitive.
e.g. She **helped** me **(to) fill** in my application form.

2 Put the verbs in brackets into the correct *infinitive form* or the *-ing form.*

1 A: Have you decided where ...*to spend*... (spend) your holiday?
   B: Yes. I would like .... (go) to a Greek island.
2 A: I hate .... (clean) the house.
   B: Me too. I wish I could afford .... (employ) a cleaner.
3 A: Jane seems .... (sleep) for hours.
   B: Yes. She must .... (be) very tired.
4 A: What are you doing this weekend?
   B: Well, Tom suggested .... (drive) to the seaside.
5 A: Steve claims .... (travel) around the world.
   B: Yes. He seems .... (go) to a lot of places.
6 A: It was nice of John .... (visit) us yesterday.
   B: Yes. I was happy .... (see) him.
7 A: I'm sure I've failed my exam.
   B: Well, there's no point in .... (worry) until you get your results.
8 A: We should .... (tell) Sue about the party.
   B: Yes. We had better .... (invite) Tony, too.
9 A: Did the police arrest that man?
   B: Yes. He admitted to .... (steal) a car.
10 A: Did you have a nice evening?
   B: Not really. I arrived home only .... (find) that I'd left my keys at work.

3 Put the verbs in brackets into the correct *infinitive form* or the *-ing form.*

1 Simon was the last person ...*to arrive*... (arrive) at the office.
2 She can't get used to .... (work) for such a large company.
3 It's no use .... (ask) Paul. He won't be able to help you.
4 Peter denied .... (break) the classroom window.
5 I will .... (feed) the dog this afternoon.
6 We had better .... (run) or we will miss the train.
7 It was kind of him .... (help) me tidy the house.
8 She refused .... (answer) his questions.
9 He is far too young .... (stay) out late at night.
10 Her teacher let her .... (bring) her lunch into the classroom.
11 I don't mind .... (help) you with your homework.
12 We don't allow students .... (talk) to each other during exams.
13 She dislikes .... (wear) suits to work.
14 It was a mistake .... (leave) the door unlocked.
15 The thieves were seen .... (drive) a stolen car.
16 I advise you .... (look for) a new job.
17 There's no point in .... (get) angry with him. It's not his fault.
18 I'll take a book .... (read) on the plane.

4 Put the verbs in brackets into the correct *infinitive form* or the *-ing form.*

A Sue has decided **1)** ...*to apply*... (apply) for a new job. Her mother advised her **2)** .... (write) to several different companies. Sue would like **3)** .... (work) for a large company where she can **4)** .... (meet) new people.

B Carol is too ill **1)** .... (go) to work today. She has managed **2)** .... (drink) some tea and now she wants **3)** .... (sleep). Her husband offered **4)** .... (call) the doctor, but Carol would prefer **5)** .... (wait) and see if she feels better tomorrow.

C Daniel would like **1)** .... (get) his teacher a present, but he doesn't know what **2)** .... (choose). He is thinking of **3)** .... (buy) her a book because he knows that she enjoys **4)** .... (read). His sister will help him **5)** .... (pick) a good one.

Infinitive/The -ing form/Too-Enough/Participles

D I dislike **1)** .... (shop) because I can't stand **2)** .... (be) in crowded places. If I have to **3)** .... (go) into town, I avoid **4)** .... (visit) shops where there are a lot of people.

E Joan can't afford **1)** .... (go) on holiday this year, but she intends **2)** .... (save) up so that she can manage **3)** .... (travel) around Europe next summer. She is looking forward to **4)** .... (visit) a lot of exciting places.

Subject of the infinitive/-ing form

◆ **The subject of the infinitive or the -ing form is omitted when it is the same as the subject of the main verb.**
   e.g. I ***would like to help*** *with the preparations.*

   When it is different, however, it is not omitted. The subject of the infinitive can be an object pronoun, a name or a noun.
   e.g. I would like ***her/Mary/my assistant to help*** *with the preparations.*

   The subject of the -ing form can be an object pronoun, a possessive adjective, a name or a possessive case.
   e.g. I remember ***him/his/Steve/Steve's*** *winning the gold medal.*

◆ **We use** *for* **+** *noun/pronoun* **to introduce the subject of the infinitive in the following cases:**
   a) **with verbs such as** *arrange, hope, long, prepare, ask, wait, etc.*
      e.g. We've ***arranged for the plumber to come*** *tomorrow.*
   b) **with adjectives such as** *anxious, cheap, convenient, dangerous, difficult, important, necessary, etc.*
      e.g. I'm ***anxious for Beth to go*** *to university.*
   c) **with nouns such as** *advantage, disadvantage, demand, disaster, idea, mistake, etc.*
      e.g. It was a ***mistake for you to lend*** *him the money.*
   d) **with too/enough.**
      e.g. It was ***easy enough for her to find*** *a job.*
   e) **when the to -infinitive expresses purpose.**
      e.g. There are benches ***for people to sit*** *on in the park.*

 5 **Rephrase the following sentences, as in the example.**

1 I don't think Ann should watch the late film.
   I don't want ...*Ann to watch the late film*....

2 She is going to tidy her clothes away. Her mother asked her to do it.
   Her mother wants ....

3 It's Mary's turn to do the washing-up. I insist on it.
   I insist on ....

4 Why don't you come to my party?
   I would like ....

5 Mark fell into the swimming pool on his wedding day. I'll never forget that.
   I'll never forget ....

6 You have to finish this project today.
   I need ....

7 I don't think my secretary should attend the meeting.
   I don't want ....

 6 **Rewrite the sentences using** *for***, as in the example.**

1 He shouldn't play his music so loud. It's too late.
   It's too late ...*for him to play his music so loud*....

2 Barry must go to the bank today. It's necessary.
   It's necessary ....

3 They must finish their homework. It's important.
   It's important ....

4 No one has taken my order yet. I'm still waiting.
   I'm still waiting ....

5 You should move to the town centre. It will be more convenient.
   It will be more convenient ....

6 John should learn a foreign language. That would be a good idea.
   It would be a good idea ....

7 There are shops in the hotel. Guests can do their shopping.
   There are shops in the hotel ....

8 The teacher spoke loudly. Everyone could hear him.
   The teacher spoke loudly enough ....
   ....

9 I've brought some magazines so that you can read them.
   I've brought some magazines ....

10 Children shouldn't play with matches. It's dangerous.
   It's dangerous ....

 7 **Complete the sentences, as in the example.**

1 The supermarket has a car park for the customers ...*to park their cars in*... .

2 The hotel has a gym for the guests ....

3 The school has a playground for the children ....
   ....

4 The office block has a restaurant for the staff ....
   ....

5 The bus has a bin for the passengers ....

6 The plane has lockers for the passengers ....

7 The youth club has a cloakroom for the members .....
   ....

33

8 **Underline the correct item.**

Countries all over the world have superstitions which some people believe and others don't. Several superstitions are the same in many countries.

Many people avoid 1) *walking*/*to walk* under ladders, as this is believed to bring bad luck. Some people expect things 2) *go*/*to go* wrong on the thirteenth day of the month, particularly if it's a Friday. Some say you must never 3) *put*/*to put* up an umbrella inside the house or 4) *to place*/*place* a pair of new shoes on the table. In many places, it is considered unlucky 5) *to see*/*seeing* a black cat, while in others this is thought 6) *to be*/*be* a symbol of good luck. 7) *Break*/*Breaking* a mirror results in seven years of bad luck and if you spill salt, you must 8) *to throw*/*throw* a pinch of it over your left shoulder immediately.

These are just a few superstitions which some people believe in. Do you know any more?

9 **Put the verbs in brackets into the correct infinitive form or the -ing form.**

1 A: Is Sue in the office today?
  B: Yes. I saw her ...*typing*... (type) a report as I came in.
2 A: I walked past the lake yesterday.
  B: So did I. I stood for a moment to watch some children .... (feed) the ducks.
3 A: Marie is good at playing the piano, isn't she?
  B: Yes. I heard her .... (perform) in a concert last week. She was wonderful.
4 A: Is Paul at home?
  B: No. I saw him .... (leave) for work as I passed by.
5 A: How do you know that Steve took the letter?
  B: I noticed him .... (put) it in his briefcase.
6 A: Did Malcolm wash up properly?
  B: Yes. I watched him .... (do) it to make sure.
7 A: Is that Joanne's fiancé?
  B: Yes. I noticed them .... (hold) hands as they went into the cinema.
8 A: Are there any children living next door?
  B: Yes. I often hear them .... (play) as I'm hanging out the washing.
9 A: Did Sarah miss the train?
  B: No, she didn't. I watched her .... (get on) the train before I left the station.

10 **Choose the correct answer.**

1 '...*B*... is very relaxing.'
  'I don't agree. I think it's boring.'
  A Fish   **B** Fishing   **C** To fish
2 'I can't decide what .... to the party.'
  'Why don't you wear your blue dress?'
  A wear   **B** wearing   **C** to wear
3 'Did you go to the cinema last night?'
  'No. My parents made me .... for the exam instead.'
  A to study   **B** studying   **C** study
4 'Did you enjoy your holiday?'
  'Yes, but I am glad .... home again.'
  A being   **B** to be   **C** be
5 'Shall we go to a restaurant this evening?'
  'I'd rather .... at home. I'm exhausted.'
  A stay   **B** staying   **C** to stay
6 'Why did you go to the library?'
  '.............. some books to read.'
  A Get   **B** Getting   **C** To get
7 'Why do you want to buy a car?'
  'Because I hate .... for the bus every day.'
  A waiting   **B** wait   **C** to wait
8 'Do you have any plans for the summer?'
  'Well, Danny suggested .... to Spain for a week.'
  A go   **B** going   **C** to go
9 'Shall we go for a picnic on the beach?'
  'Oh, no! It's far too cold .... to the beach today.'
  A going   **B** to go   **C** go
10 'What is the matter with Peter?'
  'There's no point in .... me. I have no idea.'
  A ask   **B** asking   **C** to ask

11 **Complete the sentences, as in the example.**

1 'Yes, I'll wash your car for you,' said Stuart.
  Stuart agreed ...*to wash*... my car.
2 Julia said to Sam, 'I didn't eat your sweets.'
  Julia denied .... Sam's sweets.
3 'I scratched the CD,' said Tom.
  Tom confessed to .... the CD.
4 Amanda said, 'I hate living in the city.'
  Amanda complained about .... in the city.
5 Mrs Smith said to the children, 'You have until Tuesday to finish your projects.'
  Mrs Smith expects the children .... their projects by Tuesday.
6 Her mother said, 'Don't touch the iron!' but she didn't listen.
  Her mother warned her about .... the iron, but she didn't listen.

Verbs taking the to-infinitive or the -ing form with a change in meaning

◆ **forget + to - inf = not remember**
e.g. I have to go out. I **forgot to buy** a newspaper.
forget + -ing form = not recall
e.g. I'll never **forget travelling** by plane for the first time.

◆ **remember + to - inf = not forget**
e.g. Did you **remember to tell** Sam about the meeting?
remember + -ing form = recall
e.g. I **remember talking** to him before.

◆ **go on + to - inf = then**
e.g. She introduced herself and **went on to talk** about her new book.
go on + -ing form = continue
e.g. He **went on writing** letters until 10.00.

◆ **mean + to - inf = intend to**
e.g. She **means to buy** a new car soon.
mean + -ing form = involve
e.g. She is determined to get a ticket for the concert, even if it **means paying** a lot of money.

◆ **regret + to - inf = be sorry to** (it is normally used in the present simple and is followed by verbs such as *say, tell, inform*)
e.g. We **regret to inform** you that you have failed.
regret + -ing form = feel sorry about
e.g. He **regretted selling** his house.

◆ **try + to - inf = attempt, do one's best**
e.g. We **tried to move** the heavy branch to the side of the road.
try + -ing form = do sth as an experiment
e.g. If you can't go to sleep, **try drinking** some milk.

◆ **stop + to - inf = stop briefly to do sth else**
e.g. He **stopped to fill** the tank with petrol, then continued driving.
stop + -ing form = finish, give up
e.g. He **stopped drinking** coffee because it upset his stomach.

◆ **be sorry + to - inf = apologise for a present action**
e.g. I'**m sorry to say** this, but your work is rather unsatisfactory.
be sorry for + -ing form = apologise for an earlier action
e.g. We **are sorry for keeping** you waiting.

◆ **like + to - inf = think that sth is good or right to do**
e.g. I **like to pay** my bills as soon as I get them.
like + -ing form = enjoy (general preference)
e.g. Tom **likes meeting** new people.
would like + to - inf = want (specific preference)
e.g. I **would like to go** to that new restaurant.

◆ **be afraid + to - inf = the subject is unwilling to do sth**
e.g. He **is afraid to touch** the dog in case it bites him.
be afraid of + -ing form = (the subject is afraid that what is described by the -ing form may happen)
e.g. She doesn't want to drive her father's car. She'**s afraid of crashing** it.

Verbs taking the to-infinitive or the -ing form without a change in meaning

◆ **begin, start, continue, propose, bother, intend**
We never have two -ing forms together.
e.g. We **continued to discuss/discussing** the plans.
Don't **bother to lay/laying** the table.
It's **starting to get** cold. (NOT: ~~It's starting getting cold.~~)

◆ **advise, allow, permit, recommend, encourage**
take the to-infinitive when they are followed by an object or when they are in the passive form. They take the -ing form when they are not followed by an object.
e.g. He **advised us to book** in advance. (object)
We **were advised to book** in advance. (passive)
We **advise booking** in advance. (no object)

◆ **need/require/want + -ing form**
This construction often shows that it is necessary to repair or improve something. 'Need' can also be followed by a passive infinitive.
e.g. The carpet **needs hoovering**.
The **carpet needs to be hoovered**.

12 **Put the verbs in brackets into the correct *infinitive form* or the *-ing form*.**

1 Jane went on ...*sleeping*... (sleep) for another two hours.
2 He told us his name and went on ....
(introduce) us to his wife.
3 We didn't mean .... (interrupt) you.
4 Being a doctor means .... (work) long hours.
5 She tried .... (finish) her homework, but it was too difficult.
6 You should try .... (eat) more fruit. It's good for your health.

7 He regrets .... (argue) with his best friend.

8 We regret .... (inform) you that tonight's performance will be cancelled.

9 Oh, no! I forgot .... (lock) the front door.

10 I'll never forget .... (meet) my favourite film star.

11 Claire likes .... (ski). She says it's very exciting.

12 I like .... (go) to the dentist every six months.

13 I must remember .... (post) these letters today.

14 I remember .... (read) the book, but I don't know who wrote it.

15 I'm sorry for .... (forget) your birthday. It was awful of me.

16 I'm sorry .... (say) that you have failed the exam.

17 She is afraid .... (climb) the tree in case she falls.

18 Mary never wears her diamond ring. She is afraid of .... (lose) it.

19 I have stopped .... (watch) horror films because they give me nightmares.

20 We stopped .... (buy) some food before continuing our journey.

Too - Enough

◆ **Too has a negative meaning. It shows that something is more than enough, necessary or wanted. It is used in the following patterns:**
a) too + adjective/adverb + to -infinitive
   e.g. It is **too cold to go** swimming.
b) too ... for somebody/something
   e.g. This coffee is **too sweet for me**.
c) too ... for somebody/something + to -infinitive
   e.g. This house is **too small for us to live** in.

◆ **Enough has a positive meaning. It shows that there is as much of something as is wanted or needed. It is used in the following patterns:**
a) adjective/adverb + enough + to -infinitive
   e.g. She is **old enough to go** out on her own.
BUT: not + adjective/adverb + enough + to - infinitive (negative meaning)
   e.g. He **did not run fast enough to win** the race.
b) enough + noun + to -infinitive
   e.g. We've got **enough room to put** you up.

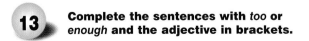

13 **Complete the sentences with too or enough and the adjective in brackets.**

1 A: Did you go to the beach yesterday?
   B: No. It wasn't ...*warm enough*... to go to the beach. (warm)

2 A: Do her new shoes fit her?
   B: No. They are .... (small)

3 A: Have you finished your homework?
   B: I can't. It's .... (difficult)

4 A: Did you hear the announcement?
   B: No. It wasn't .... (loud)

5 A: Can you open the window, please?
   B: I can't. I'm not .... to reach it. (tall)

6 A: It's .... in here. (hot)
   B: Why don't you take your coat off, then?

7 A: Did you enjoy the party last night?
   B: No. We were .... to enjoy it. (tired)

8 A: Why don't you drink your tea?
   B: It's not .... for me to drink. (sweet)

14 **Fill in *too* or *enough* and one of the adjectives from the list to write sentences as in the example. Add an object where necessary.**

heavy, cold, old, quiet, tired, cool, tall, boring

1 I went to bed early last night because I was ...*too tired to stay*... (stay) up late.

2 The soup is too hot. It isn't .... (eat) yet.

3 She isn't .... (reach) the top shelf, so she uses a ladder.

4 The children aren't .... (attend) school yet.

5 It's .... (go) outside without a coat today.

6 The film was .... (watch), so we went for a meal instead.

7 Close the door, please. It isn't .... (work) in here.

8 The bag is .... (carry). Someone else will have to take it.

15 **Complete the sentences, as in the example.**

1 He is very short. He can't be a basketball player.
   He is too ...*short to be a basketball player*....

2 She has saved enough money. She can go on holiday.
   She has saved ....

3 This tea is very hot. I can't drink it.
   This tea is ....

4 Daisy is very young. She can't go to school.
   Daisy is ....

5 They have got lots of space. They can have a party.
   They have got ....

6 Paul is rich. He can buy a yacht.
   Paul is ....

7 It's hot outside. You can't wear a coat.
   It's ....

8 Mary is mature. She can make her own decisions.
   Mary is ....

9 This flat is small. We can't live in it any more.
   This flat is ....

10 Ron has a lot of patience. He can look after the children.
   Ron has ....

Participles

The participles are:

a) present participles (staying, leaving, etc.),
b) past participles (stayed, left, etc.) and
c) perfect participles (having left, etc.).

◆ Present and past participles can be used as adjectives. The present participle (-ing) describes what somebody or something is (it answers the question 'What kind?'). The past participle (-ed) describes how somebody feels (it answers the question 'How do you feel?').

e.g. It was an **embarrassing** situation.
(What kind of situation? Embarrassing.)
He was **embarrassed**. (How did he feel? Embarrassed.)

Participles can also be used:

◆ instead of a relative pronoun and full verb.
e.g. The woman **waving** at me is my aunt.
(= The woman **who is waving** at me is my aunt.)
The new shampoo **advertised** on TV is very expensive.
(= The new shampoo **which is advertised** on TV is very expensive.)

◆ to express reason.
e.g. **Feeling shy**, Laura didn't talk to Ben.
(= **Because she was shy**, ...)
Having seen the film before, I decided to stay at home.
(= **Because I had seen the film** before, I decided to stay at home.)

◆ to express time.
e.g. **After taking/having taken his Master's degree**, he applied for a job.
Having taken his Master's degree, he applied for a job.
(= After he had taken his Master's degree, he applied for a job.)
We met John **while shopping**.
(= We met John **while we were shopping**.)

◆ instead of the past simple in narratives when we describe actions happening immediately one after the other.
e.g. **Hearing** the news, she **fainted**.
(= She heard the news and she fainted.)

◆ to avoid repeating the past continuous in the same sentence.
e.g. He was walking down the street **whistling** a tune.
(= He was walking down the street **and he was whistling** a tune.)

16 Underline the correct word.

1 A: Did you enjoy the horror film?
   B: No. It was very *frightened*/*frightening*.
2 A: Mark is always biting his nails.
   B: I know. It's an extremely *annoyed*/*annoying* habit.
3 A: Why doesn't John study French?
   B: He is not *interested*/*interesting* in learning a foreign language.
4 A: What did you think of that new restaurant?
   B: It was awful! The food was *disgusted*/*disgusting*.
5 A: Miss Shaw is a wonderful teacher.
   B: Yes. She is always *encouraged*/*encouraging* in her attitude towards the students.
6 A: Do you like windsurfing?
   B: Yes. I find it very *excited*/*exciting*.
7 A: Vicky is good at art, isn't she?
   B: Yes. I was *impressed*/*impressing* by her paintings.
8 A: Did you see the fireworks last night?
   B: Yes. It was an *amazed*/*amazing* display.

17 Rewrite the sentences using participles.

1 Because she was tired, Katie went to bed.
   ...*Being tired, Katie went to bed*....
2 He was sitting in the garden and he was drinking his tea.
   ....
3 After Janet had made dinner, she called the children.
   ....
4 The boy who is standing by the door is my brother.
   ....
5 Simon cut his hand while he was chopping some wood.
   ....
6 Donna had a shower before she went to bed.
   ....
7 Because we were late, we took a taxi.
   ....
8 Gary opened the window and breathed the fresh air.
   ....
9 She was lying on her bed and she was reading a book.
   ....
10 The jewels which were taken by the thieves were very valuable.
   ....
11 Amy picked up her pen and started to write the letter.
   ....
12 The man who is walking towards us is a relative of mine.
   ....
13 After the teacher had explained the exercise, he asked the students to do it.
   ....
14 Because she had forgotten to take her purse, she had to borrow some money from a colleague.
   ....

18 Put the verbs in brackets into the correct *infinitive form* or the *-ing form*.

Flight Attendant: Welcome aboard, sir. I hope you enjoy the flight.

Passenger: Thank you. Unfortunately, I'm afraid of **1)** ...*flying*... (fly).

Flight Attendant: Don't worry, sir. Just remember **2)** .... (fasten) your seatbelt and everything will be fine.

Passenger: I don't mean **3)** .... (be) difficult, but I would like **4)** .... (sit) next to the window. Is that alright?

Flight Attendant: Of course. This seat is free. You can sit here. Would you like a newspaper to read?

Passenger: No, thank you. I prefer **5)** .... (read) books to reading newspapers.

Flight Attendant: Well, I must **6)** .... (check) on the other passengers now.

Passenger: Oh. I'm sorry for **7)** .... (talk) too much. I'm just very nervous about the flight.

Flight Attendant: Just try **8)** .... (relax) a little bit, sir. I'll stop **9)** .... (see) how you are later.

Passenger: Thank you very much. I hate **10)** .... (be) so much trouble.

19 Complete the sentences using an *infinitive* or an *-ing form*.

1 They delayed ...*taking*... the decision until they had read the report.

2 He refused .... the book back to the shop.

3 We'd rather not .... with you. We'll stay at home.

4 It's not worth .... John to the party. He won't come.

5 I'm really looking forward to .... to the theatre on Saturday.

6 Mark was kind .... you home after the party.

7 They were very happy .... the good news.

8 You can all .... now if you want.

9 She walked out of the office without .... goodbye.

10 They made her .... the letter again.

11 She has gone to the post office .... some stamps.

12 You must .... hard for your exams.

13 You had better .... or you'll miss the train.

14 She spends most of her spare time .... the piano.

15 You're too young .... at home by yourself.

16 He opened the door only .... that the room was empty.

IN OTHER WORDS

Study these examples. The second sentence has a similar meaning to the first sentence.

1 I think it's difficult to raise children nowadays.
raising I think **raising children is** difficult nowadays.

2 It's too dark to see anything in here.
bright It **isn't bright enough** to see anything in here.

3 She made him accept full responsibility for the accident.
was He **was made to accept** full responsibility for the accident.

4 Could you post this letter for me, please?
mind Would **you mind posting** this letter for me, please?

5 She was amused by the story and burst out laughing.
found She **found the story amusing** and burst out laughing.

6 He had difficulty finding her house.
difficult It was **difficult for him to find** her house.

7 They let me watch the rehearsal.
allowed I **was allowed to watch** the rehearsal.

8 The party was so boring that we didn't enjoy ourselves.
too The party was **too boring for us to** enjoy ourselves.

9 Someone saw Ben throw an envelope in the rubbish bin.
was Ben **was seen to throw** an envelope in the rubbish bin.

10 Using the office photocopier is not allowed.
allow We do not **allow anyone to use** the office photocopier.

20 Complete each sentence with two to five words, including the word in bold.

1 Could you give me a lift to the office, please?
mind Would ...*you mind giving*... me a lift to the office, please?

2 The ring was so expensive that he couldn't afford to buy it.
too The ring was .... to buy.

3 I think it's interesting to learn about other cultures.
learning I think .... interesting.

4 They let Edward go out with his friends last night.
allowed Edward .... with his friends last night.

5 They heard Fiona quarrel with her brother last night.
was Fiona .... with her brother last night.

6 Mum was annoyed by Tina's behaviour and sent her to her room.

found Mum .... and sent her to her room.

7 This knife is too blunt for me to cut the bread with.

sharp This knife isn't .... to cut the bread with.

8 He made us help with the cleaning.

were We .... with the cleaning.

9 She had difficulty reading his handwriting.

difficult It was .... his handwriting.

10 Making personal phone calls is not allowed.

allow We do not .... personal phone calls.

11 The pool isn't deep enough for you to dive into.

shallow The pool .... to dive into.

Common mistakes

- **Eating** junk food **it** is unhealthy. ✗
  Eating junk food **is** unhealthy. ✓

- I'd **better to leave** now. ✗
  I'd **better leave** now. ✓

- You **would better** see a doctor. ✗
  You **had better** see a doctor. ✓

- They **made me to reveal** the plans. ✗
  They **made me reveal** the plans. ✓

- He **stopped to eat** fried food as it gave him indigestion. ✗
  He **stopped eating** fried food as it gave him indigestion. ✓

- Did you **remember buying** some bread? ✗
  Did you **remember to buy** some bread? ✓

- I'd **like going** to the cinema tonight. ✗
  I'd **like to go** to the cinema tonight. ✓

- You **must to work** harder. ✗
  You **must work** harder. ✓

- The soup is too hot to eat **it**. ✗
  The soup is too hot to eat. ✓

- Would you **mind to give** me a lift? ✗
  Would you **mind giving** me a lift? ✓

- I am **enough strong** to lift this box. ✗
  I am **strong enough** to lift this box. ✓

- She left the house **without to lock** the door. ✗
  She left the house **without locking** the door. ✓

- I went to the library **for to borrow** some books. ✗
  I went to the library **to borrow** some books. ✓

- I **saw** a burglar **to break into** my neighbour's house. ✗
  I **saw** a burglar **break into** my neighbour's house. ✓

 21 **Correct the mistakes.**

1 You would better stay in bed today.
2 Mum has stopped to drink fizzy drinks. She is on a diet.
3 This bag is too expensive for me to buy it.
4 Smoking it is dangerous for your health.
5 Would you mind to open the window?
6 I'd love eating a pizza tonight.
7 I stopped at the bakery for to buy some bread.
8 They made me to pay for the broken window.
9 I heard the Taylors to argue.
10 I'd better to ask someone for help.
11 I forgot calling you last night. I'm sorry.
12 He left the shop without to pay for the shirt.
13 You shouldn't to be rude to your parents.
14 He is enough old to drive a car.

 22 **Cross out the unnecessary word.**

1 He went to the florist's for to buy a bouquet of flowers.
2 Emily is not so talented enough to enter the competition.
3 I don't go for camping very often.
4 Mrs Keaton made her daughter to stay at home during the holidays.
5 I hope that to hear from you soon.
6 We saw Helen to get into her car and drive away at top speed.
7 Bungee jumping it is a dangerous activity.
8 She will always remember about cruising the Caribbean.
9 The tickets were too expensive for me to buy them.
10 He dislikes to being alone at the weekends.
11 You had better not to leave without your passport.
12 The house needs being painting.
13 Children would love being given toys.
14 To spending a lot of money on clothes is foolish.

23 **Underline the correct *preposition*.**

1 Adam complained *of*/*about*/*for* having a sore throat.
2 She was concentrating *of*/*on*/*for* writing the report when the phone rang.
3 The two men were charged *for*/*with*/*of* armed robbery.
4 I take care *about*/*for*/*of* my neighbour's cat when she goes on holiday.
5 The politician refused to comment *on*/*for*/*about* the new law.
6 Sheila's friends congratulated her *on*/*for*/*about* passing her exams.
7 Contrary *with*/*of*/*to* what had been written in the papers, the three women were proved innocent.
8 The new teacher found it hard to cope *about*/*for*/*with* the naughty children.

Phrasal Verbs

bring about:	(tr) cause to happen
bring forward:	suggest an idea (often passive)
bring on:	(tr) cause (usu sth unpleasant)
bring out:	(tr) publish; put on the market
bring round:	1) (tr) make sb regain consciousness; **bring to**, 2) (tr) persuade; **bring over (to)**
bring up:	1) (tr) raise a child, 2) mention; introduce a subject
call back:	(int) return a phone call
call for:	1) (tr) need; demand, 2) demand (sth); ask for
call off:	(tr) cancel
call out:	shout; yell
be carried away:	be very excited
carry off:	(tr) do sth successfully
carry on:	continue (after interruption)
carry out:	(tr) 1) fulfil (order, tasks), 2) conduct (an experiment)

24 Fill in the correct particle.

1 When the noise stopped, she carried ...*on*... as if nothing had happened.
2 It's difficult to bring .... children alone.
3 The heavy rains brought .... severe flooding.
4 My favourite singer has just brought .... a new record.
5 Paul carried .... his plan very successfully.
6 I'm busy now, so I'll call you .... later.
7 Some excellent ideas were brought .... at the annual meeting.
8 Scientists carry .... experiments in their laboratories.
9 I'm trying to bring my father .... to my ideas.
10 This job calls .... knowledge of a foreign language.
11 The audience was carried .... by the singer's performance.
12 Janet's asthma attack was brought .... by the smoky atmosphere.
13 When their son was ill, they called .... the doctor.
14 The children carried .... their tasks quickly and quietly.
15 Having fallen in the river, the woman called .... for help.
16 Dad brought .... the subject of holidays during dinner last night.
17 The football match was called .... due to bad weather.
18 The nurse used smelling salts to bring the patient ....

Revision Box

25 Choose the correct answer.

1 'What do you do for a living?'
'I ...*C*... portraits of famous people.'
A am painting　B paints　　C paint

2 'Did you find Tom?'
'Yes. He .... in his study when I found him.'
A worked　　B was working　C works

3 'Where .... when you went to London?'
'In a small family hotel.'
A were you staying　B did you stay　C do you stay

4 'Did you speak to Kate on the phone last night?'
'Yes, but I .... for ages before I finally got through.'
A am trying　　　　　B have been trying
C had been trying

5 'Could you take the rubbish outside for me, please?'
'I .... it.'
A have already done　　　B already do
C had already done

6 'Where is your brother?'
'He .... in the garden, I think.'
A is playing　　B plays　　　C played

7 'Do you see Catherine very often?'
'We .... for lunch twice a month.'
A have met　　B meet　　　C are meeting

8 'What are you doing?'
'I .... for the recipe I want to use tonight.'
A looked　　　B look　　　C am looking

9 'Why is Linda so tired?'
'She .... very hard recently.'
A works　　B is working　　C has been working

10 'You're very late. Where have you been?'
'Well, I ..... home from work when the car broke down.'
A was driving　B am driving　C drove

11 'Have you got your exam results yet?'
'Yes. I .... all of them.'
A am passing　B passed　　C pass

12 '........... your homework yet?'
'No, I'm still busy doing it.'
A Have you finished　　　B Are you finishing
C Do you finish

13 'Sorry I'm late. .... very long?'
'No, only five minutes.'
A Are you waiting　　　　B Do you wait
C Have you been waiting

Infinitive/The -ing form/Too-Enough/Participles

Revision Box

26 **Put the verbs in brackets into the correct tense.**

1 A: I ...'ve seen... (see) three films this week.
  B: I haven't seen any, I'm afraid.
2 A: Why .... (you/taste) the stew?
  B: I think I've put too much salt in it.
3 A: Where is Jack?
  B: He .... (go) to the park with Paul.
4 A: I haven't seen Tom for a long time.
  B: I know. He .... (study) a lot since September.
5 A: John paid for the cinema tickets last night.
  B: Really? He .... (be) very generous these days.
6 A: The children are exhausted.
  B: They .... (play) for hours, that's why.
7 A: I had a very bad day at work yesterday.
  B: So did I. First, the computer .... (break down) and then I .... (spill) coffee on some papers.
8 A: Has Arthur retired now?
  B: Yes. He .... (work) for the same company for forty years when he decided to retire.
9 A: Where are the children?
  B: Oh, Stan .... (take) them to the zoo.
10 A: Have the Smiths moved yet?
  B: Actually, they .... (move) next Saturday.
11 A: .... (you/recognise) that man over there?
  B: No. I don't think I've ever seen him before.
12 A: Shall we stay in tonight?
  B: Actually, I .... (go) to my friend's birthday party.
13 A: Do you want to come to the cinema with me?
  B: Yes, but remember, I .... (not/like) horror films.
14 A: I found a ring while I .... (plant) a tree yesterday.
  B: Really? Can I see it?
15 A: Life .... (be) a lot better fifty years ago.
  B: I agree. People .... (have) more fun.
16 A: I .... (try) to phone you since this morning.
  B: Oh, I have been out shopping with my sister.
17 A: Why are you annoyed with Jason?
  B: Because he .... (always/forget) important things.
18 A: The orchestra played very well last night.
  B: Yes. They .... (practise) together for weeks before they held the concert.

ORAL Activity

Maria Callas was a famous opera singer. Peter Jordan is a reporter who is writing an article about her life. Look at his notes and make sentences, as in the example.

e.g. She went to Athens to study opera in 1937.

- go to Athens / study / opera in 1937
- go on / perform / in many opera houses in America and Europe
- people / enjoy / hear / her sing
- could / sing / in French, German and Italian
- well-known for / sing / difficult roles
- famous for / have / bad temper
- she / be used to / appear / famous venues
- manage / earn / reputation as / excellent singer and actress
- spend / some time / teach / opera at Juilliard
- decide / give / final world concert tour in 1972-73
- retire after / perform / forty / different roles
- consider / be / one of greatest opera singers of the 20th century

WRITING Activity

Peter Jordan is now writing his article about Maria Callas. Look at the Oral Activity again and complete the article.

Maria Callas was born in New York in 1923. She went to Athens to study opera in 1937. After that, she
....
....
....
....
She died in Paris in 1977.

Adjectives

*It's a **cold** day.
The people are skiing on the **crisp white** snow.*

*Life can be very **enjoyable** for **retired** people.
They have a lot of **spare** time and can take up **interesting** hobbies.*

◆ **Adjectives describe nouns. They have the same form in the singular and plural. They go before nouns** (e.g. a *small house*) **but after the verbs be, look, smell, sound, feel, taste, seem, appear, become, get, stay,** etc. (e.g. *She* is *beautiful*. *They* seem *unhappy*.)

◆ **There are opinion adjectives and fact adjectives. Opinion adjectives such as** *boring, exciting*, etc. **show what a person thinks of somebody or something. Fact adjectives such as** *tall, thin, new*, **etc. give us factual information about age, size, colour, origin, material, etc.**

◆ **There are also compound adjectives which are formed with: a) present participles** e.g. a **never ending** journey, **b) past participles** e.g. a **brokendown** washing machine, **c) cardinal numbers + nouns** e.g. a **three-hour** delay (NOT: ~~a three-hours delay~~),

d) **well, badly + past participle**
e.g. **well-behaved** children, **badly-made** furniture

◆ **We can also use nouns as adjectives before other nouns. In this case the nouns have no plural form.** e.g. **morning** paper - **morning** papers, **coffee** table - **coffee** tables

◆ **The following adjectives have a difference in meaning:**
a) *He gave her a **gold** ring. (= ring made of gold) They walked on the **golden** sand. (= sand the colour of gold)*
b) *She bought a **silk** blouse. (= blouse made of silk) This new shampoo promises to give you **silky** hair. (= hair which feels like silk)*
c) *They walked up the **stone** path. (= path made of stone) The man had a **stony** look on his face. (= cold look - like stone)*

ORDER OF ADJECTIVES

◆ **When there are two or more adjectives in a sentence, they usually go in the following order:**

Opinion Adjectives	Fact Adjectives						
	size	age	shape	colour	origin	material	used for/be about	noun
It's a fantastic	small	new	round	red	Swiss	plastic	alarm	clock

◆ *Ordinal numbers* **(first, second, third, etc.) go before** *cardinal numbers* **(one, two, three, etc.)** e.g. the **first two** weeks (NOT: ~~the two first weeks~~)

◆ **The adjectives** *afraid, alike, alive, alone, ashamed, asleep, awake, content, glad, ill, pleased*, **etc. are not followed by nouns.** e.g. *The man was **alive**. Karen is **ill** today.*

◆ **The adjectives** *chief, elder, eldest, former, indoor, inner, main, only, outdoor, outer, principal, upper* **are always followed by nouns.** e.g. *This is my **elder son**.*

◆ **We do not usually use a long list of adjectives before a single noun. A noun is usually described by one, two or three adjectives at the most.** e.g. a **beautiful blue evening** dress

◆ **Certain adjectives can be used with 'the' as nouns to refer to groups of people in general. These are: elderly, middle-aged, old, young, blind, dead, deaf, disabled, living, sick, homeless, hungry, poor, rich, strong, unemployed, weak,** etc.
e.g. **The young** have a lot of energy. (We refer to young people in general.) **but: The young people** of our town are organising a charity concert. (We refer to a specific group of young people).
When we talk about one person we say A/The young man/woman, A/The blind man/woman, etc.
e.g. **The young woman** who lives next door is a medical student.

Underline the opinion adjectives, circle the fact ones, then put them in order.

1 (lace)/ (blue)/ beautiful / handkerchief
...*a beautiful blue lace handkerchief*...

2 a(n) stone / ancient / small / cottage
....

3 a(n) English / huge / wooden / wardrobe
....

4 a(n) Chinese / amazing / old / story
....

5 a(n) American / new / exciting / film
....

6 a pair of / wire / old / reading / glasses
....

7 a(n) wooden / lovely / old-fashioned / table
....

8 a(n) white / linen / Irish / tablecloth
....

9 a chocolate / large / delicious / cake
....

10 a(n) orange / ugly / velvet / sofa
....

 Put the adjectives in the correct order.

Dear Aunt Margaret,

I'm just writing to thank you for the money you sent me last month. It was very generous of you. I've spent it on some lovely things for my new house.

For the living room I bought a lovely pair of 1) ...*blue velvet*... (velvet/blue) curtains and for the bedroom I got a(n) 2) .... (round/large/antique) mirror. While I was shopping I found some 3) .... (silver/ beautiful/tall) candlesticks, which I have put in the dining room. I also bought some 4) .... (soft/cotton/ thick) towels for the bathroom and a 5) .... (green/square/woollen) rug for the guest room. Finally, I went to an auction where I bought a 6) .... (oak/fabulous/English) table for the kitchen.

Thank you once again for the gift.

I hope you'll visit me soon.

Love, Susie

 Fill in: *the + adjective* **or** *the + adjective + people.*

1 This charity provides shelter for ...*the homeless people*... (homeless) of London.

2 It is important to look after .... (elderly), especially in winter.

3 Ambulances took .... (injured) to hospitals in the area.

4 .... (old) in the village are upset about the new road.

5 They are changing the building to make it easier for .... (disabled) to get around.

6 .... (young) in the audience cheered loudly at the end of the concert.

7 .... (poor) of our town receive help from the council.

8 Christine is a nurse who looks after .... (sick).

9 .... (strong) in the group carried the heavy equipment.

10 .... (rich) can afford to live in luxury.

 Make compound adjectives to describe the following:

1 A walk that takes ten minutes.
...*A ten-minute walk*....

2 A story which is written well.
....

3 A building which has twelve storeys.
....

4 A train which moves fast.
....

5 A student who works hard.
....

6 An office which has good lighting.
....

7 A holiday which lasts two weeks.
....

8 A report which has ten pages.
....

 Underline the correct item.

While Lizzie was tidying the attic of her grandmother's house, she came across an old 1) **wooden/wood** chest. When she looked inside, she found a doll wrapped in 2) **silk/silky** paper. The doll had 3) **gold/golden** hair and was wearing a long 4) **woollen/wool** coat. She was beautiful and Lizzie had never seen her before. She sat down on the cold 5) **stony/stone** floor to examine the doll more carefully. She was wearing a real 6) **gold/ golden** necklace and, underneath the coat, a 7) **silky/silk** dress. The doll had belonged to her grandmother when she was young. Lizzie carefully wrapped her up again and placed her gently back in the box.

Adverbs

*Sprinters run **quickly**. They wake up **early in the morning** and train **hard all day**.*

◆ Adverbs usually describe verbs, adjectives, other adverbs or sentences.

◆ An adverb can be one word (*carefully*) or a phrase (*in the morning*). Adverbs can describe manner (how), place (where), time (when), frequency (how often), degree (to what extent), etc.
  e.g. a) He drives **carefully**. (How does he drive? Carefully. - adverb of manner)
  b) Your bag is **here**. (Where is it? Here. - adverb of place)
  c) They'll leave **tomorrow**. (When will they leave? Tomorrow. - adverb of time)
  d) He **sometimes** goes fishing at the weekend. (How often does he go fishing? Sometimes. - adverb of frequency)
  e) She is **very** polite. (How polite is she? Very. - adverb of degree)

Formation of Adverbs

◆ **We usually form an adverb by adding -ly to the adjective.**
  e.g. serious - serious**ly**

◆ **Adjectives ending in -le drop the -e and take -y.**
  e.g. gent**le** - gent**ly**

◆ **Adjectives ending in consonant + y drop the -y and take -ily.**
  e.g. happ**y** - happ**ily**

◆ **Adjectives ending in -l take -ly.**
  e.g. awfu**l** - awfu**lly**

◆ **Adjectives ending in -ic usually take -ally.**
  e.g. drama**tic** - drama**tically**   But: public - pub**licly**

◆ **Adjectives ending in -e take -ly.**
  e.g. poli**te** - poli**tely**   But: true - truly

◆ The following words end in -ly, but they are adjectives: *elderly, cowardly, friendly, likely, deadly, lively, lonely, silly, ugly, lovely*, etc.
  e.g. She's a **lively child**.

  We use the words *way/manner* to form their adverbs.
  e.g. She greeted me **in a friendly way/manner**.
  He complained in a **cowardly way/manner**.

◆ The adverbs *loud(ly), cheap(ly), quick(ly), tight(ly), fair(ly)* and *slow(ly)* are often used without -ly in everyday English.
  e.g. Come here **quick/quickly**.

◆ Some adverbs have the same form as adjectives. These include: *hard, fast, free, high, low, deep, early, late, long, near, straight, right, wrong*. Also *hourly, daily, weekly, monthly* and *yearly*.
  e.g. The lake is **deep**. (adjective)
  They went **deep** into the forest. (adverb)
  These biscuits are very **hard**. (adjective)
  He tried **hard** in order to succeed. (adverb)
  'Bella Donna' is a **weekly** magazine. (adjective)
  It comes out **weekly**. (adverb)

◆ The adverbs below have two forms, each with a different meaning:

● The treasure was buried **deep** underground. (= a long way down)
  He is **deeply** in love with her. (= very)
● The hotel guests can use the swimming pool **free**. (= without payment)
  The animals in the safari park can roam **freely**. (= without limit or restriction.)
● The kite flew **high** in the sky. (= at/to a high level)
  He is a **highly** respected doctor. (= very much)
● She arrived **late** for the meeting. (= not early)
  He hasn't been feeling well **lately**. (= recently)
● Which of his songs do you like **most**? (= superlative of much)
  I'm **mostly** interested in modern art. (= mainly)
● As he came **near**, I realised that something was wrong. (= close)
  She **nearly** fainted when she heard the news. (= almost)
● He is a **pretty** strange man. (= rather)
  The bridesmaids were **prettily** dressed in pink. (= in a pretty way)
● He is working **hard** these days. (= with a lot of effort)
  They **hardly** go anywhere now that they have children. (= almost never)

Note: *Hardly* has a negative meaning and is often used with: *any, anyone, anywhere, anything* and *ever*.

6 **For each gap, turn the adjective into an adverb.**

Julia was walking **1)** ...*quickly*... (quick) down the street when she heard someone call her name **2)** .... (loud). She looked **3)** .... (nervous) behind her, but the street was **4)** .... (complete) empty. There was nobody there. **5)** .... (Sudden), she heard her name again. She turned to see her brother running towards her, smiling **6)** .... (cheerful). 'Didn't you hear me?' he laughed **7)** .... (happy). 'Nick!' gasped Julia. 'You **8)** .... (near) frightened me to death!'

 7 **Underline the correct item.**

1 This is a **pretty**/**prettily** complicated situation.
2 They had **hard**/**hardly** been home for a minute when the phone rang.
3 My friends are **most**/**mostly** vegetarians.
4 Her loose outfit allowed her to move **free**/**freely**.
5 The shelf was so **high**/**highly** that he couldn't reach it.
6 John may be **late**/**lately** home tonight, as he has a lot of work to do.
7 The room was **pretty**/**prettily** decorated.
8 Children under five years old travel **free**/**freely**.
9 Sue has **near**/**nearly** finished her homework.
10 They have been going out a lot **late**/**lately**.
11 This college is **high**/**highly** recommended for its range of courses.
12 The miners dug **deep**/**deeply** to find coal.
13 The new supermarket is very **near**/**nearly** our house.
14 He is **deep**/**deeply** involved in the scandal.
15 We found it **hard**/**hardly** to get used to living in a foreign country.
16 Which of Mel Gibson's films do you like **most**/**mostly**?

 8 **Underline the correct item.**

It was Lucy's birthday and she was very **1)** **sad**/**sadly**. She had been waiting **2)** **hopeful**/**hopefully** all morning for the postman to arrive. **3)** **Sudden**/**Suddenly**, the letterbox rattled **4)** **gentle**/**gently** and an envelope fell **5)** **soft**/**softly** onto the doormat. Picking it up, Lucy noticed **6)** **miserable**/**miserably** that it was a bill. There were no cards, no presents and no **7)** **pretty**/**prettily** bouquets of flowers. Lucy **8)** **near**/**nearly** burst into tears. Just then, there was a **9)** **loud**/**loudly** knock on the door. Opening the door **10)** **slow**/**slowly**, Lucy saw all her friends holding **11)** **brightly**/**bright** wrapped gifts and shouting 'Happy Birthday'. Lucy **12)** **immediate**/**immediately** cheered up and greeted her friends **13)** **warm**/**warmly**.

ORDER OF ADVERBS

◆ **Adverbs usually go after verbs but before adjectives, other adverbs and participles.**
  e.g. He **speaks softly.**
  She is **amazingly beautiful.**
  He drove **very fast.**
  Computers are **extensively used** *nowadays.*

◆ **Adverbs of manner go before the main verb, after the auxiliary verb or at the end of the sentence.**
  e.g. She **easily passed** *the exam.*
  We are **eagerly waiting** *for his letter.*
  He acted **foolishly.**

◆ **Adverbs of degree (*absolutely, completely, totally, extremely, very, quite, rather, etc.*) go before an adjective, an adverb or a main verb, but after an auxiliary verb.**
  e.g. This is **totally** *unacceptable.*
  They arrived **rather** *early.*
  We **absolutely** *love her sense of humour.*
  I don't **quite** *understand what you mean.*

◆ **Adverbs of frequency go after auxiliary verbs and the verb *to be*, but before main verbs.**
  e.g. He **is always** *ready to help.*
  Sam **often complains** *about his salary.*

◆ **Adverbs of place and time usually go at the end of the sentence.**
  e.g. There is a café **nearby.**
  I'll meet you **tomorrow.**

Some one-syllable adverbs of time such as *soon, now* and *then*, go before the main verb, but after the auxiliary verb or the verb *to be*.
  e.g. She **then told** *him what had happened.*
  He **will soon** *inform us about his decision.*

◆ **We can put an adverb at the beginning of a sentence if we want to emphasise it.**
  e.g. **Slowly,** *he closed the door behind him. (manner)*
  In the living room, *there is an antique grandfather clock. (place)*
  Yesterday, *I met the President. (time)*

◆ **When there are two or more adverbs in the same sentence, they usually come in the following order: manner – place – time.**
  e.g. The baby slept **quietly in his cot all night long.**

If there is a verb of movement, such as *go, come, leave* in the sentence, then the adverbs come in the following order: place – manner – time.
  e.g. He came **to work by bus this morning.**

9 Put the adverbs in brackets in the correct place in the sentences, as in the example.

One of the most famous fashion designers of the 20th century was Gianni Versace.

1 At the age of eighteen, Versace began working for his mother and learned the skills of dressmaking and design. (quickly)

At the age of eighteen, Versace began working for his mother and ...*quickly*... learned the skills of dressmaking and design.

2 He enjoyed designing coloured clothes. (brightly)
....

3 He worked throughout his career. (very hard)
....

4 By 1982, he was famous and had won the first of many awards. (incredibly)
....

5 His clothes were popular with famous musicians, such as Elton John and George Michael. (extremely)
....

6 He was asked to design costumes for ballets, shows and concerts. (frequently)
....

7 He was respected by other fashion designers. (greatly)
....
....

8 Versace died in 1997, at the age of fifty. (sadly)
....
....
....

10 Say the sentences in as many ways as possible, using the adverbs in brackets.

1 I will cut the grass. (on Sunday).
...I will cut the grass on Sunday./On Sunday, I will cut the grass....

2 Joanne has been writing letters to her friends. (all day)
3 He has been working. (all day/in his office)
4 We placed the box. (on the table/carefully)
5 They bought some fruit. (yesterday/at the market)
6 He walked. (quietly/out of the room/during the film)
7 The party was amazing. (utterly)
8 We were lost. (completely)
9 Jenny has been reading her magazine. (all morning/in the garden)
10 They knew they had lost the match. (then)
11 They have been talking. (in the hall/for hours)
12 She changed her clothes. (quickly)
13 I was feeling tired. (extremely)
14 He is doing his homework. (quietly/in his bedroom)
15 We watched a film. (last night/at the cinema)

Fairly - Quite - Rather - Pretty

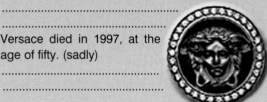

| fairly expensive | quite expensive | rather/pretty expensive | very expensive |

◆ **a/an + fairly**
 e.g. *This is **a fairly good** CD, but it's not the best they've made.*

◆ **a) quite + a/an (= enough)**
 e.g. *This is **quite a good** CD. You ought to buy it.*

 b) quite + adjectives such as *horrible, ridiculous, brilliant, amazing, extraordinary, useless, impossible, true, exhausted, certain*, etc. (= completely, totally)
 e.g. *This machine is **quite useless**.*
 *I'm **quite certain** about this.*

◆ **a) rather + a/an OR a/an + rather (= more than usual, more than wanted, expected, etc.)**
 e.g. *She has **rather a soft**/**a rather soft** voice.*
 *I expected the book to be boring, but it was **rather interesting**.*

 b) rather + comparative form/too
 e.g. *Ted is **rather more experienced** than Alec.*
 *She spends **rather too** much money on clothes.*

◆ **a/an + pretty (= usually in everyday English)**
 e.g. *He had **a pretty nasty** accident the other day.*

11 Underline the correct word.

1 Being a nurse is a *quite*/*pretty* stressful job.
2 He has *rather*/*fairly* a funny name.
3 Jane is *rather*/*quite* more athletic than Susan.
4 She stayed out *rather*/*fairly* too late last night.
5 That story was *quite*/*rather* true.
6 She is *quite*/*fairly* a friendly woman.
7 I didn't expect to enjoy the film, but it was *fairly*/*rather* brilliant.
8 He is *rather*/*fairly* good at his job, but he sometimes makes mistakes.
9 It was a *fairly*/*quite* interesting book, but it wasn't the best I've read.
10 This tin opener doesn't work. It's *fairly*/*quite* useless.
11 It was *pretty*/*rather* a long way from the station to the hotel.
12 It was *rather*/*pretty* a waste of time watering the plants. It's raining now.

Adjectives - Adverbs - Comparisons

Comparisons

ticket: £20
London-Leeds: 4.5 hrs

The coach is **cheap**.
It is **slow**, though.

ticket: £45
London-Leeds: 2 hrs

The train is **more expensive**
than the coach. It is also **faster**.

ticket: £100
London-Leeds: 40 mins

The plane is **the most expensive**
of all. It is also **the fastest**.

◆ For comparison, adjectives have got two forms: the comparative and the superlative.

◆ We use the comparative form + than to compare two people, things, etc.
e.g. Tina is **shorter than** Pam.
This chair is **more comfortable than** the other one.

◆ We use the + superlative form + of/in to compare one person, thing, etc with more than one person, thing, etc. in the same group. We use *in* when we talk about places.
e.g. Peter is **the smartest of all** my students.
'Don's' is **the most expensive** restaurant **in** our town.

◆ The comparative of one-syllable adjectives is formed by adding -er, and the superlative by adding -est. e.g. soft - soft**er** - soft**est** The comparative of *real, right* and *wrong* is formed with more and the superlative with most. e.g. real - **more** real - **most** real
Some one-syllable adjectives of abstract meaning such as *clear, safe, true, free, wise,* etc. take either -er/-est or more/most. e.g. clear - clear**er** - clear**est** OR clear - **more** clear - **most** clear

◆ The comparative of two-syllable adjectives ending in -y is formed by adding -ier and the superlative by adding -iest. e.g. easy - eas**ier** - eas**iest** (more usual)
Also easy - **more** easy - **most** easy (less usual)

◆ Some two-syllable adjectives such as: *clever, common, stupid, narrow, gentle, friendly, simple,* etc. take either -er/-est or more/most.
e.g. common - **commoner** - **commonest**
OR common - **more common** - **most common**

◆ The comparative of adjectives ending in -ing (interesting), -ed (pleased), -ful (careful) and -less (careless) is formed with more and the superlative with most. e.g. thrill**ing** - **more** thrilling - **most** thrilling

◆ The comparative of adjectives of three or more syllables is formed with more and the superlative with most.
e.g. intelligent - **more** intelligent - **most** intelligent

Comparative and Superlative Forms of Adverbs

The comparative and superlative forms of adverbs are formed in the same way as those of adjectives.

◆ Adverbs which have the same form as the adjective usually take -er in the comparative and -est in the superlative.
e.g. hard - hard**er** - hard**est**   late - lat**er** - lat**est**

◆ Adverbs formed by adding -ly to the adjective take more in the comparative and most in the superlative form.
e.g. comfortably - **more** comfortably - **most** comfortably

Irregular Comparatives and Superlatives

adjective/adverb	comparative	superlative
good/well	better	best
bad/badly	worse	worst
much/many/a lot of	more	most
little	less	least
far	further/farther	furthest/farthest

Note:
a) further/farther (adv) = longer (in distance)
e.g. Barclays Bank is **further/farther** away than Lloyds.
further (adj) = more   e.g. Let's hope there won't be any **further** delays. (NOT: ... farther delays)
b) elder/eldest (+noun) (adj) = for members of a family e.g. My **elder** brother is a doctor.
But: My brother is **older** than me. (NOT: elder than)

Adjectives - Adverbs - Comparisons

We use adjectives or their comparative or superlative forms with the following words:

a) **very + adjective**
   e.g. It's **very cold** today.

b) **even / a lot / much / far / a bit / a little / slightly + comparative**
   e.g. He seems **much better** today.

c) **by far + superlative**
   e.g. She's **by far the most beautiful** woman I've ever seen.

d) **most + adj/adv = very**
   e.g. This is **most unusual**. (It is **very** unusual.)

e) **any/no + comparative (it is used in questions and negations)**
   e.g. The days aren't getting **any warmer**.
   I want **no more** of that kind of behaviour.

12 Put the adjectives in brackets into the comparative or superlative form, adding any necessary words.

1 A: Did you enjoy the film?
   B: Yes. It was ...*the funniest*... (funny) film I've ever seen.
2 A: James is very tall.
   B: Yes. He's .... (tall) boy in our class.
3 A: Was it a good party?
   B: Yes. I left far .... (late) I had intended to.
4 A: Did you like the black dress?
   B: Yes, but it was far .... (expensive) the blue one.
5 A: Why do you want to go to Spain?
   B: Because it's much .... (warm) England.
6 A: Do you enjoy your job?
   B: Oh, yes. It's .... (good) job I've ever had.
7 A: If you need any .... (far) help, just ask me.
   B: Thank you. That's very kind of you.
8 A: My teacher is very clever.
   B: Yes. She's .... (intelligent) woman I've ever met.
9 A: Dinosaurs were .... (big) houses.
   B: I know. They were enormous.
10 A: How much did you pay for that bag?
   B: £5. It was .... (cheap) one I could find.
11 A: That exam was really difficult.
   B: I agree. It was a lot .... (difficult) I had expected.
12 A: Have you heard James playing the piano lately?
   B: Yes, but he doesn't seem to be getting .... (good).

13 Fill in the gaps with the correct form of the adjective/adverb in brackets.

1 I like living in the country. It's a lot ...*more peaceful*... (peaceful) than the city.
2 I felt very ill last week, but I'm slightly .... (good) now.
3 I can't hear you. Could you speak a little ....
   (loud) please?
4 Steven is .... (tall) boy in the basketball team.
5 This computer is very old. I need something ....
   (modern).
6 The new library is far .... (close) to my house than the old one.
7 Jane's new haircut makes her look much ....
   (attractive).
8 This jacket was by far .... (expensive) in the shop.

14 Put the adjectives in brackets into the comparative or superlative form, adding any necessary words.

Dear Anita,

   I'm writing to tell you about the auction I went to last weekend. It was held in 1) ..*the largest* ...(large) house in the village and the items being sold were far 2) ....
.... (beautiful) I had expected.
   I saw 3) .... (pretty) vase I've ever seen, but it was also 4) .... (expensive) item there, so I couldn't afford to buy it. I bid for some chairs. They were far 5) .... (nice) mine, but unfortunately someone made a 6) .... (good) offer than me and I couldn't afford to make a 7) .... (high) bid.
   In the end, I bought 8) .... (small) item of all, although it was not 9) .... (cheap) of all! It was a gold locket, which I'm going to give to my 10) ....
(old) daughter on her 18th birthday. I think it's 11) ....
.... (lovely) necklace I've ever seen and it was 12) .... (easy) to carry home than a set of chairs!
   I enjoyed the auction very much and hope to go to another one soon. Perhaps next time you'll come with me. Write soon and tell me all your news.

                                    Love,
                                    Maggie

15 Write the correct form of the comparative or superlative and complete the sentences with your own ideas.

1 In my opinion, ...*the tiger is the most dangerous*... (dangerous) animal of all.
2 .... is .... (nice) place I have ever been to.
3 .... (sweet) sugar.
4 I can .... (good), but I can .... even .... (good).
5 I think .... (difficult) subject of all.
6 .... (valuable) rubies.
7 .... (healthy) food of all.
8 .... (efficient) old ones.
9 .... (intelligent) person I have ever met.
10 .... (expensive) silver jewellery.

Types of Comparisons

♦ **as + adjective + as**
not so/as + adjective + as
*e.g. She is **as tall as** I am.*
*It is **not so/as hot as** it was yesterday.*

♦ **twice/three times, etc./half as + adjective + as**
*e.g. Their car was **twice as expensive as** ours.*

♦ **the same ... as**
*e.g. Your dress is **the same** colour **as** mine.*

♦ **less + (adjective) ... than**
the least + (adjective) ... of/in
*e.g. The Park Hotel is **less expensive than** the Plaza.*
*The King George is **the least expensive of** all.*

♦ **the + comparative ..., the + comparative**
*e.g. **The earlier** we set off, **the earlier** we'll arrive.*

♦ **comparative + and + comparative**
*e.g. The weather is getting **warmer and warmer**.*

---

16 Fill in the blanks, as in the examples.

1 The noise got ...*louder and louder*... (loud) until I couldn't bear it any longer.
2 ...*The harder*... (hard) he works, ...*the more successful*... (successful) he becomes.
3 It rained .... (hard) until the river burst its banks.
4 .... (cold) it got, ... (many) clothes they had to put on to keep warm.
5 Jake ran .... (fast) and won the race.
6 .... (high) he jumped, ... (loud) the crowd cheered.
7 Cars are getting .... (cheap) as the years go by.
8 .... (young) you are, ... (easy) you find it to learn things.
9 .... (many) people are opening their own businesses these days.
10 .... (old) he gets, ... (tall) he grows.

---

17 Compare the following hobbies using the adjectives from the list.

artistic, easy to learn, tiring, expensive, cheap, relaxing

painting   golf   carpentry

e.g. *Painting is the most artistic of all.*
Golf isn't so/as artistic as carpentry.

Like/As

Like is used:

♦ **for similarities.** *e.g. She swims **like** a fish.*

♦ **after feel, look, smell, sound, taste + noun.**
*e.g. It feels **like** silk.*

♦ **with nouns, pronouns or the -ing form to express similarity or contrast.**
*e.g. There's no place **like** home.*
*No one can sing **like** him.*

As is used:

♦ **to say what sb or sth really is (jobs or roles).**
*e.g. She works **as** a tour guide. (She is a tour guide.)*
*Harrison Ford was great **as** Indiana Jones.*

♦ **in certain expressions: as usual, as ... as, as much, such as, the same as.**
*e.g. He started complaining **as usual**.*

♦ **after accept, be known, class, describe, refer to, regard, use.**
*e.g. He **is known as** the father of modern medicine.*

♦ **in clauses of manner to mean 'in the way that'.**
*e.g. Do **as** I tell you.*

---

18 Fill in the gaps with *like* or *as*.

1 A: Tara is a wonderful artist.
B: Yes. No one else can paint ...*like*... her.
2 A: I wish Sarah would stop being so immature.
B: I agree. She acts .... a child sometimes.
3 A: How shall I tie my shoelaces?
B: Do it .... we taught you.
4 A: The play last night was fantastic.
B: Yes. The lead actor was wonderful .... Macbeth.
5 A: What does Mark do for a living?
B: He works .... a hotel manager.
6 A: What kind of meat is this?
B: I'm not sure. It tastes .... beef.
7 A: I've just bought this dress.
B: Gosh! It's exactly the same .... the one I bought!
8 A: I'm sure I know that man.
B: Me too. He looks .... my old maths teacher.
9 A: It was far too hot in that room.
B: I know. It was .... being in an oven.
10 A: Eric Clapton is very talented, isn't he?
B: Yes. He is known .... one of the greatest rock musicians of our time.
11 A: What is Peter cooking?
B: I don't know. It smells .... fish.

Common mistakes

- The coffee is quite strong **to drink**. ✗
  The coffee is quite strong. ✓

- Pam is taller **than I**. ✗
  Pam is taller **than me**. ✓
  Pam is taller **than I am**. ✓

- Jack is **not as clever than** Mike. ✗
  Jack is **not as clever as** Mike. ✓

- I'm older than you **two years**. ✗
  I'm **two years** older than you. ✓

- Dad works **hardly**. ✗
  Dad works **hard**. ✓

- He spoke to me **angrier** than usual. ✗
  He spoke to me **more angrily** than usual. ✓

- This car is **twice more expensive than** that one. ✗
  This car is **twice as expensive as** that one. ✓

- My sister is five years **elder than** me. ✗
  My sister is five years **older than** me. ✓

- The Nile is **the more longer** river in the world. ✗
  The Nile is **the longest** river in the world. ✓

- Tom is **a better student from** his sister. ✗
  Tom is **a better student than** his sister. ✓

- Mount Everest is the highest mountain **of the world**. ✗
  Mount Everest is the highest mountain **in the world**. ✓

- Their house is **modern as** ours. ✗
  Their house is **as modern as** ours. ✓

- The little girl **looked as** an angel. ✗
  The little girl **looked like** an angel. ✓

- He **smiled friendly**. ✗
  He **smiled in a friendly way**. ✓

- It is **cold extremely** today. ✗
  It is **extremely cold** today. ✓

- Call me if you need **farther information**. ✗
  Call me if you need **further information**. ✓

- He is **a quite tall** man. ✗
  He is **quite a tall** man. ✓

- The new sofa is **quite bigger** than the old one. ✗
  The new sofa is **rather bigger** than the old one. ✓

19 **Correct the mistakes.**

1 I'm shorter than you three inches.
2 Steve is older than I.
3 The little boy sang as a bird.
4 Paul is not as handsome than Tom.
5 She is a quite pretty girl.
6 Sally is the more taller girl in our class.
7 Let me know if you need any farther help.
8 Tracey studies hardly.

9 My best friend is two years elder than me.
10 The church is the oldest building of the village.
11 She did her homework more careful than usual.
12 His flat is big as mine.
13 Her new car is quite faster than her old one.
14 This cake is quite sweet to eat.
15 The green dress is twice cheaper than the black one.
16 I feel ill very today.
17 She laughed happy.

20 **Cross out the unnecessary word.**

1 He is much more taller than his brother.
2 As time went by, I got the more and more nervous.
3 I hardly not know anyone in my new job.
4 Going on holiday abroad is very more exciting than staying at home.
5 This flat is so bigger than the one we saw yesterday.
6 Her brooch is twice as more expensive as mine.
7 The more time you spend with your children, the more than they appreciate it.
8 This is the most funniest book I've ever read.
9 This chewing gum tastes as like cinnamon.
10 She invited the most of her friends to a barbecue.
11 Your handbag is the same colour as to mine.
12 He is regarded as like the best author of the century.
13 The weather is becoming hotter and even hotter.
14 Talking to him was as like talking to a brick wall.
15 It was a quite an interesting lecture.
16 Paul is as much old as Michael.
17 This ring is by far prettier than the other one we saw.
18 This house is the less expensive than the others.

21 **Read the text and fill in the word which best fits each space. Use only one word in each space.**

New York City is one of **1)** ...*the*... largest cities **2)** .... the world. It is also one of the most densely populated, with an estimated 7,400,000 inhabitants. Manhattan is the **3)** .... popular area of the city with tourists and has **4)** .... interesting sights. There is also **5)** .... a large number of businesses in this area of the city, including the head offices of some of the world's leading companies. New York's subway system provides transport for more **6)** .... 33% of the city's work force.

New York is also regarded **7)** .... a centre of entertainment. Broadway is the scene of many box-office hits, Carnegie Hall is one of the **8)** .... famous concert halls in the world and the city is also the home of several opera and ballet companies.

With **9)** .... choice of food, entertainment and social life than any other city, it is **10)** .... any wonder that people flock to New York to experience life in the Big Apple.

Phrasal Verbs

come across:	(tr) meet/find by chance; **run across**
come along:	(int) 1) hurry up; **come on**, 2) appear; arrive by chance
come by:	(tr) obtain
come down with:	(tr) become ill; **go down with**
come into:	(tr) inherit
come off:	1) (int) succeed, 2) leave (sth)
come out:	1) go on strike, 2) (of flowers) begin to blossom, 3) (int) be published; **bring out**, 4) (news, truth) be revealed; **bring out**
come over:	(int) visit
come round:	1) visit casually, 2) (int) regain consciousness; **come to/bring round**, 3) change one's point of view
come up:	1) (int) be mentioned; **bring up**, 2) arise; occur
come up against:	(tr) encounter (difficulties); **run up against**
come up with:	(tr) find; think of (a solution, an answer, etc)
cut down:	(tr) 1) cause to fall by cutting, 2) (int) reduce sth
cut down on:	(tr) reduce consumption; **cut back on**
cut into:	interrupt; **break in**
cut off:	1) disconnect, 2) (usu passive) isolate
cut out:	(tr) take out, omit
be cut out for/ to be:	be suited for (a profession)

22 **Fill in the correct particle.**

1 The truth came ...*out*... when the police started their investigation.
2 I came .... my old school books yesterday when I was tidying the attic.
3 My house has a beautiful garden. Why don't you come .... and see it?
4 I'm sorry to cut .... your conversation, but I'd like to ask a question.
5 The private detective came .... the case when he couldn't solve it.
6 I don't think Alison is cut .... to be a nurse. She faints at the sight of blood.
7 I was waiting for the bus when Emma came .... It was a lovely surprise to see her!
8 The boys came .... a brilliant idea for raising money.

9 Ellen is in bed. She's come .... the flu.
10 They decided to cut .... some of the text to make it shorter.
11 You ought to cut .... the amount of sugar you eat.
12 Come .... boys; Let's get going.
13 The electricity was cut .... when they didn't pay the electricity bill.
14 I wish Dad would come .... to the fact that I'm not a child any more.
15 How did you come .... that beautiful necklace?
16 His new novel has just come ...., and it is bound to be a best-seller.
17 The village was cut .... during the heavy snowstorm.
18 A few problems came .... during the course of the project.
19 He came .... a fortune when his father died.
20 The patient slowly came .... after his operation.
21 The builders came .... some major problems while they were laying the foundations.

23 **Underline the correct preposition.**

1 This antique table dates back *from/to/in* 1872.
2 There is great demand *from/for/of* fresh products.
3 The manager demands respect *of/from/to* his employees.
4 My plants died *from/by/in* lack of water.
5 Princess Diana died *of/from/in* an accident.
6 One disadvantage *of/to/in* smoking is that it is bad for your health.
7 There are some disadvantages *of/in/to* owning a car.
8 John is an expert *at/on/of* the subject of British history.
9 Mandy is an expert *in/with/on* a needle and thread.
10 Adam is engaged *with/to/in* a famous actress.
11 Mr Hills is engaged *to/in/with* an important meeting.
12 I dreamt *of/about/for* taking my exams last night.
13 I often dream *from/of/about* travelling abroad.
14 There is a difference *between/of/from* being alone and being lonely.
15 He differs *from/of/between* his brother in many ways.
16 Small children are dependent *on/of/with* their parents.
17 A good friend is someone you can depend *by/for/on* in difficult times.
18 Having a broken arm, he had difficulty *by/in/of* dressing himself.
19 Jake was disappointed *by/with/of* his exam results.
20 My parents disapprove *with/for/of* motorbikes.
21 We were dissatisfied *with/by/of* the hotel service, so we complained to the manager.
22 Kate is experienced *of/with/in* working with children.
23 There was no excuse *of/for/against* his behaviour.
24 He promised to pay for the damage *to/for/of* my car.
25 The children were very excited *by/about/for* the trip.

Adjectives - Adverbs - Comparisons

IN OTHER WORDS

Study these examples. The second sentence has a similar meaning to the first sentence.

1 Beth is more intelligent than Kate.
   as   Kate **isn't as/so intelligent as** Beth.
   less   Kate **is less intelligent than** Beth.
2 Can't you drive any faster than that?
   fastest Is that **the fastest you can** drive?
3 Fiona has received the same number of letters as me.
   many   Fiona has received **as many letters as** me.
4 I've never read such an interesting book.
   the   It's **the most interesting book** I've ever read.
5 Nora is the most careful driver of all.
   as   No one else **drives as carefully as** Nora does.
   than   Nora is **more careful than any** other driver.
              Nora is a **more careful driver than** anyone else.
              Nora **drives more carefully than** anyone else.
6 As she gets older, she becomes more sophisticated.
   the   The older she gets, **the more sophisticated** she becomes.

24 **Complete the sentences with two to five words, including the word in bold.**

1 I've never heard such a silly excuse.
   the   It's ...*the silliest excuse*... I've ever heard.
2 Jane's car was cheaper than Adam's.
   less   Jane's car .... Adam's.
3 As we got closer, I became more nervous.
   the   The closer we got, ... I became.
4 Tom has bought the same number of sweets as Lucy.
   many   Tom has bought .... Lucy.
5 Ben is smarter than Steve.
   as   Steve .... Ben.
6 Can't you eat any more than that?
   most   Is that ....you can eat?
7 As I study more, I get better grades.
   the   The more I study, ... I get.
8 I've never known such an independent young woman.
   the   She's .... I've ever known.
9 Josie has the same number of CDs as David.
   many   Josie has ....David.
10 Keith is the best tennis player of all.
   than   Keith... anyone else.

25 **Choose the correct answer.**

1 'You ...*B*... a mess.'
   'Sorry. I'll tidy up.'
   A always make   **B** are always making
   C will always make
2 'You had better .... that letter today.'
   'OK. I'll do it.'
   A posting   **B** to post   **C** post
3 'It's not worth .... the house now. It's winter.'
   'I agree. Let's wait till spring comes.'
   A painting   **B** to paint   **C** paint
4 'You look happy.'
   'I am. I .... my holiday.'
   A think about   **B** am thinking about
   C thought about
5 'Jenny has been writing letters all morning.'
   'Yes. She .... six letters so far.'
   A wrote   **B** has been writing   **C** has written
6 'Bill looks very tired.'
   'Yes. He .... the house all afternoon.'
   A has been cleaning   **B** has cleaned
   C had been cleaning
7 'Have you seen Jackie recently?'
   'No. I haven't seen her .... May.'
   A since   **B** for   **C** before
8 'Pauline always sits by herself.'
   'Yes, she is too shy .... to anyone.'
   A to talk   **B** talking   **C** talk
9 'Peter has been spending a lot of money lately.'
   'I know. He .... a new computer yesterday.'
   A has bought   **B** bought   **C** had bought
10 'Did John visit you last night?'
   'Yes. I .... on the phone when he arrived.'
   A talked   **B** am talking   **C** was talking
11 'Joanne is a secretary, isn't she?'
   'Yes. She .... as a secretary for seven years.'
   A has been working   **B** is working   **C** works
12 'Is Katie enjoying her university course?'
   'Yes. She .... the lectures very interesting.'
   A found   **B** had found   **C** finds
13 'Why are you all so excited?'
   'Dad suggested .... the weekend in the mountains.'
   A spend   **B** to spend   **C** spending

Adjectives - Adverbs - Comparisons

Revision Box

You are interviewing people for a position within your company. Look at the information below and make comparisons using the adjectives and adverbs in the list, as in the example.

qualified, fluently, experienced, reliable, friendly, fast

e.g. *Miss Houston is more qualified than Mr Spencer. Mrs Thompson is the most qualified of all.*

26 Expand the notes into sentences to complete the letter.

Dear Sir/Madam,

I / write / to you / to apply for / position / of / science teacher / which / advertise / Evening Argus newspaper last Friday.

I / graduate / from university five years ago and I / teach / science / Baker Comprehensive School since then. I / also organise / extra activities / for children / after school / for / last three years.

I / enjoy teaching / and / I / be very patient / with young children. I / attend / several seminars / on subject / teaching science / primary school children.

I / ask / my current employer / for / time off / to attend interviews / so / I / be free to / visit your school if / you / wish to meet me.

I / hope / hear / from you soon.

Yours faithfully,
Gary Taylor

Qualifications: Bachelor of Arts
Experience: 3 years in similar position
Languages: fluent French
Skills: types 100 words per minute
Personality: very reliable, quite friendly

Miss Houston

Qualifications: 4 A-levels
Experience: 1 year in similar position
Languages: a little French
Skills: types 80 words per minute
Personality: not very friendly, quite reliable

Mr Spencer

Qualifications: Bachelor of Arts,
Master of Arts
Experience: 2 years in similar position
Languages: working knowledge of French
Skills: types 120 words per minute
Personality: very friendly, not very reliable

Mrs Thompson

27 Complete the sentences with two to five words, including the word in bold.

1 My parents don't allow me to go out alone.
   let   My parents ...*don't let me go*... out alone.
2 The horse isn't fast enough to win the race.
   slow   The horse is .... the race.
3 She prefers reading to watching television.
   read   She ....
             watch television.
4 Would you open the door for me, please?
   kind   Would you be .... the door
             for me, please?
5 I was so angry that I couldn't speak.
   too   I was .... speak.
6 He spent weeks writing the report.
   took   It .... the report.
7 We found the news very disturbing.
   were   We .... the news.
8 She has difficulty in making new friends.
   difficult It is .... new friends.
9 They made me work late last night.
   was   I .... last night.
10 They heard Tom argue with the boss.
   was   Tom..
             with the boss.

You now have to write a report for your boss, comparing the three candidates. Look at the Oral Activity again and complete the report below.

TO: Mrs K. Athow
FROM: Miss R. Allchin
DATE: 3rd June

  I interviewed three candidates for the position of Personal Assistant to Head of Sales in France: Miss Houston, Mr Spencer and Mrs Thompson. Miss Houston is more qualified than Mr Spencer, but Mrs Thompson is the most qualified of all as she has a Bachelor of Arts and a Master of Arts Degree. ....

....

  I personally believe that Miss Houston is the best candidate for the job, as she has all the necessary qualifications.

Revision 1 (Units 1 - 3)

1 Choose the correct answer.

1 ...*B*... did Susie leave home?
   A How long   **B** How long ago   **C** While

2 I don't remember .... that shop before.
   A see   **B** to see   **C** seeing

3 His car is not .... as mine.
   A as modern   **B** more modern   **C** most modern

4 The teacher made me .... behind after school.
   A to stay   **B** stay   **C** staying

5 We couldn't find anywhere .... the car.
   A park   **B** to park   **C** parking

6 He is thinking about .... to Spain this summer.
   A go   **B** to go   **C** going

7 .... to Mike today? I need to ask him something.
   A Will you be speaking   **B** Will you have spoken
   C Will you have been speaking

8 He's .... the cleverest boy in the school.
   A far   **B** by far   **C** much

9 Mr Johnson is regarded .... a very successful lawyer.
   A like   **B** so   **C** as

10 I .... my work by 4 o'clock, so I went home.
   A had finished   **B** was finishing   **C** will have finished

11 The weather is getting hotter and ....
   A the hotter   **B** hottest   **C** hotter

12 I haven't played tennis .... I was at school.
   A for   **B** since   **C** just

13 That was .... party I have ever been to.
   A the best   **B** the better   **C** best

14 My new bed is .... than my old one.
   A comfortable   **B** more comfortable
   C most comfortable

15 .... is a great way to relax.
   A Read   **B** To read   **C** Reading

16 There's no point in .... angry. He didn't mean to annoy you.
   A get   **B** to get   **C** getting

17 My new house is much .... than my old one.
   A big   **B** bigger   **C** biggest

18 Jessica Blake .... her first novel when she was twenty.
   A wrote   **B** was written   **C** had written

19 Claire is .... runner on the team.
   A fast   **B** faster   **C** the fastest

20 Colin is not .... as Martin.
   A strong   **B** as strong   **C** stronger

21 You will soon .... to living in the city.
   A be used   **B** used   **C** get used

22 I .... to the supermarket. Do you need anything?
   A go   **B** will go   **C** am going

23 We can't decide what .... for dinner.
   A have   **B** to have   **C** having

24 The athlete .... for hours and he needed a rest.
   A had trained   **B** was training
   C had been training

25 Mark .... a lot of overtime these days. He must need the money.
   A works   **B** is working   **C** worked

26 She .... a film when the telephone rang.
   A was watching   **B** has watched
   C has been watching

27 She swims .... a fish.
   A as   **B** like   **C** so

28 I haven't been to the library ....
   A yet   **B** until   **C** just

29 The man .... near the door is my boss.
   A standing   **B** to stand   **C** stands

30 I .... you to the fair unless you behave yourselves.
   A won't be taking   **B** won't take
   C won't have taken

31 The film was .... funnier than I expected.
   A by far   **B** very   **C** even

32 Janice .... very quiet today. I wonder what's wrong.
   A be   **B** is being   **C** will have been

33 I wonder if Sally .... to the disco.
   A will come   **B** will be coming   **C** will have come

34 He is used .... alone now.
   A living   **B** to live   **C** to living

35 She prefers .... trousers to skirts.
   A wear   **B** to wear   **C** wearing

36 The meeting .... at nine o'clock. Don't be late.
  A started   **B** is starting   **C** starts

37 'How long .... Tony?' 'Since we were children.'
  A did you know   **B** have you known
  C do you know

38 The taxi .... here soon. Are you ready?
  A will be   **B** is   **C** will have been

39 It is difficult .... a good job these days.
  A find   **B** to find   **C** finding

40 My father .... to be a teacher, but now he has retired.
  A is used   **B** got used   **C** used

2 **Put the verbs in brackets into the correct tense.**

1 A: Did you have a good evening?
  B: Yes, thank you. We ...*went*... (go) to see a play.
2 A: Cats .... (wash) themselves.
  B: I know. They are very clean animals.
3 A: Why are you so dirty?
  B: I .... (work) in the garden all morning.
4 A: I want to phone Jane.
  B: Well, don't phone her now. She .... (study).
5 A: You look busy.
  B: I am. I .... (write) a letter to my brother.
6 A: I would like a new bicycle.
  B: Me too. My parents .... (buy) me one for Christmas.
7 A: What time are the guests arriving?
  B: They .... (be) here in ten minutes.
8 A: Are you excited about your trip?
  B: Yes. This time next week, I .... (sail) across the Atlantic.
9 A: I'm going to the supermarket.
  B: You'd better be quick, then. It .... (close) at eight o'clock.
10 A: You sounded tired when I spoke to you last night.
  B: Well, I .... (paint) the house all day.
11 A: What .... (you/do) when I called?
  B: I .... (water) the plants.
12 A: Have you sent those letters yet?
  B: Yes. I .... (post) them yesterday.
13 A: Are there any biscuits left?
  B: No, sorry. I .... (eat) them all.
14 A: Why was Julie crying this morning?
  B: Because she .... (hurt) her leg.
15 A: Paul is going to collect us at ten o'clock.
  B: Yes. By the time he arrives, we .... (have) breakfast.

16 A: Do you enjoy playing tennis?
  B: Oh, yes. I .... (play) since I was six years old.
17 A: Have you been working here long?
  B: Yes. By next June, I .... (work) here for ten years.
18 A: It's nine o'clock.
  B: Yes. The postman .... (deliver) Mum's parcel by now.
19 A: I liked your speech.
  B: Thank you. I .... (practise) for hours before I made it.
20 A: Did Martin help you clean the house yesterday?
  B: No. By the time he got up, I .... (do) everything.

3 **Underline the correct item.**

1 You must **brush**/to brush/brushing your teeth twice a day.
2 He has decided **look**/**to look**/**looking** for a new job.
3 Peter enjoys **to watch**/**watch**/**watching** adventure films.
4 We are tired of **live**/**living**/**to live** in such a noisy area.
5 She claims **to have repaired**/**to repair**/**repairing** the car herself.
6 I would rather **eat**/**to eat**/**eating** pizza than spaghetti.
7 We refused **lend**/**to lend**/**lending** him the car.
8 He was too young **go**/**to go**/**going** to the party alone.
9 He denied **take**/**to take**/**taking** the money.
10 You really should **to spend**/**spend**/**spending** more time studying.

4 **Complete the sentences.**

1 It's cold outside. You can't wear a T-shirt.
  It's ...*too cold outside for you to wear a T-shirt.* ...
2 Sam is clever. He can go to university.
  Sam is ....
3 She is very tired. She can't watch the late film.
  She is ....
4 Mary has a lot of money. She can go on holiday.
  Mary has ....
5 He has bought a lot of sugar. He can make a cake.
  He has bought ....
6 This soup is very salty. I can't eat it.
  This soup is ....
7 This painting is very special. I can't sell it.
  This painting is ....
8 Carol is very pretty. She could be a model.
  Carol is ....
9 He has got lots of time. He can go to the cinema.
  He has got ....
10 Paul is ill. He can't go to work.
  Paul is ....

11 The weather is warm. We can go for a picnic.
    The weather is ....

12 She is very full. She can't eat any more.
    She is ....

5 **Underline the correct item.**

1 I have been working very hard **late/lately**.
2 The mountain was so **high/highly** that they couldn't climb it.
3 Hurry up! It is **near/nearly** time to go.
4 Her books are **most/mostly** romance novels.
5 He found it **hard/hardly** to explain his problem.
6 That man is a **high/highly** respected doctor.
7 Our new house is **near/nearly** the city centre.
8 Which of these dresses do you like **most/mostly**?
9 I had **hardly/hard** finished cooking when the guests arrived.
10 The girls were **pretty/prettily** dressed for the party.
11 I got this lipstick **free/freely** with a magazine.
12 He is always **late/lately** for work.
13 The exam was **pretty/prettily** difficult, but we all passed.
14 She was **deep/deeply** absorbed in her work and didn't hear me call.
15 Her hair blew **free/freely** around her head in the breeze.

6 **Put the adjectives in brackets into the comparative or superlative form, adding any necessary words.**

1 A: Mark is very confident.
   B: Yes. He is certainly ...*more confident than*... (confident) his brother.
2 A: Did you enjoy your holiday?
   B: Oh, yes. It was .... (good) holiday I've ever had.
3 A: You're late home tonight.
   B: I know. The work took .... (long) I had expected.
4 A: Did you like the brown shoes?
   B: Yes, but they were by far .... (expensive) shoes in the shop.
5 A: Have you put the heating on?
   B: Yes. I'm much .... (warm) now.
6 A: Do you like your new job?
   B: Yes. The staff are .... (friendly) people I've ever met.
7 A: The new cinema is great.
   B: Yes. It's .... (big) cinema I've ever been to.
8 A: Your new car looks good.
   B: It is. It's much .... (fast) my old car.
9 A: Thank you for the information.
   B: No problem. If you want any .... (far) information, just ask.

10 A: This bag is very cheap.
   B: Yes, but look. This one is even .... (cheap).
11 A: Why are we going this way?
   B: Because it's .... (short) route to the beach.
12 A: The children are so noisy today.
   B: I know. I wish they would be .... (quiet).

7 **Rewrite the sentences using participles.**

1 The boy who is taking photographs is my cousin.
   ...*The boy taking photographs is my cousin.* ...
2 Because she felt hungry, Julie bought a sandwich.
   ....
3 After she had sold her flat, she moved into a house.
   ....
4 He fell asleep while he was watching TV.
   ....
5 Paul saw the rain clouds and started to hurry.
   ....
6 She was standing at the window and she was looking at the garden.
   ....
7 Because we had finished the job, we went home.
   ....

8 **Underline the correct preposition.**

1 We found it hard to cope **about/with/for** such noisy children.
2 The boy complained **of/about/for** having too much homework.
3 The mechanic charged me £50 **of/with/for** servicing my car.
4 He seems to be very anxious **for/of/about** the exam results.
5 There was no reason **of/for/about** him to shout at her.
6 He was dissatisfied **by/with/of** his new computer.
7 She dreamt **of/for/about** being a pop star last night.
8 According **with/to/by** the weather forecast, it will be sunny today.
9 My mother took care **about/for/of** my plants while I was away.
10 I am very angry **with/about/at** you for disobeying my orders.
11 I know I can count **against/on/for** my parents for support.
12 She accused me **of/for/about** stealing her necklace.
13 I don't always agree **at/on/with** the decisions he makes.
14 One advantage **of/for/about** living in the country is that it is quiet.
15 The taxi arrived **at/to/in** the hotel at half past two.

9   **Fill in the gaps with the correct particle from the list.**

down on, for, into, off, on, up, down with, out, down

1   We are trying to cut ...*down*... on fuel this year. It is so expensive.
2   She is not cut .... to be a teacher. She has no patience at all.
3   I can't print the files. The computer has broken ....
4   He missed the party because something came ....
5   She came .... a cold and had to cancel her holiday.
6   The manager brought .... the subject of overtime at the meeting.
7   She was .... all night preparing for the presentation.
8   Being an athlete calls .... a lot of stamina.
9   He was .... school for two weeks when he had measles.
10   The business deal came .... and the company made a lot of money.
11   The children carried .... with their work when the teacher left the room.
12   The stress of the accident brought .... one of her asthma attacks.
13   There is a good film .... television this evening.
14   He had to break .... his house because he had lost his keys.
15   The village was cut .... after the snowstorm.

10   **Complete each sentence with two to five words, including the word in bold.**

1   I got this job three months ago.
   for   I ....*have had this job for* .. three months.
2   That test was easier than the last one.
   less   That test .... the last one.
3   Mark is shorter than Paul.
   as   Mark .... Paul.
4   We haven't finished decorating the house yet.
   still   We .... decorating the house.
5   As it got later, I became more tired.
   the   The later it got, ... I became.
6   Some people say it is bad for your eyes to watch too much TV.
   watching   Some people say ....
      .... is bad for your eyes.
7   She moved here when she was eighteen.
   since   She ....
      she was eighteen.

8   Could you help me make dinner, please?
   mind   Would ....
      me make dinner, please?
9   He has difficulty in expressing his feelings.
   difficult   It is ....
      his feelings.
10   They heard the boss shouting at her secretary yesterday.
   was   The boss ....
      .... at her secretary yesterday.
11   Carl has got the same number of videos as Andrew.
   many   Carl has got ....
      Andrew.
12   Sarah was charmed by the silver earrings and bought them immediately.
   found   Sarah ....
      and bought them immediately.
13   This tea is too cold for me to drink.
   warm   This tea ....
      for me to drink.
14   He has never travelled by ship before.
   the   It's ....
      he has travelled by ship.
15   She made me stay in my bedroom.
   was   I ....
      in my bedroom.
16   We haven't been to the theatre for months.
   time   The ....
      to the theatre was months ago.
17   We were on the point of going out when the phone rang.
   about   We ....
      when the phone rang.
18   It was the first time she had driven a car.
   never   She ....
      a car before.
19   I think it's important to travel to other countries.
   travelling   I think ....
      is important.
20   Wearing jeans in the office is not allowed.
   allow   We do not .... in the office.

11   **Cross out the unnecessary word.**

1   I'll make the dinner when I ~~will~~ get home.
2   She went to the market for to buy some fruit.
3   I heard Michael to phone and book the tickets.
4   The question was too difficult for me to answer it.
5   He left the house without to saying goodbye to me.
6   He's much more younger than he looks.
7   Bob was feeling the more and more tired.
8   She spent the most of the day lying on the beach.
9   He can hardly not see anything without his glasses.
10   Learning to drive it is difficult.
11   You had better to eat all of your dinner.
12   Karen made her brother to apologise to her.

Nouns

- Nouns are: **abstract** (*love, freedom, etc.*), **proper** (*Joe, Europe, etc.*), **group** (*family, team, crowd, group, etc.*) **or common** (*chair, hat, boy, etc.*).

- Most nouns which refer to jobs, social status, etc. have the same form for men and women *e.g. doctor, teacher, etc.*

Others have different forms:

actor - actress
(bride) groom - bride
duke - duchess
hero - heroine
host - hostess

king - queen
monk - nun
prince - princess
waiter - waitress
widower - widow, etc.

Countable Nouns/Uncountable Nouns

Scientists do a lot of research in order to find cures for various diseases. A lot of money is spent on equipment every year, but the information collected is invaluable.

- **Countable nouns** are nouns which we can count. They have singular and plural forms. We usually form the plural by adding -s. (Look at Appendix 1).

- **Irregular Plurals:** man - **men**, woman - **women**, foot - **feet**, tooth - **teeth**, louse - **lice**, mouse - **mice**, child - **children**, goose - **geese**, ox - **oxen**

- Some nouns have the same form in the singular and the plural. These are:
  a) some kinds of animals (*sheep, deer*) **and fish** (*trout, cod, salmon,* **etc.**)
     e.g. **A sheep was** *grazing in the field.* **Some sheep were** *grazing in the field.*
  b) the words *aircraft, spacecraft, hovercraft, etc.*
     e.g. **One hovercraft was** *approaching the port.* **Two hovercraft were** *approaching the port.*
  c) some nouns ending in -s: *crossroads, means, series, species, works, etc.*
     e.g. A car is a **means** *of transport. Cars* **are a means** *of transport.*

- **Uncountable nouns** are nouns which we cannot count. They do not have different plural forms. Uncountable nouns include:
  a) **many types of food:** *flour, yoghurt, butter, meat, cheese, spaghetti, rice, sugar, etc.*
  b) **liquids:** *coffee, lemonade, oil, petrol, wine, water, etc.*
  c) **materials:** *crystal, wood, plastic, silver, china, glass, etc.*
  d) **abstract nouns:** *knowledge, beauty, justice, help, freedom, education, love, etc.*
  e) **others:** *research, luggage, baggage, hair, weather, behaviour, advice, news, accommodation, information, fun, equipment, litter, rubbish, furniture, crockery, cutlery, jewellery, machinery, money, etc.*

- We use the following nouns with uncountable nouns to show quantity: *a* **piece** *of cake/paper/news/ advice/information/furniture, a* **glass/bottle** *of water, a* **jar** *of jam/honey, a* **rasher** *of bacon, a* **packet** *of rice/ tea, a* **loaf/slice** *of bread, a* **pot** *of yoghurt/honey, a* **pot/cup** *of tea, a* **kilo** *of meat, a* **tube** *of toothpaste, a* **bar** *of chocolate/soap, a* **can** *of soda, a* **carton** *of milk, a* **bowl** *of sugar/soup, etc.*
  Some of the above nouns can also be used with plural countable nouns.
  e.g. a kilo of tomatoes, a bowl of cherries

Countable nouns:

◆ **can take singular or plural verbs.**
 e.g. *The window is open.*
 The windows are open.

◆ **always go with a/an/the/my, etc. in the singular.**
 e.g. *I paid the bill. This is my pen.*

◆ **can be used alone or with some/any/many/few in the plural.**
 e.g. *I love apples.*
 I bought some apples to make a pie.

Uncountable nouns:

◆ **always take singular verbs.**
 e.g. *Gold is more expensive than silver.*
 Milk comes from cows.

◆ **do not go with a/an/one/two, etc.**
 e.g. *Water is good for you.*

◆ **can be used alone or with some/any/much/little/ the/my, etc.**
 e.g. *Don't forget to buy (some) coffee.*

Note: We use *a/an, one/two*, etc. with uncountable nouns such as *coffee, tea, beer*, etc. when we order something in a restaurant, café, etc.
 e.g. *We'll have three beers, please.*

Some nouns can be used as countable or uncountable, with a difference in meaning.

● *Would you like a glass of lemonade?*
 Tina can't see without her glasses. (spectacles)
 The vase is made of glass. (the material)

● *He went to the newsagent's to buy a paper.* (newspaper)
 He wrote my phone number on a piece of paper. (the writing material)
 Don't forget to bring all the necessary papers. (documents)

● *Susan has got short, dark hair.* (all the hair on her head)
 There is a hair in my soup!

● *I've bought an iron as a wedding gift for Tom and Jane.* (for ironing clothes)
 This chair is made of iron. (the material)

● *You shouldn't eat too much chocolate.*
 We gave her a box of chocolates.

● *Your room is a mess!*
 We haven't got enough room to put you up. (space)

● *The table is made of wood.* (the material)
 A lot of wolves live in the woods. (forest)

● *Mr Davis has a lot of experience in accounting.* (length of time doing it)
 He had a few unpleasant experiences while living abroad. (events)

● *I haven't got any time to lose.*
 How many times did Rick phone? (occasions)

◆ *A couple of, several, (a) few, many, a (good, large, great) number of and both are used with countable nouns.* e.g. *a couple of friends. (Too) much, (a) little, a great/good deal of, a small/large amount/quantity of are used with uncountable nouns.* e.g. *a small amount of money. A lot of, lots of, (hardly) any, some, no, plenty of are used with countable and uncountable nouns.* e.g. *plenty of friends/money*

Compound Nouns

◆ **Compound nouns are nouns that are made of two or more parts and are formed as follows:**

 a) **noun + noun. The plural is usually formed by adding -s/-es to the second noun.**
 e.g. *ticket inspector → ticket inspectors*

 b) **-ing form/adjective + noun. The plural is formed by adding -s/-es to the noun.**
 e.g. *swimming pool → swimming pools*
 e.g. *greenhouse → greenhouses*

 c) **noun + in-law. The plural is formed by adding -s to the noun.**
 e.g. *sister-in-law → sisters-in-law*

 d) **noun + adverb. The plural is formed by adding -s to the noun.**
 e.g. *runner-up → runners-up*

 e) **verb + adverb particle. The plural is formed by adding -s to the word.**
 e.g. *breakthrough → breakthroughs*

UNIT 4
Nouns - Articles - Word Formation

Singular/Plural Verb Forms

We use singular verb forms with:

◆ a) nouns which refer to school subjects: *economics, physics, mathematics (maths), politics*, etc.

b) nouns which refer to sports: *gymnastics, athletics, bowls*, etc.

c) nouns which refer to games: *billiards, dominoes, darts, draughts*, etc.

d) nouns which refer to illnesses: *measles, mumps*, etc,

e) the word *news*.

e.g. *I think **physics is** a very interesting subject.*
*The **news isn't** very encouraging, I'm afraid.*

◆ plural nouns when we talk about an amount of money, a time period, weight, distance, etc.

e.g. ***Five hundred thousand pounds was** donated to build a new hospital wing.*

◆ group nouns such as *jury, family, team, group, crew, crowd, class, audience, committee, council, army, club, press, government, company*, etc. when we mean the group as a unit. But we use plural verbs when we mean the individuals who make up the group.

e.g. *The **jury is** ready to give the verdict. (We mean the jury as a unit.)*
*The **jury are** all staying at the Park Hotel. (We mean the individual members of the jury.)*

We use plural verb forms with:

◆ nouns such as: *clothes, people, police, stairs, (good) looks, surroundings, outskirts, premises, earnings, wages, cattle, poultry*, etc.

e.g. *Designer **clothes are** rather expensive.*

◆ nouns which refer to objects that consist of two parts, such as: *trousers, binoculars, shorts, shoes, gloves, pyjamas, tights, glasses, earrings, socks, scissors*, etc.

We do not use *a/an* or a number with these words. We use the phrase *pair of ...* instead.

e.g. *Where **are** your **gloves**?*
*I was given a **pair of gloves**.*

---

1 **Fill in the gaps with an appropriate *noun* + *of* to indicate quantity.**

1 a ...*carton/glass/jug of*... orange juice
2 a .... cheese
3 a .... bread
4 a .... coffee
5 a .... water
6 a .... wine
7 a .... chocolate
8 a .... crisps
9 a .... honey
10 a .... meat
11 a .... spaghetti
12 a .... flour

---

2 **Fill the gaps with *a, an*, or *some* where necessary.**

1 a) We had ...*some*... delicious food last night.
   b) We had ...*a*.. delicious meal last night.
2 a) There is .... beautiful furniture in that shop.
   b) There is .... beautiful table in that shop.
3 a) I'm thirsty. I need .... drink.
   b) I'm thirsty. I need .... water.
4 a) She's just bought .... expensive clothes.
   b) She's just bought .... expensive dress.
5 a) They booked .... room in advance.
   b) They booked .... accommodation in advance.
6 a) The band played .... lovely song.
   b) The band played .... lovely music.
7 a) We had .... heatwave last week.
   b) We had .... hot weather last week.
8 a) I can't do this job alone. I need .... assistant.
   b) I can't do this job alone. I need .... help.
9 a) He has got .... heavy luggage to carry.
   b) He has got .... heavy suitcase to carry.
10 a) I need .... cutlery to eat this food with.
    b) I need .... knife and fork to eat this food with.
11 a) She has got .... important job to do.
    b) She has got .... important work to do.
12 a) He found .... coin on the ground.
    b) He found .... money on the ground.

---

3 **Complete the sentences using the *noun* in brackets in the singular or plural form and *a/an* where necessary.**

1 He gave me a box of my favourite ...*chocolates*.... (chocolate)
2 His favourite food is .... (chocolate)
3 She bought .... on her way to work. (paper)
4 He placed all the important .... in his briefcase. (paper)
5 I need some .... to write this message on. (paper)
6 Hurry up! We don't have much .... (time)
7 She has visited us several .... this month. (time)
8 He has no ...., but he is keen to learn. (experience)
9 She had a lot of exciting .... during her travels. (experience)

10 We went for a walk in the .... after lunch. (wood)

11 His desk is made of .... (wood)

12 Jane is in her .... reading a book. (room)

13 We have got plenty of .... for a party in here. (room)

14 I am going to have my .... cut tomorrow. (hair)

15 There was .... in my soup. (hair)

16 I'm thirsty. I need .... of water. (glass)

17 Susan only wears her .... when she reads. (glass)

18 This ornament is made of coloured .... (glass)

19 Helen bought .... in the sale at the electrical store. (iron)

20 The old gate was made of .... (iron)

4 **Cross out the expressions which cannot be used with the nouns, as in the example.**

1 There are **several, many,** ~~much,~~ **plenty of,** ~~too little~~ things you can do to help.

2 He has met **a couple of , a few, very little, plenty of, too much** interesting people.

3 She earns **few, hardly any, plenty of, several, a great deal of** money.

4 We have got **no, many, lots of, a great deal of, a few** work to do.

5 Don't worry, there's **a little, plenty of, a couple of, many, a lot of** time.

6 **Both, Several, A large quantity of, Plenty of, Too much** students applied for the course.

7 He's got **no, hardly any, a little, some, a small amount of** qualifications.

8 She's got **hardly any, several, a little, a few, a lot of** experience in dealing with customers.

9 There is **too much, a lot of, hardly any, few, several** salt in this soup.

10 There is **a little, many, too much, a great number of, some** traffic on the roads today.

5 **What do we call the following things or people?**

1 A person who drives a bus is ...*a bus driver*....

2 The screen of a computer is ....

3 The juice from an orange is ....

4 A stick for walking with is ....

5 A curtain around the shower is ....

6 Someone who cleans windows is ....

7 Your husband's mother is your ....

8 A chair which rocks is ....

9 A brush for your hair is ....

10 Someone who passes by a place or incident is ....

11 The keys to your house are ....

6 **Underline the correct word.**

1 A: I have a Physics exam tomorrow.
   B: Oh dear. Physics **is**/**are** a very difficult subject.

2 A: My office is three miles from my house.
   B: Three miles **is**/**are** a long way to walk to work.

3 A: My little brother has got measles.
   B: Oh dear. Measles **is**/**are** quite a serious illness.

4 A: Jane looked nice today, didn't she?
   B: Yes. Her clothes **were**/**was** very smart.

5 A: I've got two pounds. I'm going to buy a CD.
   B: Two pounds **is**/**are** not enough to buy a CD.

6 A: The classroom was empty when I walked past.
   B: Yes. The class **was**/**were** all on a school outing.

7 A: Have you just cleaned the stairs?
   B: Yes, so be careful. They **is**/**are** very slippery.

8 A: Did you ask John to fix your car?
   B: Yes. His advice **was**/**were** that I take it to a garage.

9 A: Did you enjoy your holiday?
   B: Yes, thank you. The weather **was**/**were** wonderful.

10 A: These trousers **is**/**are** very old.
    B: You should buy a new pair.

11 A: How **is**/**are** the company doing lately?
    B: Great. We opened up two more branches.

12 A: I am going to travel for two years when I finish school.
    B: Two years **is**/**are** a long time to be away from home.

7 **Finish the sentences, as in the example.**

1 You need a lot of experience to do this job.
   A lot of experience ...*is needed to do this job*....

2 They gave us some interesting information.
   The information ....

3 She likes Maths more than any other subject.
   Maths ....

4 We had mild weather this winter.
   The weather ....

5 We called the police immediately.
   The police ....

6 I told them some exciting news.
   The news ....

7 He was irritated because of the bad traffic.
   He was irritated because the ....

8 I stayed in very luxurious accommodation.
   The accommodation ....

9 The driver took the luggage out of the car.
   The luggage ....

10 She gave me very sensible advice.
    The advice she gave me ....

11 These shorts are too big for me.
    This pair of shorts ....

12 The hotel is in magnificent surroundings.
    The hotel surroundings ....

13 She's got long blonde hair.
    Her hair ....

UNIT 4
Nouns - Articles - Word Formation

The Indefinite Article 'A'/'An' - One/Ones

'A'/'An'

We use a/an:

- with singular countable nouns when we talk about them in general.
  e.g. I want to buy **a** dress. (any dress)
- with the verbs *to be* and *have (got)*.
  e.g. Mary **has (got) a** dog. It's a German Shepherd.
- before *Mr/Mrs/Miss/Ms* when we refer to an unknown person.
  e.g. **A Mrs Jones** called you this morning. (A person that we don't know.)
- to show: a) price in relation to weight (two pounds **a** kilo), b) distance in relation to speed (80km **an** hour) and c) frequency (twice **a** week).

We do not use a/an:

- with uncountable nouns or plural countable nouns. We use *some* instead of *a/an*.
  e.g. We need **some milk** and **some flour**.
       They bought **some flowers**.
- before an adjective if it is not followed by a noun.
  e.g. This ring is **expensive**.
  But: This is **an expensive ring**.

A(n)/One

- We use a/an to refer to an unspecified thing with the meaning 'any one'. We use one when we are counting, to put emphasis on number.
  e.g. He bought **a** tie. (We are not talking about a specific tie.)
  e.g. He bought **one** tie. (He didn't buy two ties.)
- We use one with the words *day, week, month, year, winter, morning, night*, etc. or with a specific day or month to say when something happened, usually in

narration.
  e.g. **One summer,** the family decided to go to Tahiti.
       One Tuesday, Kate was walking home from work.

We can use *one day* to refer to the future.
  e.g. **One day,** you will regret this.

- We use one or one of ... when we mean one person/thing out of many. It usually contrasts with *another/other(s)*.
  e.g. **One** bus was full, but **the others** were empty.
       One of my colleagues is from Italy.
- We use a/an or one with no difference in meaning when counting or measuring distance, weight, time, etc.
  e.g. I paid **a/one** hundred pounds for this bracelet.
       We bought **a/one** carton of milk.
       They spent **a/one** month cruising down the Nile.

One/Ones

- We use one in the singular and ones in the plural to avoid repeating the noun when it is clear what we mean.
  e.g. My house is the **one** with the red front door.
- We use a/an with one when there is an adjective before one.
  e.g. I want to buy a jacket. I want **a leather one**.
  BUT: I want to buy a jacket. I want **one** with a fur collar.
- We use one/ones with *this/that*.
  e.g. I don't like this pair of shoes, but I like **that one**.
- We use which one(s) in questions.
  e.g. I like the yellow blouse best. **Which one** do you like?

8 Fill in *a, an, one* or *ones*.

1 I'm making ...a... sandwich. Would you like ....?
2 There was only .... sandwich left. All the others had been eaten.
3 We saw .... giraffe and .... alligator at the zoo.
4 These biscuits are nicer than the .... I normally buy.
5 She paid .... thousand pounds for her car.
6 .... day, I will buy a house of my own.
7 I'd love .... car like that .... over there.
8 .... of my brothers is .... policeman.
9 I'm looking for .... dress. I'd like a blue ....
10 I heard .... amusing joke yesterday.
11 I like these three pairs of trousers. Which .... do you like best?
12 Simon enjoys swimming. He goes to his local pool three times .... week.
13 I'm tired. I need .... rest.
14 .... Mr Green came to see you. He's waiting in your office.
15 We had .... exciting holiday. It was better than the .... we had last year.

Nouns - Articles - Word Formation

The Definite Article *The*

We use *the:*	We do not use *the:*

We use *the:*

◆ with nouns when we are talking about something specific, that is, when the noun is mentioned for a second time or is already known. In other words, when we can answer the question 'Who?' or 'Which?'
*e.g. I bought a shirt and a dress. **The** dress is blue and **the** shirt is green.*

◆ with nouns which are unique.
*e.g. **the** sun, **the** Eiffel Tower*

◆ with the names of cinemas *(the Rex)*, hotels *(the Carlton)*, theatres *(the Globe)*, museums *(the British Museum)*, newspapers/magazines *(the Times* but: *Time magazine)*, ships *(the Mary Rose)*, organisations *(the EU)*, galleries *(the Tate Gallery)*

◆ with the names of rivers *(the Nile)*, seas *(the Caspian Sea)*, groups of islands *(the Canary Islands)*, mountain ranges *(the Alps)*, deserts *(the Sahara Desert)*, oceans *(the Atlantic)*, canals *(the Panama Canal)*, countries when they include words such as *state, Kingdom, republic,* etc. *(the United Kingdom)* and names or nouns with 'of' *(the Leaning Tower of Pisa)*
NOTE: *the equator, the North/South Pole, **the** north of England, **the** south/west/north/east*

◆ with the names of musical instruments and dances.
*e.g. **the** piano, **the** tango*

◆ with the names of families *(the Windsors)*, and nationalities ending in -sh, -ch or -ese *(the French, the Scottish, the Japanese,* etc.). Other plural nationalities are used with or without the *(the Americans, the Greeks,* etc.)

◆ with titles *(the King, the Prince of Wales, the President)*
BUT: 'The' is omitted before titles with proper names. *Queen Victoria*

◆ with adjectives/adverbs in the superlative form.
*e.g. He's **the most respected** man in the firm.*
BUT: When 'most' is followed by a noun, it does not take 'the'.
*e.g. **Most** children like cartoons.*

◆ with the words *morning, afternoon, evening* and *night*.
*e.g. We eat dinner in **the** evening. but: at night, at noon, at midnight, by day/night, at 4 o'clock,* etc.

◆ with historical periods/events. *the Middle Ages, **the** Crimean War (**but**: World War II)*

◆ with the words *only, last, first* (used as adjectives).
*e.g. He was **the first** person to arrive.*

We do not use *the:*

◆ with uncountable and plural countable nouns when talking about something in general, that is, when we cannot answer the question 'Who?' or 'Which?'.
*e.g. **Fish** live in water.*

◆ with proper nouns. *e.g. **Mark** lives in **Brighton**.*

◆ with the names of sports, games, activities, days, months, celebrations, colours, drinks, meals and languages (when they are not followed by the word 'language'). *e.g. I often play **chess**. We speak **German**. but: **The German language** is difficult to learn.*

◆ with the names of countries *(Italy,* but: *the Netherlands, the Lebanon, the Sudan, the Vatican City)*, cities *(Paris)*, streets *(Oxford Street,* but: *the High Street, the Strand, the Mall, the London road, the A19, the M6 motorway)*, squares *(Trafalgar Square)*, bridges *(Tower Bridge* but: *the Bridge of Sighs, the Humber Bridge)*, parks *(Hyde Park)*, railway stations *(Victoria Station)*, mountains *(Ben Nevis)*, individual islands *(Tahiti)*, lakes *(Lake Geneva)*, continents *(Africa)*

◆ with *possessive adjectives* or the *possessive case*.
*e.g. That is **my** car.*

◆ with two-word names when the first word is the name of a person or place *Gatwick Airport, Windsor Castle* BUT: *the White House (because 'White' is not the name of a person or place)*

◆ with names of pubs, restaurants, shops, banks and hotels named after the people who started them and end in -s or -'s. *(Lloyds Bank, Harrods, Dave's Pub* but: *the Red Lion (pub) (because 'Red' is not the name of a person or place)*

◆ with the words *bed, church, college, court, hospital, prison, school, university* when we refer to the purpose for which they exist.
e.g. Sarah went to school. (She is a student.)
BUT: *Her father went to **the school** to see her teacher yesterday. (He went to the school as a visitor.)*

◆ with the word *work* (= place of work).
*e.g. He is at **work**.*

◆ with the words *home, Father/Mother* when we talk about our own home/parents. *e.g. **Father** is at **home**.*

◆ with *by + means of transport:* by bus/car/train/ plane, etc. *e.g. She travelled **by bus**.*
BUT: *She left **on the 8 o'clock bus** this morning.*

◆ with the names of illnesses. *e.g. He's got malaria. but: flu/the flu, measles/the measles, mumps/the mumps*

Nouns - Articles - Word Formation

NOTE:

◆ We use *the* with the words *beach, station, cinema, theatre, coast, country(side), ground, jungle, seaside, weather, world, shop, library, city, sea* (BUT *to be at sea = to be sailing*), etc.
  e.g. Let's go to the beach.
  We spent the weekend in the countryside.
  The weather is awful today.

◆ We usually don't use *the* with the word *television*.

  e.g. I like watching television in the evenings.
  BUT: Turn on the television, please. (the television set)

◆ *The* is optional with seasons.
  e.g. My favourite season is (the) spring.

◆ We use the + adjective to refer to a group of people usually with the adjectives: *poor, rich, sick, injured, elderly, unemployed, homeless, disabled, young, old, dead, blind, deaf, handicapped, mentally ill.*
  e.g. The young are usually impatient.

◆ When we refer to a group of people, animals or things we use:
  1 *a/an* or *the* with singular countable nouns.
    e.g. A/The dolphin is a clever creature.

  2 plural countable nouns without *a/an* or *the*.
    e.g. Dolphins are clever creatures.
        (NOT: ~~The dolphins are clever creatures.~~)

9 Fill in the gaps with one of the words from the list adding 'the' where necessary. Use each word twice.

prison, school, bed, sea, hospital

1 The minute we reached the beach, the children ran into ...*the sea*... to swim.
2 My brother is in the navy. He is at .... for months sometimes.
3 I usually go to .... at about 11 pm to get a good night's sleep.
4 The cat is sitting on ....
5 The Prime Minister visited .... yesterday and talked to the prisoners.
6 The men who robbed the bank are in .... now.
7 The ambulance took the injured people to ....
8 I must go to .... to visit my aunt. She's had an operation.
9 We saw the children in their classrooms as we walked past ....
10 I want to go to university when I leave ....

10 Choose the correct alternative.

1 Catherine loves **cats**/**the cats**.
2 Look at **cats**/**the cats**! They are chasing a bird.
3 I don't like **coffee**/**the coffee**, but I like **tea**/**the tea**.
4 You cut **the cake**/**cake** and I'll pour **coffee**/**the coffee**.
5 **Life**/**The life** will be very different in the future.
6 **Life**/**The life** of a mayfly is extremely short.
7 I enjoy **swimming**/**the swimming** in the sea.
8 **Children**/**The children** usually like playing games.
9 **Children**/**The children** have gone to the park.
10 All **people**/**the people** in this room are my relatives.
11 All **people**/**the people** should have freedom of speech.
12 **Villages**/**The villages** in this part of the country are very beautiful.
13 **Breakfast**/**The breakfast** is the most important meal of **day**/**the day**.
14 Paul was **only**/**the only** person who remembered me.
15 In **Stone Age**/**the Stone Age**, people lived in caves.
16 I would like to travel to **Spain**/**the Spain**.
17 We travelled to London by **train**/**the train**.
18 He is learning to play **flute**/**the flute**.

11 Fill in *a*, *an* or *the* where necessary.

1 A: Shall we go to ...*the*... cinema tonight?
   B: Yes. It's a long time since I saw .... film.
2 A: Have you ever been to .... Copenhagen?
   B: Yes. I think it's .... prettiest city in Europe.
3 A: Did you see all .... sights in Paris?
   B: Yes, but .... Eiffel Tower and .... Louvre were my favourites.
4 A: What did you have for .... lunch today?
   B: I had .... sandwich in .... office canteen.
5 A: Do you buy .... newspaper every day?
   B: Yes. I usually buy .... Independent and my wife reads .... Times.
6 A: Danny plays .... golf very well, doesn't he?
   B: Yes, he practises every weekend with his friends.
7 A: Which station are you meeting John at?
   B: .... Waterloo Station. It's .... big place. I hope I find him easily.
8 A: Are you going on holiday this summer?
   B: Yes. We've booked .... holiday for three weeks in .... Canary Islands.
9 A: What did you see on your tour today?
   B: .... Buckingham Palace and .... Houses of Parliament.
10 A: .... Duponts, who live next door to us, are French.
   B: .... French are very friendly people, aren't they?
11 A: That's .... beautiful dress. Where did you get it?
   B: In .... summer sale at .... Harrods, actually.
12 A: Who is going to open .... new shopping centre?
   B: I heard that .... Queen is going to do it.

12   **Fill in a, an or the where necessary.**

A   **1)** ...The... football team who have won **2)** .... World Cup **3)** .... most times is **4)** .... Brazil. They have won **5)** .... competition five times. **6)** .... team also hold **7)** .... record for **8)** .... greatest number of **9)** .... goals scored overall and have played in every one of **10)** .... tournament's finals.

B   **1)** .... tallest man in **2)** .... world was born in **3)** .... USA in 1918. His name was **4)** .... Robert Wadlow and **5)** .... last time he was measured, in 1940, he had reached a height of 2.72 m. His hands were 32.4 cm from **6)** .... wrist to **7)** .... tip of **8)** .... middle finger.

C   **1)** .... David was waiting at **2)** .... King's Cross station. He was about to travel to **3)** .... Newcastle by **4)** .... train for **5)** .... job interview. However, **6)** .... train was late and he had been standing on **7)** .... platform for over **8)** .... hour.

D   I take **1)** .... bus to **2)** .... school every day. I leave **3)** .... house at eight o'clock in **4)** .... morning. It is **5)** .... five-minute walk from my house to **6)** .... bus-stop. **7)** .... journey to school takes about **8)** .... quarter of **9)** .... hour.

E   **1)** .... Queen is going to visit **2)** .... Bridgeford next week to open **3)** .... new hospital which has been built in **4)** .... town. It will be **5)** .... exciting event which all **6)** .... local people will attend.

F   **1)** .... Stuart has got **2)** .... cold, so he has to stay in **3)** .... bed. His mother has made him **4)** .... bowl of soup and he has got **5)** .... box of **6)** .... tissues on his **7)** .... bedside table. He will probably spend most of **8)** .... day sleeping.

13   **Read the following proverbs and fill in a, an, the or —.**

1   ... — .. Rome wasn't built in .... day.
2   .... actions speak louder than .... words.
3   .... apple .... day keeps .... doctor away.

4   When in .... Rome, do as .... Romans do.
5   Where there's .... will there's .... way.
6   You can't teach .... old dog .... new tricks.
7   You can't get .... blood out of .... stone.
8   You cannot make .... omelette without breaking .... eggs.
9   .... more you get, ... more you want.
10   .... more .... merrier.
11   .... home is where .... heart is.
12   Fire is .... good servant but .... bad master.

14   **Choose the correct alternative.**

1   **Historian/<u>A historian</u>** is a person who studies **history/ the history**.
2   **Panda/The panda** is a large mammal which lives in **China/the China**. **Pandas/The pandas** have black and white fur and eat **bamboo/the bamboo** shoots.
3   We visited **wildlife park/a wildlife park** last week. It was **interesting experience/an interesting experience**.
4   Sally's going to buy **the new car/a new car** next month. She wants one which runs on **lead-free petrol/the lead-free petrol**.
5   We stayed at **hotel/a hotel** by the **sea/sea**. **Room/The room** was very comfortable and **a view/the view** was fantastic.
6   Simon was **last/the last** person to arrive at **party/the party**. He had been waiting for **the taxi/a taxi** for an hour.
7   Susan doesn't believe in **ghosts/the ghosts**. She thinks that **the supernatural/a supernatural** is **a product/ product** of **people's/the people's** imagination.
8   **Clothes/The clothes** I bought yesterday were very cheap. There was **sale/a sale** in one of **department stores/the department stores** in **a city centre/the city centre**.

15   **Fill in the gaps with a, an, the or —.**

1   A: Have you got ...a... car?
    B: Yes, I bought .... second-hand one last winter.
2   A: How often do you take .... holiday?
    B: I go to my house in .... country about twice .... year.
3   A: I can't find .... shoes I wanted to wear for my party.
    B: Have you looked in .... cupboard in .... hall?
4   A: Did you have fun at .... theatre last night?
    B: Yes, it was .... enjoyable evening and .... play was great.
5   A: That's .... interesting painting.
    B: I know. I found it in .... attic.
6   A: Did you stay in .... hotel when you went to .... London?
    B: Yes. We had .... beautiful room in .... King hotel.

UNIT 4
Nouns - Articles - Word Formation

Word Formation

◆ Prefixes are syllables which we add before certain words to form new words. The meaning of the new word depends on the prefix that has been used.

anti-	=	against	e.g. **anti**social
bi-	=	two	e.g. **bi**annual
co-	=	with	e.g. **co**-driver
ex-	=	previous, former	e.g. **ex**-husband
inter-	=	between	e.g. **inter**national
mis-	=	done wrongly or badly	e.g. **mis**behave
mono-	=	one	e.g. **mono**rail
multi-	=	many	e.g. **multi**national
non-	=	not	e.g. **non**-fiction
out-	=	more, better	e.g. **out**number
over-	=	(done) to a great extent	e.g. **over**work
post-	=	after	e.g. **post**date
pre-	=	before	e.g. **pre**historic
pro-	=	in favour of	e.g. **pro**-government
re-	=	again	e.g. **re**decorate
semi-	=	half	e.g. **semi**-final
sub-	=	under, less	e.g. **sub**marine
super-	=	big, more	e.g. **super**human
trans-	=	(travel) from one side, group etc to another	e.g. **trans**continental
under-	=	not enough	e.g. **under**cooked

◆ The prefixes below are used to express opposite meanings.

de-	e.g. **de**frost, **de**compose
dis-	e.g. **dis**honest, **dis**like
in-	e.g. **in**direct, **in**dependent
BUT:	il- (before l) e.g. **il**logical
	im- (before m, p) e.g. **im**moral, **im**practical
	ir- (before r) e.g. **ir**responsible
	but: **un**reliable, **un**reasonable
non-	e.g. **non**-smoker, **non**-stop
un-	e.g. **un**acceptable, **un**employed

◆ Suffixes are syllables which we add to the end of certain words to form new words.

◆ Nouns referring to people

- verb + er/or/ar
  e.g. teach - teach**er**, sail - sail**or**, beg - begg**ar**
- noun/verb/adjective + ist
  e.g. motor - motor**ist**, tour - tour**ist**, national - national**ist**

- verb + ant/ent
  e.g. contest - contest**ant**, study - stud**ent**
- noun + an/ian
  e.g. republic - republic**an**, library - librar**ian**
- verb + ee (passive meaning).
  e.g. train - train**ee**

◆ Nouns formed from verbs

-age	e.g. pack - pack**age**
-al	e.g. refuse - refus**al**
-ance	e.g. accept - accept**ance**
-ation	e.g. realise - realis**ation**
-ence	e.g. differ - differ**ence**
-ion	e.g. revise - revis**ion**
-ment	e.g. enjoy - enjoy**ment**
-sion	e.g. comprehend - comprehen**sion** (verbs ending in -d/-t)
-sis	e.g. hypnotise - hypno**sis**
-tion	e.g. prescribe - prescrip**tion**

◆ Nouns formed from adjectives

-ance	e.g. important - import**ance**
-cy	e.g. vacant - vacan**cy**
-ence	e.g. competent - compet**ence**
-ion	e.g. desolate - desolat**ion**
-ness	e.g. lonely - loneli**ness**
-ity	e.g. formal - formal**ity**
-ty	e.g. loyal - loyal**ty**
-y	e.g. modest - modest**y**

◆ Adjectives formed from nouns

-ous	e.g. fame - fam**ous**
-al	e.g. addition - addition**al**
-ic	e.g. hero - hero**ic**
-ive	e.g. expense - expens**ive**
-ful (with)	e.g. care - care**ful**
-less (without)	e.g. care - care**less**
-y	e.g. health - health**y**
-ly	e.g. friend - friend**ly**

◆ Adjectives formed from verbs

-able	e.g. like - like**able**
-ible	e.g. defend - defens**ible**
-ive	e.g. conclude - conclus**ive**

◆ Verbs formed from adjectives

-en	e.g. light - light**en**
-ise	e.g. legal - legal**ise**

16 **Add the correct prefixes to the words in bold.**

1 Kate is now doing a ...*post*... **graduate** degree.
2 Mr Bell is an ....-**teacher**. He retired ten years ago.
3 This is an ....**national** company. It has offices all over the world.
4 Sharon is ....**weight** for her age and height. She eats very little.
5 John is very ....-**social**. He is often rude to people.
6 The ....-**finals** of the championship are next week.
7 You can ....**book** a vegetarian meal on this flight.
8 The men tried to ....**code** the secret message.
9 The restaurant ....**charged** us by £20 for our meal, but we refused to pay until they had checked the bill.
10 When you've finished reading, please ....**place** the books on the shelves.

17 **Add the correct prefixes to form the opposite of the words in bold.**

1 He's an ...*un*... **interesting** person. In fact, he's rather boring.
2 Driving a car without a licence is ....**legal**.
3 I'm afraid I ....**agree** with what you just said.
4 I can't do this puzzle. It's ....**possible**!
5 The cake was ....**resistible**, so she ate three pieces.
6 The waiting room is a ....**smoking** area.
7 He is ....**literate**. He can't read or write.
8 I am ....**decisive** about where to go on holiday.
9 The telephone company ....**connected** the phone when he failed to pay the bill.
10 His comment was ....**relevant** to our discussion.

18 **Fill in the correct form of the words in brackets.**

A Sophie can be very 1) ...*careless*... (care) at times. Although she tries to be 2) .... (help) and is always willing to offer her 3) .... (assist), more often than not her 4) .... (clumsy) causes great 5) .... (frustrate) to her family and friends.

B The 1) .... (organise) of the firework display had been a difficult job, but now the children were shrieking with 2) .... (excite) as each 3) .... (colour) 4) .... (explode) lit up the sky. In the warm glow of the bonfire we could see that every child wore an 5) .... (express) of great 6) .... (happy).

C We are having an 1) .... (extend) built to our house. The 2) .... (build) have been working on its 3) .... (construct) for two weeks and now it looks quite 4) .... (impress). The extra space will be very 5) .... (use).

Common mistakes

- Both my **brother-in-laws** work in a bank. ✗
  Both my **brothers-in-law** work in a bank. ✓
- Two **aircrafts** are flying in the sky. ✗
  Two **aircraft** are flying in the sky. ✓
- My favourite TV **series are** 'Eastenders'. ✗
  My favourite TV **series is** 'Eastenders'. ✓
- Could you help me carry my **luggages**? ✗
  Could you help me carry my **luggage**? ✓
- What **are** the latest **news**? ✗
  What **is** the latest **news**? ✓
- **Two kilometres are** a long way to go on foot. ✗
  Two kilometres is a long way to go on foot. ✓
- The **police is** after the escaped prisoners. ✗
  The **police are** after the escaped prisoners. ✓
- **The most of** my friends live nearby. ✗
  Most of my friends live nearby. ✓
- He goes to work **by the train**. ✗
  He goes to work **by train**. ✓
- The robbers were taken to **the court**. ✗
  The robbers were taken to **court**. ✓

19 **Correct the mistakes.**

1 We lost our luggages at the airport.
2 We went to Bath by the car.
3 The police is searching for the stolen painting.
4 Twenty kilometres are too far to travel to school.
5 A very reliable means of transport are the train.
6 The criminal was sentenced to ten years in the prison.
7 Two hovercrafts almost collided at sea yesterday.
8 I have three sister-in-laws.
9 The most people enjoy listening to music.
10 The news are on TV at six o'clock every evening.

20 **Cross out the unnecessary word.**

1 She likes all the kinds of films.
2 There is a great film on the TV tonight.
3 Millions of people were killed in the World War II.
4 I spent a week looking for an accommodation.
5 Jason is at the work. He'll be back at six o'clock.
6 I want a new car. I want one car with a sunroof.
7 A lot of children learn the English nowadays.
8 She is seriously ill. She's got the malaria.
9 The most people enjoy spending their holidays by the seaside.

Phrasal Verbs

do away with:	(tr) 1) abolish, 2) murder
do up:	(tr) 1) fasten; tie, 2) wrap, 3) repair; redecorate, 4) make oneself more attractive, dress up
do with:	(tr) want; need
do without:	(tr) live/continue without having sb/sth
draw in:	1) (int) (of a bus/train) slow down to stop, 2) (tr) attract people
draw up:	1) (of a vehicle) stop, 2) (tr) write sth (a will/a contract, etc)
fall apart:	1) (int) break into pieces, 2) (int) end in failure
fall back on:	turn to sb/sth for help when other plans have failed; **turn to**
fall behind:	(int) 1) fail to keep up with, 2) be late (with payment)
fall for:	(tr) 1) be deceived, 2) fall in love with sb
fall in with:	(tr) agree with; **go along with**
fall out (with):	quarrel

21 Fill in the correct particle.

1 This book is so old that it's falling ...*apart*....
2 We could do .... a new washing machine. This one is very old.
3 I think Kate and Peter have fallen .... They aren't speaking to each other.
4 The car drew .... next to me, and the driver asked for directions.
5 The slowest runner fell .... very quickly after the race had started.
6 It's about time the government did .... housing tax.
7 We bought an old house last year and now we're doing it ....
8 Mike was so handsome and charming that Sarah fell .... him immediately.
9 The train drew .... to the station exactly on time.
10 The politician thought that someone was trying to do .... him, so he hired a bodyguard.
11 Lots of people fell .... the conman's tricks before he was caught by the police.
12 The landlord drew .... a contract for the new tenant.
13 Until you can afford to buy a car, you'll have to do .... one.

14 Don't forget to do .... your shoe laces or you'll trip over them.
15 Despite months of preparation, their plans fell .... at the last minute.
16 Jenny's doing herself .... at the moment because she's going to a party tonight.
17 If you fall .... with the payments, we may take legal action.
18 The parcel that was delivered to my house was done .... with string.
19 You can always fall .... your skills as a teacher if you don't make it as an artist.
20 I'll fall .... whatever you plan for the weekend.

22 Underline the correct preposition.

1 She had never heard **for/of/from** the effects of global warming.
2 Did you hear **of/about/from** the robbery which took place yesterday?
3 I haven't heard **of/about/from** Terry since he moved to Australia.
4 I am fed up **of/for/with** tidying up after those boys.
5 She is very fond **with/by/of** her baby sister.
6 I have forgiven David **of/for/from** breaking my stereo.
7 Eating fruit and vegetables is very good **to/of/for** your health.
8 Peter is very good **at/to/for** Mathematics.
9 My brother is very good **at/to/for** me. He always looks after me.
10 Tom was upset by his failure **of/in/with** the exam.
11 Richard Branson failed **in/to/with** his attempt to cross the Atlantic in a hot air balloon.
12 Her car failed **in/to/with** start this morning, so she had to call a taxi.
13 I am very grateful **to/of/for** you for all your help with the arrangements.
14 That man looks familiar **to/with/by** me.
15 I am not familiar **to/with/of** the workings of this company yet.
16 He was found guilty **about/of/for** theft and sentenced to three months in prison.
17 She felt very guilty **of/about/for** lying to her parents.
18 Car exhaust fumes are harmful **for/to/of** the environment.
19 Tony hopes **of/for/from** a rise in salary and a promotion this year.
20 I hope **for/of/to** travel the world when I finish university next year.
21 There is no hope **for/of/to** finding a solution to this problem.
22 Vincent Van Gogh is famous **of/to/for** his beautiful paintings.

Revision Box

23 **Choose the correct answer.**

1 Sam hopes ...*B*... an astronaut one day.
   A becoming   B to become   C become

2 I .... you to the airport in my car if you like.
   A will take   B 'm going to take
   C have taken

3 Jane's work is .... than Sarah's.
   A good   B better   C best

4 It's cold. I think I .... another jumper.
   A will put on   B am putting on   C put on

5 Jake .... at his friend's house last night.
   A stayed   B was staying   C had stayed

6 They advised her .... a new lock for the door.
   A buy   B to buy   C buying

7 I have .... money than David.
   A little   B less   C least

8 Would you like .... to my party tonight?
   A come   B to come   C coming

9 Lisa .... the house when her husband came home.
   A paints   B was painting   C has painted

10 Sally .... by the time I get home tonight.
   A is leaving   B will leave   C will have left

11 Ellen .... all her money by the time the shops closed.
   A had spent   B was spending   C spent

12 You should .... the windows more often.
   A cleaning   B clean   C to clean

13 Paul .... for three hours before he left the disco.
   A danced   B had been dancing   C was dancing

14 This time next month we .... for our holiday.
   A are packing   B will pack   C will be packing

15 This is the .... day of the year.
   A hot   B hotter   C hottest

16 That dress is rather .... I can't afford to buy it.
   A expensive   B more expensive
   C most expensive

17 Dad has finally managed .... the television.
   A to fix   B fix   C fixing

18 The doctor made John .... in bed for a week.
   A staying   B stay   C to stay

19 Jenny seems .... very happy these days.
   A to be   B being   C be

20 You had better .... now or you'll be late.
   A leaving   B leave   C to leave

ORAL Activity

ORAL Activity

Maxine recently won a competition. The prize was a free ticket to see her favourite band in concert and a chance to meet the band. Look at the prompts and say what Maxine did, using *a, an, some* or *the* where necessary, as in the example.

e.g. She bought some new clothes to wear to the concert.

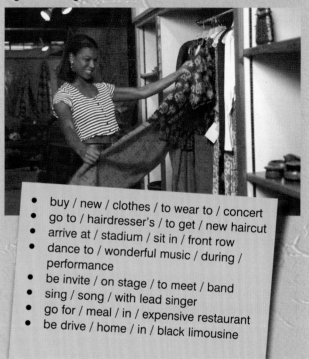

- buy / new / clothes / to wear to / concert
- go to / hairdresser's / to get / new haircut
- arrive at / stadium / sit in / front row
- dance to / wonderful music / during / performance
- be invite / on stage / to meet / band
- sing / song / with lead singer
- go for / meal / in / expensive restaurant
- be drive / home / in / black limousine

WRITING Activity

Maxine has been asked to write an account of her evening for a music magazine. Look at the Oral Activity again and complete the article.

When I heard that I had won the competition to see 'Starstruck', I was very excited. First of all, I bought some new clothes to wear to the concert and I went ...

....
....
....
....
....
....
....
....
....

... It was a fantastic evening which I will never forget.

UNIT 5
Modal Verbs

The verbs *can, could, may, might, must, will, would, shall, should* and *ought* are modal verbs. They do not take a suffix (*-s, -ing* or *-ed*). e.g. *He should stay* here. They are followed by a bare infinitive, except for *ought* which is followed by a to-infinitive. e.g. *They may come* tonight. *You ought to get* a job. They go before the subject in questions and are followed by *not* in negations. e.g. *Can I* say something? *I couldn't* understand him. Modal verbs do not usually have tenses. They can refer to the present or the future. e.g. *I must* go now. (present) *You must* call me early tomorrow morning. (future)

Ability (Can-Could-Be able to)

He was able to climb up the tree.

Can is used in the present and future. *Could* is the past tense of *can*. We use be able to to form all the other tenses.

- Can = be able to - ability in the present
  e.g. Tom **can** play the guitar.

- will be able to - ability in the future
  e.g. When you graduate, you **will be able to** get a job. But we use *can* when we decide now about something we will do in the near future.
  e.g. I haven't got any money now, but I **can** pay you tomorrow. (= I decide now about something I will do tomorrow.)

- Could = used to be able to
  ability in the past (repeated past action)
  We can use was/were able to with no difference in meaning.
  e.g. I **could**/**was able to** run fast when I was young.

- was/were able to = managed to do
  ability in the past (single past action)
  We use *was/were able to* to show that someone had the ability to do something in a particular situation in the past.
  e.g. Although it was dark, he **was able to** find his way.

- We normally use could with the verbs *see, hear, smell, taste, feel, understand, guess* and *remember*.
  e.g. She listened carefully and she **could hear** people talking in the next room.
  (NOT: ... ~~she was able to hear~~ ...)

- In negations we can use couldn't or wasn't/weren't able to with no difference in meaning.
  e.g. I **couldn't**/**wasn't able to** reach him on the phone.

Obligation/Duty/Necessity (Must-Have to-Should/Ought-Need)

Everyone should recycle their rubbish.

We use *must* to refer to the present or future.

- must = *it is your duty/you are obliged to do sth*
  e.g. You **must** listen to your teacher.

- have to = *it is necessary to do sth*
  e.g. We **have to be** at the airport at 9 o'clock.
  We use *must* when the speaker decides that something is necessary. We use *have to* when somebody else other than the speaker has made the decision.
  e.g. I **must** finish the report by tomorrow. (The speaker decides.)
  I **have to** finish the report by tomorrow. (Somebody else has made the decision.)

- *Must* and *have to* have different meanings in questions.
  e.g. **Must** I tidy my room? (= **Do you insist** that I tidy my room?)
  Do I have to tidy my room? (= **Is it necessary** for me to tidy my room?)

- Have got to has the same meaning as *have to*, and is often used in everyday speech.
  e.g. '**I've got to** phone Mum tonight.'

- We use *have to* when we need to use other tenses.
  e.g. We **had to** call for the doctor when Aunt Lucy fainted last night.

- should/ought (less emphatic than must)
  Should and ought express duty.
  e.g. People **should** take/**ought** to take better care of the environment.

- need = *it is necessary to*
  e.g. **Need I talk** to the boss right away?

70

NOTE: *Need* can be used as a main verb or as a modal verb with no difference in meaning. When it is used as a main verb it is followed by a to - infinitive and takes -s in the third person singular. We form questions and negations with *do/does*. e.g. Mike **needs to buy** some new clothes. You **don't need to do** this right now.
Need is used as a modal verb mainly in questions and negations. e.g. **Need I book** a room in advance? (Also: Do I need to book ...?) You **needn't give** me a lift home. (Also: You don't need to ...)

Absence of Necessity
(Needn't/Don't have to/Don't need to-Didn't need to-Needn't have done)

*You **don't need to** look up his phone number. I've got it right here.*

◆ **needn't/don't have to/don't need to + present infinitive (present or future) = it isn't necessary to do sth**
   e.g. You **needn't/don't have to/don't need to** work tonight. (It isn't necessary for you to work tonight.)

◆ **didn't need to/didn't have to = it was not necessary to do sth**
   This structure suggests that an action did not happen in the past because we knew then that it was not necessary.
   e.g. She **didn't need to/didn't have to** take a taxi. (It wasn't necessary, so she didn't.)

◆ **needn't + bare perfect infinitive = it was not necessary to do sth, but it was done**
   This structure shows that an action happened in the past, even though it was not necessary.
   e.g. You **needn't have bought** any bread. I'd already bought some. (It wasn't necessary, but you did.)

Prohibition (Mustn't/Can't)

SPEED LIMIT 35

◆ **mustn't/can't = it is forbidden to do sth/you are not allowed to do sth/it is against the rules/law to do sth**
   e.g. You **mustn't/can't** drive over 35 mph. (= It's against the law. You are not allowed to drive over 35 mph.)

1 Fill in the gaps with *can, can't, could, couldn't* or *was/wasn't able to*.

1 I had my hands full, so I ...*couldn't/wasn't able to*... open the door.
2 When I was young, I .... stand on my head.
3 Although he felt ill, he .... finish all the paperwork.
4 Tony is clever. He .... speak three languages.
5 I .... afford that bag. It's too expensive.
6 Although it was dark, he .... find his way through the woods.
7 I heard his voice calling me, but I .... see him.
8 We're busy tonight, so we .... come to the party.
9 When I entered the house, I .... smell fresh bread baking.
10 I .... drive a car. I learnt when I was eighteen.

2 Fill in the gaps with *must, mustn't* or *needn't/don't have to*.

1 A: You ...*must*... study hard to pass the exams.
   B: I know. I study every evening.
2 A: You .... be late for your job interview.
   B: I know. I'll leave early so as to get there on time.
3 A: Shall I collect the children from the party?
   B: No, you .... collect them. Mrs Shaw is giving them a lift home.
4 A: Do you want me to wait for you after work?
   B: No, you .... wait. I can walk home by myself.
5 A: You .... interrupt while people are talking.
   B: No. It's very bad manners to do that.
6 A: My dog has been ill all week.
   B: Oh dear! You .... take him to the vet.
7 A: It's Sally's birthday on Wednesday.
   B: I know. I .... remember to buy her a present.
8 A: Shall I wash the dishes for you?
   B: No, you .... do that. I'll do them later.

3 Fill the gaps with *needn't have* or *didn't need to* and the correct form of the verb in brackets.

1 I ran all the way to work, but I ...*needn't have hurried*... (hurry) because I was the first person to arrive.
2 We .... (hurry), so we stopped to have lunch on the way.
3 I went to college today, but I .... (go) as all the lectures were cancelled.
4 I............................... (ask) the way to Lewes, since I'd been there before.
5 I .... (buy) any food, so I didn't go to the supermarket.
6 I .... (buy) any food after all, because we had plenty at home.
7 I .... (pack) my shorts, as it rained all week.
8 We .... (pack) many things, as we would only be away for one night.

Logical Assumptions (Must-Can't/Couldn't)

They're wearing light clothes.
*It **must** be summer.*
*It **can't** be winter.*

◆ must = I'm sure/certain that sth is true
Must is used in affirmative sentences and expresses positive logical assumptions.
   e.g. *It is Sunday. He **must** be at home. (I'm sure he is at home.)*

◆ can't/couldn't = I'm sure that sth isn't true, real, etc.
Can't and *Couldn't* are used in negations and expresses negative logical assumptions.
   e.g. *It is Sunday. He **can't**/**couldn't** be at work. (I'm sure he isn't at work.)*

Probability (Should/Ought)

*It's four o'clock. The children **should** be/**ought** to be home by now.*

◆ should/ought = probably
Should and *ought* are used to express that something is likely to happen in the present or future.
   e.g. *It's 10 o'clock. He **should** be/**ought** to be at work.*

Possibility (Can-Could/May-Might)

*John isn't answering his phone. Where **can** he be?*

*I don't know. He **could** be in the manager's office.*

◆ can + present infinitive = general possibility - it is theoretically possible
This structure is used in affirmative sentences to show that something is possible theoretically or in general, that is, when we are not referring to a specific situation.
   e.g. *This road **can** get very busy.*
      (In general, not in a specific situation.)

Could/May/Might + present infinitive = it is possible/it is likely/perhaps
It is used to show that something is likely to happen in a specific situation.
   e.g. *The roads **could**/**may**/**might** get very busy tomorrow afternoon because there is a demonstration. (NOT: The roads can get ...)*
NOTE: In questions we use can (to talk about general or specific possibility), could or might. We do not use *may*.
   e.g. *'I got a bouquet of flowers, but there was no card.' 'Who **can**/**could**/**might** they be from?'*

◆ could/might + perfect infinitive (refers to the past) = it was possible, but it didn't happen
   e.g. *Yesterday, I left the car unlocked. It **could**/**might have been stolen**, but luckily it wasn't.*

---

 4 **Look at the pictures and answer the questions using *must/can't*, as in the example.**

   e.g. *No, they can't be in the city.*

A	B	C	D

Are they in the city? Are they tired? Do they know each other?	Do they go fishing often? Is it winter? Are they bored?	Did they walk up the mountain? Do they enjoy walking? Is the weather very hot?	Has she been interviewing the man? Is she a reporter? Are they in an office?

Study these examples:

I'm sure she **knows** him well. Perhaps he **will be** late.	present inf.	She must **know** him well. He may **be** late.
It's possible that he**'s working** late tonight. I'm sure she**'ll be working** tomorrow.	present cont. inf.	He could **be working** late tonight. She must **be working** tomorrow.
I'm sure he **didn't know** the truth. Perhaps they **have missed** the bus. It's possible he **had got** lost.	perfect inf.	He can't **have known** the truth. They might **have missed** the bus. He may **have got** lost.
I'm certain he **was sleeping**. Perhaps she **has been lying**. It's likely they **had been hiding**.	perfect cont. inf.	He must **have been sleeping**. She may **have been lying**. They could **have been hiding**.

5 **Complete the sentences using** *must* **or** *can't,* **as in the example.**

1 I'm sure she has gone on holiday.
   She ...*must have gone on holiday*....

2 I'm certain he doesn't know the secret.
   He ....

3 I'm certain Mike hasn't got a new car.
   Mike ....

4 I'm sure Susan has paid the phone bill.
   Susan ....

5 I'm sure they don't live here.
   They ....

6 I'm sure they left the party early.
   They ....

7 I'm certain he didn't call me.
   He ....

8 I'm certain Marie sent you a birthday card.
   Marie ....

9 I'm sure she has been keeping secrets from me.
   She ....

10 I'm certain she is looking for a new job.
   She ....

11 I'm sure David didn't go to the supermarket.
   David ....

12 I'm certain he is working at the library.
   He ....

6 **Rephrase the following sentences in as many ways as possible.**

1 It's likely she has forgotten about the meeting.
   She ...*may/might/could have forgotten about the meeting*....

2 Perhaps he will be home soon.
   He ....

3 Perhaps we won't stay in a hotel.
   We ....

4 It's possible she has been delayed in traffic.
   She ....

5 It's likely they have gone to the cinema.
   They ....

6 Perhaps they are asleep already.
   They ....

7 It's likely he hasn't been promoted.
   He ....

8 It's possible she called while we were out.
   She ....

9 It's likely we will go shopping this afternoon.
   We ....

10 Perhaps he is outside in the garden.
   He ....

11 It's possible they didn't receive our message.
   They ....

12 Perhaps she is visiting a friend.
   She ....

7 **Fill in** *can, can't, must, mustn't, needn't* **or** *have to.*

1 A: Is Jason at work today?
   B: He ...*can't*... be. His car isn't in the car park.

2 A: I can't do my German homework. It's too difficult.
   B: I'll help you. I .... speak German.

3 A: I'm going to watch television.
   B: Alright, but you .... stay up too late.

4 A: We .... book a taxi to take us to the airport.
   B: I'll do it now.

5 A: I didn't know Rachel was in the choir.
   B: Oh yes. She .... sing beautifully.

6 A: Shall I cook dinner tonight?
   B: No, you .... We're going to a restaurant.

7 A: Has Tim bought a car yet?
   B: He .... have. I saw him on the bus yesterday.

8 A: She .... be very rich.
   B: Yes. She's got a huge house and an expensive car.

9 A: I did the washing-up for you.
   B: Oh, you .... have, but it was kind of you.

10 A: Would you like to come to my party on Saturday night?
   B: I'd like to, but Mum says I .... visit my grandparents.

Permission
(Can/Could/May/Might)

Can I look at the figures, please?

Asking for permission

◆ **Can/Could/May/Might I ...?** = **Do you/Would you mind if ...?**
Could and *may* are more polite than *can*. *Might* is formal. *May* and *Might* are used to ask for permission when we do not know the other person very well. We normally reply with: *'Certainly.'/ 'Of course.'/ 'Why not?'/'No, I'm afraid you can't.'*
e.g. *'Can I use your pen for a minute?' 'Of course.'*
'May I see the manager, please?' 'Certainly.'

Giving permission

◆ **can/may** = you are allowed to do sth
(**can** - informal, **may** - formal)
May is usually used in writing.
e.g. *You may make a phone call here.*
We do not use could or might to give permission.
e.g. *'Could I borrow your dictionary?' 'Yes, you can.'/ 'Yes, you may.'* (NOT: *Yes, you could.*)

Refusing permission

◆ **can't/mustn't/may not** = you are not allowed to do sth
May not is formal and is usually used in writing.
e.g. *I'm sorry, but you can't/mustn't use the fax.*
Customers may not enter this area.
We do not use couldn't to refuse permission.
e.g. *'Could I stay a little longer?' 'I'm sorry, but you can't.'* (NOT: *I'm sorry, but you couldn't.*)

Talking about permission

◆ **We use can and be allowed to to refer to laws or regulations.**
e.g. *All citizens over the age of 18 can/are allowed to vote. (law)*

There is a difference in meaning between *may* and *be allowed to* in questions.
Study the examples:
e.g. a) **May I** use your phone? (= *Will you allow me to use your phone?*)

b) **Are we allowed to** use the office phone?
(= *What is the rule?*)

◆ We use *could* or *was/were allowed to* to say that we had general permission to do something in the past.

We use *was/were allowed to* and not *could*, to say that we had permission to do something in a particular situation in the past.

e.g. *I could/was allowed to go to parties when I was young. (I was allowed to go to parties in general.)*

BUT: *I was allowed to go to John's party last night.*
(NOT: *I could go ... as this is a particular situation.)*

 8 **Fill in the gaps with *could* or *was/were allowed to*.**

1 The children ...*were allowed to*... go to the cinema on their own yesterday.
2 When I was young, we .... wear whatever we liked to school.
3 Peter .... watch a concert on TV last night, although it was on quite late.
4 When we were children, we .... play outside until it got dark.
5 Yesterday, we .... bring our favourite toys to school.
6 When Dennis lived with his parents, he .... come in at whatever time he liked.

 9 **Underline the correct word(s).**

1 A: Could I sleep at my friend's house tonight?
   B: Yes, of course you **could/can**.
2 A: I **could/was allowed to** go to the disco last night.
   B: Was it good fun?
3 A: **Can/Might** I have a biscuit please, Mum?
   B: Of course. Help yourself.
4 A: Excuse me, sir. **May I/Am I allowed to** leave the room?
   B: Yes, but don't be too long.
5 A: **Must/Might** I borrow these files for a moment, sir?
   B: Certainly. Take whatever you need.
6 A: Might I use your pen?
   B: Of course you **may/might**.
7 A: **May I/Am I allowed to** park in the company car park?
   B: Of course you are!

Requests (Can/Could/Will/Would/May/Might)

> **Could you** send the samples to my office, please?

◆ **Can/Could/Will/Would you ...?**
We use this structure to ask someone to do something for us. *Can* and *will* are informal. *Would* and *could* are more polite than *can* and *will*.
e.g. **Can/Will you** get me a glass of water? (informal)
Could/Would you type these letters for me, please? (more polite)
We normally reply with: *'Yes, I'd (would) be happy to.'/'Yes, I'd be glad to.'* / *'Certainly.'* / *'Of course.'* / *'I'm sorry, but I can't.'*

◆ **May/Might/Can/Could I ...?**
We use this structure to ask for something politely. *Might* is formal and is not often used.
e.g. **Can/Could/May I** have a piece of that cake, please?
We normally reply with: *'Certainly.'* / *'Yes, certainly.'* / *'Of course.'* / *'Yes, of course.'*

Offers (I'll-Shall/Can/Could)

> **Shall I** explain it again?

◆ **I'll** = I'm willing to do something (informal)
e.g. You look tired. **I'll** do the ironing for you.

◆ **Shall/Can/Could I/we ...?** = Would you like me/us to ...?/Do you want me/us to ...?
e.g. **Shall/Can/Could I** give you a hand with the preparations?

Suggestions (Shall/Can/Could)

> We **could** have the meeting on Tuesday instead.

◆ **Shall I/we ...?**
I/We can/could } = **Why don't we ...?/How about ...?/What about ...?/Let's ...**
e.g. *'**Shall we** go the theatre tomorrow night?'*
*'I'd rather not. We **can/could** go to the cinema instead.'*

◆ We use *shall* in questions when we are asking for suggestions or instructions.
e.g. *'Where **shall** I put these flowers?'*
'In this vase.'

Advice (Should/Ought/Must)

You **should** always wear a life jacket when you go canoeing.

◆ **should/ought + present infinitive = I advise you to/You had better do sth**
e.g. It's late. You **should go/ought to go** home as soon as possible.

◆ We use *must* to give strong advice. Compare the examples:
e.g. *'You **must** follow a healthy diet,'* the doctor said to me. (an order which is likely to be obeyed)
e.g. *'You **should** follow/**ought to** follow a healthy diet,'* my friend said to me. (a piece of advice which may or may not be followed)

Criticism (Should/Ought)

*The owners **shouldn't have left/ought not to have left** the window unlocked.*

◆ **should/ought + perfect infinitive = it would have been better if you had ...**
We use these structures to criticise someone else's actions.
*e.g. You **should have come/ought to have come** to me for help. (But you didn't.)*

10 Fill in *shall* or *will*.

1 A: ...*Shall*... I help you with the washing-up?
  B: No, I can manage by myself.
2 A: .... we have pizza for dinner tonight?
  B: I'd rather have steak.
3 A: .... you carry this for me, please?
  B: Certainly. It looks heavy.
4 A: What .... we buy for Bob's birthday?
  B: I think he'd like a book.
5 A: .... you answer the phone, please?
  B: Of course.
6 A: Where .... we sit in the classroom?
  B: Next to the window.
7 A: .... you take the rubbish outside for me, please?
  B: Yes, in a minute.
8 A: .... we have a barbecue next weekend?
  B: Yes, if the weather's fine.
9 A: .... you babysit for me tonight?
  B: I'm sorry, but I can't.
10 A: .... we try this new recipe tonight?
  B: Yes. We've got all the ingredients.

11 Read the situations and complete the sentences with *should/shouldn't, ought to/ought not to* and the correct tense of the infinitive.

1 Your friend didn't see a film on TV last night. You saw it and it was very good.
  You ...*should/ought to have seen*... (see) the film.

2 Liz bought an expensive jacket yesterday and now she hasn't got enough money for the rest of the week.
  She .... (buy) such an expensive jacket.
3 Your sister eats a lot of junk food which is bad for her health.
  You .... (eat) so much junk food.
4 Mr Jackson had a stiff back. He lifted some heavy boxes and now his back is worse.
  He .... (lift) those heavy boxes.
5 Tony always drives too fast. Yesterday, he was arrested for speeding.
  He .... (drive) more slowly.
6 Sally is clumsy. She is always breaking things.
  She .... (be) more careful.
7 Paul didn't do his homework. The teacher punished him.
  He .... (do) his homework.
8 Amy borrowed her brother's car without asking. He was very angry.
  She .... (borrow) his car without asking.

12 Underline the correct word(s) in bold.

1 A: I found a briefcase on the train.
  B: You **ought to/can** take it to the police station as soon as possible.
2 A: Did you get some money from the bank?
  B: No, I **didn't need to/needn't**. I had enough in my wallet.
3 A: Sorry I'm late again.
  B: You **should/might** wear a watch.
4 A: **Couldn't/May** I speak to Claire, please?
  B: Just a moment, please. I'll call her.
5 A: We **could/must** go out for a meal this evening, if you like.
  B: Oh, yes. That would be nice.
6 A: I wonder if Paul and Jim have got lost.
  B: They **can't/mustn't** have got lost because I gave them a map.
7 A: **Could/Would** I use your telephone, please?
  B: Yes, of course.
8 A: Was the exam very difficult?
  B: Yes, but I **can/was able to** answer all the questions.
9 A: We **mustn't/needn't** go shopping this week. We've got plenty of food.
  B: Alright. We'll go next week instead.
10 A: **Should/May** I sit down, please?
  B: Yes, of course. Make yourself at home.
11 A: When **will/shall** I visit you next?
  B: You **can/must** call in tomorrow, if you like.
12 A: Helen should be here by now.
  B: She **ought to/could** have missed the train.

Expressions Similar to Modal Verbs

◆ **Be supposed to + infinitive (= should)**
This structure is used to show that someone else expects us to do something.
e.g. I'm supposed to work this weekend. (My boss expects me to do so.)

◆ **Be to + infinitive (= must)** is used to give orders.
e.g. You are to stay here until I return.
This medicine is to be taken three times a day.

◆ **Be likely to + infinitive/It is likely that + clause (= probably - more emphatic than may but less emphatic than should/ought). They are used to express possibility.**
e.g. The Austrian racing driver is likely to win the race.
It is likely that the Austrian racing driver will win the race.
Is Mary likely to get the job she applied for?

13 Match the items in column A to their synonyms in column B.

A	B
1 You mustn't ...	a You are supposed to ...
2 You can't be ...	b It wasn't necessary for us to ... (but we did)
3 You needn't ...	c Let's ...
4 They ought to ...	d He managed to ...
5 She didn't need to ...	e They had better ...
6 You should ...	f It is forbidden ...
7 May I ...?	g I'm sure they are ...
8 We needn't have ...	h Do you mind if I ...?
9 He was able to ...	i You are to ...
10 Shall we ...?	j It isn't necessary for you to ...
11 You must ...	k I'm certain you aren't ...
12 They must be ...	l It wasn't necessary for her to ...

14 Rephrase the following sentences in as many ways as possible.

1 **It is possible that Sue will** be late this evening.
Sue may/might/could be late this evening./ Sue is likely to be late this evening.

2 **I'm sure David isn't** going to the party tonight.
....

3 **The guests are supposed** to arrive at 8 o'clock.
....

4 **It wasn't necessary for Toby to** go to school today.
....

5 **I advise you to** book a table in advance.
....

6 **They are obliged to** wear helmets at work.
....

7 **You are to** wait here until the manager arrives.
....

8 **Steve managed to** repair the bike after trying for two hours.
....

9 **Perhaps we will** go to Italy for a holiday next summer.
....

10 **We are obliged to** wear a uniform for school.
....

11 **You aren't allowed to** run in the corridors.
....

12 **How about** inviting some friends over to dinner?
....

13 **It isn't necessary for you to** buy me a present.
....

14 **Do you mind if I** use your telephone?
....

15 **Would you like me to** clean the windows for you?
....

16 **How about** going for a walk this afternoon?
....

15 Answer the questions using a suitable modal verb.

1 Are the men criminals?
They may be criminals.
2 Are they trying to escape?
3 Are they in the countryside?
4 Is it a cloudy day?
5 Is this their own boat?
6 Are they going to a hiding place?
7 Are the police chasing them?

Functions of Modal Verbs

Expressing ability

a) Terry is twenty years old. He **can** drive a car. (present)
b) When he was ten, he **could/was able to** ride a bicycle. (past repeated action)
c) Paula **was able to** climb to the top of the mountain. (managed to do; past single action)

Expressing lack of ability

a) Sue **can't** dance. (present)
b) He **couldn't/wasn't able to** play chess when he was younger. (past repeated action)
c) She **couldn't/wasn't able to** finish the book. (past single action)

Expressing obligation/duty/necessity

a) You **must** attend the meeting. (You are obliged to/You have to/You need to/It is necessary.)
b) I **must** attend the meeting. (I have decided.)
c) I **have to** attend the meeting. (Someone else has decided.)
d) We **ought to/should** respect the elderly. (less strong than must)
e) **Need** I **buy** her a present? (Is it necessary?)

Expressing absence of necessity

a) She **doesn't need to/doesn't have to/needn't** do the shopping. I'll do it later. (It isn't necessary.)
b) She **didn't need to/didn't have to** do the shopping as I had already done it. (It wasn't necessary for her to do it.)
c) She **needn't have done** the shopping. (It wasn't necessary for her to do the shopping, but she did.)

Expressing prohibition

You **mustn't/can't** be late for work. (it's forbidden/you aren't allowed to/it's against the rules/law)

Expressing certainty

a) He **must** be at home. (positive; I'm sure he is.)
b) He **can't** be sleeping. (negative; I'm sure he isn't.)

Expressing probability

He **ought to/should** be in now. (He is probably in.)

Expressing possibility

a) It **can** get very hot in July. (it is theoretically possible)
b) We **could/may/might** be a little late. (it is possible)
c) He **could/might have been** injured. (but he wasn't)

Asking for permission

a) **Can** I ask you a question, please? (informal)
b) **Could** I ask you a question, please? (more polite)
c) **May/Might** I ask you a question, please? (formal)

Giving/Refusing permission

a) You **can** park your car here. (informal)
b) You **may** park your car in this area. (formal - usually written)
c) You **can't/mustn't** use this phone. (informal)
d) You **may not** use this phone. (formal - usually written)

Talking about permission

a) All students **can/are allowed to use** the library. (regulation)
b) I **could/was allowed to go** out alone when I was 18. (general permission)
c) I **was allowed to go** out alone last night. (permission for one particular action)

Making requests

a) **Can/Will** you explain this to me? (informal)
b) **Could/Would** you explain this to me? (more polite)
c) **Can** I have some water? (informal)
d) **Could/May** I have some water? (formal)
e) **Might** I have some water? (very formal)

Making offers

a) **I'll** help you with your essay. (I'm willing to help you.)
b) **Shall/Can/Could** I carry this bag for you? (Would you like me to/Do you want me to do it?)

Making suggestions

a) **Shall** we visit Grandma this weekend?
b) We **can/could** go to a concert tonight.
(Why don't we....?/How about....?/What about...?/ Let's ...)
c) Where **shall** we go? (What is your suggestion?)

Giving advice

a) You **ought to/should** study harder. (I advise you to)
b) You **must** study harder. (I strongly advise you to.)

Expressing criticism

a) You **ought to/should** have been more careful. (It would have been better if you had been more careful.)

16 Rephrase the following sentences in as many ways as possible.

1 You had better ask your teacher to help you with your studies.
   ...*You ought to/should ask your teacher to help you with your studies*....
2 Can you hold this bag for me, please?
   ....
3 Why don't we go for a picnic this weekend?
   ....
4 It wasn't necessary for John to go to work because it was Sunday.
   ....
5 We managed to do the puzzle, although it was difficult.
   ....
6 You are to report to the manager as soon as you reach Manchester.
   ....
7 You are forbidden to enter this area.
   ....
8 Do you mind if I take this chair?
   ....
9 You don't need to feed the dog. I've already done it.
   ....
10 You ought to have locked the doors when you went out.
   ....
11 I strongly advise you to take legal action.
   ....
12 We are supposed to obey the law.
   ....

17 Choose the correct answer.

1 Shall I make you a cup of tea?
   (A) Yes, please.   B No, you won't.
2 Would you help me please? My car won't start.
   A I'd be happy to.   B Yes, I would.
3 Could you open the door for me, please?
   A Yes, I could.   B Of course.
4 Can you do the washing-up for me, please?
   A No, I may not.   B No problem.
5 We could go for a walk this afternoon.
   A That's a nice idea.   B No, we might not.
6 Could I sit down for a minute, please?
   A Yes, of course.   B No, you couldn't.
7 Can I get you anything, madam?
   A No, you can't.   B No, thank you. I'm just looking.
8 Can I go and play football now, please?
   A Not at all.   B Yes, if you like.
9 Shall I pick you up from work this evening?
   A Yes, please.   B No, you won't.
10 Will you hold this box for me, please?
   A Yes, I may.   B Certainly.

18 Complete the sentences, as in the example. Sometimes more than one answer is possible.

Modal	Use
1 You ...*can*... go to the cinema.	giving permission
2 You .... have any sweets.	refusing permission
3 .... we go for a walk?	making a suggestion
4 .... I stay at Paul's house tonight, please?	asking for permission
5 You .... have worked harder.	expressing criticism
6 You .... talk in the library.	expressing prohibition
7 Sally .... invite us to her party.	expressing possibility
8 They .... be lost.	expressing a positive logical assumption
9 You .... do your homework before you go out.	expressing obligation
10 She .... be older than me.	expressing a negative logical assumption
11 Steve .... walk. He's broken his leg.	expressing lack of ability
12 .... I paint the fence for you?	making an offer

19 Rephrase the following sentences in as many ways as possible.

1 Why don't we go to Spain on holiday this year?
   ...*We can/could go to Spain on holiday this year*....
2 Perhaps Tony has gone to work early.
   ....
3 Policemen are obliged to wear a uniform while on duty.
   ....
4 Simon managed to climb the mountain, although it was steep.
   ....
5 It is forbidden to sound the alarm for no reason.
   ....
6 How about watching a video this evening?
   ....
7 I'm certain Martin heard me calling him.
   ....
8 I'm sure Paul isn't an engineer.
   ....

UNIT 5
Modal Verbs

20 **Choose the correct answer.**

1 ...B... I borrow your pen? Mine doesn't work.
   A Needn't   B Can   C Ought

2 I .... go to the bank. I haven't got any money.
   A must   B mustn't   C may

3 Lizzie .... spell her name before she was three.
   A might   B could   C must

4 .... you help me with the shopping, please?
   A Must   B Shall   C Will

5 You .... go to the post office. I'll go later.
   A needn't   B might   C must

6 You .... to study hard for your exams.
   A need   B can't   C shall

7 You .... to be at work by nine o'clock.
   A must   B should   C are

8 No reporters .... approach the scene of the accident.
   A might have   B were allowed to   C needn't

9 We .... phone Mary. It's her birthday today.
   A needn't   B ought to   C are able to

10 What time .... I pick you up from work?
   A mustn't   B will   C shall

21 **Choose the correct answer.**

1 'You ...C... pay the bills today.'
   'I know. I promise I won't forget.'
   A would   B shall   C must

2 '............. we go to the beach tomorrow?'
   'Yes. That's a great idea.'
   A Shall   B Mustn't   C Would

3 'I'm going to the cinema. Do you want to come with me?'
   'No, thank you. I .... do my homework.'
   A could   B would   C have to

4 'You .... put that shirt in the washing machine.'
   'I know. It has to be dry-cleaned.'
   A must   B mustn't   C couldn't

5 'Was your suitcase very heavy?'
   'Yes, but I .... carry it by myself.'
   A was able to   B can't   C ought

6 '............. you drive?'
   'Yes, but I haven't got my own car.'
   A Might   B Should   C Can

7 'I .... ride a bicycle until I was eight.'
   'Neither could I.'
   A couldn't   B could   C can't

8 '............. you open the door for me, please?'
   'Yes, certainly.'
   A Shall   B Must   C Would

9 'Ben had a hard time trying to find the leak in the pipe.'
   'But he .... stop it, wasn't he?'
   A was allowed to   B was able to   C could

10 'I saw Tina in town last night.'
   'You .... have seen her. She's on holiday in Spain.'
   A would   B could   C can't

11 'Where's Colin?'
   'I'm not sure. He .... be in the study.'
   A might   B will   C ought

12 'I feel very tired today.'
   'You .... have stayed up so late last night.'
   A shouldn't   B could   C might

13 'Did you phone Alan yesterday?'
   'No, I .... He came round to see me.'
   A didn't need to   B needn't   C have to

14 '............. you give me a lift to work tomorrow?'
   'Yes. I'll pick you up at eight o' clock.'
   A May   B Shall   C Will

15 '............. I help you, madam?'
   'Yes, I'm looking for the manager.'
   A Would   B Must   C May

22 *Imagine you're a detective. You are at the scene of a crime and have found some clues.* **Look at the things you have found and answer the questions below using** *must* **and** *can't*.

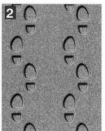

1 Were the thieves wearing gloves?
   ...*They can't have been wearing gloves*....
2 How many thieves were there?
3 How did they get into the house?
4 Did they have a getaway car?
5 Were they looking for something?
6 Did they want money?

IN OTHER WORDS

Study these examples. The second sentence has a similar meaning to the first sentence.

1 It's forbidden to go near the launch pad.
   mustn't You **mustn't go** near the launch pad.
   allowed You **aren't allowed to go** near the launch pad.

2 I advise you to send them a letter of apology.
   should You **should send** them a letter of apology.
   ought You **ought to send** them a letter of apology.

3 I'm certain Andrew didn't reveal your secret.
   can't Andrew **can't have revealed** your secret.

4 Let's discuss this over lunch.
   can We **can discuss** this over lunch.

5 Do you think Laura will leave for Chicago earlier than she thought?
   likely Is Laura **likely to leave** for Chicago earlier than she thought?

6 It isn't necessary for Ron to pay for our tickets.
   have Ron **doesn't have to pay** for our tickets.
   need Ron **doesn't need to pay** for our tickets.

7 I'm sure Robert realised how wrong he was.
   must Robert **must have realised** how wrong he was.

8 It is possible that they will sell their house.
   may They **may sell** their house.

9 It wasn't necessary for her to come early, but she did.
   have She **needn't have come** early.

10 Everyone is supposed to pay taxes to the government.
   should Everyone **should pay** taxes to the government.

23 **Complete each sentence with two to five words, including the word in bold.**

1 I'm sure the books are in this cupboard
   must The books ...*must be in this*... cupboard.

2 Let's have lunch in half an hour.
   can We .... in half an hour.

3 It isn't necessary for you to work on Saturday.
   have You .... on Saturday.

4 I advise you to open a bank account.
   should You .... a bank account.

5 It is possible that she has forgotten to call.
   may She .... to call.

6 It wasn't necessary for him to buy a gift, but he did.
   have He .... a gift.

7 Perhaps Alice is at the hairdresser's.
   could Alice .... the hairdresser's.

8 I advise you to have your car serviced.
   should You .... car serviced.

9 I'm sure Sylvia didn't mean what she said.
   can't Sylvia .... what she said.

10 It wasn't necessary for him to help me, but he did.
   have He .... me.

11 It's forbidden to take your bag into the building.
   mustn't You .... into the building.

12 I'm sure she understood what I was saying.
   have She .... what I was saying.

13 Perhaps he took the train to work this morning.
   may He ....
   the train to work this morning.

14 Running in the corridors is forbidden.
   allowed You .... in the corridors.

15 Is it possible that Jane is leaving school at the end of this week?
   be Could ....
   at the end of this week?

16 We'll probably have a party for Simon's birthday.
   likely It's ....
   a party for Simon's birthday.

17 I'd better start studying for my exams soon.
   ought I .... for my exams soon.

24 **Underline the correct word(s).**

1 A: *Shall/Would/<u>Could</u>* I speak to the manager, please?
   B: I'm afraid he's busy at the moment.

2 A: The Taylors brought us a bottle of wine for our anniversary.
   B: They *needn't/couldn't/mightn't* have done that, but it was very kind.

3 A: *Could/May/Shall* you tell me where the bank is, please?
   B: Certainly. It's on the corner.

4 A: You *mustn't/needn't/couldn't* clean the floor.
   B: Oh, have you done it already?

5 A: *Would/Shall/Will* we go for a walk this afternoon?
   B: Why not? It's a lovely day.

6 A: *Can/Shall/Would* I have a milkshake, please?
   B: Yes, of course. What flavour would you like?

7 A: *May/Should/Would* I borrow your pen, please?
   B: Yes, of course. Be my guest.

8 A: *Shall/Will/Would* I pour you a glass of orange juice?
   B: Yes, please. *Could/May/Shall* you put some ice in it, too?

9 A: I put your blue trousers in the washing machine.
   B: Oh, no! You *shouldn't/mustn't/can't* have done that. They have to be dry-cleaned.

10 A: Where's Alan?
   B: Well, it's five o'clock. He *ought/mustn't/needn't* to be here by now.

11 A: What are you doing on Saturday morning?
   B: I *have to/will/should* go into the office for a couple of hours.

12 A: I want to get a better job.
   B: You *didn't need to/should/needn't* get some more qualifications.

25 Add the correct prefixes to form derivatives.

1 Carl is very ...*anti*...social and doesn't like to be with other people.
2 The fact that Tony and Sue caught the same plane was a ....incidence.
3 Simon is ....lingual — he is fluent in both French and English.
4 The thieves managed to ....activate the alarm before entering the building.
5 This exam gives you an ....nationally recognised degree.
6 I forgot to set my alarm and I ....slept.
7 After the earthquake, the town was slowly ....built.
8 Tara was so nasty to Bob — her behaviour was ....forgivable.
9 Brian had to ....write several chapters of his book before it could be published.
10 Daniel is very ....reliable — he never turns up for anything.

26 Fill in the the blanks with the correct form of the word in brackets.

1 His ambition in life is to become a famous ...*actor*.... (act)
2 The fireworks at the party were very .... (impress)
3 Body language is an important part of .... (communicate)
4 He is very .... and uses hand gestures to emphasise whatever he says. (express)
5 The .... was very proud of his time machine. (invent)
6 Many jobs require workers to wear .... clothing. (protect)
7 The .... from the gas plant took us all by surprise. (explode)
8 His most valuable .... is a gold pocket-watch. (possess)
9 Her knowledge of the region is quite .... (extend)
10 She has an amazing .... of seashells. (collect)
11 One of the most popular .... at the funfair is the Ghost Train. (attract)
12 Claire is a .... girl and gets upset very easily. (sense)
13 The audience showed their .... of the performance by cheering loudly. (appreciate)
14 Although she will be ninety this year, she is still a very .... woman. (act)
15 These chemicals are .... and should be treated with extreme care. (explode)
16 We could tell from the .... on his face that he was very angry. (express)

- You **should to exercise** regularly. ✗
  You **should exercise** regularly. ✓

- I **must study** very hard **last week**. ✗
  I **had to study** very hard **last week**. ✓

- Although he didn't feel well **yesterday**, he **could** finish his work. ✗
  Although he didn't feel well **yesterday**, he **was able to** finish his work. ✓

- **Need I to pay** cash for my ticket? ✗
  Need I pay cash for my ticket? ✓

- The shops **can be very crowded tomorrow** because it's the last shopping day before Christmas. ✗
  The shops **could/may/might be very crowded tomorrow** because it's the last shopping day before Christmas. ✓

- **May** this letter be from my friend? ✗
  Can/Could/Might this letter be from my friend? ✓

- 'Could you lend me some money?' '**Of course I could.**' ✗
  'Could you lend me some money?' '**Of course I can.**' ✓

- I **could watch** the late film on TV **last night**. ✗
  I **was allowed to watch** the late film on TV **last night**. ✓

27 Correct the mistakes.

1 'Could you help me lift this box?' 'Of course I could.'
2 I could go to Emma's party last Saturday.
3 Need I to book a table in advance?
4 May these flowers be from your fiancé?
5 Although she was exhausted, she could finish the race.
6 You should to brush your teeth twice a day.
7 I must have my car repaired last month.
8 The bus can be late today because there is a lot of traffic.

28 Cross out the unnecessary word.

1 They shouldn't to have called the police.
2 Paul was been able to change the flat tyre by himself.
3 She needn't to have bought such an expensive dress.
4 The Prime Minister is to will give a speech at the conference tomorrow.
5 Jennifer is likely that to look for another job.
6 How about we driving to the coast?
7 That can't to have been Paul. He's on holiday in Jamaica.
8 Would you mind if my staying here for a couple of days?
9 They might have been forgotten about our meeting.
10 Jack has had to see the General Manager yesterday.

Phrasal Verbs

get across:	(tr) communicate ideas; become understood
get along (with):	be on friendly terms; get on (with)
get at:	1) (tr) reach; find, 2) (int) imply
get away:	avoid capture
get away from:	avoid
get away with:	(tr) 1) escape punishment for wrong-doing, 2) escape capture with stolen goods
get by:	(int) survive despite difficulties
get down to:	(tr) start doing sth seriously
get off:	1) (int) avoid punishment, 2) start a journey
get off with:	(tr) not be punished; be treated leniently
get on:	1) (int) advance; make progress, 2) become late; get nearer 3) (int) have a friendly relationship with; get along
get on with:	(tr) 1) be on good terms with; get along with, 2) continue after an interruption
get over:	1) recover, 2) overcome
get round:	(int) to spread (news)
get round to:	(tr) find the necessary time to do sth
get through:	1) (tr) finish (a piece of work), 2) (int) survive through difficult times, 3) (tr) use up all of sth (supplies, money, etc), 4) (tr) reach sb by telephone; get through to
get to:	(tr) have an effect on sb's feelings

29 **Fill in the correct particle.**

1 I generally get ...*on/along with*... my boss, although we disagree sometimes.
2 You really must get .... work. The exams start next week!
3 The teacher tried to get .... the main ideas of the theory to her class without confusing them.
4 We have to get .... early to get to London on time.
5 I haven't got .... ironing those clothes yet. I've been very busy.
6 I earn enough money to get ...., but I haven't managed to save much lately.
7 I don't understand what you're getting .... Can you explain what you mean?
8 We get .... two loaves of bread a day.
9 After the phone call, I got .... my work.
10 Because it was his first offence, he got .... a warning from the judge.

11 There's no getting .... paying taxes.
12 What he said really got .... her, and she started to cry.
13 Despite the cold, they got .... the winter without too many problems.
14 Bill got .... his illness quickly and returned to work.
15 By the time we got home, it was getting .... for midnight.
16 The burglars got .... the jewellery.
17 After several attempts, I finally got .... the radio station.
18 No one should get .... breaking the law.
19 The news got .... the office fast.
20 No problem is too big to get ....
21 The thieves managed to get .... even though the police were looking for them.
22 I can't get .... that box because the shelf it's on is too high.
23 Susan got .... the work quickly, so she was able to leave early.

30 **Underline the correct preposition.**

1 I have a high opinion *of*/*on*/*for* Sarah's teacher.
2 Tom refused to join *on*/*of*/*in* the football match.
3 I've lost my earring. Will you help me look *after*/*for*/*at* it?
4 I need someone to look *at*/*after*/*for* my children while I'm at work.
5 I looked closely *after*/*at*/*for* the man, but I didn't recognise him.
6 I mistook that woman *for*/*of*/*about* my French teacher.
7 She earns hardly enough money to live *on*/*with*/*for*.
8 Since the company changed management there has been an increase *on*/*of*/*in* profits.
9 It is rude to laugh *at*/*with*/*for* other people.
10 What he lacks *of*/*in*/*to* size he makes up for in strength.
11 Her lack *of*/*in*/*with* confidence was the reason she didn't get the job.
12 I have no intention *of*/*for*/*to* selling my car.
13 There is no need *of*/*about*/*for* such childish behaviour.
14 Some people had objections *about*/*to*/*for* the proposed changes.
15 The new teacher made a great impression *on*/*by*/*with* the class.
16 The manager was impressed *with*/*on*/*of* the new player's technique.
17 Jane likes to be comfortable, so she is not keen *in*/*at*/*on* camping.
18 Sam is keen *on*/*to*/*of* join the army when he leaves school.
19 Take no notice *from*/*for*/*of* Amanda. She's showing off.
20 I don't want to get involved *on*/*about*/*in* this argument.
21 Julia insisted *in*/*for*/*on* paying for lunch.
22 She is completely ignorant *for*/*about*/*to* computer technology.

Revision Box

31 **Put the verbs in brackets into the correct tense.**

Dear Phil,

I **1)** ...'m writing... (write) to tell you about the plans for the school Summer Fun Day. We **2)** .... (already/put) some tables in the school field, but I don't think there **3)** .... (be) enough, so we **4)** .... (probably/borrow) some more.

I **5)** .... (arrange) for the mayor to come and open the event. He **6)** .... (arrive) at ten o 'clock on the day and the headmaster, Mr Pearson, **7)** .... (take) him on a guided tour of the school.

We **8)** .... (go) shopping yesterday to buy some prizes for the competitions. We also **9)** .... (buy) some coffee, tea, orange juice and biscuits for the refreshments stall.

Anyway, as you can see, everything is almost ready. I hope everything **10)** .... (go) well.

See you on Saturday at the fair!

Lily

32 **Put the verbs in brackets into the correct tense.**

1 A: What does Tony do for a living?
   B: He ...works... (work) for a large company in London.
2 A: Are you busy this evening?
   B: Yes. I .... (meet) some friends at eight o'clock.
3 A: Mum .... (bake) all morning.
   B: I know. She .... (make) a lot of cakes.
4 A: Is Simon going to school today?
   B: No. He .... (feel) ill all week, so he's going to stay in bed.

5 A: .... (you/ever/go) to Spain?
   B: No, but Chris .... (go) there last summer.
6 A: Were you at home when I called you?
   B: Yes, but I .... (cut) the grass and I didn't hear the phone.
7 A: Steve is a famous singer now.
   B: Yes. He .... (make) his first record in 1993.
8 A: Why did you pay for the meal last night?
   B: Because Joe .... (lose) his wallet, so he couldn't pay.
9 A: Why are you in such a hurry?
   B: Because I'm going to the theatre and the play .... (start) in ten minutes.
10 A: Shall we go for a picnic tomorrow?
   B: I can't. My cousins .... (come) to visit tomorrow.
11 A: I can't believe we're going on holiday in a few days.
   B: Just think. This time next week, we .... (ski) in the Alps.

33 **Choose the correct answer.**

When Simon woke up, he knew it **1)** ...B... a good day. The sun was shining through the curtains and he felt strangely **2)** .... Today was **3)** .... day he had been waiting for. Six weeks **4)** ...., Simon had taken his school exams. He had been **5)** .... nervous, but he had told himself, 'I **6)** .... for months and I know I can pass. I'll stay calm and, by the time the exam finishes, I'll have answered every question as **7)** .... as I can.'

And now the day when Simon would **8)** .... his results had come. He ran down the stairs and picked up the large envelope which **9)** .... on the mat. His hands were shaking as he read the results. He **10)** .... with top marks!

	A	B	C
1	is going to be	was going to be	will be
2	excited	excite	exciting
3	one	the	a
4	since	before	after
5	very	far	much
6	have been studying	had been studying	was studying
7	good	well	best
8	to get	getting	get
9	was lying	lies	is lying
10	passed	had passed	has passed

34   Underline the correct word.

1 Tony's new job involves **travelling**/**to travel** around the country.
2 David is eighteen. He is too old **to join**/**joining** the youth club.
3 We considered **to go**/**going** to France, but then we decided **to go**/**going** to Italy.
4 Sarah learnt how **to sew**/**sewing** when she was eight.
5 The thief finally confessed to **steal**/**stealing** the jewels.
6 I regret **to speak**/**speaking** so angrily to my brother.
7 Try **eat**/**eating** more fruit. You will feel much healthier.
8 Mary is busy **to clean**/**cleaning** the house.
9 He would like **going**/**to go** to the cinema this evening.
10 Gary opened the door only **to find**/**finding** that there was nobody there.

35   Complete each sentence with two to five words, including the word in bold.

1 We haven't been on holiday for five years.
  since   It's ...*five years since we went*... on holiday.
2 The last time she went to a party was three months ago.
  been   She ....
       a party for three months.
3 I've never heard such a funny joke.
  funniest   It's .... I've ever heard.
4 How long ago did you take your driving test?
  took   How long ....
       your driving test?
5 He hasn't tidied his room yet.
  still   He .... his room.
6 'No, I didn't take your wallet,' the young man said.
  denied   The young man ....
       my wallet.
7 Mark is more energetic than his brother.
  as   Mark's brother isn't ....
       Mark.
8 He is interested in literature. That's why he buys so many books.
  finds   He ....
       That's why he buys so many books.
9 Sally is the most graceful dancer of all.
  as   No one else ....
       Sally does.
10 They made me reveal the secret.
  was   I .... the secret.

ORAL Activity

Look at the pictures and the prompts below and, in pairs, ask and answer questions using appropriate modal verbs, as in the example.

e.g. SA: Is he happy?
     SB: He can't be happy. He must be angry, etc.

1 Is he happy?
2 Is he a businessman?
3 Does he want someone to help him?
4 Is he worried about something?

1 Have they jumped out of a plane?
2 Are they frightened?
3 Do they enjoy doing this?
4 Will they land safely?

1 Is he at school?
2 Is he enjoying himself?
3 Is he jumping up and down?
4 Will he be told off by his parents?

1 Has she been sleeping?
2 Is it late at night?
3 Has the phone call woken her up?
4 Is it an emergency?

UNIT 6
The Passive – Have Something Done

The Passive

*The Forbidden City **is situated** in the centre of Beijing. It **was built** as the Imperial Palace for the emperors of China. It **was named** the Forbidden City because no common or foreign person **was allowed** to go inside without special permission.*

We form the passive with the verb to be and the past participle of the main verb.

	Active	Passive
Present Simple	He **delivers** the parcels.	The parcels **are delivered**.
Present Continuous	He **is delivering** the parcels.	The parcels **are being delivered**.
Past Simple	He **delivered** the parcels.	The parcels **were delivered**.
Past Continuous	He **was delivering** the parcels.	The parcels **were being delivered**.
Future Simple	He **will deliver** the parcels.	The parcels **will be delivered**.
Present Perfect	He **has delivered** the parcels.	The parcels **have been delivered**.
Past Perfect	He **had delivered** the parcels.	The parcels **had been delivered**.
Future Perfect	He **will have delivered** the parcels.	The parcels **will have been delivered**.
Present Infinitive	He must **deliver** the parcels.	The parcels must **be delivered**.
Perfect Infinitive	He must **have delivered** the parcels.	The parcels must **have been delivered**.
Simple -ing form	I object to his **delivering** the parcels.	I object to the parcels **being delivered**.
Perfect -ing form	**Having delivered** the parcels, ...	The parcels **having been delivered**, ...
Modals + be + p.p.	He **should deliver** the parcels.	The parcels **should be delivered**.

◆ The present perfect continuous, the future continuous, the past perfect continuous and the future perfect continuous are not normally used in the passive.

◆ We can use the verb *to get* instead of the verb *to be* in everyday speech when we talk about things that happen by accident or unexpectedly.
  e.g. *Four people **got hurt** in the car crash.*
  (= *Four people were hurt ...*)

Use

We use the passive:

a) when the person who carries out the action is unknown, unimportant or obvious from the context.
  e.g. a) *My flat **was broken into** last week. (We do not know who broke into the flat.)*
  b) *Coffee beans **are grown** in Brazil. (It is not important to know who grows the coffee.)*
  c) *My car **was serviced** yesterday. (It is obvious that a mechanic serviced it.)*

b) when the action itself is more important than the person who carries it out, as in news headlines, newspaper articles, formal notices, instructions, advertisements, processes, etc.
  e.g. a) *The new hospital **will be opened** by the Queen on May 15th. (formal notice)*
  b) *Then, the milk **is taken** to a factory where it **is pasteurised**. (process)*

c) when we refer to an unpleasant event and we do not want to say who or what is to blame.
  e.g. *A lot of mistakes **have been made**. (instead of 'You have made a lot of mistakes'.)*

The Passive - Have Something Done

Changing from active into passive

To change a sentence from the active into the passive:

a) the object of the active sentence becomes the subject in the passive sentence.

b) the active verb remains in the same tense, but changes into a passive form.

c) the subject of the active sentence becomes the agent, and is either introduced with the preposition by or omitted.

	subject	verb	object
active	Tom	invited	me.

	subject	verb	agent
passive	I	was invited	by Tom.

◆ Only transitive verbs (verbs followed by an object) can be changed into the passive.

    e.g. **active:** *Grandma **knitted my jumper**. (transitive verb)*

    passive: *My jumper **was knitted** by Grandma.*

    But: *They **travelled to** Lisbon last summer. (intransitive verb)*

Some transitive verbs such as *have, fit, suit, resemble*, etc. cannot be changed into the passive.

    e.g. *I have a shower every morning. (NOT: A shower is had by me ...)*

◆ We use by + agent to say who or what carries out the action. We use with + instrument/material/ingredient to say what the agent used.

    e.g. *The pancakes were made **by Claire**. They were made **with eggs, flour and milk**.*

◆ The agent is often omitted in the passive sentence when the subject of the active sentence is one of the following words: people, one, someone/somebody, they, he, etc.

    e.g. **active:** ***Somebody** has rearranged the furniture.*

    passive: *The furniture has been rearranged.*

But: The agent is not omitted when it is a specific or important person or when it is essential to the meaning of the sentence.

    e.g. a) *The 'Mona Lisa' **was painted** by Leonardo da Vinci.*

    b) *A new law **has been passed** by the government.*

◆ Object pronouns (me, you, him, etc.) become subject pronouns (I, you, he, etc.) in the passive.

    e.g. **active:** *They arrested **him**.*

    passive: ***He** was arrested.*

◆ With verbs which take two objects such as bring, tell, send, show, teach, promise, buy, throw, write, award, hand, sell, owe, grant, allow, feed, pass, post, read, take, offer, give, pay and lend we can make two different passive sentences.

    active: *Patrick gave **Laura some flowers**.*

    passive: a) ***Laura was given** some flowers by Patrick. (more usual)*

        b) ***Some flowers were given** to Laura by Patrick. (less usual)*

◆ When the verb of the active sentence is followed by a preposition, the preposition is kept in the passive sentence as well.

    e.g. **active:** *They **presented** him **with** a medal.*

    passive: *He **was presented with** a medal.*

◆ When we want to find out who or what did something, then the passive question form is as follows: Who/What ... by?

    e.g. ***Who** was Australia discovered **by**?*

    ***What** was the fire caused **by**?*

◆ The verbs *hear, help, see* and *make* are followed by the bare infinitive in the active but by the to-infinitive in the passive.

    e.g. **active:** *They **saw** him **leave** the building.*

    passive: *He **was seen to leave** the building.*

    But: hear, see, watch + -ing form (active and passive)

    e.g. **active:** *They **saw** him **running** down the stairs.*

    passive: *He **was seen running** down the stairs.*

Personal/Impersonal Construction

The verbs *think, believe, say, report, know, expect, consider, understand*, etc. are used in the following passive patterns in personal and impersonal constructions.

    active: *People **believe** that he lied in court.*

    passive: a) ***It is believed** (that) he lied in court. (impersonal construction)*

        b) ***He is believed to have lied** in court. (personal construction)*

    active: *They **expect** him to arrive soon.*

    passive: c) ***It is expected** (that) he will arrive soon.*

        d) ***He is expected to arrive** soon.*

UNIT 6
The Passive – Have Something Done

1 *What happens in Luigi's restaurant before it opens for the evening?* **Look at the prompts and make sentences using the present simple passive, as in the example.**

1 the carpets/vacuum
...*The carpets are vacuumed*....
2 the tables/wipe
3 the cutlery/polish
4 the places/set
5 the menu/check
6 the food/prepare
7 the ovens/heat
8 the flowers/arrange/in vases
9 the salt and pepper pots/fill
10 the candles/light

2 **Put the verbs in brackets into the correct passive tense.**

1 A: That's a lovely shirt. Is it new?
   B: Yes. It ...*was bought*... (buy) for me by my grandmother.
2 A: When do you have to have this report ready?
   B: Well, it .... (must/hand in) by Tuesday.
3 A: Did you read the newspaper this morning?
   B: No. It .... (not/deliver) by the time I left for work.
4 A: Where is your car?
   B: At the garage. It .... (repair).
5 A: Do you know your exam results yet?
   B: No. They .... (not/announce) yet.
6 A: Are you going to make dinner tonight?
   B: No. It .... (make) by Simon. He promised to do it.
7 A: Have you finished your homework yet?
   B: No, but it .... (finish) by eight o'clock.
8 A: Who waters your plants for you when you're away?
   B: They .... (water) by my neighbour.

3 **Rewrite the newspaper headlines as complete sentences.**

1 FIVE-DAY STRIKE TO BE HELD BY CUSTOMS OFFICERS

2 MONEY BEING RAISED FOR CHILD'S OPERATION IN AMERICA

3 DECISION MADE ABOUT NEW EXAMS

4 SHOPPING CENTRE TO BE OPENED BY MAYOR TOMORROW

5 ESCAPED PRISONER STILL? NOT CAUGHT

6 FAMILY RESCUED FROM BURNING HOUSE LAST NIGHT

1 *A five-day strike is to be held by customs officers.*
2 ....
3 ....
4 ....
5 ....
6 ....

4 **Put the verbs in brackets into the correct passive tense.**

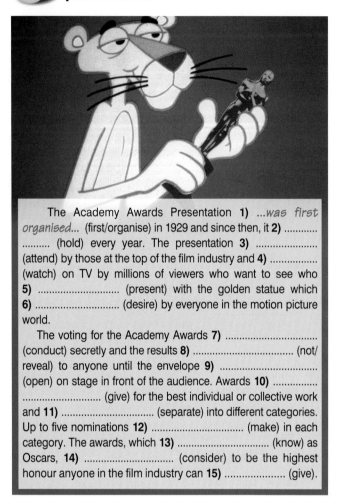

The Academy Awards Presentation **1)** ...*was first organised*... (first/organise) in 1929 and since then, it **2)** .... (hold) every year. The presentation **3)** .... (attend) by those at the top of the film industry and **4)** .... (watch) on TV by millions of viewers who want to see who **5)** .... (present) with the golden statue which **6)** .... (desire) by everyone in the motion picture world.
   The voting for the Academy Awards **7)** .... (conduct) secretly and the results **8)** .... (not/reveal) to anyone until the envelope **9)** .... (open) on stage in front of the audience. Awards **10)** .... (give) for the best individual or collective work and **11)** .... (separate) into different categories. Up to five nominations **12)** .... (make) in each category. The awards, which **13)** .... (know) as Oscars, **14)** .... (consider) to be the highest honour anyone in the film industry can **15)** .... (give).

5 **Rewrite the sentences in the passive, where possible.**

1 Her mother drives her to school every day.
   ...*She is driven to school by her mother every day.* ...
2 Paul drives to work every day.
   ...*It cannot be changed*...
3 I woke up late on Sunday morning.
   ....
4 Her mother woke her up at seven o'clock.
   ....
5 Sue asked the waiter to bring some water.
   ....
6 David asked for some help.
   ....
7 Simon is moving house next month.
   ....
8 Michael moved the boxes out of the way.
   ....
9 Sandra walks on the beach regularly.
   ....
10 The boys walk the dog every day.
   ....

6 Fill in *by* or *with*.

1 She was woken up ...*by*... a loud noise.
2 The parcel was tied up .... string.
3 John was told off .... his mother.
4 This picture was painted .... a famous artist.
5 The chair was covered .... a woollen blanket.
6 The walls were decorated .... posters.
7 My car was repaired .... my father.
8 This dessert was made .... fresh cream.

7 Rewrite the sentences in the passive. Omit the agent where possible.

1 Do they sell clothes in this shop?
...*Are clothes sold in this shop?*...
2 Someone is cleaning the windows.
....
3 She tapped him on the hand with her pen.
....
4 I don't like people laughing at me.
....
5 People spend a lot of money on food.
....
6 Is Sue washing the car?
....
7 Who made this mess?
....
8 Grandfather is going to tell the children a story.
....
9 They will open the new sports centre soon.
....
10 They made him confess to the robbery.
....
11 Liz showed me some holiday pictures.
....
12 Sam remembers his friend telling him about the party.
....
13 They heard him calling for help.
....
14 Who broke this mug?
....
15 The jury will have reached a verdict by the morning.
....
16 The teacher will mark the essays.
....
17 People make jam from fruit.
....
18 They sent for the doctor.
....
19 Clive hasn't cut the grass yet.
....
20 They may not repair the car this week.
....

8 Complete the sentences, as in the example.

1 It is said that this orchestra is the best in the world.
This orchestra ...*is said to be the best in the world.*
2 It is believed that the thieves have left the country.
The thieves..
3 The fire is reported to have started by accident.
It ....
4 He is known to be making a lot of money.
It ....
5 It is expected that they will arrive in time for dinner.
They ....
6 She is said to know a lot about gardening.
It ....
7 It is thought that he will be attending the meeting.
He..
8 It is believed that we are able to win the competition.
We ....
9 The company is thought to be making a big profit.
It ....
10 It is reported that the government has reached a decision.
The government ....
11 It is said that they were responsible for the damage.
They ....
12 She is expected to break the world record.
It ....
13 He is known to have several foreign bank accounts.
It ....
14 They are reported to have financial problems.
It ....

9 Underline the correct answer.

A large amount of valuable jewellery **1) has stolen/ has been stolen** from Forest Manor. A man **2)arrested/was arrested** yesterday and **3) is questioned / is being questioned** by the police at the moment. He **4) thought/is thought** to **5) have committed/ have been committed** the crime, although so far no proof **6) has found/has been found**. The robbery **7) believed/is believed** to **8) have carried out/have been carried out** by two men, but so far no clue **9) has discovered/has been discovered** as to the second man's identity. The police say that he may **10) have left/have been left** the country.

UNIT 6
The Passive – Have Something Done

10 Rewrite the following passages in the passive.

A Yesterday afternoon, the school held a sports day. John's teacher entered him for the 100m race because people thought John was the fastest runner in the school. John's teacher blew the whistle and the race started. Loud cheers filled the air as John's friends cheered him on. John overtook all the other runners and, as people had expected, John won the race. The headmaster gave him a trophy as a prize.

....
....
....
....
....
....
....
....

B Do you think that people will ever use electric cars? Someone has already invented the electric car, but at the moment they are too expensive for most people to buy. Also, you have to recharge their batteries frequently. However, if people drove electric cars instead of the cars we use today, the air we breathe would be cleaner, as they would not pump exhaust fumes into the atmosphere.

....
....
....
....
....
....
....

C Last week, the Prime Minister visited Dawston. The Mayor of the town greeted him when he arrived and gave him a tour. He introduced the Prime Minister to some important businessmen and took him to lunch in a local restaurant. In the afternoon, the Mayor held a meeting and the Prime Minister addressed the citizens of Dawston. He told them that he had enjoyed his visit very much.

....
....
....
....
....
....
....

11 Rewrite the sentences in the active.

1 Her excuse may not be believed by her parents.
...*Her parents may not believe her excuse*....
2 The painting has been valued by an expert.
....
3 He likes being given presents.
....
4 The bill must be paid immediately.
....
5 Hot water is provided by the hotel 24 hours a day.
....
6 Our newspaper is delivered by a boy every morning.
....
7 Her wedding dress will be made by a designer in Paris.
....
8 The meeting was attended by several important art critics.
....
9 Preparations are being made by the event organisers.
....
10 An interesting book has been published by the company.
....

12 Put the verbs in brackets into the correct *passive* or *active* tense.

Coffee **1)** ...*is said*... (say) to originate from Kaffa in Ethiopia and most species of coffee plant **2)** .... (find) in the tropics of the Eastern Hemisphere. The species which **3)** .... (think) to be the earliest coffee plant **4)** .... (ever/cultivate) by man is Coffea arabica. Today it **5)** .... (grow) mostly in Latin America.

The coffee shrub **6)** .... (reach) a height of 8-10 metres and **7)** .... (have) white scented flowers. It **8)** .... (produce) a red fruit which **9)** .... (call) a cherry. The cherry **10)** .... (contain) two seeds which **11)** .... (join) together. These seeds, which **12)** .... (also/know) as beans, **13)** .... (first/roast) and then they **14)** .... (grind) to make coffee. The grounds **15)** .... (then/process) in a variety of different ways. Sometimes they **16)** .... (filter) and sometimes they **17)** .... (soak) in water to make the drink which is popular with so many people. Coffee is available as grounds or as instant coffee powder and **18)** .... (drink) by one third of the world's population.

Have something done

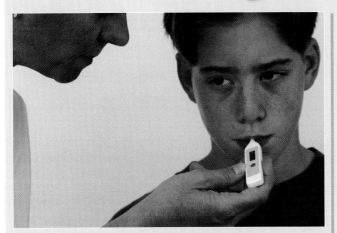

*Simon **is having** his temperature **taken**.*
His mother is taking his temperature.

We use **have** + object + past participle to say that we have arranged for someone to do something for us.
*e.g. We **had new cupboards made by the carpenter**. (We didn't make them ourselves. The carpenter made them for us.)*

◆ Questions and negations of the verb *have* are formed with do/does or did.
*e.g. **Did you have** your car serviced?*

◆ We can also use have something done to say that something unpleasant happened to somebody.
*e.g. Paul **had his bike stolen** yesterday. (= Paul's bike was stolen.)*

◆ We can use the verb *get* instead of the verb *have* only in informal conversation.
*e.g. You must **get/have** your hair cut this week.*

present simple	He **paints** the house.	He **has the house painted**.
present continuous	He **is painting** the house.	He **is having the house painted**.
past simple	He **painted** the house.	He **had the house painted**.
past continuous	He **was painting** the house.	He **was having the house painted**.
future simple	He **will paint** the house.	He **will have the house painted**.
future continuous	He **will be painting** the house.	He **will be having the house painted**.
present perfect	He **has painted** the house.	He **has had the house painted**.
present perfect cont.	He **has been painting** the house.	He **has been having the house painted**.
past perfect	He **had painted** the house.	He **had had the house painted**.
past perfect cont.	He **had been painting** the house.	He **had been having the house painted**.
infinitive	He must **paint** the house.	He must **have the house painted**.
-ing form	It's **worth painting** the house.	It's **worth having the house painted**.

13 Write a correct sentence for each picture, as in the example.

1 Jack / paint / fence
...Jack is painting the fence....

2 Melanie / take / picture
....
....

3 Paul / fill / tooth
....
....

4 Helen / mop / floor
....
....

5 Jane/ paint / nails
....
....

6 Tim / prune / tree
....
....

14 Connie moved to a new town last week. She knows nothing about the town, so this morning she has decided to have a look at the shops. Look at the pictures and the prompts below and say what Connie thinks when she sees the signs, as in the example.

e.g. *I can have my garden tidied by them.*

A
- I can / garden / tidy by them

B
- I can / my living room / design here

C
- I will/my suits/clean here

D
- I will/my hair/cut here

E
- I can / new locks / make / for the house here

F
- I will my clothes / mend here

15 Read the situations, then write sentences using *have something done.*

1 John's suit is dirty. It has to be dry-cleaned. What should he do?
   ...He should have his suit dry-cleaned...
2 All Linda's clothes are made specially for her. What does she do?
   ....
3 They arranged for their house to be painted last week. Now it has been done. What have they done?
   ....
4 Malcolm's car was broken into last night. What happened to him? ....
5 Her bag was stolen yesterday. What happened to her?
   ....

6 A printer has printed party invitations for Emma. What has Emma done? ....
7 Diana is at the hairdresser's. The hairdresser is cutting her hair. What is Diana doing? ....
   ....
8 Robert is taking his car to the garage for a service tomorrow. What's he going to do? ....
   ....
9 Their roof has a hole in it. What should they do?
   ....
10 Tracey's bicycle has got a puncture. What should she do? ....

16 Complete the following conversation using *have something done.*

A: I **1)** ...'*m having an extension built*... (an extension/build) on my house this week.
B: That's nice. When it's finished, **2)** ....
   .... (it/decorate)?
A: No, I'm going to do that myself. First, though, I **3)** ....
   .... (double glazing/fit).
A: **4)** .... (carpets/lay)?
B: I'm not sure yet. How about you? **5)** ....
   .... (you/your curtains/deliver) last week?
A: Yes. They're really nice. I also **6)** ....
   .... (the carpets/clean), so everything looks lovely now.

17 Rewrite the sentences using *have something done.*

1 His teeth are checked twice a year.
   ...He has his teeth checked twice a year....
2 Her skirt is being cleaned at the moment.
   ....
3 My hair is trimmed once a month.
   ....
4 Central heating is going to be installed in our house next month.
   ....
5 Sam's burglar alarm was fitted last week.
   ....
6 My car is being repaired at the moment.
   ....
7 The band's new single has just been recorded.
   ....
8 Our new furniture is going to be delivered tomorrow.
   ....
9 Their new house is being decorated at the moment.
   ....
10 The windows will be cleaned.
   ....
11 A new jumper has been knitted for me.
   ....
12 The lock has to be fixed.
   ....
13 A new pair of glasses is going to be made for him.
   ....

18 **Rewrite the sentences using** *have something done.*

1 Their windows need to be cleaned.
   ...*They need to have their windows cleaned*....

2 The hairdresser was styling Mrs Brown's hair.
   ....

3 She told her son to carry the shopping to the house.
   ....

4 Dad is going to arrange for someone to cut the grass.
   ....

5 They used to employ a cleaner who cleaned the house.
   ....

6 Did the mechanic repair Paul's motorbike?
   ....

7 The boss asked his assistant to type the letter.
   ....

8 A plumber fixed the dripping tap for Joe.
   ....

9 Have you told the secretary to make some photocopies?
   ....

10 The chef was cooking Tom's lunch.
   ....

11 Did you tell the shop to deliver the sofa to you?
   ....

12 My purse was stolen last Friday.
   ....

13 Did you employ a painter to decorate your house?
   ....

14 The builders are putting a new roof on Adam's house at the moment.
   ....

15 She asked the maid to polish the silver.
   ....

16 The man had asked the porter to take his luggage to his room.
   ....

17 Did you ask Jenny to arrange the flowers for you?
   ....

18 When will your glasses be made?
   ....

19 I hired a professional to cater for my party.
   ....

20 Did you ask anyone to sweep the chimney?
   ....

21 She asked him to do the shopping.
   ....

22 Their house was burgled last night.
   ....

23 He employed a carpenter to build the fence.
   ....

24 Julie's housekeeper irons all her clothes.
   ....

25 His shop's windows were smashed in the riot.
   ....

IN OTHER WORDS

Study these examples. The second sentence has a similar meaning to the first sentence.

1 It is known that the explosion caused major damage to the buildings.
   have The explosion is known **to have caused** major damage to the buildings.

2 The Lumière brothers invented the first film-making equipment.
   was The first film-making equipment **was invented by** the Lumière brothers.

3 Bob doesn't like people asking him questions about his job.
   being Bob **doesn't like being asked** questions about his job.

4 They hired a famous architect to design their house.
   had They **had their house designed** by a famous architect.

5 Someone stole his bike while he was in the bank.
   had He **had his bike stolen** while he was in the bank.

6 They will punish you if you go on causing trouble.
   get You **will get punished** if you go on causing trouble.

 19 **Complete each sentence with two to five words, including the word in bold.**

1 The boss will shout at you if you're late again.
   get You ...*will get shouted at*... if you're late again.

2 People say that a problem shared is a problem halved.
   be A problem shared .... a problem halved.

3 John repaired the fence after the storm.
   was The fence .... John after the storm.

4 Ann likes people listening to her when she is talking.
   being Ann .... when she is talking.

5 Mum will tell you off if you don't stop fighting.
   will You .... if you don't stop fighting.

6 Daniel hasn't locked the doors yet.
   been The doors .... yet.

7 Are the local artists organising a new exhibition this year?
   organised Is a new exhibition .... the local artists this year?

8 They expect the police to be present at the demonstration.
   expected The police .... at the demonstration.

9 Janet needs someone to teach her how to drive.
   be Janet needs .... how to drive.

10 Someone should tell Pauline about the new arrangements.
   be Pauline .... about the new arrangements.

93

11 Colin is mending the broken table.
by The broken table .... Colin.

12 Someone told us about the party.
were We .... the party.

13 She will get a famous designer to design her wedding dress.
have She will .... by a famous designer.

14 Two of his teeth were broken in a fight.
had He .... broken in a fight.

15 They will give Lily a pay rise this month.
be Lily .... a pay rise this month.

20 Fill in the gaps with the correct form of the word in brackets.

1 It is hard to tell the ...*difference*... between the twins, as they are identical. (differ)
2 I received a large .... in the post this morning. (pack)
3 I value my .... highly, and so I enjoy living alone. (independent)
4 There was a very high .... at yesterday's meeting. (attend)
5 The .... was a great success and the audience enjoyed themselves. (perform)
6 We spent a very .... weekend in the country. (please)
7 She gives the .... of being shy, but in fact she is quite self-assured. (impress)
8 My father is very fit and leads a .... lifestyle. (health)
9 I have received no .... from David since he moved away. (correspond)
10 She was .... of the fact that air pollution can cause so many health problems. (ignore)
11 The teacher made .... to a book we had been studying. (refer)
12 The noise from outside spoilt his .... of the performance. (enjoy)
13 His .... was noticed by the manager. (absent)
14 We apologise for any .... this delay will cause. (inconvenient)
15 Great .... is placed on exam results in this school. (important)
16 The police discovered vital .... which led to the arrest of the thief. (evident)
17 His .... was proved in court and he was set free. (innocent)
18 The .... of the headmaster made the children nervous. (present)
19 Scenes of .... on television can have a negative effect on children. (violent)
20 The invention of personal computers was one of the greatest .... of this century. (achieve)

Common mistakes

- The photocopier **has serviced** recently. ✗
  The photocopier **has been serviced** recently. ✓
- A famous TV star **is resembled by Steve**. ✗
  Steve resembles a famous TV star. ✓
- This omelette **was made by** eggs and cheese. ✗
  This omelette **was made with** eggs and cheese. ✓
- Who was this portrait **painted**? ✗
  Who was this portrait **painted by**? ✓
- The woman **was heard scream**. ✗
  The woman **was heard to scream**. ✓
- **He is said he has stolen** some money. ✗
  He is said to have stolen some money. ✓
- How often **have you** your house painted? ✗
  How often **do you have** your house painted? ✓

21 Correct the mistakes.

1 He is said he has been promoted.
2 This pie was made by shortcrust pastry.
3 Who was this cake made?
4 Have you your car serviced often?
5 Green clothes are suited by Katie.
6 The man was seen hit the police officer.
7 The house has decorated recently.

22 Cross out the unnecessary word.

1 Valerie was being sent on an important mission last month.
2 She doesn't mind to having her house photographed for interior decoration magazines.
3 The famous star is believed to have been signed a new multi-million dollar contract.
4 This car it is expected to be very popular with the younger generation.
5 She was seen to entering the Plaza Hotel late last night.
6 The painting was disappeared from the owner's house yesterday.
7 Did you have had the food provided by a caterer?
8 The Prime Minister is said that to be thinking of introducing a new tax.
9 You should to have an extension built as soon as possible.
10 She insists on having been her breakfast brought to her room at nine o'clock sharp.

Phrasal Verbs

give away:	(tr) 1) reveal sth; betray sb, 2) lose or waste (sth)
give in:	1) (int) surrender, 2) (tr) hand in
give off:	(tr) emit (heat, fumes, smell, etc.)
give out:	1) (int) come to an end, 2) (tr) distribute, hand out
give up:	(tr) 1) stop/abandon an attempt, habit, etc. 2) surrender; offer oneself as a prisoner, 3) stop doing or having sth
go ahead:	continue
go along:	(int) advance; make progress; **go on**
go along with:	(tr) 1) agree with sb/sth, 2) advance with sth
go back:	(int) date back to
go back on:	(tr) break a promise or agreement
go by:	(int) 1) (of time) pass, 2) (of a chance) let it pass without taking it
go down:	(int) 1) be reduced, 2) (of the sun/moon) set
go down with:	(tr) become ill
go in for:	(tr) take part in (a competition)
go into:	(tr) investigate thoroughly
go off:	(int) 1) (of a bomb) explode; (of an alarm) ring, 2) be switched off, 3) (of food) go bad
go on:	(int) 1) happen, 2) make progress, 3) be turned on
go out:	(int) stop burning, be extinguished
go over:	(tr) 1) examine details, 2) repeat
go round:	(int) 1) be enough for everyone to have a share, 2) visit; look round, 3) (of news, a disease) spread; circulate
go through:	(tr) 1) examine carefully; go over, 2) (of money, food, etc.) use up; spend, 3) experience; endure
go through with:	complete sth in spite of opposition; carry out
go up:	(int) rise (in price); increase
go without:	(tr) endure the lack of sth; do without

23 **Fill in the correct particle.**

1 They went ...*through*... the survey results carefully.
2 The price of petrol has gone   again; the cost of running a car is increasing.
3 You must give .... your assignments at the end of the week.
4 Let's sit and watch the sun go .... from your balcony.
5 The candle went .... when a gust of wind blew through the window.

6 Pam isn't in today. She's gone .... the flu.
7 When their supplies gave ...., the team decided to abandon their trip.
8 He has gone .... some difficult periods this year.
9 They had a difficult childhood — they often had to go .... things they needed.
10 Please could you go .... what you said again?
11 My alarm went .... at 6 o'clock this morning.
12 The fraud team are going .... the matter thoroughly.
13 Robert has decided to go .... his plan to change jobs this year.
14 Things are going .... fine at the moment. There are no problems.
15 House prices are going ...., which is good news for buyers.
16 Someone is giving .... secret information.
17 Did you go .... the poetry competition?
18 Go .... with the project since you have already started it.
19 This fire gives .... a lot of heat, doesn't it?
20 Time goes .... very quickly when you're enjoying yourself.
21 The electricity went .... when there was a power cut this afternoon.
22 Is there enough coffee to go ...., or shall I make some more?
23 She gave .... her chances of promotion when she shouted at her boss.
24 The thieves gave themselves .... and were taken to prison.
25 The records in the office go .... ten years.
26 The teacher gave .... the exam papers after everyone had sat down.
27 The accountant went .... the receipt book to try to find the mistake.
28 Put the milk in the fridge, otherwise it will go ....
29 I hope he doesn't go .... his promise.
30 The news went .... the office quickly.

24 **There are eight unnecessary words in the text below. Cross them out.**

1 Ten-year-old Martin Witts, who was been rescued
2 from a fire at his home last week, has to
3 been discharged from hospital today. He is said
4 by to be fully recovered from his injuries. The
5 fire it was started by accident when a
6 pan was knocked over. Smoke was seen to
7 coming from the house by Mr. Steven Free, who
8 did broke down the door and rescued Martin
9 and his parents, who they were not seriously
10 injured. Mr Free was awarded a medal for
11 the bravery.

25 **Underline the correct preposition.**

1 May I pay **by**/for/in cheque, please?
2 He offered to pay by/**for**/at dinner, but I wouldn't let him.
3 We paid by/for/**in** cash when we bought our television.
4 She persists on/**in**/to playing that dreadful song again and again.
5 We had the pleasure **of**/for/in meeting the conductor after the concert.
6 He was very pleased of/for/**with** his new stereo.
7 This group are very popular in/**with**/for young people.
8 I prefer reading of/**to**/with watching television.
9 John has a preference of/to/**for** milk chocolate rather than dark chocolate.
10 The police surrounded the bank to prevent the robbers of/to/**from** escaping.
11 Rachel prides herself **on**/to/in being the cleverest girl in the class.
12 Mary takes pride of/to/**in** being a brilliant musician.
13 We were very proud on/in/**of** Martin when he won the competition.
14 The government provided the victims of the earthquake of/**with**/by temporary shelter.
15 Sam is not qualified of/**for**/to such difficult work.
16 Jane is always quick **at**/by/for answering the teacher's questions.
17 Her reaction **to**/for/of the news was most surprising.
18 He has a reputation **for**/on/by doing excellent work.
19 The headmaster referred **to**/at/with a famous poem during his speech.
20 Tim is regarded of/by/**as** the best lawyer in the area.
21 What is the relationship **between**/with/to Tony and Claire?
22 Did you know that Ruth is related **to**/for/in a famous musician?
23 Steven has an open relationship between/**with**/to his parents.
24 That information is hardly relevant **to**/for/of this subject.
25 I must remind Simon **about**/on/from tomorrow's meeting.
26 The management will not be held responsible of/from/**for** any damage.
27 Who knows what will result in/**from**/of his irresponsible behaviour?
28 Such careless driving is certain to result of/from/**in** an accident.
29 His successful career was the result **of**/from/in hard work.
30 He had a lot of injuries resulting **from**/of/in the accident.
31 I've had this cold for weeks. I can't get rid **from**/of/by it.
32 She feels great pity on/to/**for** the homeless.
33 The woman took pity **on**/to/for the stray dog and gave it some food.
34 There is no reason **for**/with/to her to be angry with me.
35 It is impossible to reason for/**with**/to Steve when he loses his temper.

Revision Box

26 **Correct the mistakes.**

1 Sally knows Jim for about six months.
2 At ten o' clock last night, I am baking an apple pie.
3 Pollution in cities becomes a serious problem.
4 Who are you talking to just now?
5 Julie writes five letters so far.
6 This time next week, Claire is flying to America.
7 We have visited our cousins last weekend.
8 The train from London is arriving at 1.15.
9 Shall you open the door for me, please?
10 I'm tired. I had been working hard all day.
11 She was used to play tennis when she was younger.
12 I will call Sam when I will have finished my homework.
13 We have done the shopping by the time the shops closed.
14 She talks on the telephone at the moment.
15 Susan can walk the dog when she will come home.
16 He had waited for half an hour before his friend arrived.
17 Paul will finish writing the report by lunchtime.
18 I am walking to school every day.
19 Last night, I am watching TV when the phone rang.
20 By the end of June, I will be working here for six months.

27 **Put the verbs in brackets into the correct infinitive form or the -ing form.**

Chris Weaver is thought **1)** ...*to be*... (be) one of the best modern artists in the world. **2)** .... (paint) and **3)** .... (make) statues are his favourite types of art but he also enjoys **4)** .... (draw). So far, he has managed **5)** .... (sell) his best pieces to collectors and galleries all over the world. As a result, he has made a lot of money. At the moment, he is planning **6)** .... (hold) an exhibition. He would like **7)** .... (have) it at the National Gallery in London, but he isn't sure whether he can **8)** .... (do) that or not. As well as **9)** .... (plan) his exhibition, Chris is also busy **10)** .... (work on) his latest statue, which was ordered two months ago by a famous actress for her new mansion in Miami.

28 **Rewrite the sentences in the passive.**

1 They gave us very expensive gifts.
The gifts ...*we were given were very expensive*....
2 Many people watch the news.
The news ....
3 You need a lot of wool to knit a jumper.
A lot of wool ....
4 The gardener planted some flowers.
Some flowers ....
5 We spent a lot of money at the supermarket.
A lot of money ....
6 Most children enjoy cartoons.
Cartoons ....
7 The resort offers excellent accommodation.
The accommodation ....
8 She washed the clothes and hung them out to dry.
The clothes ....
9 They examined the information before writing the article.
The information ....
10 She told the police about the robbery.
The police ....
11 We entertain guests in the living room.
Guests ....
12 The optician repaired and cleaned her glasses.
Her glasses ....

29 **Underline the correct word.**

1 A: Jane works very *quick/ quickly*, doesn't she?
B: Yes, but if she worked *slow/slowly* she might not be so *careless/carelessly*.
2 A: It's so *peaceful/peacefully* here.
B: It *certain/certainly* is. I'm having a *wonderful/ wonderfully* holiday.
3 A: This film is so *sad/sadly*. I can't watch any more.
B: Oh, you should. I'm sure it will end *happy/happily*.
4 A: Close the door *careful/carefully*. We don't want to wake the children.
B: Don't worry. I'm being as *quiet/quietly* as I can.
5 A: Tom behaved *terrible/terribly* today. He was very *rude/rudely* to his teacher.
B: Oh dear! He knows he should speak *polite/politely* to other people.
6 A: I wish you would discuss this *serious/seriously*. It isn't *funny/funnily*.
B: I'm sorry. I'm only trying to be *cheerful/cheerfully*.
7 A: Gary left rather *sudden/suddenly* last night.
B: I know. He doesn't enjoy talking to people he *hard/ hardly* knows.

Look at the prompts below and make passive sentences about the Forbidden City, as in the example.

e.g. The construction of the Forbidden City was completed in 1420.

- construction of / Forbidden City / complete / in 1420
- protect / high walls and a moat on all four sides
- country / govern / from the Forbidden City for nearly 500 years
- in 1924 / Forbidden City / rename / Palace Museum and / open / to / public
- visit / thousands of people every year
- use / as / set for / film 'The Last Emperor' / which / direct / Bernardo Bertolucci
- might / use / again / in future / for / similar project

Now write a passage about the Forbidden City using passive sentences, as in the example.

e.g. The Forbidden City is situated in Beijing, China. ....

Revision 2 (Units 1 - 6)

1   **Choose the correct answer.**

1 You ...A... write and thank Aunt Louise for your present.
   A must   **B** need   **C** can

2 No announcement about the results .... so far.
   A has made   **B** has been made   **C** was made

3 He .... his teeth checked once every six months.
   A is having   **B** has had   **C** has

4 You .... wear a coat. It is very warm outside.
   A must   **B** needn't   **C** could

5 I can't come to the cinema tonight. I .... work.
   A could   **B** needn't   **C** have to

6 The children are at .... school at the moment.
   A –   **B** a   **C** the

7 She got .... of presents on her birthday.
   A several   **B** a great deal   **C** a great number

8 I brush my teeth twice .... day.
   A a   **B** the   **C** one

9 The play was said .... because the lead actor was ill.
   A to be cancelled   **B** to have been cancelled
   C to have cancelled

10 He was very nervous. He .... for this moment all his life.
   A had waited   **B** had been waiting
   C has been waiting

11 The advice you gave me .... really useful.
   A were   **B** are   **C** was

12 I read .... interesting article in the newspaper today.
   A a   **B** an   **C** the

13 No information .... to the new staff yet.
   A has given   **B** has been given   **C** was given

14 It's late. Mark .... have forgotten about the meeting.
   A might   **B** will   **C** ought

15 He .... be at work. His car isn't outside his house.
   A would   **B** can't   **C** must

16 .... we have lunch in the garden today?
   A Shall   **B** Mustn't   **C** Would

17 Sam .... carry the box. It was too heavy.
   A couldn't   **B** could   **C** can't

18 We .... go shopping because we had plenty of food.
   A needn't have   **B** didn't need to   **C** need to

19 She spends .... of her income on clothes.
   A a large amount   **B** many   **C** a large number

20 The football team which he supports .... a large fan club.
   A have   **B** is having   **C** has

21 The news .... at six o'clock last night.
   A announced   **B** were announced
   C was announced

22 Could you get me two .... of bread from the bakery, please?
   A loaves   **B** packets   **C** kilos

23 He always catches .... 8 o'clock train to work.
   A a   **B** the   **C** –

24 It was very dark, but he .... find his way.
   A was able to   **B** could   **C** couldn't

25 She .... be on holiday. I saw her this morning.
   A can't   **B** would   **C** must

26 Two months .... a long time to wait for a reply.
   A are   **B** were   **C** is

27 .... you help me with my homework, please?
   A Will   **B** Shall   **C** Must

28 Steve fell asleep on .... sofa last night.
   A a   **B** the   **C** one

29 She .... her hair cut yesterday afternoon.
   A will have   **B** had   **C** has had

30 .... day, I will buy a big house with a garden.
   A One   **B** A   **C** The

31 Matthew is busy .... for his interview.
   A prepare   **B** to prepare   **C** preparing

32 A lot of children .... to boarding school in the old days.
   A are sent   **B** is sent   **C** were sent

33 Simon is .... friendly than Jason.
   A the least   **B** as   **C** less

34 She heated up a .... of soup for her dinner.
   A bar   **B** tin   **C** plate

35 Her feet ache. She .... all day.
   A has stood up   **B** has been standing up
   C had been standing up

36 Be careful. This saucepan is .... hot.
   A much   **B** by far   **C** very

37 Paul is not .... as Charles.
   A as handsome   **B** more handsome
   C most handsome

38 A lot of people .... by this company last year.
   A hired   **B** are hired   **C** were hired

39 .... Queen is going to visit this town next month.
   A A   **B** An   **C** The

40 Cathy is .... the fastest runner in the school.
   A much   **B** by far   **C** very

2 Complete the sentences.

1 He told me a wonderful story.
   The story ...*he told me was wonderful*....
2 She was angry because of the man's rudeness.
   She was angry because the ....
3 She bought some very expensive luggage.
   The luggage ....
4 His secretary had booked his accommodation.
   His accommodation ....
5 These trousers are too small for me now.
   This pair of trousers ....
6 The house is surrounded by beautiful gardens.
   Beautiful gardens ....
7 She's got short brown hair.
   Her hair ....
8 You need a lot of patience to be a teacher.
   A lot of patience ....
9 They cooked us a delicious meal.
   The meal ....
10 She likes chocolate more than any other food.
   Chocolate ....
11 They had great weather during their holiday.
   The weather ....
12 He called the fire brigade immediately.
   The fire brigade ....

3 Rewrite the sentences in the passive. Omit the agent where possible.

1 Jack must have sent this letter.
   ...*This letter must have been sent by Jack*....
2 He should plant some more flowers.
   ....
3 I object to her using my computer.
   ....
4 Does she train all the new staff?
   ....

5 We will have finished the project by next Friday.
   ....
6 Having posted the letters, John went back to the office.
   ....
7 What did they open the safe with?
   ....
8 You must inform the contestants about the rules of the game.
   ....
9 She had made all the beds.
   ....
10 Has Danny written a poem for you?
   ....
11 The children were feeding the dog.
   ....
12 She locked all the doors before she went on holiday.
   ....
13 Is Mark repairing my bicycle ?
   ....
14 Dad decorated the living room last week.
   ....
15 People believe that he should be given a medal.
   ....
16 They heard him making the arrangements.
   ....
17 Everyone knows that she is a successful businesswoman.
   ....
18 Who broke this teapot?
   ....
19 We expect him to arrive early in the morning.
   ....
20 Why did they pull down that building?
   ....
21 People say that he is a very wealthy man.
   ....
22 When will they repair my car?
   ....

4 Fill in the correct form of the word in brackets.

1 The ...*construction*... **(construct)** of the new shopping centre is almost complete.
2 You must be very .... **(care)** not to break these glasses.
3 He always offers his .... **(assist)** when he sees someone in trouble.
4 She has some very .... **(colour)** flowers in her garden.
5 He is just giving some directions to a .... **(tour)**.
6 She changed the .... **(arrange)** for the outing at the last minute.
7 The wedding .... **(receive)** was held in a small hotel.
8 He gave the policeman a .... **(describe)** of the thieves.

Revision 2 (Units 1 - 6)

9 That author is a distant .... (**relate**) of mine.

10 I'm sorry. I didn't mean to .... (**fright**) you.

11 He couldn't contain his .... (**excite**) about the coming holiday.

12 Luckily, no one was injured in the .... (**explode**).

13 He had a worried .... (**express**) on his face throughout the exam.

14 Some of the paintings we saw were very .... (**impress**).

15 He has made a very .... (**attract**) offer for our house.

5 Complete each sentence with two to five words, including the word in bold.

1 Wearing jewellery to school is forbidden.
   allowed   You ...*are not allowed to wear*... jewellery to school.

2 Someone should invite Kerry to the party.
   be   Kerry .... to the party.

3 I'm sure Michael has been promoted.
   must   Michael .... promoted.

4 They will sack you if you are caught making personal calls.
   be   You .... you are caught making personal calls.

5 I advise you to mend those trousers.
   ought   You .... those trousers.

6 Sally cleaned the house before the guests arrived.
   was   The house .... before the guests arrived.

7 Perhaps she has gone on holiday.
   may   She .... on holiday.

8 I spilt my coffee when I knocked the table.
   got   My coffee .... when I knocked the table.

9 People say that Martin is a good sportsman.
   be   Martin .... a good sportsman.

10 I'm sure he hasn't forgotten your birthday.
   can't   He .... your birthday.

11 It isn't necessary for you to attend the meeting.
   have   You .... the meeting.

12 I'd better go and tidy my bedroom.
   should   I .... my bedroom.

13 Steve likes people to ask him about his work.
   being   Steve .... about his work.

14 Dad hasn't tidied the garage yet.
   been   The garage .... yet.

15 We'll probably go to visit my parents at the weekend.
   likely   It is .... to visit my parents at the weekend.

16 People think that he will be discharged from hospital tomorrow.
   thought   It .... will be discharged from hospital tomorrow.

17 Perhaps David has been held up in traffic.
   could   David .... in traffic.

18 It's forbidden to smoke in the waiting room.
   mustn't   You .... in the waiting room.

19 Claire needs someone to show her to the dining room.
   be   Claire needs .... the dining room.

20 It wasn't necessary for him to lock the door.
   have   He .... the door.

6 Rephrase the following sentences in as many ways as possible.

1 Perhaps she has got a new job.
   ...*She may/might/could have got a new job*....

2 I'm sure he isn't a policeman.
   ....

3 It is likely that they will move house this month.
   ....

4 I'm certain she made this cake herself.
   ....

5 It's possible he posted the letters yesterday.
   ....

6 Perhaps we have won a prize.
   ....

7 I'm sure they don't eat meat.
   ....

8 I'm certain she lives with her parents.
   ....

9 It is likely that I will be late for work tomorrow.
   ....

10 Perhaps he has gone to the doctor's.
   ....

11 I'm sure we haven't missed the bus.
   ....

12 It's possible they have been invited to the party.
   ....

7 Cross out the expressions which cannot be used with the nouns.

1 ***Both, Several, A large quantity*** of, ***Many of, Too much*** employees were made redundant last year.

2 She's got ***hardly any, several, a little, a few, a lot of*** spare time these days.

3 There is ***too much, a lot of, hardly any, few, many*** noise in here.

4 There's ***a little, plenty of, a couple of, many, a lot of*** soup left. Would you like some?

5 He passed ***no, hardly any, a little, some, a small amount of*** exams at school.

6 She owns ***few, hardly any, plenty of, a great deal of, several*** property.

7 There is ***a little, many, too much, a great number of, some*** ice on the roads today.

8 There are ***several, many, much, plenty of, very little*** ways to solve this problem.

Underline the correct preposition.

1 He is completely ignorant *for/about/to* British history.
2 Did you hear *of/about/from* Clive's new job?
3 She prides herself *on/to/in* keeping the house clean and tidy.
4 We must remind the staff *about/on/from* the new policy.
5 She is very pleased *of/for/with* her new flat.
6 Will you help me look *at/after/for* my contact lens, please?
7 He can afford a holiday. He earns more than enough to live *on/with/for*.
8 I haven't heard *of/about/from* my friend for weeks.
9 The children took no notice *from/of/for* the new teacher.
10 Sandra is keen *on/to/for* join the choir.
11 My next-door neighbour is related *for/with/to* a famous actor.
12 His lack *in/with/of* money meant that he had to sell his car.
13 I cannot forgive him *about/to/for* insulting my brother.
14 He felt very guilty *of/for/about* forgetting her birthday.
15 This restaurant is regarded *of/by/as* one of the best in the country.

 Fill in the gaps with the correct particle from the list.

> on, away with, behind, up, off, in, back on

1 The manager drew ...*up*... a contract for the new employee.
2 Please give .... your assignments at the end of the lesson.
3 I have never really got .... with my next-door neighbours.
4 She has given .... eating chocolate in order to lose weight.
5 It is a good idea to have some savings to fall .... in difficult times.
6 The school is going to do .... the old uniform.
7 My brother's hobby is doing .... old cars.
8 He has fallen .... with his school work recently.
9 The fire was not giving .... enough heat to warm the room.
10 It was unfair of him to go .... his promise to help me.
11 The thieves panicked when the burglar alarm went ....
12 He thought he would get .... parking on the double yellow line.
13 The meeting went .... until after lunchtime.
14 The bus drew .... to the bus station and we all got off.
15 The boys got .... with a warning from the police, but they had learnt their lesson.

 Cross out the unnecessary word.

1 I would love to be able to speak ~~the~~ French.
2 He needn't to have bought me a present.
3 He might have been missed the train.
4 Mark has had to take his car to the garage last week.
5 She eats all the kinds of food.
6 I need a new bike. I want one bike with lots of gears.
7 You can't to have seen Jane. She is in America.
8 We are likely that to be moving house soon.
9 The team were been able to win the game after all.
10 I don't mind to lending you the money.
11 How about we watching a video this evening?
12 He insists on having been his hair cut every three weeks.
13 Mike is in the hospital. He has broken his arm.
14 Sue was being sent a bunch of flowers yesterday.
15 She shouldn't to have spoken to me like that.

11 **Rewrite the sentences using** *have something done.*

1 Her hair was cut by her best friend.
   ...*She had her hair cut by her best friend.*...
2 Tony's car will be taken to the garage tomorrow.
   ....
3 Jane's bag was stolen last night.
   ....
4 Paul's jaw was broken in a boxing match.
   ....
5 The new lock will be fitted on Monday.
   ....
6 His passport has just been stolen.
   ....
7 Their house is decorated every year.
   ....
8 Our rooms were cleaned by our mother this morning.
   ....
9 Sally's wedding dress is going to be made next month.
   ....
10 My salary is deposited in my bank account every month.
   ....
11 Our grass is cut by the gardener.
   ....
12 My window was broken during the storm.
   ....
13 His photograph will be taken by his friend.
   ....
14 His case was carried to the car by the chauffeur.
   ....
15 Their windows are cleaned once a month.
   ....
16 How often is your eyesight checked by the optician?
   ....

We will have to spend a lot of money on the construction of these buildings.

What did Mr Lee tell his partner yesterday?
He told his partner, '**We will have to spend a lot of money on the construction of these buildings.**'
                    OR
He told his partner (that) **they would have to spend a lot of money on the construction of the buildings.**

◆ We can report people's words by using *direct speech* or *reported speech*. Direct speech is the exact words someone used. We use quotation marks (' ') in direct speech. *e.g. 'I'm tired,'* Helen said. Reported speech is the exact meaning of what someone said, but not the exact words. We do not use quotation marks in reported speech. We can either use the word that after the introductory verb (*say, tell,* etc.) or we can omit it.

◆ Personal pronouns, possessive adjectives/ possessive pronouns change according to the meaning of the sentence.
*e.g. Helen said **(that) she was tired**.*

◆ We can report someone's words either a long time after they were said (out-of-date-reporting) or a short time after they were said (up-to-date reporting).

Say - Tell

We can use the verbs *say* and *tell* both in direct and reported speech.

◆ Say is used with or without a personal object. When used with a personal object, it is always followed by the preposition *to* (said to me).
*e.g. He **said**, 'I'm cold.'*
    *He **said** (that) he was cold.*
    *He **said to me**, 'I'm cold.'*
    *He **said to me** (that) he was cold.*

◆ Tell is always followed by a personal object (told me). *e.g. He **told me**, 'I'm cold.'*
*He **told me** (that) he was cold.*

Expressions with *say* and *tell*:

say	good morning/afternoon etc, something/nothing etc, a prayer, so, a few words, etc.
tell	the truth, a lie, a secret, a story, a joke, the time, the difference, sb one's name, sb the way, one from another, one's fortune, sb so, etc.

1 **Fill in the gaps with *say* or *tell* in the correct tense.**

A 'This sugar-free chocolate is delicious', 1) ...*said*... Sandra. 'I can't 2) .... the difference between this chocolate and the one containing sugar.' 'I like it, too', 3) .... Mark. 'I wish someone had 4) .... me about it sooner. I could have lost so much weight!' 'To 5) .... you the truth, I don't think you should lose weight,' 6) .... Sandra. 'I like you just the way you are,' she 7) .... him.

B 'I saw Paul in town today', Steve 1) .... Louise. 'I 2) .... good afternoon to him and I noticed that he'd had his hair cut. I should have 3) .... something about it, but it looked awful, so I didn't mention it'. 'You did the right thing', Louise 4) .... him. 'It's better to 5) .... nothing than to 6) .... a lie.'

C At Alison's wedding reception, her father stood up and 1) .... the guests that he would like to 2) .... a few words. He started to 3) .... a story about when Alison was young. Alison felt embarrassed, but she didn't 4) .... so. Then, her father 5) .... the guests some jokes, which everyone found very funny. Finally, he 6) .... a prayer for the happy couple.

Reported Statements

◆ **Verb tenses and time expressions change in reported speech:**

a) **when the introductory verb is in a past tense.**
   e.g. *'I'm moving to a new flat next week,'* she said.
   She **said** (that) she **was moving** to a new flat **the following week**.

b) **in out-of-date reporting.**
   e.g. (Monday 2 May) Mike said, *'I **borrowed** some money from my parents.'*
   (Thursday 5 May) Mike said (that) he **had borrowed** some money from his parents.

c) **when we consider what the speaker says to be untrue.**
   e.g. *'Paula and I **are** best friends,'* Jack said to me.
   Jack said to me that he and Paula **were** best friends, but Paula had never actually met him.

The tenses change as follows:

present simple → past simple
*'I **need** a new car,'* Greg said.
Greg said (that) he **needed** a new car.

present continuous → past continuous
*'He'**s sleeping**,'* she said.
She said (that) he **was sleeping**.

present perfect → past perfect
*'I'**ve** already **seen** this film,'* he said.
He said (that) he **had** already **seen** the film.

past simple → past simple or past perfect
*'I **got up** late,'* Tonia said.
Tonia said (that) she **(had) got up** late.

past continuous → past cont. or past perfect cont.
*'I **was working** at four o' clock,'* Tim said.
Tim said (that) he **was working/had been working** at four o' clock.

future (will) → conditional (would)
*'I'**ll call** you tomorrow,'* Rea said.
Rea said (that) she **would call** me the following day.

The past perfect and past perfect continuous remain the same.

◆ **Some words and time expressions change according to the meaning of the sentence:**

now → **then, at that time, immediately**
today, tonight → **that day, that night**
yesterday → **the day before, the previous day**
tomorrow → **the next day, the following day**
this week → **that week**
last week → **the week before, the previous week**
next week → **the week after, the following week**
two days ago → **two days before**
here → **there**
come → **go**

◆ **When this/these are used in time expressions, they change to that/those.**
e.g. **this** week → **that** week, **these** days → **those** days

When this/these/that/those are not used in time expressions, they change as follows:

a) **they change to the when used as adjectives, that is, when they are followed by a noun.**
   e.g. *'**This film** is boring,'* Claire told me.
   Claire told me (that) **the film** was boring.

b) **they change to it or they/them when used as pronouns, that is, when they are not followed by a noun.**
   e.g. *'**This** is an unusual situation,'* Dad said.
   Dad said (that) **it** was an unusual situation.

◆ **Certain modal verbs change as follows:**

will → would
He said, *'One day I'**ll** be able to afford a car.'*
He said (that) one day he **would** be able to afford a car.
can → could
He said, *'I **can** speak French.'*
He said (that) he **could** speak French.
can → could/would be able to (future reference)
He said, *'We **can** meet tomorrow.'*
He said (that) we **could/would be able to** meet the next day.
may → might
He said, *'I **may** call you.'*
He said (that) he **might** call us.
shall ⌐→ should (asking for advice)
       └→ offer (expressing offers)
He said, *'When **shall** I come?'*
He asked when he **should** come.
He said, *'**Shall** I help you?'*
He **offered** to help me.
must → must/had to (obligation)
He said, *'You **must** finish this.'*
He said (that) I **must/had to** finish it.
needn't → needn't/didn't need to/didn't have to
He said, *'You **needn't** pay in cash.'*
He said (that) I **needn't/didn't need to/didn't have to** pay in cash.

***Would, could, might, should, ought, had better, used to** and **mustn't** do not change. **Must** does not change when it expresses a logical assumption.*
e.g. a) *'I **might** talk to her,'* Danny said.
   Danny said (that) he **might** talk to her.
   b) *'You **must** be tired,'* Paul told Susan.
   Paul told Susan (that) she **must** be tired.

◆ **In Type 1 conditionals tenses change in reported speech as follows: the *present simple* becomes *past simple* in the if-clause and *will* becomes *would* in the main clause.**
e.g. *'If you **ask** Liz, she'**ll help** you,'* he said.
   He said (that) if I **asked** Liz, she **would help** me.

◆ **In Type 2 and Type 3 conditionals tenses do not change.**

e.g. a) *'If I* **had** *more time, I* **would** *take up a hobby,'*
Eric said to me.
Eric told me (that) if he **had** more time, he **would** take up a hobby.

b) *'If I* **hadn't parked** *my car on a double yellow line, I* **wouldn't have got** *a ticket,'* Sam said.
Sam said (that) if he **hadn't parked** his car on a double yellow line, he **wouldn't have got** a ticket.

The verb tenses remain the same in reported speech when the introductory verb is in the present, future or present perfect.

---

e.g. Mum **says**, *'Dinner* **is** *ready.'*
Mum **says** (that) dinner **is** ready.

The introductory verb is in the present tense:
a) when we pass on messages. *e.g. Debbie* **says** *she needs the car tonight.* **b) when we report the content of a letter, article, etc. while reading it.** *e.g. The article* **says** *that people use too much water.* **c) when we refer to something someone says very often.** *e.g. Mum often* **says** *that I shouldn't talk to strangers.*

◆ **The verb tenses can either change or remain the same in reported speech:**

a) in up-to-date reporting.
b) when reporting a general truth or law of nature.

e.g. The teacher said, *'Paris* **is** *the capital of France.'*
The teacher said (that) Paris **is/was** the capital of France.

---

2 *Ruth met lots of students when she went to visit a* **university last month. Read their words, then report what they said.**

e.g. **1** *Sarah told her (that) she had made lots of friends.*

1 I've made lots of friends. (Sarah)

2 The library is huge. (Tina)

3 I'm learning lots of interesting things. (Paul)

4 The teachers are very friendly. (Simon)

5 I will always remember my time here. (Elaine)

6 I'm taking my final exams next month. (Roger)

---

3 **Turn the following sentences into** *reported speech.*

1 Robert said, 'This film is very funny'.
...*Robert said (that) the film was very funny*....

2 'I'm starting a new job next week,' she said.
....

3 'I got my exam results last week,' he told them.
....

4 'I can't afford to buy this dress,' said Sally.
....

5 'I would buy a car if I had enough money,' he said to her.
....

6 Frank said, 'That's the house where I was born.'
....

7 'That was a wonderful party,' said Jill.
....

8 'Oranges grow in hot countries,' the teacher said.
....

9 'A lot of people visit museums,' he said.
....

10 'This is a very famous statue,' the tour guide told us.
....

11 'I don't like that jacket,' said Bob.
....

12 'I'm lost,' the boy said. (up-to-date reporting)
....

13 'I may be a little late this evening,' she said.
....

14 'You'd better clean up this mess,' Mum said to Claire.
....

15 'I've already done the shopping,' she said. (up-to-date reporting)
....

16 'I found this note under the sofa,' said Sue.
....

17 'I won't be late again,' he said to us.
....

18 'If I finish work early, I'll call you,' she said.
....

19 'I've been training hard recently,' he told the reporters.
....

20 'Shall I make some tea?' said Zoë.
....

21 'We must go home now,' said the man to his children.
....

22 'Those are the boys who chased me,' Sarah said.
....

23 'I'm going to a party tonight,' Lynne told her friends. (up-to-date reporting)
....

24 'I used to have long hair,' Laura said.
....

25 'There is too much violence on TV,' said Grandad.
....

26 'You ought to make a decision soon,' Andrew told her.
....

4 Complete the sentences with your own ideas using *reported speech*, as in the example.

1 'I bought a new dress yesterday.'
'Did you? But you told me ...*you had bought trousers.*'...

2 'Bill is moving house on Saturday.'
'Is he? ....'

3 'I like Chinese food a lot.'
'Do you? ....'

4 'Tom can speak German fluently.'
'Can he? ....'

5 'I haven't seen Anna for months.'
'Haven't you? ....'

6 'Sam is working for his father at the moment.'
'Is he? ....'

7 'I'm afraid I have to work this weekend.'
'Do you? ....'

8 'Janet knows about the surprise party.'
'Does she? ....'

5 Turn the sentences into *reported speech*. In which of the following sentences do the tenses not change? In which do they not have to be changed? Why?

1 The instructions say, 'The camera needs two batteries.'
The instructions say (that) the camera needs two batteries.
The tenses do not change because the introductory verb is in the present simple.

2 'I've finished the letters you asked me to write,' Jill said.
....

3 'Pandas live in China,' the teacher said.
....

4 Dad says, 'It's time for bed.'
....

5 'I have to tidy my bedroom now,' Toby said.
....

6 The article says, 'There has been an increase in the number of university students.'
....

7 Mr Brown says, 'My son is going to work abroad.'
....

8 'I should have bought her a present,' he said.
....

9 'I'm never going to have a pet,' my sister always says.
....

10 Alison says, 'The taxi is here.'
....

11 Mr Collins says, 'You needn't work late this evening.'
....

12 'I'll pick you up at eight o' clock,' she told me.
....

13 'Coal is found underground,' he said.
....

14 'You ought to go to the doctor's,' she said to her son.
....

15 'It is raining hard today,' she said.
....

16 They said, 'We've never travelled by plane before.'
....

17 'We might go to the cinema tonight,' they said.
....

18 Mum always says, 'You should wear warmer clothes.'
....

6 Lucy's grandmother was a famous actress. Now that she has retired, she is showing Lucy reviews from some of the films she made. Using the prompts below, make sentences, as in the example.

e.g. 'When I starred in 'The Love Affair' in 1952, 'Movie World' said that I was an extremely talented actress. 'The Stars' said that ...

'The Love Affair' — 1952
• 'Frances Garner is an extremely talented actress.' *Movie World*
• 'Garner gives an amazing performance in this film.' *The Stars*

'Over the Moon' — 1958
• 'Garner brings any character to life.' *Film Stars*
• 'Frances Garner is always a pleasure to watch.' *Movie News*

'The Secret House' — 1961
• 'Ms Garner is the best actress ever seen on screen.' *Film Weekly*
• 'Garner has a gift which is very rare.' *Movie Times*

'Only for You' — 1963
• 'Frances Garner has made this film a success.' *Film World*
• 'Garner truly is a star of the screen.' *Screen Play*

Reported Questions

Why are you mixing the liquids?

Shall we take notes?

Yesterday, they carried out an experiment.

*One student **asked** the teacher **why he was mixing the liquids.***
*The other student **asked** the teacher **if/whether they should take notes.***

◆ Reported questions are usually introduced with the verbs ask, inquire, wonder or the expression want to know. The verb is in the affirmative. The question mark and words/expressions such as *please, well ..., oh,* etc. are omitted. The verb tenses, pronouns and time expressions change as in statements.

  e.g. *'What did you make for dinner yesterday?' Bob asked me.*
  *Bob asked me **what I had made for dinner the day before**.*

◆ When the direct speech begins with a question word (*who, where, how old, how long, when, why, what,* etc.), the reported question is introduced with the same question word. When the direct question begins with an auxiliary (*is, do, have*) or a modal verb (*can, may,* etc.), then the reported question begins with if or whether.

  e.g. *'Why do you want to leave your job?' Pam asked me.*
  *Pam asked me **why** I wanted to leave my job.*
  *'**Do** you like rock music?' he asked us.*
  *He asked us **if/whether** we liked rock music.*
  *'**Can** you ride a motorcycle?' Ben asked David.*
  *Ben asked David **if/whether** he could ride a motorcycle.*

7 Turn the questions into *reported speech*. Begin each one with *I asked the ...* and give the name of the person who does the job, as in the example.

1 'Do I need another filling?'
  ...*I asked the dentist if I needed another filling....*
2 'How much does this blouse cost?'
3 'How many tablets should I take each day?'
4 'Can I borrow the book for another week?'
5 'Will it cost very much to repair the television?'
6 'May I look at the menu, please?'

7 'What do I have to do for homework?'
8 'When will the report be typed?'
9 'Will you be able to deliver the flowers today?'
10 'Can I make an appointment to have my hair cut?'

8 Turn the following into *reported questions*.

1 'What is your name?' he asked me.
  ...*He asked me what my name was....*
2 'Where are your parents?' Uncle Bill asked us.
  ....
3 'Will you help me carry the box, please?' Dad asked.
  ....
4 'What time will you be home?' Mum asked me.
  ....
5 'Can you play the guitar?' he asked her.
  ....
6 'Who was at the door?' David asked Janet.
  ....
7 'Where is the post office?' they asked us.
  ....
8 'When will you do your homework?' Meg asked me.
  ....
9 The boss asked me, 'Have you finished those reports?'
  ....
10 John asked Sam, 'Do you like computer games?'
  ....
11 'Will you give me a lift to work, please?' he asked her.
  ....
12 'Where is your jacket?' she asked him.
  ....

9 *Yesterday, Simon interviewed a famous actor. He asked him the following questions.* **Turn them into *reported questions*.**

1 'Do you enjoy being famous?'
  ...*Simon asked him if/whether he enjoyed being famous....*
2 'What is the best part of your job?'
  ....
3 'What do you find difficult about acting?'
  ....
4 'How many films have you starred in?'
  ....
5 'What is your favourite film?'
  ....
6 'Have you met many other famous people?'
  ....
7 'Where would you most like to make a film?'
  ....
8 'Have you visited many interesting places?'
  ....
9 'What are your plans for the future?'
  ....
10 'Are you happy with your life?'
  ....

Reported Commands/ Requests/Suggestions

Inform the manager immediately.

Let's call the computer expert.

Please don't tell anyone about this.

*Lorna **asked** them **not to tell** anyone about it.*
*Peter **told them to inform** the manager right away.*
*Jim **suggested calling** the computer expert.*

◆ **To report commands, instructions, requests or suggestions in reported speech, we use an appropriate introductory verb (*ask, order, beg, suggest, tell*, etc.) and the to-infinitive, -ing form or that-clause depending on the introductory verb (see page 109).**

e.g. a) *'Stop the car!' the policeman said to him.*
   *The policeman **ordered him to stop** the car.*
 b) *'Put all the ingredients in a bowl,' she said to me.*
   *She **told me to put** all the ingredients in a bowl.*
 c) *'Will you please hold this bag for me?' Laura said to Helen.*
   *Laura **asked Helen to hold** the bag for her.*
 d) *'How about going to the cinema?' I said to them.*
   *I **suggested going** to the cinema.*

10 **Turn the following sentences into *reported speech.***

1 The teacher said to the student, 'Come and see me after the lesson.'
   ...The teacher asked the student to go and see him/ her after the lesson....

2 He said, 'Shall we go out for dinner?'
   ....

3 Colin said to Dave, 'Please hold this book for me.'
   ....

4 He said to her, 'Close the door, please.'
   ....

5 Father said, 'How about going to the beach?'
   ....

6 She said, 'Let's watch the game on TV.'
   ....

7 He said to them, 'Please, please don't hurt me.'
   ....

8 The policeman said to the thieves, 'Put your hands up!'
   ....

9 The man said to the waiter, 'Can you bring me some water, please?'
   ....

10 Jason said to his father, 'Please, please let me go to the party.'
   ....

11 The librarian said to the boys, 'Don't make so much noise.'
   ....

12 The chef said to me, 'Put the cake in the oven.'
   ....

11 **First read, then report what the teacher told the students before the exam.**

1 Please leave your bags at the front of the room.

2 Don't talk during the exam.

3 Raise your hand if you need anything.

4 Write all your answers in pen.

5 Answer all the questions.

6 Don't forget to write your name at the top of the page.

7 Check your answers again before you hand the paper in.

8 Please leave quietly when you finish.

1 *...He asked the students to leave their bags at the front of the room....*

2 ....

3 ....

4 ....

5 ....

6 ....

7 ....

8 ....

Reported Speech

12 Study the speech bubbles, then complete the sentences below using *reported speech*, as in the example.

Hurry up!

We'll discuss it later.

Let's go to the theatre.

I won't be home tonight, Dad.

Be quiet!

Can I have a biscuit, please, Mum?

Will you help me with these bags, please, Jim?

I'm going to bed.

1 It was very late, so I ...*said I was going to bed*...........
2 Clare was planning to stay with friends, so she ....
   ....
3 I was hungry, so I ....
   ....
4 The shopping was very heavy, so Sarah ....
   ....
5 Mark wasn't ready for school, so his brother ....
   ....
6 The children were shouting, so the teacher ....
   ....
7 Susie wanted to watch a play, so she ....
   ....
8 Pam was busy when I asked for some advice, so she
   ....

13 Turn the following sentences into *reported speech.*

1 'Where are you going?' she said to them.
   ...*She asked them where they were going*....
2 'I'm going shopping,' said Anna. (up-to-date reporting)
   ....
3 'Go away!' said his friend.
   ....
4 She asked me, 'Are you ready to leave?'
   ....
5 'I'll pick you up at five o'clock,' he said to her.
   ....
6 'It's time for lunch,' Ruth says.
   ....
7 'When did you arrive?' asked Marilyn.
   ....
8 'The meeting started ten minutes ago,' she said.
   (up-to-date reporting)
   ....

9 My father said to me, 'Don't be late.'
   ....
10 'Tom has already left,' said Pam to us.
   ....
11 'Who's there?' said Joe.
   ....
12 'What colour skirt did you buy?' she asked me.
   ....
13 They said to him, 'We're leaving early in the morning.'
   (up-to-date reporting)
   ....
14 'Don't go near the fire,' Dad said to the boys.
   ....
15 'Let's have a barbecue this weekend,' said Liz.
   ....

14 Choose the correct answer.

1 She said that it was going to be a wonderful party.
   a 'It was going to be a wonderful party.'
   ⓑ 'It's going to be a wonderful party.'

2 He said the bus might be a little late that day.
   a 'The bus was a little late today.'
   b 'The bus might be a little late today.'

3 She told him that he should study harder.
   a 'You should study harder.'
   b 'You should have studied harder.'

4 He said that the fire had done a lot of damage to the building.
   a 'The fire had done a lot of damage to the building.'
   b 'The fire has done a lot of damage to the building.'

5 He said that Michael was the best student he had ever taught.
   a 'Michael is the best student I have ever taught.'
   b 'Michael was the best student I have ever taught.'

6 She told us that the new furniture had been delivered the day before.
   a 'The new furniture had been delivered yesterday.'
   b 'The new furniture was delivered yesterday.'

7 They said that the manager would inspect the office the following day.
   a 'The manager will inspect the office the following day.'
   b 'The manager will inspect the office tomorrow.'

8 He said that if we hadn't acted so quickly, the accident would have been even worse.
   a 'If you hadn't acted so quickly, the accident would have been even worse.'
   b 'If you haven't acted so quickly, the accident would be even worse.'

Introductory Verbs

introductory verb	direct speech	reported speech
+ to - inf agree *claim demand offer *promise refuse *threaten	'Yes, I'll lend you the money.' 'I saw the robbers.' 'Give me the money.' 'Would you like me to help you?' 'I'll return the book to you soon.' 'No, I won't call her.' 'Stop shouting or I'll punish you.'	He **agreed to lend** me the money. He **claimed to have seen** the robbers. He **demanded to be given** the money. He **offered to help** me. He **promised to return** the book to me soon. He **refused to call** her. He **threatened to punish** her if she didn't stop shouting.
+ sb + to - inf advise allow ask beg command forbid invite order *remind warn	'You should eat more fruit.' 'You can go to the party.' 'Could you do me a favour?' 'Please, please don't hurt me.' 'Put your hands up.' 'You mustn't stay out late.' 'Will you come to my wedding?' 'Go to your room!' 'Don't forget to buy some milk.' 'Don't touch the iron.'	He **advised me to eat** more fruit. He **allowed me to go to** the party. He **asked me to do** him a favour. He **begged them** not to hurt him. He **commanded them to put** their hands up. He **forbade me to stay out** late. He **invited me to (go to)** his wedding. He **ordered me to go** to my room. He **reminded me to buy** some milk. He **warned me not to touch** the iron.
+ -ing form accuse sb of *admit (to) apologise for *boast about/of *complain to sb of *deny *insist on *suggest	'You committed the crime.' 'Yes, I gave away your secret.' 'I'm sorry I'm late.' 'I'm the best student in my class.' 'I have noisy neighbours.' 'No, I didn't use your computer.' 'You must finish by Friday.' 'Let's go out to dinner.'	He **accused her of committing/having committed** the crime. He **admitted (to) giving/having given away** my secret. He **apologised for being** late. He **boasted about/of being** the best student in his class. He **complained of having** noisy neighbours. He **denied using/having used** my computer. He **insisted on me/my finishing** by Friday. He **suggested going out** to dinner.
explain to sb + **how**	'That's how it works.'	He **explained to us how it** worked.
+ that - clause explain inform sb exclaim/remark	'I don't like him because he's rude.' 'The results will come out tomorrow.' 'What a glorious day!'	She **explained that** she didn't like him because he was rude. He **informed us that** the results would come out the next day. He **exclaimed/remarked that** it was a glorious day.

* Note: The verbs marked with an asterisk can also be followed by a that - clause in reported speech.

e.g. He **claimed that** he had won a prize.
He **promised that** he would call.
He **threatened that** he would leave.
He **reminded** me **that** I had a meeting that afternoon.
He **admitted that** he was wrong.

He **boasted that** he was very rich.
He **complained that** he didn't earn enough money.
He **denied that** he had taken the money.
He **insisted that** I (should) work on Saturday.
He **suggested that** we (should) take out a loan.

15 Complete the sentences.

1 'You should spend more time studying.'
The teacher advised ...*me to spend more time studying*...

2 'Don't forget to lock the door before you leave.'
Sam reminded ....

3 'I'm sorry I forgot to call you.'
Jim apologised ....

4 'You never listen to me, Stuart.'
Mary complained ....

5 'Shall we go bowling this evening?'
Mark suggested ....

6 'You mustn't play near the road.'
Father forbade ....

7 'This man stole my wallet!'
Mr Brown accused ....

8 'I'm the best basketball player in the school.'
Steve boasted ....

9 'Yes, I took the letter.'
Claire admitted ....

10 'You must stay for lunch, Sarah.'
Mrs Stamp insisted ....

11 'Please, please, let me borrow your bicycle.'
Martin begged ....

12 'Don't touch the oven. It's hot.'
Mother warned ....

16 Fill in the gaps with one of the introductory verbs from the list below in the past simple.

deny	suggest	boast	agree
insist	accuse	promise	complain
advise	threaten	warn	remind

1 'I'm the fastest runner on the team,' he said.
He ...*boasted*... about being the fastest runner on the team.

2 'I didn't take your jacket,' he said to her.
He .... taking her jacket.

3 'You should go to the doctor's,' Mum said to me.
Mum .... me to go to the doctor's.

4 'I'll call you next week,' she said to him.
She .... to call him next week.

5 'Yes, I'll set the table for dinner,' he said to her.
He .... to set the table for dinner.

6 'He always forgets my birthday,' she said.
She .... that he always forgot her birthday.

7 'Let's go for a walk,' she said.
She .... going for a walk.

8 'Leave, or I'll shoot,' the man said to them.
The man .... to shoot them if they didn't leave.

9 'Don't forget to feed the cat,' she said to him.
She .... him to feed the cat.

10 'You broke my CD player,' she said to him.
She .... him of breaking her CD player.

11 'Don't go near the edge of the cliff,' Dad said to them.
Dad .... them not to go near the edge of the cliff.

12 'You must do your homework before you go out,' she said to us.
She .... on us doing our homework before we went out.

17 Turn the sentences into *reported speech* using an appropriate introductory verb.

1 'No, I won't do your homework for you,' she said to me.
...*She refused to do my homework for me*....

2 'You lied to me,' Dennis told Ann.
....

3 'I promise I won't tell anyone your secret,' Tara said to Diana.
....

4 'Don't forget to post the letters,' Mum said to me.
....

5 'I'm sorry I ruined your shirt,' Sarah told Frances.
....

6 'No, I didn't use Tim's computer,' George said.
....

7 'Don't get too close to the fire,' Mike said to the children.
....

8 'Let's have a party,' Simon said.
....

9 'I'll punish you if you behave badly,' Mum told the twins.
....

10 'It was me who broke the vase,' she said.
....

11 'Could I use your phone, please?' David asked me.
....

12 'Yes, I'll help you with the washing-up,' Sandra told me.
....

13 'Everyone stop talking!' Mr Jones told the class.
....

14 'Please, please, don't tell anyone about this,' he said to us.
....

15 'You should go to the dentist's,' she told her brother.
....

16 'Children, sit down!' the school bus driver said.
....

17 'Throw down your weapons!' the policeman said to the robbers.
....

18 'No, you may not stay out late tonight,' Dad said to Louise.
....

19 'You must wash your hands before eating dinner,' she told the children.
....

20 'That's the most beautiful necklace I've ever seen!' Amanda said.
....

Exclamations – Yes/No Short answers – Question Tags

◆ We use the verbs **exclaim/say that** to report exclamations which begin with 'What a/an ...' or 'How ...' in direct speech.

e.g. '**What an** unusual design!' he said.
  He **exclaimed/said that** it was an unusual design.
  He **exclaimed/said that** the design was unusual.

But with exclamations such as '**Splendid!'**, '**Great!'**, '**Good!'**, '**Excellent!'**, '**Oh!'**, '**Oh dear!'** etc. we use the expression **give an exclamation of delight/ disgust/ relief/surprise**, etc.

e.g. '**Wow!**' he said as he unwrapped his gift.
  He **gave an exclamation of surprise** as he unwrapped his gift.

◆ Study the following examples:

e.g. a) They said, '**Thank you.**' → They **thanked** us.
  b) '**You fool!**' she said. → She **called** him a fool.
  c) '**Happy Birthday!**' we said to Tamzin.
    → We **wished** Tamzin a happy birthday.
  d) '**Congratulations!**' they said to us.
    → They **congratulated** us.

◆ Yes/No short answers are expressed in reported speech with subject + appropriate auxiliary verb/ introductory verb.

e.g. 'Will you help me decorate the cake?' she asked him. 'Yes,' he said.
  She asked him to help her decorate the cake and **he said he would/he agreed**.

◆ Question tags are omitted in reported speech. We use an appropriate introductory verb to convey the same meaning.

e.g. 'You won't tell anyone, **will you**?' she said to him.
  She **asked** him not to tell anyone.

18 Turn the following sentences into *reported speech.*

1 'Will you call me?' he asked. 'Yes, of course,' she said.
  ...He asked her to call him and she said she would....
2 'Wow!' they said as the fireworks exploded in the sky.
  ....
3 'You'll try to visit John, won't you?' he said to us.
  ....
4 'How delicious!' she said as she tasted the dessert.
  ....
5 'What a surprise!' he said when he saw the present.
  ....
6 'Amazing!' she said when she saw the magician's act.
  ....
7 'Well, good luck, then,' she said to him.
  ....
8 'Can you do this puzzle?' she asked. 'No,' he said.
  ....

Reporting a Dialogue

In dialogues we use a mixture of statements, questions, commands, requests, etc. In reported speech, we use: *and, as, adding that, and (he/she) added that, because, but, since, and then (he/she) went on to say (that), while, then,* etc. to link the sentences in a dialogue. We can also use introductory verbs in the present participle form (*offering, begging, explaining,* etc.).

a 'I'm exhausted,' she said to him. 'Can you make me a cup of tea?'

  She exclaimed that she was exhausted **and** asked him to make her a cup of tea.

b 'I'll take a taxi home. It's getting late', he said.

  He said that he would take a taxi home **as/ because/since** it was getting late.

c Mr Adams: Can I talk to Mr Stephens?
  Secretary: I'm sorry, but he's not here. Would you like me to take a message?
  Mr Adams: No, thank you. I need to see him in person.

  Mr Adams asked to talk to Mr Stephens. His secretary said that he wasn't there **and offered** to take a message. Mr Adams declined, **explaining** that he needed to see him in person.

 19 Turn the following sentences into *reported speech.*

1 'I'm hungry,' she said. 'I haven't eaten all day.'
  ...She said that she was hungry, explaining that she hadn't eaten all day....
2 'Let's go to the cinema,' he said. 'We haven't seen a film for months.'
  ....
3 Tim: Dave is ill. He can't come to the party.
  Mike: What's wrong with him?
  Tim: He's got flu. He has to stay in bed.
  ....
  ....
  ....
4 'You're early,' he said to her. 'I'm not ready yet.'
  ....
5 'Hurry up!' she told him. 'We're going to miss the bus.'
  ....
6 'Have you got your key?' she said. 'I've forgotten mine.'
  ....

7 'I'm going out,' Colin said. 'I might be back late.'

....

8 Sally: I've bought a car. It's being delivered tomorrow.
John: What kind of car is it?
Sally: It's a sports car. It was very expensive.

....
....
....

9 'I'm sorry I'm late. I overslept,' he said to them.

....

10 Martin: Can you help me? I need some advice.
James: What's the problem?
Martin: I don't know what to buy my mother for her birthday. I want to get something special.

....
....
....

Punctuation in Direct Speech

◆ We put the speaker's words in quotation marks and we capitalise the first word of the direct speech. When the speaker is mentioned *before* the direct speech, we put the comma outside the quotation marks. When the speaker is mentioned *after* the direct speech, we put the comma inside the quotation marks.
e.g. **He said,** 'I love Paris in the winter.'
OR: 'I love Paris in the winter,' **he said**.

◆ If the direct speech is a question and the person being spoken to comes after it, we put a question mark and not a comma.
e.g. 'Shall we go now**?**' he asked her.
OR: He asked her, 'Shall we go now**?**'

20 Punctuate the following, making any other necessary changes.

1 would you like a drink she asked me.
...'Would you like a drink?' she asked me....
2 shall we go out tonight Bill asked
....
3 David said shut the door please
....
4 why are you crying Steve asked Jenny
....
5 I'm sorry I'm late he said I was stuck in traffic
....
6 Rachel said I'm afraid I can't help you
....
7 I don't want eggs she said to her mother I'd rather have a steak
....

8 we have to leave in five minutes Sally said can you call us a taxi
....
9 did you go to the library today Sean asked me
....
10 Daniel said stop talking I can't concentrate
....

21 Turn the following sentences into *direct speech*, as in the example.

1 He threatened to tell the headmaster if we didn't behave properly.
...'I'll tell the headmaster if you don't behave properly,' he said....
2 She invited me to go to the cinema with her.
....
3 He offered to help me clean the house.
....
4 We explained that we were late because we had missed the bus.
....
5 She advised me to see a professional.
....
6 She admitted to reading my diary.
....
7 She agreed to help me interview the candidates.
....
8 He accused me of breaking his glasses.
....
9 We apologised for missing their dinner party.
....
10 Edward complained that the children were always disturbing him.
....

22 Turn the following sentences from *direct* into *reported speech* or vice versa.

1 'What are your plans for the weekend?' he asked her.
...He asked her what her plans for the weekend were....
2 Malcolm suggested that they go fishing that afternoon.
....
3 Simon denied having damaged the car.
....
4 'Could you open the door for me, please?' Kate asked Harry.
....
5 Julia claimed to have met Kevin Costner.
....
6 'You never listen when I'm talking to you,' she said.
....
7 The instructor said, 'This is how you open the parachute.'
....

8 'I promise I won't lose your necklace,' she told her friend.

....

9 Stuart begged his parents to let him go to the disco.

....

10 His father said to him, 'No, you can't go to the concert.'

....

11 'Yes, you may stay out late on Saturday,' said Mum.

....

12 The man demanded to speak to his lawyer.

....

13 'I'm afraid there are no tickets left,' he said to us.

....

14 'The path is very slippery,' the guide said to the climbers.

....

15 He asked her to write to him while she was away.

....

23 Turn the following into *reported speech.* Use appropriate introductory verbs.

1 Sam: 'We're having trouble finding a good sales assistant.'

   ...Sam complained that they were having trouble finding a good sales assistant....

2 Dave: 'We've been interviewing people for two weeks.'

   ....

3 Lucy: 'Why don't you contact the Job Centre?'

   ....

4 Ann: 'I think that Julie Smith is looking for a job.'

   ....

5 Tom: 'Yes, right. We forgot that she has been looking for a job.'

   ....

6 Dave: 'Actually, Julie might be perfect for the job. Ann, do you have her phone number?'

   ....

7 Ann: 'Yes, I do. I'll give her a call if you like.'

   ....

8 Sam: 'Don't forget to ask her if she can work flexible hours.'

   ....

Common mistakes

- She **told to me** that she was late. ✗
  She **told me** that she was late. ✓

- Colin said, 'I met them last week.'
  Colin said he had met them **last week**. ✗
  Colin said he had met them **the week before/the previous week**. ✓

- 'This is a mistake,' she told me.
  She told me that **that** was a mistake. ✗
  She told me that **it** was a mistake. ✓

- 'Derek must be very rich,' Samantha told me.
  Samantha told me that Derek **had to be** very rich. ✗
  Samantha told me that Derek **must be** very rich. ✓

- Peter says, 'Everybody is in the garden.'
  Peter says that everybody **was** in the garden. ✗
  Peter says that everybody **is** in the garden. ✓

- 'Where did you find this ring?' Karen asked me.
  Karen asked me where **had I found** the ring. ✗
  Karen asked me where **I had found** the ring. ✓

24 Correct the mistakes.

1 Anna says that lunch was ready.
2 They told me that that was a photograph of their family.
3 Brian told to me that he had a new car.
4 Linda said she had seen the film last month.
5 Tim asked me where had I been on holiday.
6 Alan told me that John had to be in the office.

25 Cross out the unnecessary word.

1 Our friends told us that we had better to avoid the city centre.
2 Annabelle asked Tony where he was being going for his holidays.
3 They asked me if I would like to buy her a gift and I said I would so.
4 Paul suggested that they should to inform the police as soon as possible.
5 Rebecca told to her husband that the postman had delivered a parcel for him.
6 The man wanted to know if where the nearest post office was.
7 Melissa promised that to call us as soon as she reached Madrid.
8 The teacher told us do not to make any noise.
9 Rhonda asked me that what I would like for my birthday.
10 He insisted on that we should tell the truth about the incident.

26 Complete each sentence with two to five words, including the word in bold.

1 'I feel very ill,' he said to her.
complained He ...*complained of feeling*... very ill.

2 'I promise I'll send you a postcard,' Julie said to Mike.
promised Julie .... Mike a postcard.

3 'I will send you to your room if you don't apologise,' she said to him.
threatened She .... to his room if he didn't apologise.

4 'Would you like to come to dinner on Friday?' they said to us.
invited They .... to dinner on Friday.

5 'What an amazing garden!' said Marie.
exclaimed Marie .... an amazing garden.

6 'I'm sorry I interrupted the meeting,' he said to her.
for He .... the meeting.

7 'You must finish that report by five o'clock,' she said to me.
on She .... the report by five o'clock.

8 'No, I won't give you any more pocket money,' Dad said to Steve.
refused Dad .... any more pocket money.

9 'Let's go for a picnic this afternoon,' Mum said.
going Mum .... that afternoon.

10 'I didn't leave the tap on,' she said.
denied She .... the tap on.

11 'Don't forget to pack your swimming costumes,' Mum said to us.
reminded Mum .... our swimming costumes.

12 'I took your new skirt,' my sister said.
admitted My sister .... my new skirt.

13 'You drank the last can of lemonade,' Sue said to Jane.
of Sue .... the last can of lemonade.

14 'Why don't we organise a party for Lucy's birthday?' Dave said.
should Dave .... organise a party for Lucy's birthday.

15 'Ok, I'll give you a chance,' she said.
agreed She .... a chance.

16 'Drop your gun!' the policeman told the man.
ordered The policeman .... his gun.

17 'Why are you making such a fuss?' Mum asked me.
was Mum wanted to know .... such a fuss.

18 'I'll give you a lift to the station,' Mike said to me.
to Mike .... a lift to the station.

19 'You should save some money every month,' Rita told her son.
advised Rita .... some money every month.

20 'I've got the fastest car of all my friends,' Daniel said.
boasted Daniel .... the fastest car of all his friends.

21 'I don't suppose you can lend me thirty pounds, can you?' Caroline said to me.
whether Caroline wanted to know .... her thirty pounds.

22 'I saw who broke into the flat,' Mrs Reeves told the police.
claimed Mrs Reeves .... who broke into the flat.

23 'Where is my purse?' she asked herself.
wondered She .... was.

24 'Why are you so upset?' Diana asked Fiona.
was Diana asked Fiona .... so upset.

27 Underline the correct preposition.

1 Colin searched everywhere **at/for/on** his missing keys.
2 I am quite satisfied **about/with/by** my new television.
3 We hurried through the storm in search **for/of/at** shelter.
4 The judge sentenced the thief **to/of/for** five years in prison.
5 The teacher shouted **to/at/about** the naughty children.
6 The boy shouted **at/to/for** his friends that he was going home.
7 This dress is similar **to/with/for** the one Sally bought.
8 Toby is a doctor who specialises **in/of/at** allergies.
9 The lifeguard saved the old lady **of/by/from** drowning.
10 They spent all their money **for/on/at** computer games, so they had to walk all the way back home.
11 Sam hopes to succeed **in/at/of** becoming captain of the football team.
12 Paula suffers **from/with/of** hay fever every summer.
13 I am not sure **about/of/on** where to go on holiday this year.
14 She is always suspicious **with/of/at** people who refuse to look her in the eye.
15 The police suspect her **for/about/of** committing a robbery.
16 I sympathise **to/with/for** you over the loss of your job. I'm out of work, too.
17 Although he is sympathetic **to/with/for** the hardships of the homeless, he doesn't do anything to help them.
18 We're in a difficult situation, but I hope we'll find a solution **for/at/to** our problem soon.

Phrasal Verbs

hold back:	1) (tr) control (tears, laughter), 2) (tr) delay, 3) (tr) keep secret, 4) (int) be reluctant to act
hold in:	(tr) restrain; keep under control
hold on:	(int) to wait (esp on the phone)
hold out:	(int) 1) persist; not give way, 2) last
hold up:	1) (tr) delay, 2) (tr) use violence in order to rob, 3) (int) last; **hold out**
keep away (from):	(tr) stay away
keep back:	(tr) conceal
keep behind:	(tr) make sb remain after others have left
keep (oneself) from:	(tr) 1) prevent from, 2) avoid
keep off:	(tr) 1) make sb stay away from, 2) avoid (food, a habit, etc); **keep away from**
keep on:	1) (int) continue in spite of difficulties, 2) (tr) continue doing sth; **carry on**
keep out of:	(tr) stay away from (trouble)
keep up:	(tr) 1) maintain sth at the same level, 2) keep sb out of bed, 3) keep sth in good condition
keep up with:	(tr) 1) proceed at an equal pace with, 2) continue to be informed (news, events)
let down:	(tr) 1) (of clothes) lengthen (opp: **take up**), 2) disappoint
let off:	(tr) 1) not punish, 2) make sth explode (fireworks)
let out:	(tr) 1) (of clothes) make wider, (opp: **take in**), 2) say sth (usu a secret) unintentionally

28 Fill in the correct particle.

1 The house is becoming too expensive for them to keep ...*up*... .
2 You shouldn't hold .... your anger. It will only make you feel worse.
3 I'm keeping .... chocolate for a while in an attempt to lose a little weight.
4 I didn't mean to let the secret .... It was an accident.
5 We were held .... in traffic. That's why we arrived late.
6 Our business is holding .... quite well, despite the economic crisis.
7 The young man was let .... because he had never been in trouble before.
8 The secretary asked me to hold .... until Mrs Harris was ready to take my call.
9 Kate is trying to keep her grades .... at the same level.
10 The jury thought that one of the witnesses was keeping some important information ....

11 The joke was so funny that Jake couldn't hold .... his laughter.
12 Sally buys a newspaper every day to keep .... the news.
13 You mustn't hold .... secrets if there's something I ought to know.
14 I've had a few problems, but I'm going to keep .... trying until I succeed.
15 This skirt is too short. I'll let it .... a bit.
16 I think our water supplies will hold .... for another four days.
17 Simon held .... because he wasn't sure if it was the right thing to do.
18 You've put on weight! I'll have to let .... the waist of your trousers for you.
19 When Jane had measles, her mother kept her .... school for two weeks.
20 The demonstrators held .... for three weeks before ending their protest outside the factory.
21 I'm counting on you. Please don't let me ....
22 Don't walk so fast. I can't keep .... you!
23 George keeps .... watering the tree in the garden, but I'm sure it's dead.
24 The noise from the party kept me .... until the early hours of the morning.
25 While we're away, please try to keep .... trouble.

29 Fill in the gaps with the correct form of the words in brackets.

A Making a cake does not require much 1) ...*intelligence*... (intelligent). All you have to do is follow the 2) .... (instruct) in the recipe book. If you pay 3) .... (attend) to the recipe and are 4) .... (care) to measure the ingredients accurately, then you should end up with a 5) .... (wonder) cake.

B The 'Spice Girls' are a very 1) .... (success) band. Their 2) .... (popular) is a result of their 3) .... (fashion) image and their 4) .... (enjoy) music. The band has many fans who watch each new 5) .... (develop) with interest.

C I have a great deal of 1) .... (admire) for doctors and nurses. Their work demands 2) .... (commit) and, of course, 3) .... (concentrate). They make difficult 4) .... (decide) every day and treat all kinds of illnesses and 5) .... (injure).

D Our trip to the theatre last night was rather a 1) .... (disappoint). A woman in the audience caused a 2) .... (distract) by coughing loudly throughout the 3) .... (perform). It totally spoilt our 4) .... (enjoy) of the play as we found the noise 5) .... ((un) bear).

Revision Box

30 **Choose the correct answer.**

1 'I'm going to take Louise to a restaurant tonight.'
 'Well, you ...*B*... book a table in advance.'
 A shall **B** ought to **C** may

2 'How is Brian today?'
 'He .... a little better, thank you.'
 A felt **B** is feeling
 C has been feeling

3 'Mr Jones won't be free for at least half an hour.'
 'That's alright. I don't mind ....'
 A wait **B** to wait **C** waiting

4 '........... fruit is good for your health.'
 'I know. I eat an apple every day.'
 A Eating **B** To Eat **C** Eat

5 'What is happening over there?'
 'A new supermarket ....'
 A is building **B** is built **C** is being built

6 'This room looks very nice.'
 'Thank you. We .... last week.'
 A have it decorated **B** had it decorated
 C are having it decorated

7 'You look tired.'
 'I am. I think I need .... holiday.'
 A the **B** an **C** a

8 'I bought these trousers from a wonderful shop.'
 'Really. What was .... name of the shop?'
 A the **B** an **C** a

9 'That's a beautiful painting.'
 'Yes. It .... by my sister.'
 A painted **B** was painted **C** is painted

10 'Sarah is in a good mood today.'
 'Yes. She looks very ....'
 A happily **B** happy **C** happier

11 'David's car isn't here.'
 'No. He .... be at work.'
 A should **B** will **C** must

12 'Do you know Steven?'
 'Yes. I .... him for years.'
 A know **B** knew **C** have known

13 'John is a lovely person.'
 'Yes. I consider him .... the nicest person I know.'
 A to be **B** being **C** be

14 'You're up very early today.'
 'I know. I don't want to be .... for my interview.'
 A late **B** lately **C** later

15 'That film was brilliant.'
 'Yes. It was .... film I've ever seen.'
 A funniest **B** the funniest **C** the funnier

16 'Grandpa wants to go to university!'
 'You're never .... old to do something like that.'
 A very **B** enough **C** too

17 'We .... in the country.'
 'When did you move to the city?'
 A are living **B** used to live **C** use to live

31 **Choose the correct answer.**

It was very 1) ...*B*... at night and Susan was fast 2) .... in bed. Suddenly, she 3) .... by a loud noise. She sat up and turned on the light. She 4) .... hear faint noises 5) .... from downstairs. Someone was in the house. Susan was very scared, but she decided to go and 6) .... what was happening. She wouldn't let her house 7) .... burgled. She didn't want to have all her belongings 8) .... Pulling on her dressing-gown, she crept slowly down the stairs. As she opened the door to the kitchen she came face to face with her brother. He 9) .... downstairs to get something to eat, but he had dropped the biscuit tin on the floor. They both laughed and 10) .... went back to bed.

1	**A** later	**B** late	**C** lately
2	**A** asleep	**B** sleepy	**C** sleeping
3	**A** was waking up	**B** woke up	**C** was woken up
4	**A** can	**B** could	**C** couldn't
5	**A** coming	**B** come	**C** to come
6	**A** to see	**B** see	**C** seeing
7	**A** being	**B** to be	**C** be
8	**A** stolen	**B** steal	**C** be stolen
9	**A** was going	**B** went	**C** had gone
10	**A** then	**B** after	**C** next

Revision Box

32 Complete each sentence with two to five words, including the word in bold.

1 I'm sure he didn't go to the cinema last night.
   have   He ...*can't have gone to*... the cinema last night.

2 It wasn't necessary for him to give me a lift because I had my own car.
   need   He .... me a lift because I had my own car.

3 I advise you to be more careful.
   should   You .... more careful.

4 I'll cut the grass for you.
   like   Would .... the grass for you?

5 Let's go for a drive in the countryside.
   about   What .... in the countryside?

6 It wasn't necessary for her to buy me a present, but she did.
   bought   She .... me a present.

7 You mustn't interrupt the teacher when she's talking.
   allowed   You .... the teacher when she's talking.

8 It's possible that you left your keys at home.
   have   You .... your keys at home.

9 You are not allowed to play football in the house.
   mustn't   You .... in the house.

10 It wasn't necessary to go shopping, so we didn't.
    need   We .... go shopping.

11 She will probably go to university.
    likely   It .... go to university.

12 It wasn't necessary for her to clean the windows, but she did.
    needn't   She .... the windows.

13 It's possible that they will sell their house.
    may   They .... their house.

14 I am certain Philip proposed to Mary last night.
    must   Philip .... to Mary last night.

15 You ought to reconsider your decision.
    better   You .... your decision.

16 'What a spectacular view!' said Virginia.
    exclaimed   Virginia .... was spectacular.

ORAL Activity

Mr Houston has recently opened a local museum which shows the history of his town. Yesterday, he was interviewed by a reporter for the local newspaper. Look at the questions and answers below and then report what was said, as in the example.

e.g. *The reporter asked Mr Houston why he had decided to open the museum.*
   Mr Houston answered that he thought everyone should have access to the town's history.

R: Why did you decide to open the museum?
H: I think everyone should have access to the town's history.
R: Where did you find all the interesting objects and pictures?
H: I have been collecting them for years.
R: Have you always been interested in history?
H: Yes. It was my favourite subject at school.
R: Do you have any other hobbies apart from history?
H: Yes. I also enjoy listening to classical music.
R: What are your hopes for this museum?
H: I hope that it will be popular with visitors and residents and that people will learn from it.

WRITING Activity

The reporter is now writing an article about Mr Houston and his museum. Look at the Oral Activity again and complete the article below.

Yesterday, I met Mr Houston, who has recently opened a local museum which shows the history of our town. I asked Mr Houston why he had decided to open the museum and he said ...

....
....
....
....

The museum is open from 9am-5pm, Monday to Saturday and is well worth a visit.

Emphasis

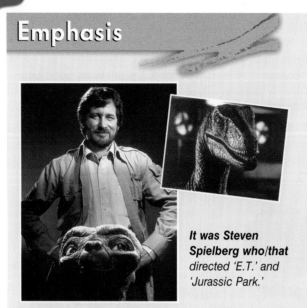

It was Steven Spielberg who/that directed 'E.T.' and 'Jurassic Park.'

We can put emphasis on certain words or parts of a sentence with:

◆ **It is/was ... who/which/that**
e.g. a) **Sheila** *is planting flowers in the garden.*
It is Sheila who/that *is planting flowers in the garden. (emphasis on the subject = Sheila)*
b) *Sheila is planting* **flowers** *in the garden.*
It is flowers that *Sheila is planting in the garden. (emphasis on the object = flowers)*
c) *Sheila is planting flowers* **in the garden**.
It is in the garden that *Sheila is planting flowers. (emphasis on the adverbial phrase = in the garden)*
d) **The dog's barking** *didn't wake me up, the alarm clock did.*
It wasn't the dog's barking **which/that** *woke me up, it was the alarm clock.*

Note: We use *who, which* or *that* to put emphasis on the subject. We normally use *that* to put emphasis on the object or the adverbial phrase.

◆ **All (that)= the only thing**
e.g. **All (that)** *she cares about* **is** *money.*
All (that) *he did* **was** *call me to say goodbye.*

◆ **What**
e.g. a) **Jogging** *keeps me in shape. (subject)*
What *keeps me in shape is jogging.*
OR *Jogging is* **what** *keeps me in shape.*
b) *I need* **a holiday.** *(object)*
What *I need is a holiday.*
OR *A holiday is* **what** *I need.*

◆ **What ... do (to put emphasis on verbs)**
e.g. a) *Sharon* **designs** *clothes.*
What *Sharon* **does** *is (to) design clothes.*

b) *Greg* **updated** *the files.*
What *Greg* **did** *was (to) update the files.*

◆ **Question word + ever (usually shows surprise)**
e.g. **Who ever** *told you I was getting married?*
Where ever *did you find this old map?*
Which and **whose** are not used in this case.
e.g. *Whose idea was it? (NOT: ~~Whose ever idea ...~~)*

**Note: *Question words + ever* (except for *why*) can be written as one word. e.g. *Whoever* told you ...?
We also use *ever* to put emphasis on negative sentences.**
e.g. **Nobody ever** *explained this to me.*
I haven't seen this man **ever** *before.*

◆ **We use do/does/did + bare infinitive in the present simple, past simple or the imperative to give emphasis.**

e.g. a) *She* **believes** *in supernatural powers.*
She **does believe** *in supernatural powers.*
b) *He* **went** *to the reception.*
He **did go** *to the reception.*
c) **Stay** *a little longer.*
Do stay *a little longer.*

 1 **Rewrite these *first aid instructions* using *what*, as in the example.**

1 You should remember to stay calm.
 ...What you should remember is to stay calm....
2 You need to act quickly.
 ....
3 You have to call an ambulance.
 ....
4 You must concentrate on helping the victims.
 ....
5 You need to check that the injury is not serious.
 ....
6 You should not allow anyone to move the injured people.
 ....
7 You should remember to keep the victims warm.
 ....
8 You have to keep the injured people calm.
 ....

 2 **Change the sentences, as in the example.**

1 I don't need a pencil, I need a pen.
 ...It's not a pencil I need, it's a pen....
2 Sam isn't a policeman, Daniel is.
 ....

3 I don't like carrots, I like potatoes.
....

4 He's not eating sweets, he's eating fruit.
....

5 We didn't watch a film, we watched a play.
....

6 I don't speak French, I speak German.
....

7 They don't want a house, they want a flat.
....

8 I didn't break a window, I broke a mirror.
....

 3 Rewrite the sentences in all possible ways, as in the example.

1 Jane moved to Italy in 1986.
   ...It was Jane who/that moved to Italy in 1986....
   ...It was Italy that Jane moved to in 1986....
   ...It was in 1986 that Jane moved to Italy....
2 Paul sold his old car last week.
3 Sarah lost her keys this morning.
4 David made dinner last night.
5 Simon published his latest novel last month.
6 I met a film star last week.
7 Alan repaired the fence this afternoon.
8 Catherine found a kitten on Monday.

 4 Read the information, then rewrite it emphasising the words in bold.

1 **Victor Fleming** directed 'Gone With the Wind.'
   ...It was Victor Fleming who/that directed 'Gone With the Wind.'...
2 **Clark Gable and Vivien Leigh** played the lead parts.
   ....
3 **Margaret Mitchell** wrote the original novel.
   ....
4 The film was released **in 1939**.
   ....
5 The film was first shown **in Atlanta**.
   ....
6 The film became a huge success **soon after its release**.
   ....
7 The film won **nine** Oscars in 1940.
   ....

 5 Rewrite the sentences putting emphasis on the highlighted words.

1 **Lydia** stole the papers from the office.
   ...It was Lydia who/that stole the papers from the office....
2 **Alison** made the bridesmaids' dresses.
   ....
3 **Where** did you meet Jason?
   ....
4 **Who** gave you this expensive necklace?
   ....
5 Are you going to buy **that cake** for the party?
   ....
6 **Steve** decorated the living room.
   ....
7 **What** made you react like this?
   ....
8 **Why** did you phone the police?
   ....
9 **Why don't** you remember my birthday?
   ....
10 We received the letter **this morning**.
   ....

 6 Rewrite the sentences using emphatic constructions, starting with the words given.

1 John set off the fire alarm.
   It was *...John who/that set off the fire alarm....*
2 Come in!
   Do ....
3 Why did they close the shop?
   Why ever ....
4 She needs a pay rise.
   What ....
5 She promised to call him.
   She did ....
6 When did you get married?
   When was ....
7 What have you done?
   Whatever ....
8 I told you to be quiet.
   I did ....
9 Annie opened the windows.
   It was ....

7 Complete the sentences, using your own ideas.

1 All I want is *...to be happy....*
2 What I would like is ....
3 What I really need is ....
4 What I enjoy is ....
5 What I hate is ....
6 What I don't understand is ....
7 What I would like to know is ....
8 What I like most is ....

Inversion

No sooner had they arrived at the station **than** the train pulled in.

There are two ways to invert the subject and the verb.

1) **be/have/modal/auxiliary verb + subject + main verb**

It is used in the following cases:

a) **in questions.**
e.g. **Is Peter taking** an exam today?

b) **after the following words or expressions, when they come at the beginning of a sentence.**

Seldom	Only in this way
Rarely	Only then
Little	Hardly (ever) ... when
Barely	No sooner ... than
Nowhere (else)	Not only ... but (also)
Never (before)	Not until/till
Not (even) once	In no way
On no account	In/Under no circumstances
Only by	Not since, etc.

e.g. **Never (before) have I seen** such a beautiful woman.
Not only did they make a donation **but** they **(also)** promised to build a shelter for the homeless.
Seldom do we go out since the baby was born.

But: *We seldom go out since the baby was born. (There is no inversion because the word seldom does not come at the beginning of the sentence.)*

Note: **When the expressions *only after, only by, only if, only when, not until/till* come at the beginning of a sentence, the inversion is in the main clause.**
e.g. **Only after** she started working **was she able to** save some money.
Only if you follow my advice **will you succeed.**

c) **with so, neither, nor, as to express agreement.**
e.g. *'I love chocolate ice cream.' 'So do I.' (We use 'so' to agree with an affirmative statement.)*
'I can't stand violent films.'
*' **Neither/Nor can I.** ' (We use 'neither/ nor' to agree with a negative statement.)*
*She was a talented musician, **as was her sister** /and **so was her sister.***

d) **with should, were, had when they come at the beginning of an if-clause instead of 'if'.**
e.g. Type 1: **Should he call**, tell him I'm out.
(= If he should call ...)
Type 2: **Were I you**, I wouldn't trust her.
(= If I were you ...)
Type 3: **Had I been** told, I would have offered my help.
(= If I had been told ...)

2) **main verb + subject**

It is used in the following cases:

a) **after verbs of movement or adverbial expressions of place when they come at the beginning of a sentence.**
e.g. **Outside the house was a sports car.**
*On the sofa **sat an old man.***
*Here **comes the bride.***
*There **goes the bus.***
If the subject is a pronoun, there is no inversion.
*Here **she comes.** (NOT: ~~Here comes she.~~)*
*Up **you get.** (NOT: ~~Up got you.~~)*

b) **in direct speech when the subject of the introductory verb is a noun.**
e.g. *'I don't like this hotel,' **said Henry**.*
(OR: ... Henry said.)
*'I'll call you a taxi,' **said the doorman**.*
(OR: ... the doorman said.)
But: *'What can I do for you?' **she asked**.*
(NOT: ... ~~asked she,~~ because the subject of the introductory verb is a pronoun.)

 8 **Fill in the gaps, as in the example.**

1 'I have a terrible cold.'
'So...*do I*.... I feel really bad.'
2 'I didn't go to the party last night.'
'Nor .... I stayed at home instead.'
3 'We went shopping yesterday.'
'So .... We bought lots of things.'
4 'I've got some good news!'
'So .... I've got a new job!'

5 'I didn't win a prize.'
'Nor .... I was very disappointed.'
6 'I'll send Kim a card.'
'So .... I'll buy one tomorrow.'
7 'I went skiing last year.'
'So .... I had a lovely time.'
8 'We're not going on holiday this year.'
'Neither .... We can't afford it.'
9 'I can play the guitar.'
'So ...., but not very well.'
10 'I'm not going to work tomorrow.'
'Neither .... My boss has given me the day off.'

9 Rewrite the sentences, beginning with the words in bold.

1 The rain came **down**.
...*Down came the rain*....
2 The birds flew **away**.
....
3 My house is **at the end of the road**.
....
4 The actors came **onto the stage**.
....
5 The aeroplane rose **up into the sky**.
....
6 The Grand Hotel stands **at the foot of the mountain**.
....
7 The policeman walked **down the street**.
....
8 The window cleaner climbed **up the ladder**.
....

10 Rewrite the sentences using the words/ phrases given.

1 I have seldom eaten at such an expensive restaurant.
Seldom ...*have I eaten at such an expensive restaurant*....
2 She had no sooner fallen asleep than the telephone rang.
No sooner ....
3 We not only got lost, but our car broke down.
Not only ....
4 I have never heard such a terrible story before.
Never before ....
5 We realised only then that the jewels had been stolen.
Only then ....
6 Business has rarely been so good.
Rarely ....
7 The boss has not once given him a bonus.
Not once ....
8 You should not enter this room under any circumstances.
Under no circumstances ....
9 I got to know Peter only after meeting him several times.
Only after ....

10 The police didn't know that the man was a criminal.
Little ....
11 I haven't been to the beach since last summer.
Not since ....
12 If I had known about the party, I would have gone.
Had ....
13 We haven't had such a wonderful time anywhere else.
Nowhere ....
14 If I were you, I would look for a new job.
Were ....
15 He had barely entered the office when the manager called him.
Barely ....

11 *Chris Young is a fashion designer. He is talking to his staff about keeping the designs for his next show a secret.* **Put the verbs in brackets into the correct form.**

Under no circumstances **1)** ...*should you tell*... (you/should/tell) anyone about the plans for the show next week and in no way **2)** .... (you/must/give) our competitors any clues about our designs. Not until the day after the fashion show **3)** .... (you/will/be able to) talk to reporters about the clothes. Only in this way **4)** ....
.... (the show/will/be) a success. If you all follow these orders, not only **5)** .... (you/will/get) a large bonus after the show, but you will also be given some time off.

12 Fill in the blanks with a suitable word or phrase.

1 Never ...*before had she seen*... such a beautiful dress.
2 No sooner .... than there was a knock at the door.
3 Only by .... did we finish the report on time.
4 On no account .... arrive late on Monday morning.
5 Not only .... my wallet, but my watch was missing, too.
6 Only when .... did I realise I had been asleep.
7 Not since I was young .... such an enjoyable day.
8 Under no circumstances .... be informed of this agreement.

13 Look at the following text and write inverted sentences using the words/ phrases in bold.

Alexander Fleming discovered penicillin in 1928. He had **no sooner** noticed an interesting mould growth in one of his glass dishes **than** he knew that it was something important. He **only later** realised what a difference it would make to our lives. There had **never** been a drug like this **before**. Patients with infections could **only** be successfully cured **by** taking penicillin. Penicillin **not only** advanced medical technology, **but also** saved thousands of lives. People **rarely** die from infections these days.

1 ...*No sooner had he noticed an interesting mould growth in one of his glass dishes than he knew that it was something important.* ....

....
....
....
....
....
....
....
....
....

14 Rewrite the sentences, as in the example.

1 Alexander Graham Bell invented the telephone.
It ...*was Alexander Graham Bell who/that invented the telephone.*...
2 Vincent Van Gogh painted beautiful pictures.
What ....
3 The only thing Mozart cared about was his music.
All ....
4 The Wright Brothers made the first aeroplane flight.
It ....
5 Writing gave Charles Dickens great pleasure.
What ....
6 The only thing Emily Pankhurst wanted was equal rights for women.
All ....
7 Tobacco was first discovered in America.
It ....
8 Margaret Thatcher became the first female Prime Minister of Britain.
It ....

15 Complete each sentence with two to five words, including the word in bold.

1 You will get there on time if you leave now.
will   Only if you ...*leave now will you*... get there on time.
2 As soon as I got into bed, I fell asleep.
sooner   No .... into bed than I fell asleep.
3 We didn't notice the time until it was too late.
did   Not until it was .... the time.
4 It was only after I drank the milk that I realised it was sour.
did   Only after I had drunk the milk .... it was sour.
5 If I were you, I would buy a computer.
you   Were .... buy a computer.
6 I only noticed the scratch on my car when I looked closely.
notice   Only when I looked closely .... the scratch on my car.
7 They had no idea it was the wrong train.
know   Little .... it was the wrong train.
8 There's no way I can meet him at the airport.
can   In no way .... at the airport.
9 We could only get there on time by taking a short cut.
could   Only by taking a short cut .... there on time.
10 She's a brilliant actress and a talented writer as well.
only   Not .... actress, but she's also a talented writer.
11 Don't open the door on any account while I'm out.
should   On no account .... the door while I'm out.
12 If I had realised how late it was, I wouldn't have stayed so long.
realised   Had .... was, I wouldn't have stayed so long.
13 I haven't eaten such delicious food anywhere.
else   Nowhere .... such delicious food.
14 You must not open this box under any circumstances.
no   Under .... this box.
15 I had never seen such a fierce dog before.
before   Never .... such a fierce dog.
16 I remembered my keys only after I had closed the door.
remember   Only after I had closed the door .... my keys.
17 We rarely had sweets when we were young.
have   Hardly ever .... we were young.

Common mistakes

- **Rarely they** travel abroad any more. ✗
  Rarely do they travel abroad any more. ✓

- **Hardly** had she left the house **than** it started raining. ✗
  Hardly had she left the house **when** it started raining. ✓

- **Not only she is** arrogant but also rude. ✗
  Not only is she arrogant but also rude. ✓

- **Only after had he finished** his work **he had** a break. ✗
  Only after he had finished his work **did he have** a break. ✓

- 'I enjoy going to open-air concerts.' **'So I do.'** ✗
  'I enjoy going to open-air concerts.' **'So do I.'** ✓

- She is a lively person, **as her** brother. ✗
  She is a lively person, **as is her** brother. ✓

- 'Where did you buy this rug?' **asked he**. ✗
  'Where did you buy this rug?' **he asked**. ✓

16 Correct the mistakes.

1 'I love chocolate biscuits.' 'So I do.'
2 'What have you been doing?' asked she.
3 Hardly had Melissa gone to bed than the telephone rang.
4 Not only he is lazy, but also stubborn.
5 He is a mechanic, as his father.
6 Seldom she goes to the theatre.
7 Only after had he closed the windows he left the house.

17 Cross out the unnecessary word.

1 Do you come in, please.
2 What I would really like it is a long holiday.
3 Only by you getting a job will you be able to pay off your debts.
4 Marion enjoys travelling abroad and so does enjoy her sister.
5 It was Angela who she told me about your accident.
6 If were I you, I would think twice before accepting his proposal.
7 All he did it was mumble an excuse.
8 Only when did I talked to him in person was the matter settled.
9 Rarely ever do we go to the opera.
10 No sooner had we finished our meal than when a fight broke out.

18 Fill in the gaps with the correct form of the words in brackets.

1 The plants flourished in the ...*warmth*... of the greenhouse. (warm)
2 Suddenly we caught .... of the glittering blue sea. (see)
3 Animals in the wild have to fight for .... (survive)
4 I lost my keys, but .... my neighbour has a spare set. (fortune)
5 My brother is a very talented .... (music)
6 We should treat all .... creatures with kindness and respect. (life)
7 The aircraft reached a .... of 35,000 feet. (high)
8 The company have received several .... about their latest product. (complain)
9 She is a very .... driver and never exceeds the speed limit. (caution)
10 Taking a computer course has been .... to my career. (benefit)
11 She has made .... useful contacts throughout her career. (number)
12 I prefer to wear clothes which are made from .... fibres. (nature)
13 Modern supermarkets offer a large .... of products. (choose)
14 .... is a good quality to have. (honest)
15 To Rick's ...., his painting won the competition. (amaze)

19 Fill in the gaps with the correct form of the words in brackets.

The Riverview is an **1)** ...*expensive*... (expense) hotel on the shore of **2)** .... (peace) Lake Bead. The hotel is very **3)** .... (attract) and is set in **4)** .... (beauty) surroundings. It has over a hundred **5)** .... (space) rooms which are very **6)** .... (luxury). Lots of **7)** .... (fame) people have stayed there in order to enjoy the **8)** .... (private) that the hotel offers them, since there are **9)** .... (secure) guards to keep photographers and reporters out.

Phrasal Verbs

look after:	(tr) take care of
look down on:	(tr) have a bad opinion of sb; disapprove of sb/sth (opp: **look up to**)
look for:	(tr) search for
look forward to:	(tr) anticipate (with pleasure)
look into:	(tr) investigate
look on:	watch (instead of doing sth)
look on/upon:	(tr) regard as; consider
look out for:	(tr) be alert in order to see/find sb/sth
look over:	1) examine carefully; **go through**, 2) revise briefly and quickly
look round:	examine (an area, place, etc.)
look through:	(tr) 1) look at quickly, 2) study sth carefully
look up:	1) (tr) look for sth (such as an address, etc) in a book or list, 2) visit sb (specially sb living far away)
look up to:	(tr) respect (opp: **look down on**)
make for:	(tr) move in the direction of
make off:	(int) run away; escape; **make away**
make out:	(tr) 1) see sb/sth clearly, 2) understand; **work out**, 3) write out; **fill in**
make sth up to sb:	compensate sb for sth
make up:	1) (tr) invent; **think up**, (a story, an excuse, etc.) 2) (tr) put cosmetics on, 3) (int) become friends again, 4) (tr) compensate, 5) form as a whole
make up for:	compensate; repay sb for
pass away:	(int) die
pass off as:	(tr) pretend to be sth/sb else successfully
pass on:	(tr) give sth (usu clothes) to younger/smaller member of family
pass out:	(int) lose consciousness

20   **Fill in the correct particle.**

1   They looked ...*round*... the village before setting off down the mountain.
2   Fred passes .... at the sight of blood.
3   The actress made herself .... before she went on stage.
4   Nurses look .... patients in hospital.
5   Look .... the turning, I don't want to miss it.
6   Two members of staff and eight parents make .... the school committee.
7   What does this word say? I can't make .... the handwriting.
8   He looks .... people who are less privileged.
9   Julie looked .... the book quickly in the shop before she bought it.
10 Sadly, the chairman of the club passed .... last weekend.

11 I looked .... your telephone number in the telephone book.
12 This school is looked .... as being one of the best in the area.
13 The doctor looked .... the patient carefully before giving his diagnosis.
14 The shoplifter was making .... the door when the security guard stopped him.
15 They gave him a free meal to make .... the bad service he received.
16 I'll make .... the cheque to you, shall I?
17 We're really looking .... your birthday party.
18 Clive made .... an excuse for his being late.
19 I am looking .... a new house at the moment.
20 Most of her clothes are passed .... from her older sisters.
21 Look .... the contract before you sign it.
22 The jeweller tried to pass the ring .... solid gold even though it wasn't.
23 The man made .... with cash from the till, but was caught by the police a short time later.
24 I was in the area so I thought I'd look you .... – we haven't seen each other for such a long time.
25 Please lend me your car this weekend. I'll make it .... you later, I promise.
26 The crowd looked .... as the athlete finished the race in record time.
27 The police are looking .... the burglary.
28 All Arthur's employees look .... him and respect him very much.
29 They had an argument yesterday, but I think they've made .... now.

21   **Underline the correct preposition.**

1   Sandra has wonderful taste *of/in/at* clothes.
2   This tea tastes *of/in/at* strawberries.
3   I was thankful *about/of/for* all his support.
4   The burglar threatened the woman *at/of/with* a knife.
5   John threw the ball *at/to/of* me, but I dropped it.
6   Jo threw the ball *at/to/of* the coconut and won a prize.
7   She is tired *from/of/by* doing the same thing every day.
8   He was tired *from/of/by* working in the garden all day.
9   The trouble *of/with/about* computers is that they are very expensive.
10 This wet weather is typical *of/from/on* England.
11 Cathy was upset *about/from/of* missing the train.
12 We tried to warn him *about/for/from* the icy roads but he wouldn't listen.
13 He wastes all his money *for/to/on* computer games and magazines.
14 The performance was worthy *of/for/from* an award.
15 These vouchers are valid *in/to/from* all good record shops.
16 This ticket is valid *of/for/from* three months.
17 I have to translate this poem *for/into/at* English for my homework.

Revision Box

 22 **Choose the correct answer.**

1 Your teacher has told you to write a story for your homework. You tell your parents.
   A I should write a story.
   B I may write a story.
   C I have to write a story.

2 You put some petrol in the car, even though your father didn't ask you to.
   A You needn't have put petrol in the car.
   B You ought to have put petrol in the car.
   C You can't have put petrol in the car.

3 You want to use your mobile phone on a plane, but the stewardess tells you it isn't allowed.
   A You needn't use your mobile phone on the plane.
   B You mustn't use your mobile phone on the plane.
   C You won't use your mobile phone on the plane.

4 You have a headache. Your friend gives you some advice.
   A You should take an aspirin.
   B You may take an aspirin.
   C You might take an aspirin.

5 Chris didn't speak to you. You are sure he didn't see you.
   A Chris can't have seen me.
   B Chris should have seen me.
   C Chris might not have seen me.

6 An old man is trying to carry a heavy box up the stairs. You offer to do it for him.
   A Shall I carry the box for you?
   B Must I carry the box for you?
   C Couldn't I carry the box for you?

7 You and your friend quarrelled about something unimportant. Your mother says it was wrong.
   A You couldn't have quarrelled.
   B You must have quarrelled.
   C You shouldn't have quarrelled.

8 A parcel arrives at your house. You are sure it is from Uncle Peter.
   A It can't be from Uncle Peter.
   B It might be from Uncle Peter.
   C It must be from Uncle Peter.

9 You offer to do the ironing, but your mother says it isn't necessary.
   A You must do the ironing.
   B You could do the ironing.
   C You needn't do the ironing.

10 You want your friend to carry your bag for you.
   A Need you carry my bag for me?
   B Would you carry my bag for me?
   C Shall you carry my bag for me?

23 **Fill in *a, an* or *the* where necessary.**

Mr Webb is 1) ...the... manager of 2) .... large company. He owns 3) .... expensive sports car which he drives to 4) .... office every morning. By the time he arrives at 5) .... work, his secretary has opened 6) .... mail and made 7) .... pot of coffee for him. In 8) .... morning, Mr Webb usually has meetings with 9) .... important clients. He has 10) .... break for 11) .... lunch at twelve o'clock and in 12) .... afternoon he spends 13) .... hour or two catching up with 14) .... paperwork. When he goes 15) .... home in 16) .... evening, he watches 17) .... television or spends 18) .... quiet evening with his family.

24 **Rewrite the following sentences in the passive.**

1 My secretary opens the mail every morning.
   ...The mail is opened by my secretary every morning....
2 A firefighter rescued the young girl.
   ....
3 A gardener is watering the flowers.
   ....
4 Caroline walks the dogs every morning.
   ....
5 Heavy rain had caused the flood.
   ....
6 Police officers were examining the evidence.
   ....
7 A spokesperson gave an interview to the reporters.
   ....
8 An official will take you to your seat.
   ....
9 We are going to announce the results on Friday.
   ....
10 The new manager has made some changes.
   ....
11 The students are making the arrangements for the party.
   ....
12 They clean the windows every week.
   ....

UNIT 9
Conditionals - Wishes - Had Better/Would Rather - Unreal Past

Conditionals

Conditionals are clauses introduced with if. The main types of conditionals are: Type 0, Type 1, Type 2 and Type 3.
Conditional clauses consist of two parts: the if - clause (hypothesis) and the main clause (result). When the if clause comes before the main clause, the two clauses are separated with a comma.

When the main clause comes before the if-clause, then no comma is necessary.

if - clause	main clause
e.g. **If** the weather is good tomorrow,	we will go to the beach.
We will go to the beach	if the weather is good tomorrow.
main clause	if - clause

Type 0 Conditionals (general truth)

If - clause	Main clause
If + present simple	present simple

They are used to express something which is always true. We can use *when* (=whenever) instead of if.

If/When it rains, the roads get slippery and dangerous.

Type 1 Conditionals (real present)

If - clause	Main clause
If + present simple/ present cont./present perfect/present perfect cont.	future/imperative can/may/might/must/ should/could + present bare infinitive

They are used to express real or very probable situations in the present or future.

If we work hard, we'll finish the project on time.

Type 2 Conditionals (unreal present)

If - clause	Main clause
If + past simple or past continuous	would/could/might + present bare infinitive

They are used to express imaginary situations which are contrary to facts in the present and, therefore, are unlikely to happen in the present or future. They are also used to give advice.

Richard is daydreaming.

If I didn't have to work such long hours, I wouldn't be so tired.

Type 3 Conditionals (unreal past)

If - clause	Main clause
If + past perfect/past perfect continuous	would/could/might + perfect bare infinitive

They are used to express imaginary situations which are contrary to facts in the past. They are also used to express regrets or criticism.

Simon made a big mistake because he wasn't careful.

If I had been more careful, I wouldn't have made such a big mistake.

Conditionals - Wishes - Had Better/Would Rather - Unreal Past

Note: Type 1 and Type 2 Conditionals refer to the present or the future. The use of Type 2 Conditionals suggests that the situation is less probable, impossible, or imaginary. Compare the examples:

e.g. a) *If I **meet** Brad Pitt, I'**ll ask** him about his next film. (comment made by a reporter who is going to Hollywood)*
*If I **met** Brad Pitt, I **would ask** for his autograph. (comment made by a teenage fan)*
b) *If I **win** the money, I'**ll buy** a new car. (comment made by a contestant on a TV game show)*
*If I **won** the money, I **would buy** a new car. (comment made by a member of the audience)*

◆ We use *if* to show that something might happen. We use *when* to show that something will definitely happen.
e.g. *If Steve calls, tell him I'll be back in ten minutes. (Steve might call.)*
When Steve calls, tell him I'll be back in ten minutes. (It is certain that Steve will call.)

◆ We can form conditionals by using words/ expressions such as *unless (Type 1 Conditionals), providing/provided that, so/as long as, on condition (that), what if, suppose/supposing, otherwise (= if not), but for, and, or (else), even if, in case of/in the event of*, etc.
e.g. a) ***Unless** you **help** me, I won't finish on time. (= If you don't help me, ...)*
b) *I'll water the plants **providing/provided (that)** I have time this afternoon. (... if I have time ...)*
c) ***So/As long as** you promise to be back by midnight, you can go to the party. (If you promise ...)*
d) *He agreed to work Saturdays **on condition that** he was paid overtime. (... if he was paid ...)*
e) *'I'll take Dad's car tomorrow night.' **'What if** he needs it?' (= What will you do if he needs it?)*
f) ***Suppose/Supposing** you were fired, what would you do? (= If you were fired, ...)*
g) *We'd better leave now. **Otherwise** we'll miss our flight. (If we don't leave now, we'll miss our flight.)*
h) ***But for** your advice, I wouldn't have been able to solve my problems. (If you hadn't advised me, ...)*
i) *Do that again **and** I'll punish you.*
j) *Don't do that again **or (else)** I'll punish you.* } *(If you do that again ...)*
k) *I wouldn't go to the party **even if** they invited me.*
l) ***In case of/In the event of** a fire, sound the alarm. (If there is a fire, ...)*

◆ We do not normally use *will, would* or *should* in an if-clause. However, we can use *will* or *would* after *if* to make a polite request or express insistence or uncertainty (usually with expressions such as *I don't know, I doubt, I wonder*, etc.) In this case, *if* means *whether*. We can also use *should* after *if* to talk about something which is possible, but not very likely to happen.
e.g. a) *If you **will wait** a minute, Mr Carrington will be able to see you. (Will you please wait ... - polite request)*
b) *If you **will go on** making so much noise, I'll send you out. (If you insist on making ... - insistence)*
c) *I **wonder if** he'll call me tomorrow. (I wonder whether ... - uncertainty)*
d) *If Paul **should** turn up, tell him to wait for me. (I don't really expect Paul to turn up.)*

◆ We can use *were* instead of *was* for all persons in the if-clause of Type 2 conditionals.
e.g. *If Andrew **was/were** taller, he could be a basketball player.*
We use *If I were you ...* when we want to give advice.
e.g. *If I **were** you, I wouldn't travel on my own.*

◆ We can omit *if* and use inversion in Type 1, 2 and 3 Conditionals. This structure is more common in formal English.
e.g. a) ***Should he** fail to be re-elected, it would be a great disappointment for him.*
***Were he** more careful, he would make fewer mistakes.*
***Had she** been asked, she would have given her permission.*

1 **Fill in the gaps with *if* or *when* and a verb in the present tense, as in the examples.**

1 We might go for a walk tomorrow. ...*If we go,*... we will take the dog with us.
2 The guests will arrive soon. ...*When they arrive,*... we will greet them at the door.
3 I am going to phone Sam in a minute. .... him, I want you to leave the room.
4 I might visit Pamela tomorrow. .... her, I will buy her a present.
5 The bus comes at eight o'clock. ...., we will all get on it.
6 She might invite us to her party. .... us, we will go.
7 The film will start soon. ...., I will record it.
8 Mark may lend me some money. .... some money, I will buy that jacket.

127

2 Match the items in column A with those in column B in order to make correct Type 0 conditional sentences, as in the example.

e.g. 1 - d ...If you wash woollen clothes in hot water, they shrink....

A	B
1 Wash woollen clothes in hot water.	a They die.
2 Put food in the fridge.	b It becomes ice.
3 Don't water plants.	c It gets rusty.
4 Put water in the freezer.	d They shrink.
5 Leave metal out in the rain.	e It falls to the ground.
6 Drop something.	f It stays fresh for longer.
7 Throw a pebble into the sea.	g You get green.
8 Mix blue and yellow.	h It sinks.

3 *A friend of yours is going to Monaco. You have been there before. What information do you give him/her? First, match the items in column A to the ones in column B, then make sentences, as in the example.*

e.g. ...If you want to stay at a five-star hotel, go to the Hotel de Paris. It's very luxurious....

A
1 stay at a five-star hotel ...g...
2 dine out ....
3 visit a museum ....
4 see a play ....
5 watch athletics events ....
6 see beautiful flowers ....
7 observe wild animals ....
8 go shopping ....

B
a Princess Grace Rose Garden (open every day)
b the Oceanographic Museum (popular with tourists)
c the Casino Square (designer shops)
d André's Restaurant (French food)
e the Louis II Stadium (international competitions)
f the Zoological Gardens (recently modernised)
g the Hotel de Paris (very luxurious)
h the Fort Antoine Theatre (open-air performances)

4 In pairs, ask and answer questions about what you would do in each of the following situations, as in the example. Use your own ideas.

SA: What would you do if you saw someone committing a robbery?

SB: If I saw someone committing a robbery, I would call the police.

1 ... you / see / someone committing a robbery
2 ... you / find / a lot of money
3 ... a fire / start / in your home
4 ... you / have / a headache
5 ... you / see / a stray dog outside your house
6 ... your boss / shout / at you

5 Read the headlines and make a conditional sentence for each, as in the example.

e.g. If the prisoner hadn't escaped, he wouldn't have robbed the bank.

1 ESCAPED PRISONER ROBS BANK

2 STUDENTS' HARD WORK RAISES THOUSANDS FOR CHARITY

3 FOOTBALLER ROWS WITH MANAGER AND QUITS TEAM

4 ACTRESS IN CAR ACCIDENT - FILMING DELAYED

5 BRAVE TEENAGER SAVES CHILD FROM DROWNING

6 HEAVY RAINS CAUSE FLOODING OF CREEK VALLEY

6 Underline the correct form of the verb.

My brother Kevin has always been a fitness fanatic. He believes that if you **1)** *look after/looked after* your body, it will look after you. Whenever anyone is ill, he **2)** *says/will say*, 'If they had taken care of themselves, they **3)** *wouldn't get/ wouldn't have got* ill. And the same thing **4)** *happens /will happen* to me if I **5)** *didn't keep fit/don't keep fit*.' I would often say to him, 'If I were you, Kevin, I **6)** *would try/would have tried* to slow down a little bit. You will wear yourself out.'

Last month, however, I went to the doctor's and he told me that I was unfit. He said that if I **7)** *don't start/didn't start* taking regular exercise, I **8)** *would be/would have been* in danger of becoming ill. I started going to the gym with Kevin and, after a week, I said to him, 'I feel better already. If I **9)** *know/had known* how good it feels to exercise, I **10)** *would start/would have started* years ago!'

Conditionals - Wishes - Had Better/Would Rather - Unreal Past

7 Put the verbs in brackets into the correct tense.

1 She would have come to dinner if we ...*had invited*... (invite) her.
2 If you had locked the door, the burglars .... (not/get) in.
3 Were I you, I .... (put on) some warmer clothes.
4 Joan .... (be able to) come to the party if she wasn't working.
5 Had I heard any news, I .... (tell) you immediately.
6 Paul .... (ruin) his shirt if he climbs that tree.
7 If Mark .... (be) younger, he could join the army.
8 She would have stayed at home if she .... (know) there would be so much traffic.
9 Should he .... (get) this job, he will be able to buy his own flat.
10 If you .... (put) your keys in your pocket, you wouldn't have lost them.
11 She will be here at eight unless she .... (lose) her way.
12 If I were you, I .... (not/go) out in this weather.
13 Emily .... (call) me if she had changed her mind.
14 If you like Tom Cruise, you .... (love) this film.
15 Dave .... (be) home at six o'clock, provided he catches the five o'clock bus.

8 Underline the correct word or expression.

1 I'll lend you the money **on condition that/unless** you pay it back soon.
2 **Even if/But for** her help, I'd be in trouble now.
3 **Unless/Provided** it stops raining, we won't be going to the park.
4 I couldn't lend them the money **even if/or** I wanted to.
5 Try to be here on time, **and/otherwise** we'll miss the beginning of the film.
6 'I'll wear Mum's necklace for the party.' '**What if/Otherwise** you lose it?'
7 **Supposing/Providing** we went to London — what could we do there?
8 Be late again **provided/and** you'll have to see the manager.
9 **In case of/On condition that** an emergency, call this number.
10 You can go to the party **in case of/as long as** you are home before 11 pm.
11 Don't shout **or/what if** you'll wake the baby.

9 Put the verbs in brackets into the correct tense.

1 A: If you ...*pass*... (pass) a bakery, ... (you/buy) some bread, please?
   B: Yes, of course. How much do you need?
2 A: Did you invite Tim to the party?
   B: No, but when I .... (speak) to him, I .... (invite) him.
3 A: May I go out now, please?
   B: Yes, provided you .... (do) your homework.
4 A: Mum seems very busy at the moment.
   B: Were I you, I .... (offer) to help her.
5 A: Hurry up, or else we .... (miss) the train.
   B: I know, I'm being as quick as I can.
6 A: Unless you .... (work) hard, you .... (fail) the exam.
   B: I know. I've been studying every evening.
7 A: I forgot to ask Simon for his phone number.
   B: If I .... (see) him today, I .... (ask) him for you.
8 A: Peter won't help me with my homework.
   B: I'm sure he .... (help) you if he .... (have) the time.
9 A: I'm not going to tell him what happened.
   B: What if he .... (find out) on his own?
10 A: If I .... (not/buy) that lottery ticket, I .... (never/win) all this money!
   B: I know. Isn't it amazing!
11 A: Unless you .... (go) to bed now, you .... (be) tired in the morning.
   B: I know. I'm going.
12 A: I need some wrapping paper.
   B: Well, if I .... (find) any at the shop, I .... (buy) some for you.
13 A: Can I have some chocolate cake, please?
   B: Well, as long as you .... (eat) all your dinner, you can have some chocolate cake.
14 A: I hate going into town.
   B: So do I. Whenever I .... (go) into town, I .... (come back) with a headache.
15 A: You'd better apologise, otherwise he .... (never/speak) to you again.
   B: You're right. I will.

10 Choose the correct answer.

1 'I can't find my wallet.'
   'If I were you, I ...A... in my jacket pocket.'
   A would look   B will look   C am looking

2 'Where is my bank book?'
   'If you .... in the drawer, you'll find it.'
   A had looked   B look   C looked

3 '............ we get up on time, we will catch the train.'
'I will set my alarm clock.'
A Supposing B Providing C Unless

4 'Can I go and play football, please, Mum?'
'If you .... your homework, you can go and play.'
A finished B had finished C have finished

5 'Dad shouted at me today.'
'Well, if you .... the window, he wouldn't have shouted at you.'
A didn't break B hadn't broken C don't break

6 'Why is the baby crying?'
'............ babies are tired or hungry, they cry.'
A When B Providing C Supposing

7 'When ice melts, it .... water.'
'Everyone knows that!'
A becomes B will become C would become

8 'I'm going to a party tonight.'
'If I wasn't ill, I .... with you.'
A come B will come C would come

9 '............ we miss the bus, what will we do?'
'Call a taxi.'
A Supposing B Providing C When

10 'If I were rich, I .... around the world.'
'Perhaps you will one day.'
A will sail B can sail C could sail

11 'Have you seen Daniel recently?'
'No. If I have time, I .... him tomorrow.'
A would visit B might visit C visit

12 'Paul lost his watch.'
'Well, if he had looked after it, he .... it.'
A wouldn't lose B won't lose C wouldn't have lost

13 '............ you hurry, you will be late for school.'
'I'm nearly ready now.'
A Unless B Providing C Supposing

14 'If you hadn't watched that film, you .... nightmares.'
'You're right.'
A wouldn't have had B won't have C don't have

11 **Complete the following sentences with an appropriate conditional clause.**

1 Were I you, ...*I'd go to the police.* ....
2 If I hadn't met her, ...
3 Only if you work hard, ...
4 If they had been more careful, ...
5 If I won a lot of money, ...
6 Unless it rains, ...
7 I would have told you earlier, ...
8 But for your suggestions, ...
9 Should Annie phone, ...
10 If you had tried harder, ...

Mixed Conditionals

We can form mixed conditionals, if the context permits it, by combining an if - clause from one type with a main clause from another.

If - clause	Main clause
Type 2	**Type 1**
If she **got** back late last night,	she **won't come** to work today.
Type 2	**Type 3**
If you **were** more sensible,	you **wouldn't have spoken** to your boss like that.
Type 3	**Type 2**
If she **hadn't missed** the bus,	she **would be** here now.

12 **Rewrite the following as mixed conditional sentences.**

1 She didn't study hard. She won't pass the exams.
...*If she had studied hard, she would pass the exams.*...
2 You didn't wake me up. Now I'm late for my appointment.
....
3 She isn't well-qualified. She didn't get the job.
....
4 We didn't go to the restaurant. We don't like fast food.
....
5 She didn't bring her umbrella. Now, she's getting wet.
....
6 I don't know them very well, so I didn't go to the party.
....
7 He isn't at the lecture because he wasn't told about it.
....
8 They didn't take a map with them. They're lost now.
....
9 The driver isn't careful. He crashed his car into a wall.
....
10 I didn't buy tickets. We can't go to the theatre tonight.
....
11 He didn't reserve a table. He has to wait for an hour.
....
12 Sue forgot to go to the bank. Now she can't go shopping.
....
13 They missed their flight. They won't arrive until tomorrow.
....

Wishes

◆ We use the verb *wish* and the expression *if only* to express a wish. *If only* is more emphatic than *I wish*.

◆ **wish/if only + past simple/past continuous**
This structure is used when we want to say that we would like something to be different in the present.

> *I wish/If only I didn't have to take the train to work every day.*

◆ **wish/if only + past perfect**
This structure is used to express regret that something happened or did not happen in the past.

> *I wish/If only I hadn't stolen the motorbike.*

◆ **wish/if only + would**
This structure is used: a) **for a polite imperative.**
b) **to express our desire for a change in a situation or someone's behaviour.**

> *I wish you would pay more attention!*

> *I wish/If only he wouldn't give me so much work.*

◆ After the subject pronouns *I* and *we*, we use *could* instead of *would*.
e.g. *I wish I could travel abroad.* (NOT: *I wish I would travel ...*)

Note: We can use *were* instead of *was* after *wish* or *if only*.
e.g. *I wish he were/was more careful.*

---

13 Match the items in column A with those in column B to make complaints using *would/wouldn't*. Then, decide which person from the list is making each complaint.

shopkeeper, businessman, traffic warden, flight attendant, doctor, campsite owner, lifeguard

e.g. *1 - e ...'I wish my staff would get to work on time', says the businessman....*

A	B
1 I wish my staff ...	**a** take their medication properly
2 If only drivers ...	**b** be more polite
3 I wish passengers ...	**c** not light fires in the forest
4 If only the customers ...	**d** park illegally
5 I wish campers ...	**e** get to work on time
6 If only patients ...	**f** follow the safety regulations
7 I wish bathers ...	**g** put their luggage in the lockers

14 Put the verbs in brackets into the correct tense.

1 A: I wish Paul ...*would tell*... (tell) me what is wrong with him.
   B: Yes. He seems very upset, doesn't he?
2 A: I wish I .... (not/shout) at the children like that.
   B: Why? They were being very naughty.
3 A: I wish you .... (tidy) your room more often.
   B: Sorry. I'll try to.
4 A: I wish I .... (practise) harder before the concert.
   B: I thought you performed very well.
5 A: If only Stuart .... (call) me.
   B: Don't worry. I'm sure he'll phone soon.
6 A: I wish I .... (be) back at school again.
   B: Those were great days, weren't they?
7 A: I wish Mark .... (stop) playing his music so loudly.
   B: Why don't you ask him to turn it down?
8 A: If only I .... (buy) those shoes we saw today.
   B: Why not go back and buy them tomorrow?
9 A: I wish you .... (try) harder with your Maths homework.
   B: Sorry. I find it very difficult.
10 A: If only we .... (go) to France last summer.
   B: We could go this year if you like.

11 A: I wish I .... (afford) some new CDs.
    B: Would you like to borrow some of mine?

12 A: If only it .... (stop) raining.
    B: Yes. Then we could go for a walk.

13 A: Are you going to Joanne's party on Saturday?
    B: No. I wish I .... (go), because I'm sure it will be fun.

14 A: I wish you .... (help) with the housework more often.
    B: What would you like me to do?

15 A: I'm bored. I wish I .... (arrange) to go out this evening.
    B: I'm going to the cinema. Why don't you come, too?

15 Look at the pictures and complete the wishes. Also make mixed conditional sentences, as in the example.

1

> I should have brought my umbrella.

I wish *I had brought my umbrella.* (not / be / so wet)
If I had brought my umbrella, I wouldn't be so wet now.

2

> I should have booked a room.

I wish ....
(have / somewhere to stay)
....

3

> I shouldn't have eaten so much chocolate.

I wish ....
(not feel / so ill)
....

4

> I shouldn't have touched the iron.

I wish ....
(my hand / not hurt so much)
....

5

> I should have got up earlier.

I wish ....
(not be / late now)
....

16 Fill in the gaps with an appropriate auxiliary verb.

1 I don't know many people, but I wish I ...*did*... .
2 He can't drive, but he wishes he ....
3 We didn't move house, but we wish we ....
4 I'm not very wealthy, but I wish I ....
5 She probably won't help me, but I wish she ....
6 He hasn't got any pets, but he wishes he ....
7 They don't go out very often, but they wish they ....
8 He won't listen to my advice, but I wish he ....

17 Read the text and complete the sentences below using *Type 3 Conditionals*, as in the example.

    The 'Titanic' was a British luxury passenger liner which sank during its maiden voyage from Southampton to New York in 1912. On 14th April, the 'Titanic' hit an iceberg in the Atlantic Ocean. Distress signals were sent to the 'Californian', a ship 20 miles away, but their radio operator was off duty and the signals were not received. Some of the passengers got into lifeboats, but, although the 'Titanic' was luxurious, it did not have enough lifeboats for all the passengers on board. As a result, the loss of life was great. Many people died because the sea was very cold. Luckily, another ship, the 'Carpathia', rescued some of the passengers. As a result of this disaster, new rules were made to ensure that sea voyages would be safer in the future. It is now believed that the 'Titanic' sank so quickly because it was too large.

1 If the ship had not hit an iceberg, ...*it wouldn't have sunk*....
2 If the 'Californian's' radio operator had been on duty, ...
....
3 If the 'Titanic' had had enough lifeboats, ...
....
4 If the sea hadn't been so cold, ...
....
5 If the 'Carpathia' had not arrived, ...
....
6 If the 'Titanic' had not sunk, ...
....
7 If the 'Titanic' had not been so big, ...
....

Had Better / Would Rather

◆ **Had better + bare infinitive (= should/ought)**
This structure is used to give advice or to say what the best thing to do in a particular situation is.
e.g. You had/'d better book your flight early.
I'd better not take out a loan; I won't be able to pay it back.

Had better is more emphatic than should/ought to, but it is not as emphatic as must.
e.g. You must see a lawyer. (strong advice)
You had better see a lawyer. (less emphatic than must)
You should/ought to see a lawyer. (less emphatic than had better)

◆ **Would rather (= would prefer to) expresses preference.**

When the subject of *would rather* is also the subject of the following verb, we use the following constructions:

a) **would rather + present bare infinitive (present/future)**
e.g. I'd rather do my shopping tomorrow.
b) **would rather + perfect bare infinitive (past)**
e.g. I'd rather not have gone to the dinner party last night.
c) **would rather + bare infinitive + than (+ bare infinitive)**
e.g. I'd rather watch a comedy than (watch) a thriller.

When the subject of *would rather* is different from the subject of the following verb, we use the following constructions:

a) **would rather + past tense (present/future)**
e.g. I'd rather Kate stayed with us tonight.
b) **would rather + past perfect (past)**
e.g. I'd rather Sam hadn't taken his father's car yesterday.

We can also use prefer in the following constructions to express preference:

a) **prefer+ -ing form + to + -ing form (general preference)**
e.g. I prefer playing tennis to playing squash.
b) **prefer+ full infinitive + rather than + bare infinitive (general preference)**
e.g. I prefer to eat fish rather than (eat) meat.
c) **prefer+ noun+ to + noun (general preference)**
e.g. He prefers basketball to football.
d) **would prefer + full infinitive + rather than + bare infinitive (specific preference)**
e.g. a) I'd prefer to walk home rather than take the bus.
b) I'd prefer to have juice rather than (have) Coke.

18 **Answer the following questions using *would rather ...... because* and your own ideas.**

1 Your parents have offered to take you to Rome on holiday and your best friend has invited you to join him/her in Majorca. Where would you prefer to go?
e.g....I'd rather go to Majorca because I love being by the sea....

2 You have received two invitations. One is for a film premiére and one is for a rock concert. Which would you rather go to?

3 You have recently won the lottery jackpot. Would you rather have all of the money at once, or a set amount every month?

4 You need some extra money. Would you rather spend your evenings babysitting or get a paper round in the mornings?

5 Your parents have offered to buy you a present. Would you rather have some new clothes or a pair of rollerblades?

6 You have lost the watch which your parents bought you and you know they will be angry. Would you rather buy yourself a new watch and pretend nothing has happened, or tell your parents the truth?

19 **Put the verbs in brackets into the correct form.**

1 A: I'm going out in a minute.
  B: So am I, so you'd better ...*take*... (take) your keys with you.
2 A: Do you watch much television?
  B: No. I prefer .... (read) books to .... (watch) television.
3 A: I didn't enjoy the concert much.
  B: Nor did I! I would rather they .... (play) more modern music.
4 A: Shall we go to that new restaurant this evening?
  B: Good idea. We had better .... (book) a table.
5 A: Shall I tidy your bedroom for you?
  B: I'd rather you .... (not/tidy) it. I'll do it later.
6 A: Shall we go for a walk this afternoon?
  B: No. I would prefer .... (stay) here and read a book.
7 A: My brother prefers .... (play) computer games to .... (do) his homework.
  B: So does mine.
8 A: Did you enjoy the play last night?
  B: No. I'd rather .... (go) to the cinema.
9 A: I'd rather you .... (not/make) so much noise.
  B: Sorry. I'll try to be quiet.
10 A: You had better .... (work) hard at your new job.
  B: I will. I want to make a good impression.

11 A: Paul has bought Tania a present.
    B: Yes, but we'd better .... (not/mention) it. It might be a surprise.

12 A: Did you enjoy the party last night?
    B: Yes, but I would rather we .... (stay) a little longer.

13 A: Shall we spend the evening together?
    B: Well, actually, I'd prefer .... (spend) some time alone.

14 A: That meal was terrible. I'd rather .... (eat) at home.
    B: It was very expensive, too.

15 A: It's the company's office party tomorrow.
    B: Yes. To be honest, I'd rather .... (not/go).

The Unreal Present and Past

The *past simple* can be used to refer to the present (unreal present) when we talk about imaginary, unreal or improbable situations which are contrary to facts in the present.

The *past perfect* can be used to refer to imaginary, unreal or improbable situations which are contrary to facts in the past (unreal past).

The past simple is used with:

- **Type 2 Conditionals**
  e.g. *If he had the money, he would buy a new car.*
- **suppose/supposing**
  e.g. *Suppose/Supposing he stood you up, what would you do?*
- **wish/if only**
  e.g. *I wish/If only I had a better job.*
- **would rather (present)**
  e.g. *I'd rather Nick drove me to the station.*
- **as if/as though**
  e.g. *Mary talks as if/as though she knew everything.*
- **it's (about/high) time**
  e.g. *It's (about/high) time you went to bed.*

The past perfect is used with:

- **Type 3 Conditionals**
  e.g. *If she hadn't fallen down the stairs, she wouldn't have broken her arm.*
- **suppose/supposing**
  e.g. *Suppose/Supposing you had been invited, would you have gone?*
- **wish/if only**
  e.g. *I wish/If only I hadn't argued with him.*
- **would rather (past)**
  e.g. *I'd rather you had kept it a secret.*
- **as if/as though**
  e.g. *He had never been abroad, but he spoke about New York as if/as though he had been there many times.*

20 Underline the correct tense.

1 I'd rather you **did**/**had done** your homework before you go out.
2 Supposing you **had heard**/**had been heard** telling me, what would have happened?
3 He acted as if he **owns**/**owned** the house.
4 I wish I **went**/**had gone** to the library yesterday.
5 I would have made a cake if I **know**/**had known** you were coming.
6 It's about time we **employed**/**had employed** some new staff.
7 If she **had won**/**won** the competition, she would have had a party.
8 I'd rather you **didn't interrupt**/**hadn't interrupted** me when I'm talking.
9 Suppose you **saw**/**had seen** a crime being committed, what would you do?
10 If only you **told**/**had told** me, I would have understood.
11 He would have sent a card if he **realised**/**had realised** it was your birthday.
12 If you **met**/**had met** John now, you wouldn't recognise him.
13 It's high time you **learnt**/**had learnt** how to drive.
14 I'd rather you **hadn't misbehaved**/**didn't misbehave** at the party last night.
15 They spoke as if they **knew**/**had known** each other for years.

21 Put the verbs in brackets into the correct form.

1 Would you rather ...*come*... (come) shopping with me or stay at home?
2 If only I .... (not/confide) in her; now everybody knows my problems.
3 Amy says she would rather .... (organise) the event herself.
4 I'd rather you .... (get) a full-time job than a part-time job.
5 Supposing I invited you to a party, ... (you/accept)?
6 I wish I .... (ask) my parents for some advice before I made up my mind.
7 Suppose you .... (meet) a film star, what would you say?
8 She didn't understand the question, but she looked as though she .... (understand) it.
9 Liz studied Art at university, but she says she would rather .... (study) History.
10 I wish Alan .... (not/move) away, as I miss him a lot.
11 It seemed as if she .... (forget) about the meeting.
12 If you hadn't left early, you .... (meet) Tim.

IN OTHER WORDS

Study these examples. The second sentence has a similar meaning to the first sentence.

1 I don't think it's a good idea to lie to your parents about what happened.

were If **I were you**, I wouldn't lie to my parents about what happened.

2 If you sit next to the fireplace, you'll get too hot.

else Don't sit next to the fireplace **or else you'll get** too hot.

3 It rained heavily all day, so they didn't go out.

for But **for the heavy rain**, they would have gone out.

4 If you don't act quickly, you may find yourself in trouble.

unless You may find yourself in trouble **unless you act** quickly.

5 Sam ran out of time; that's why he didn't go shopping.

would If Sam hadn't run out of time, he **would have gone** shopping.

6 If Helen gets a grant, she will be able to continue her studies.

provided Helen will be able to continue her studies **provided she gets** a grant.

7 Tony wants to buy a new car, but he hasn't got enough money.

wishes Tony **wishes he had** enough money to buy a new car.

8 Jack would prefer to learn Italian rather than learn German.

rather Jack **would rather learn** Italian than German.

9 Mary regrets not studying hard for her exams.

wishes Mary **wishes she had studied** hard for her exams.

10 You should join a gym.

better You **had better join** a gym.

11 Why don't you make an effort to improve your life?

would I **wish you would make** an effort to improve your life.

12 It's a pity I missed your graduation.

wish I **wish I hadn't missed** your graduation.

---

22 **Complete each sentence with two to five words, including the word in bold.**

1 You will be late for school unless you leave now.

if You will be late for school ...*if you don't leave*... now.

2 If you touch the iron, you will burn your fingers.

else Don't touch the iron, ... burn your fingers.

3 I don't think it's a good idea to buy that jacket.

were If ...., I wouldn't buy that jacket.

4 I want to have a party, but my flat isn't big enough.

wish I .... big enough for me to have a party.

5 You shouldn't go out tonight; you have to go to school tomorrow.

better You .... out tonight; you have to go to school tomorrow.

6 John would prefer to eat pizza rather than chips.

rather John .... pizza than chips.

7 Jane regrets spending all that money on new clothes.

wishes Jane .... all that money on new clothes.

8 It's a pity I didn't make it to your wedding.

wish I .... it to your wedding.

9 Colin wishes he hadn't missed the bus; now he is late for work.

missed If Colin .... the bus, he wouldn't be late for work.

10 If the weather gets better, we'll go on a sailing trip tomorrow.

provided We'll go on a sailing trip, ... better tomorrow.

11 You should write a letter to your pen-friend.

better You .... to your pen-friend.

12 Samantha wants to be a model, but she isn't tall enough.

wishes Samantha .... to be a model.

13 Why don't you wipe your feet when you come back from the park?

would I .... your feet when you come back from the park.

14 If you don't stop being naughty, I will tell the headmaster.

else Stop being naughty, ... the headmaster.

15 Sam would prefer to go out rather than stay at home.

rather Sam .... than stay at home.

16 It's a pity I didn't go to that party.

wish I .... that party.

17 I didn't know your address; that's why I didn't send you a postcard.

would If I had known your address, I .... you a postcard.

18 He wouldn't have finished his report if you hadn't helped him.

for But ...., he wouldn't have finished his report.

19 If you exceed the speed limit, you'll have to pay a fine.

else Don't exceed the speed limit, ... have to pay a fine.

20 If you don't practise daily, you will never learn to play the piano.

unless You will never learn to play the piano .... daily.

23 Fill in the gaps with the correct form of the words in brackets.

1 She has lost a lot of ...*weight*... recently. (weigh)
2 Due to his .... to add up properly, he made a big mistake in the accounts book. ((in) able)
3 I .... with what you are saying. In fact, I am of the exact opposite opinion. (agree)
4 He has made many successful .... investments. (finance)
5 That man is involved in lots of .... activities, but the police can't prove anything at the moment. (legal)
6 A mistake in this chemical formula could be .... (disaster)
7 I don't want him to babysit for me. He's too .... (responsible)
8 Tom is very .... and works hard to achieve his goals. (ambition)
9 The project is .... There is no way we can make it work. (practical)
10 He doesn't speak very good French, which is why he .... the woman's question. (understand)
11 Mr Webb is a very .... man in the business world. (influence)
12 It's .... that the plan will go ahead, since there is very little money available at the moment. (likely)
13 I am often .... of the water in foreign countries. (suspicion)
14 It must be wonderful to be .... (wealth)
15 His good .... background helped him to get the job. (education)
16 We found his collection of modern paintings quite .... He even possessed a genuine Picasso! (impress)

24 Fill in the gaps with the correct form of the words in brackets.

A Tom made the **1)** ...*decision*...(decide) to have a party. He sent **2)** .... (invite) to twenty of his friends and all of them came, with the **3)** .... (except) of David, who had already made **4)** .... (arrange) for that evening.

B Alison attended a job interview last week and the company made her a very **1)** .... (attract) offer. She has just written a letter of **2)** .... (accept) to the **3)** .... (manage) of the company and she hopes to receive **4)** .... (confirm) of her **5)** .... (employ) soon.

C My aunt collects **1)** .... (value) paintings. It is a rather **2)** .... (expense) hobby, but she considers each picture she buys to be an **3)** .... (invest). If she ever sold her **4)** .... (collect), it would make an **5)** .... ((un)believe) amount of money.

Common mistakes

- **If you will finish** early, give me a call. ✗
  If you finish early, give me a call. ✓

- **Unless we don't pay** the bill, the phone will be cut off. ✗
  Unless we pay the bill, the phone will be cut off. ✓

- **I wish we would** buy a bigger house. ✗
  I wish we could buy a bigger house. ✓

- We'd **better to cut down on** our expenses. ✗
  We'd **better cut down on** our expenses. ✓

- **You'd not better talk** to him about it. ✗
  You'd better not talk to him about it. ✓

- We **would better** leave now. ✗
  We **had better** leave now. ✓

- **I'd rather** Greg **goes** to medical school. ✗
  I'd rather Greg **went** to medical school. ✓

- **It's high time** you **redecorate** your flat. ✗
  It's high time you **redecorated** your flat. ✓

25 Correct the mistakes.

1 You'd not better be late for your interview.
2 We would better go soon.
3 It's high time you tidy your bedroom.
4 We'd better to do the washing-up.
5 I'd rather the guests come at eight o'clock.
6 Unless you don't study, you won't pass the exams.
7 I wish we would afford a new car.
8 If you will need any help, just call me.

26 Cross out the unnecessary word.

1 You'd better to apply to a university in your country.
2 As long as you will book early, you won't have a problem finding a seat.
3 I wish if someone would do something about it.
4 John would rather his sister had made less noise every time she comes back from a party.
5 It's time Paul had stopped acting like a child.
6 They won't let you in unless you will wear a suit and tie.
7 Unless you not ask him, he won't come.
8 Even if he offered to lend me the money, or I wouldn't take it.
9 I prefer playing cards than to playing board games.
10 Had if we been there, we would have offered to help.
11 Emma would rather to study Medicine than Chemistry.
12 If they will practise hard, they may win the match.

Conditionals - Wishes - Had Better/Would Rather - Unreal Past

Phrasal Verbs

pay back:	(tr) 1) return money owed, 2) get revenge on sb
pay for:	(tr) receive punishment for a wrongdoing
pull down:	(tr) demolish a structure
pull in:	(int) (of trains, etc) arrive, **draw in** (opp: **pull out**)
pull through:	(int) survive
pull up:	(int) slow down and stop
put aside:	(tr) save; **put by**
put away:	put sb into prison or mental hospital
put back:	(tr) cause to be delayed
put down:	(tr) 1) make a note; **write down**, 2) pay a deposit for sth
put down to:	(tr) attribute sth to sth else
put off:	(tr) 1) postpone, 2) discourage sb from liking sth
put on:	(tr) 1) dress oneself in, 2) increase (in weight), 3) switch on, 4) pretend, 5) cause to take place (show/performance)
put out:	(tr) 1) extinguish (fire, etc), 2) cause inconvenience to sb
put through:	(tr) 1) connect by telephone, 2) make sb undergo or suffer sth
put up:	(tr) 1) offer sth for sale 2) (of prices) increase, 3) offer hospitality (put sb up)
put up with:	tolerate; bear

27 Fill in the correct particle.

1 The train pulled ...in... at the station and hundreds of people got off.
2 The taxi pulled .... outside my house. I paid the driver and got out.
3 Put your ideas .... on paper and I'll look at them later.
4 I'll put you .... to the correct department, madam.
5 Put .... your gloves. It's very cold outside.
6 Walter's parents tried to put him .... becoming an artist.
7 She put her tiredness .... the fact that she had been working very hard.
8 Ignore James. He's not really ill, he's just putting it ....
9 That shop has put .... its prices again.
10 Kelly is trying to put .... some money every week for her summer holidays.
11 The firemen put the fire .... very quickly.
12 You'll just have to put .... the noise until the repairs are finished, I'm afraid.
13 The snowstorm caused the team's expedition to be put .... a few days.

14 Gordon vowed to pay Steve .... for what he had done to him.
15 We put .... going on holiday because I was very busy at work.
16 The drama group are putting .... their first performance next month.
17 Alice said to Jane, 'You'll pay .... this one day.'
18 The young soldiers were put .... strict training in the first few weeks.
19 His house was put .... for sale after he lost his job.
20 He put .... a deposit of £100 when he booked the holiday.
21 He borrowed £20 from me but he still hasn't paid it ....
22 I'll put you .... for the night if you can't find a hotel.
23 It was a serious operation, but the patient pulled ....
24 If you don't stop eating sweets, you'll put .... weight.
25 I don't want to put you ...., but could you babysit for me tonight, please?
26 All the old buildings in this area are going to be pulled ....
27 Put the television .... if you're bored.
28 The public called for the criminal to be put .... for a long time.

 28 Fill in the gaps with the correct preposition from the list. Some prepositions can be used more than once.

at, by, for, in, on, out of, off, under, to, with

1 She wrote the report ...by... hand, as the computer wasn't working.
2 You look worried. What's .... your mind?
3 .... Tim's surprise, his boss gave him a bonus.
4 Passengers must check in .... arrival at the airport.
5 He's saving money .... a view to buying a car.
6 Don't worry. I've got everything .... control.
7 He was .... breath after running for ten minutes.
8 I think I'll have a sandwich. .... second thoughts, I'll have a salad.
9 Steve has not been .... touch with us recently.
10 We must put out the fire .... all costs.
11 People living in developing countries are .... need of our help.
12 Where have you been? I've been waiting .... ages.
13 James is .... a bad mood today.
14 Medicine should be kept .... reach of children.
15 This hotel is the cheapest on the island .... far.
16 Her name is Joanna, but we call her Jo .... short.
17 She searched .... vain for the missing money.
18 I don't believe in love .... first sight.

Revision Box

29 Choose the correct answer.

1 'You ...*B*... talk during the exam.'
  'I know. I'll be quiet.'
  A needn't   **B** mustn't   **C** must

2 '............ you carry this bag for me, please?'
  'Yes, of course.'
  A Must   **B** Shall   **C** Can

3 'James apologised .... shouting at me.'
  'That's good.'
  A at   **B** to   **C** for

4 'I'll give you .... your book tomorrow.'
  'Okay. I don't need it at the moment.'
  A back   **B** off   **C** out

5 'The roads are clear now.'
  'Yes. The snow .... by the Council this morning.'
  A is cleared   **B** was cleared   **C** cleared

6 'Dinner .... by Mark tonight.'
  'That's very kind of him!'
  A cooked   **B** is cooked   **C** will be cooked

7 'What is Jeff worried .... ?'
  'I don't know.'
  A with   **B** of   **C** about

8 'They own a yacht.'
  'I know. They .... be well-off.'
  A can   **B** can't   **C** must

9 'I think the milk has gone ....'
  'Throw it away, then.'
  A off   **B** out   **C** after

10 'The doors ....'
  'Good. Let's go to bed, then.'
  A have been locked   **B** were being locked
  C locked

11 'Is Peter good .... Science?'
  'Yes, he's the best in the class.'
  A for   **B** at   **C** in

12 'That parcel .... yesterday.'
  'I wonder who it's from.'
  A was delivered   **B** is delivered   **C** are delivered

13 'I .... clean the house today. It's dirty.'
  'I'll help you this afternoon.'
  A must   **B** can   **C** mustn't

14 'You .... make a noise in the library.'
  'I know. People are trying to read.'
  A can   **B** mustn't   **C** won't

30 Choose the correct answer.

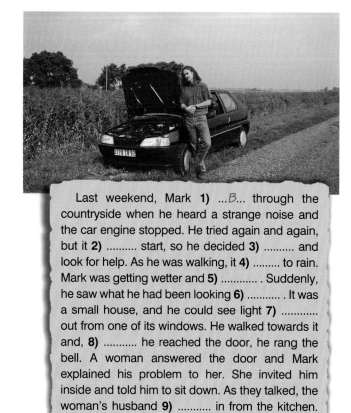

Last weekend, Mark **1)** ...*B*... through the countryside when he heard a strange noise and the car engine stopped. He tried again and again, but it **2)** .... start, so he decided **3)** .... and look for help. As he was walking, it **4)** .... to rain. Mark was getting wetter and **5)** .... Suddenly, he saw what he had been looking **6)** .... It was a small house, and he could see light **7)** .... out from one of its windows. He walked towards it and, **8)** .... he reached the door, he rang the bell. A woman answered the door and Mark explained his problem to her. She invited him inside and told him to sit down. As they talked, the woman's husband **9)** .... in from the kitchen. When Mark's clothes had dried a little, the man suggested **10)** .... Mark back to his car. Mark asked the man if he could take him home instead, and said that he **11)** .... and collect his car **12)** ....

1 **A** drove   **B** was driving   **C** had driven
2 **A** wouldn't   **B** couldn't   **C** wasn't able to
3 **A** getting out   **B** to get out   **C** get out
4 **A** was starting **B** had started   **C** started
5 **A** wet   **B** wettest   **C** wetter
6 **A** for   **B** after   **C** at
7 **A** shine   **B** shining   **C** to shine
8 **A** when   **B** while   **C** before
9 **A** would come   **B** had come   **C** came
10 **A** driving   **B** drive   **C** to drive
11 **A** will go back **B** would go back   **C** went back
12 **A** tomorrow   **B** next morning   **C** the next morning

138

Conditionals - Wishes - Had Better/Would Rather - Unreal Past

Revision Box

 31 **Turn the following sentences into reported speech.**

1 'Why are you in such a hurry?' she asked me.
   ...*She asked me why I was in such a hurry*....

2 'I met some friends in town,' Brian said. (up-to-date reporting)
   ....

3 'Where did you go last night?' he asked her.
   ....

4 'I would go out tonight if I didn't have to work,' she said.
   ....

5 'You should ask your teacher for help,' he told her.
   ....

6 'Clean up this mess!' he said to them.
   ....

7 'Birds make nests in trees,' he said to me.
   ....

8 'Belgium is a small country,' he told us.
   ....

9 'I'll help you paint the garage,' he said. (out-of-date reporting)
   ....

10 'You can visit whenever you like,' she said to him. (up-to-date reporting)
   ....

 32 **Write sentences using *have something done*, as in the example.**

1 Josie's mum is going to cut her hair for her.
   ...*Josie is going to have her hair cut by her mum*....

2 We must ask the carpenter to mend those cupboards.
   ....

3 Ask Sam to do the shopping for you.
   ....

4 Tony's tooth was taken out yesterday.
   ....

5 The doctor is examining Claire's broken leg.
   ....

6 James asked for the parcel to be sent first-class.
   ....

7 We didn't go out. We asked for a pizza to be delivered.
   ....

8 Frank asked the shop assistant to wrap the gift for him.
   ....

 **ORAL**
Activity

Answer the questions below using *I wish ...*, then justify your answer using the correct conditional type, as in the example.

1 Which country in the world would you most like to visit?
   e.g. I wish I could visit India. If I ever visited India, I would visit the Taj Mahal.

2 What object would you most like to own?
   e.g. I wish I had ...

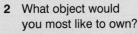

3 Who would you most like to meet?
   e.g. I wish I could meet ...

4 What talent would you most like to have?
   e.g. I wish I could ...

5 What period in history would you most like to have lived in?
   e.g. I wish I had lived in ...

6 What do you regret having done?
   e.g. I wish I hadn't ...

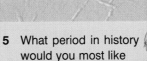

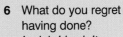

139

Revision 3 (Units 1 - 9)

1   Choose the correct answer.

1 If you ...*C*... your room, you can go out to play.
A tidied   **B** had tidied   **C** have tidied

2 Alan apologised for .... Jane's birthday.
A forgetting   **B** to forget   **C** forget

3 You .... report the burglary to the police.
A can't   **B** might   **C** ought to

4 If I feel better tonight, I .... to the party.
A would go   **B** might go   **C** go

5 Malcolm hates ...., so he often eats out.
A cook   **B** cooking   **C** to cook

6 That picture .... by someone very famous.
A painted   **B** is painting   **C** was painted

7 Sam .... for his wallet for hours before he found it.
A has been searching   **B** had been searching
C had searched

8 They advised me .... for some help.
A asking   **B** ask   **C** to ask

9 They are identical twins and I can't .... one from the other.
A told   **B** tell   **C** say

10 That office block is much .... than this one.
A taller   **B** tall   **C** tallest

11 They had lots of potatoes so they .... buy any more.
A didn't need to   **B** mustn't   **C** couldn't

12 .... the bank is closed, what will we do?
A Unless   **B** Providing   **C** Supposing

13 Jack broke his leg while he .... last winter.
A is skiing   **B** was skiing   **C** skiied

14 If you .... in such a hurry, you wouldn't have forgotten the file.
A hadn't left   **B** didn't leave   **C** haven't left

15 If I were you, I .... a letter of complaint.
A write   **B** will write   **C** would write

16 Melissa .... in a very busy office now.
A works   **B** has worked   **C** was working

17 He denied .... his mother's vase.
A break   **B** breaking   **C** to break

18 .... he's with his friends, he's very talkative.
A Providing   **B** When   **C** Supposing

19 The boys admitted .... the window.
A smash   **B** to smash   **C** smashing

20 I don't mind .... In fact, I quite enjoy it.
A iron   **B** to iron   **C** ironing

21 He .... me not to go near the river.
A exclaimed   **B** warned   **C** demanded

22 Nothing will stop her from .... out.
A move   **B** to move   **C** moving

23 He was the .... person in the competition. He knew all the answers.
A cleverest   **B** clever   **C** cleverer

24 If the temperature rises above 0°C, ice ....
A melts   **B** would melt   **C** might melt

25 They .... be friends. They never speak to each other.
A would   **B** could   **C** can't

26 If you .... to open the box, you wouldn't have broken it.
A didn't try   **B** hadn't tried   **C** haven't tried

27 He enjoys .... time by himself.
A to spend   **B** spending   **C** spend

28 .... I take your order now, madam?
A Should   **B** Must   **C** May

29 You .... finish that exercise before you leave today.
A must   **B** can't   **C** would

30 You .... close the door. I like to leave it open.
A couldn't   **B** must   **C** needn't

31 .... you leave now, you won't miss the start of the film.
A Supposing   **B** Providing   **C** Unless

32 If you had arrived earlier, you .... dinner.
A wouldn't have missed   **B** won't have missed
C won't miss

33 If he had some money, he .... on holiday.
A could go   **B** can go   **C** will go

34 He .... that she was the most beautiful girl he'd ever seen.
A warned   **B** denied   **C** exclaimed

35 They .... on paying for the meal.
A claimed   **B** demanded   **C** insisted

2 Complete each sentence with two to five words, including the word in bold.

1 'You must pay for the tickets by Friday,' he said to me.
on He ...*insisted on my paying*... for the tickets by Friday.

2 I didn't see the car until it was too late.
did Not until it was .... the car.

3 You will miss the bus unless you leave now.
if You will miss the bus ....
.... now.

4 I want to go on holiday, but I can't afford it.
wish I .... to go on holiday.

5 If I were you, I would apologise.
you Were .... apologise.

6 'Don't forget to lock the car door,' Dad said to Bill.
reminded Dad .... the car door.

7 She had no idea she had gone to the wrong house.
know Little .... had gone to the wrong house.

8 If you wake up early tomorrow, we'll go shopping together.
provided We'll go shopping together ....
.... early tomorrow.

9 'I broke Jane's doll,' the boy said.
admitted The boy .... Jane's doll.

10 If you don't stop shouting, I will tell the teacher.
else Stop shouting, ... the teacher.

11 If you don't study hard, you won't pass your exams.
unless You won't pass your exams ....
.... hard.

12 Don't touch anything while I'm away on any account.
should On no account ....
.... anything while I'm away.

13 'I don't suppose you know where Alison is, do you?' Liz said to me.
whether Liz wanted to know ....
.... Alison was.

14 They had never heard such an interesting story before.
before Never .... such an interesting story.

15 Ruth would prefer to stay at home than go to the party.
rather Ruth .... than go to the party.

16 'I didn't leave the gate open,' he said.
denied He .... the gate open.

17 Caroline regrets shouting at her friend yesterday.
wishes Caroline .... at her friend yesterday.

18 I rarely went to the cinema before I got married.
go Hardly ever .... the cinema before I got married.

19 If I had realised what time it was, I wouldn't have called.
realised Had .... was, I wouldn't have called.

20 'What a fantastic view!' they said.
exclaimed They .... a fantastic view.

3 Turn the following sentences into reported speech.

1 'Be quiet!' the teacher said to the boys.
...*The teacher ordered the boys to be quiet*....
2 'Would you like to come to my party?' she said to him.
3 'I'm the fastest runner in the school,' Paul said.
....
4 'I'll phone you every week while I'm away,' she said to him.
....
5 'Don't go near the waterfall,' he said to us.
....
6 'Could you lend me some money?' she said to her brother.
....
7 'Everyone wait outside!' the boss said to his employees.
....
8 'Can I borrow your pen?' she said to the man.
....
9 'Would you like to help me make dinner?' Mum said to me.
....
10 'I didn't borrow your football,' he said to Tom.
....
11 'Don't forget to water the plants,' Mum said to me.
....
12 'I'm sorry I was late,' he said to her.
....
13 'Let's go for a walk,' Linda said.
....
14 'I've got toothache,' Adam said.
....
15 'Please, please help me,' she said to him.
....

4 Put the verbs in brackets into the correct tense.

1 I wish I ...*hadn't broken*... (not/break) my favourite toy.
2 If only she .... (listen) to what I tell her.
3 I wish I .... (not/go) to bed late last night.
4 If only Linda .... (apply) for that job.
5 If only the boys .... (not/arrive) so late last night.
6 If only we .... (have) enough money to buy a car.
7 I wish I .... (be) rich.
8 If only we .... (be) old enough to live alone.

Revision 3 (Units 1 - 9)

9   I wish my neighbours .... (not/have) parties every weekend.

10 If only I .... (apologise) for my bad behaviour yesterday.

11 I wish I .... (not/make) such a big mistake.

12 I wish my brother .... (not/borrow) my favourite clothes.

13 If only Trevor .... (remember) to post the letter.

14 If only I .... (invite) more people to the party.

15 Tara wishes she .... (know) more people in the area.

5   **Rewrite the sentences using the words/ phrases given.**

1   He not only dropped the eggs, but he slipped on them.
Not only ...*did he drop the eggs, but he slipped on them*....

2   She has seldom been to such a good party.
Seldom ....

3   I have rarely met such polite people.
Rarely ....

4   They have not once visited the museum in the town.
Not once ....

5   I realised only then that the window was broken.
Only then ....

6   I not only took the picture, but I developed it.
Not only ....

7   They have never taken such an important exam before.
Never before ....

8   I had no sooner closed the door than Bill opened it again.
No sooner ....

9   He has seldom heard such an amusing joke.
Seldom...

10 They have rarely taken a day off work.
Rarely ....

11 He has not once asked us to help him.
Not once ....

12 They had no sooner sat down than the film started.
No sooner ....

13 He noticed only then that the music had stopped.
Only then ....

14 She has never attended an audition before.
Never before ....

15 I not only broke the glass, but I cut my finger on it.
Not only ....

6   **Underline the correct word(s) in bold.**

1   A: **Should/May** I speak to you in private, please?
B: Of course. Come into my office.

2   A: When **shall/will** we meet to discuss the plans?
B: Next week.

3   A: Those files **mustn't/couldn't** be moved.
B: Alright. I'll leave them where they are.

4   A: I've been feeling very tired recently.
B: You **couldn't/ought to** have a holiday.

5   A: **Would/Could** you tell me where the accounts department is, please?
B: It's on the third floor.

6   A: **Can/Must** you cook?
B: Not very well, although I enjoy it.

7   A: Why are you working late?
B: I **ought to/have to** finish updating the files by tomorrow morning.

8   A: There were lots of fast runners in the race, weren't there?
B: Yes, but Alex **was able to/could** finish second.

9   A: Shall I take the rubbish outside?
B: No, you **didn't need to/needn't**. I'll take it in a minute.

10 A: I phoned Jill and Martin, but there was no answer.
B: They **must/can** have gone to the supermarket.

11 A: Barbara's late. I wonder where she is.
B: She **could/should** have got stuck in traffic.

12 A: **Might/May not** I speak to Miss Andrews, please?
B: One moment, please. I'll see if she's available.

13 A: **Will/Shall** we rent a video this evening?
B: That's a good idea.

14 A: You **should/must** wear protective clothing in here. It's a rule.
B: Yes, I know.

15 A: Where is Angela?
B: She **may/can** be in her bedroom, studying.

7   **Rewrite the sentences in the passive.**

1   The police found the missing jewels.
...*The missing jewels were found by the police*....

2   A wealthy businessman donated the money.
....

3   Scientists made an important discovery last weekend.
....

4   Who painted Susan's portrait?
....

5   Simon paid the deposit for the new flat.
....

6   They did the washing-up before they watched TV.
....

7   Jenny made the arrangements for the school trip.
....

8   What destroyed the village?
....

9   Melissa ate all the fruit.
....

10 Mother decorated Jim's birthday cake.
....

11 Gordon introduced me to the managing director of the company.
....

12 The cat broke the vase in the dining room.
....

8   **Underline the correct preposition.**

1 He was sentenced <u>**to**</u>/**at**/**for** two years in prison for his crime.
2 Your sister is very similar **with**/**for**/**to** a girl I used to know.
3 Is James worried? He seems to have something **in**/**on**/**off** his mind.
4 Alison suffers **from**/**of**/**for** lots of allergies.
5 He was very upset **of**/**for**/**about** failing the exam.
6 That entry wasn't worthy **to**/**of**/**for** winning first prize.
7 It's typical **for**/**of**/**from** Lilian to be late.
8 I'm not sure **on**/**for**/**about** the answer to that question.
9 She has terrible taste **in**/**from**/**of** clothes.
10 You should be suspicious **at**/**of**/**for** anyone who you don't know well.
11 Her novels have been translated **for**/**to**/**into** twelve languages.
12 The fire brigade soon had the blaze **into**/**under**/**out of** control.
13 They emptied all the cupboards in search **for**/**of**/**to** the money.
14 You waste too much money **on**/**for**/**with** sweets and magazines.
15 **At**/**To**/**By** my surprise, he bought me flowers.

9   **Fill in the gaps with the correct particle from the list.**

> *away, on, off, out, back, up, up to*

1 The fact that the house was very isolated put me ...*off*... buying it.
2 The car pulled .... outside the house and a man got out.
3 The criminals were put .... for five years after they were found guilty.
4 The man asked me to hold .... while he answered the door.
5 I'm tired of telling him to do things. He keeps .... ignoring me.
6 You must tell me everything. Don't keep anything .... .
7 Keep .... from the main road. It's very dangerous.
8 Do you think the wood supplies will hold .... until the spring?
9 Annie looks .... her older sister.
10 She thought of a way to pay him .... for his lies.
11 It's too dark in here. I can't make .... where the light switch is.
12 This skirt is too tight. I'll ask Mum to let it .... for me.
13 The prices in the supermarket have been put .... this week.
14 The thief made .... with the money from the safe.
15 I'll look .... John's telephone number in my address book.

10   **Cross out the unnecessary word.**

1 Rarely ~~ever~~ do I go to the theatre.
2 Tony likes horror films and so does like Marilyn.
3 You'd better to tell the boss what has happened.
4 I wish if they would stop giving me so much work to do.
5 All they did it was to move the furniture.
6 It was Brian who he borrowed the bicycle.
7 No sooner had he locked the door than when the phone rang.
8 What I really like to do it is eat out with my friends.
9 He said that everyone should to sign the card.
10 I asked her that what she would like to drink.
11 Do you help yourself to coffee and biscuits, please.
12 If you will get up early, you may catch the early train.
13 Jack prefers reading magazines than to reading novels.
14 She told to him that she had made a mistake.
15 Mum told me do not to touch the oven.

11   **Fill in the correct form of the word in brackets.**

1 My uncle knows lots of ...*famous*... (fame) people.
2 Have you made a .... (decide) about which job to take yet?
3 The sunflower grew to a .... (high) of two metres.
4 He is well-known for his .... (kind) to others.
5 Everyone who knows him admires his .... (generous).
6 He passed the exams because he had done a lot of .... (revise).
7 Gunpowder is a highly .... (explode) substance.
8 I have no .... (complain) about the service in that hotel.
9 Sarah's .... (impatient) makes her unpopular with lots of people.
10 She felt a sense of .... (relieve) when she realised that she hadn't lost her bag.
11 The sports car was so .... (expense) that he needed a loan to buy it.
12 My contacts in the business world have been .... (benefit) to my career.
13 Our neighbours have had a large .... (extend) built on their house.
14 This document requires a .... (sign) from the manager.
15 The .... (compete) was won by a young boy from the village.
16 New technology makes .... (communicate) between countries very easy these days.
17 Sarah has always been a .... (sense) girl. She rarely takes risks.
18 Kerry has a very .... (act) lifestyle. That's why she's very fit.

UNIT 10
Clauses - Linking Words

Time Clauses

*They **had booked** tickets **before** they **went** to the cinema. They **will go** home **when** the film **is** over.*

♦ We use the following time conjunctions to introduce time clauses.

> *when - as - while - before - after - since - until/till - whenever - as long as - by the time - as soon as - the moment that - no sooner ...than - hardly ... when - once - immediately - the first/last/next time etc.*

♦ When the time clause precedes the main clause, a comma is used.
  e.g. *Whenever he is in town, he visits us.*

time clause | main clause
He visits us whenever he is in town.

main clause | time clause

Sequence of Tenses

♦ Time clauses follow the rule of the sequence of tenses. That is, when the verb of the main clause is in a present or future form, the verb of the time clause is in a present form. When the verb of the main clause is in a past form, the verb of the time clause is in a past form too.

Main clause		Time clause
present / future / imperative	→	present simple or present perfect

*She **takes off** her shoes **the moment that** she **gets** home.*
*I'll **call** you **as soon as** I **get** to my hotel.*
***Turn off** the lights **before** you **leave**.*

| past simple / past perfect | → | past simple or past perfect |

*He **took** a shower **after** he **had finished** painting the room.*
*They **had reserved** a table **before** they **went** to the restaurant.*

Time Conjunctions

♦ ago - before

ago = before now
e.g. *My parents **got** married twenty years **ago**.*
    (= twenty years before now)

before = before a past time
e.g. *Helen and Mike got married last month.*
    *They **had met** six months **before**. (= six months before last month)*

♦ until/till - by the time

until/till = up to the time when
e.g. *You must stay in the office **until/till you finish/have finished** the report.*
    (= up to the time when you finish the report)
    *They'll be at their summer house **until/till Sunday**.*
    (= up to Sunday)

by the time + clause = not later than the moment something happens
e.g. *I will have set the table **by the time** you **come** home. (= before, not later than the moment you come home)*

by = not later than
e.g. *I'll let you know my decision **by** Friday. (= not later than Friday)*

Note: a) not ... until/till
        e.g. *I **won't** have finished my work **until/till/before** Thursday.*
      b) Both *until/till* and *before* can be used to say how far away a future event is.
        e.g. *There's only one week **until/till/before** my summer holidays.*

♦ during - while/as

during + noun = in the time period
e.g. *We learnt several interesting facts **during the lecture**.*

while/as + clause = in the time period
e.g. *We learnt several interesting facts **while/as we were listening to the lecture**.*

♦ **when = (time conjunction) + present tense**
e.g. *We'll order some pizzas **when** our friends **get** here.*

♦ **when = (question word) + will/would**
e.g. *I'm not sure **when** his next book **will be published**.*

Clauses - Linking Words

1 **Fill in the gaps with** *by, until, while, before, hardly ... when, as soon as, when, as long as* **or** *by the time.*

1 You can keep those CDs for ...*as long as*... you like.
2 I can't do any washing .... the washing machine is repaired.
3 We saw the smoke .... we turned into our street.
4 We had .... gone to bed .... there was a knock at the door.
5 Sarah parked the car .... Paul dashed into the bank.
6 I have to finish these letters .... I can leave the office.
7 Wait here .... I get back.
8 I was washing my hair .... the phone rang.
9 You must be home .... eleven o'clock tonight.
10 .... Sue reached the bank, it had closed.

2 **Put the verbs in brackets into the correct tense.**

1 A: I must tell Steve the good news.
  B: Don't worry. I ...*'ll tell*... (tell) him when I ...*see*.. (see) him.
2 A: How did your tear your dress?
  B: I .... (step) on it as I .... (get) out of the car.
3 A: Have you finished with the newspaper?
  B: Almost. You can have it after I .... (read) the sports section.
4 A: When will they announce the results?
  B: They .... (not/announce) them until they .... (mark) all the papers.
5 A: When did you realise you had been burgled?
  B: I knew it the moment I .... (arrive) home.
6 A: You should be in bed by now.
  B: I .... (go) to bed as soon as I .... (finish) this chapter.
7 A: Has your boss signed the contract yet?
  B: No. I'm not sure when he .... (sign) it.
8 A: Have you spoken to Uncle John?
  B: Yes. I .... (phone) him before I .... (leave) the house.
9 A: Did your friends organise a surprise party for your birthday?
  B: Yes! No sooner .... (I/open) the door than all my friends .... (jump) out to surprise me!
10 A: Do you see Catherine very often?
  B: We meet whenever she .... (have) the time.
11 A: Can I borrow your dictionary, please?
  B: You can have it once I .... (finish) with it.
12 A: Has Lee cleaned his room yet?
  B: No, but he will have done it by the time Mum .... (get) home.

3 **Underline the appropriate time phrases and put the verbs into the correct tense.**

1 I'll call you *while*/*the moment* I ...*get*... (get) home.
2 You can visit me *whenever*/*till* you .... (want) to.
3 We went for a walk *after*/*until* we .... (eat) breakfast.
4 *Once*/*Before* he .... (read) the manual, he knew how to operate the machine.
5 I was doing the ironing *during*/*while* he .... (wash) the car.
6 They didn't get married *until*/*by the time* they .... (save) enough money for their honeymoon.
7 I'll write to you *as soon as*/*immediately* I .... (have) the results.
8 I got to the station *till*/*just as* the train .... (pull in).
9 We won't move to a new house *since*/*before* the children .... (leave) school.
10 They had fixed the roof *until*/*by the time* John .... (come) back.
11 The students don't know *when*/*till* the results .... (announce).

4 **Complete each sentence with two to five words, including the word in bold.**

1 As soon as he woke up, he jumped out of bed.
  moment He jumped out of bed ...*the moment he woke*... up.
2 She did some research before she wrote her report.
  after She wrote her report .... some research.
3 I had no sooner entered the house than the phone rang.
  hardly I had .... the phone rang.
4 Simon hurt his leg climbing a tree.
  while Simon hurt his leg .... a tree.
5 We can't go. We have to wait for the taxi to arrive.
  until We can't go .... arrives.
6 We opened the gate. The dog ran towards us.
  sooner We had .... than the dog ran towards us.
7 The shop will open at nine o'clock. The staff will have come in to work by then.
  time The staff will have come in to work .... the shop opens.
8 Moira bought the ring only after she had made sure it was solid gold.
  before Moira made sure the ring was solid gold .... it.
9 Her phone card ran out during her conversation with her mother.
  while Her phone card ran out .... her mother.

Clauses - Linking Words

Clauses of Result

*Dolphins are **so appealing** (that) it is hard not to like them. They are **such intelligent creatures** (that) they can communicate with each other.*

Clauses of result are used to express the result of something. They are introduced with the following words/expressions:

> **as a result - therefore - consequently/as a consequence - so - so/such ... that etc.**

◆ **as a result/therefore/consequently**
   e.g. *The president was taken ill and, **as a result/therefore/consequently** the summit meeting was cancelled.*
   *The president was taken ill. **As a result/therefore/consequently**, the summit meeting was cancelled.*

◆ **so** e.g. *It was hot, **so** I turned on the air-conditioning.*

◆ **such a/an + adjective + singular countable noun**
   e.g. *It was **such an interesting book** (that) I couldn't put it down.*

◆ **such + adjective + plural/uncountable noun**
   e.g. *They are **such good friends** (that) they've never had an argument.*
   *It was **such expensive jewellery** (that) it was kept in a safe.*

◆ **such a lot of + plural/uncountable noun**
   e.g. *She invited **such a lot of guests** to her party that there wasn't enough room for all of them.*
   *He has **such a lot of money** (that) he doesn't know what to do with it.*

◆ **so + adjective/adverb**
   e.g. *He is **so devoted** that he deserves praise.*
   *He speaks **so quickly** that I can't understand him.*

◆ **so much/little + uncountable noun**
   so many/few + plural noun
   e.g. *There is **so much traffic** that we won't be on time.*
   *He pays **so little attention** to what I say that it makes me angry.*
   *He made **so many mistakes** that he failed.*
   *There are **so few wolves** left that we have to protect them.*

---

5   **Fill in** *so, such* **or** *such a/an.*

1 The party next door last night was ...*so*... loud that I couldn't sleep.
2 They sell .... lovely things in that shop.
3 I bought .... lot of shopping that I couldn't carry all the bags.
4 It was .... late when I got home that I didn't have dinner.
5 She dresses .... elegantly that everyone admires her.
6 I had .... bad headache yesterday that I had to leave work and go home.
7 I'm .... hungry that I could eat anything for lunch.
8 He had put .... little salt in the soup that it was tasteless.
9 It was .... amusing film that I laughed all the way through.
10 They have got .... fashionable furniture in their house that it is often photographed for magazines.
11 She is .... interesting person that I could spend hours talking to her.

6   **Complete each sentence with two to five words, including the word in bold.**

1 I had a lot of homework to do, so I couldn't go out.
   so   I had ...*so much homework*... to do that I couldn't go out.
2 The bus was very late. We decided to take a taxi.
   so   The bus was .... we decided to take a taxi.
3 He was sleeping soundly. We couldn't wake him.
   so   He was .... we couldn't wake him.
4 It was very exciting news and I couldn't wait to tell everyone.
   such   It was .... I couldn't wait to tell everyone.
5 She is a very clever girl and her parents are very proud of her.
   such   She is .... her parents are very proud of her.
6 Jane doesn't spend much time studying. She may fail her exams.
   little   Jane spends .... she may fail her exams.
7 Peter did a lot of work yesterday, so he has nothing to do today.
   much   Peter did .... yesterday that he has nothing to do today.
8 His luggage was heavy. He decided to call a porter.
   such   He had .... that he decided to call a porter.

Clauses – Linking Words

Clauses of Reason

*Traffic is getting worse **because/as** more people are buying cars. Traffic is getting worse **on account of the fact that** more people are buying cars.*

Clauses of reason are used to express the reason for something. They are introduced with the following words/expressions:

> **because - as/since - the reason for/why - because of/on account of/due to - now that - for etc.**

◆ **because** *e.g. I took a taxi **because** it was raining.* ***Because** it was raining, I took a taxi.*

◆ **as/since** (=because) *e.g. They bought him a gift **as/since** it was his birthday. **As/Since** it was his birthday, they bought him a gift.*

◆ **the reason for + noun/-ing form**
the reason why + clause
*e.g. **The reason for** his **resignation** was (the fact) that he had been offered a better job.*
*The fact that he had been offered a better job was **the reason for** his **resigning**.*
***The reason why** he resigned was (the fact) that he had been offered a better job.*

◆ **because of/on account of/due to + noun**
because of/on account of/due to the fact that + clause
*e.g. All flights were cancelled **because of/on account of the thick fog.***
*All flights were cancelled **due to the thick fog.***
*He asked for a few days off **because of/on account of the fact that he was exhausted.***
*He asked for a few days off **due to the fact that he was exhausted.***

◆ **now (that) + clause** *e.g. **Now (that) they have children**, they have less free time.*

◆ **for = because (in formal written style)**
A clause of reason introduced with *for* always comes after the main clause.
*e.g. The citizens of Harbridge were upset, **for** a new factory was to be built near their town.*

7 **Rewrite the sentences using the word(s) in brackets.**

1 She went to bed because she was tired. **(since)**
...She went to bed since she was tired....

2 The singer cancelled her appearance. She was feeling unwell. **(on account of)**
....

3 She hadn't eaten all day, and therefore she was hungry. **(as)**
....

4 He was rude and, as a result, the teacher punished him. **(because of)**
....

5 The reason why the Prime Minister did not attend the press conference was that he was out of the country. **(for)**
....

6 He has passed his exams, so his parents are pleased with him. **(now that)**
....

7 The job was very dangerous, so she turned it down. **(the reason for)**
....

8 His car ran out of petrol, so it wouldn't move. **(due to)**
....

9 He was late. He took a taxi. **(since)**
....

8 **Complete each sentence with two to five words, including the word in bold.**

1 It was very cold, so I wore my coat.
as   I wore my coat ...*as it was*... very cold.
2 We didn't go for a walk because it was raining.
account   We didn't go for a walk ....
.... the rain.
3 He didn't tidy his room. As a result, his mother shouted at him.
because   His mother shouted at him ....
.... his room.
4 She didn't close the gate. As a result, the dog escaped.
due   The dog escaped ....
.... she didn't close the gate.
5 The reason why she got a lot of presents was that it was her birthday.
for   The fact that it was her birthday was ....
.... a lot of presents.
6 We didn't understand the lecture, so we asked the tutor to explain.
since   We asked the tutor to explain, ...
.... the lecture.
7 The car skidded on the road because it was icy.
due   The car skidded on the road .... ice.
8 I couldn't sleep because it was noisy.
of   I couldn't sleep ....
noise.

Clauses of Purpose

They met in a café **to discuss** their holiday.
They met in a café **so that they could** discuss their holiday.

Clauses of purpose are used to express the purpose of an action. That is, they explain why someone does something. They are introduced with the following words/expressions:

> **to** - **in order to/so as to** - **so that/in order that** - **in case** - **for** etc.

◆ **to -infinitive**
e.g. She went shopping **to look for** some new clothes.

◆ **in order to/so as to + infinitive (formal)**
e.g. He did a postgraduate course **in order to/so as to widen** his knowledge of international politics.

In negative sentences we use *in order not to* or *so as not to*. We never use *not to* alone.
e.g. He wrote the number down **in order not to/so as not to** forget it.

◆ **so that + can/will (present or future reference)**
e.g. Emma has booked a first-class ticket **so that** she **can** travel in comfort.

so that + could/would (past reference)
e.g. He recorded the match **so that** he **could** watch it later.

Note: *In order that* has the same structure as *so that*. However, it is not used very often as it is formal.
e.g. We will send you the forms **in order that** you **can** make your application.

◆ **in case + present tense (present or future reference)**
in case + past tense (past reference)
In case is never used with *will* or *would*.
e.g. Take your credit card **in case** you **run out of** cash.
He took a jumper **in case** it **got** cold.

◆ **for + noun (when we want to express the purpose of an action)**
e.g. He went to the doctor's **for a check-up**.

for + -ing form (when we want to express the purpose or function of something)
e.g. We use a spade **for digging**.

Clauses of purpose follow the rule of the sequence of tenses, like time clauses (page 144).
e.g. He **borrowed** some money **so that** he **could** pay his phone bill.

Note: We can express negative purpose by using:

a) **prevent + noun/pronoun + (from) + -ing form**
e.g. She covered the sofa with a sheet **to prevent it (from) getting** dirty.

b) **avoid + -ing form**
e.g. They set off early in the morning **to avoid getting stuck** in traffic.

9 **Underline the correct word.**

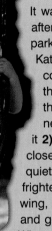

It was three o'clock on Saturday afternoon and Ben was in the park. He had taken his sister, Katy, with him **1) so that / for** she could play on the swings. While they were playing, Ben noticed that a small bird was sitting near a tree. He walked towards it **2) in order to / so that** have a closer look. He walked slowly and quietly **3) not to / so as not to** frighten it. The bird had a broken wing, so Ben and Katy went home and got a box **4) for / to** carry it in. When they had put it in the box, they took it to the vet **5) to / for** treatment. The vet was very gentle **6) in order to / so that** he wouldn't hurt it. The bird recovered a few weeks later and the vet released it in the park again.

10 **Join the sentences using the word(s) in brackets.**

1 He got the car out of the garage. He wanted to wash it. **(so that)**
   ...He got the car out of the garage so that he could wash it....

2 I always lock the doors and windows. I don't want to be burgled. **(avoid)**
   ....

3 The doctor examined the patient. He wanted to find out what was wrong with him. **(so as to)**
   ....

4 I've taken out a loan. I want to buy a car. **(to)**
   ....

5 We'll take some food with us. We might get hungry. **(in case)**
   ....

6 She is studying medicine. She wants to become a doctor. **(so that)**

....

7 He put his keys in his briefcase. He didn't want to lose them. **(in order not to)**

....

8 They will take some magazines with them. They may get bored. **(in case)**

....

9 She set her alarm clock. She didn't want to oversleep. **(so that)**

....

10 We put the letters on the table. We didn't want to forget to post them. **(so as not to)**

....

 11 **Complete each sentence with two to five words, including the word in bold.**

1 We took a taxi. We didn't want to be late.
  not   We took a taxi ...*so as not to*... be late.
2 Tony is employing more staff. He wants to expand his business.
  that   Tony is employing more staff ....
  .... his business.
3 Take your mobile phone. It is possible that someone may call you.
  case   Take your mobile phone ....
  .... you.
4 We use a microwave to cook food quickly.
  for   We use a microwave ....
  food quickly.
5 We took a camera. We wanted to take some photographs.
  that   We took a camera ....
  .... some photographs.
6 She applied sunscreen. She didn't want to get sunburnt.
  not   She applied sunscreen ....
  .... sunburnt.
7 I did my homework. I didn't want the teacher to be angry with me.
  that   I did my homework ....
  .... not be angry with me.
8 Mark called John. He wanted to ask him for some advice.
  to   Mark called John ....
  .... for some advice.
9 He checked his answering machine. There may have been a message for him.
  case   He checked his answering machine ....
  .... message for him.
10 She put her jewellery in the hotel safe. She didn't want it to get stolen.
  prevent   She put her jewellery in the hotel safe ......
  .... stolen.

Exclamations

Exclamations are words or sentences used to express admiration, surprise, etc.

To form exclamatory sentences we can use *what (a/an), how, such, so* **or a** *negative question.*

◆ **so + adjective/adverb**
  e.g. *This cake is* **so tasty**!
  He works **so hard**!

◆ **such + a/an (+ adjective) + singular countable noun**
  e.g. *This is* **such an original design**!

◆ **such (+ adjective) + uncountable/plural noun**
  e.g. *You gave me* **such valuable information**!
  She's wearing **such elegant clothes**!

◆ **what + a/an (+ adjective) + singular countable noun**
  e.g. **What a lovely view**!
  What an unusual pattern! **What a day**!

◆ **what (+ adjective) + uncountable/plural noun**
  e.g. **What expensive furniture**!
  What comfortable shoes!

◆ **how + adjective/adverb**
  e.g. **How clever** he is! **How well** she behaved!

◆ **negative question (+ exclamation mark)**
  e.g. **Isn't she** a graceful dancer!

 12 **Fill in** *what (a/an), how, so* **or** *such (a/an).*

1 ...*How*... sweetly she sings!
2 .... scary film that was!
3 She's .... pretty!
4 .... loud music!
5 .... clever man he is!
6 This is .... great news!
7 .... tired they look!
8 He behaved .... rudely!
9 .... awful thought!
10 It's .... tiring journey!
11 .... lazy of you to stay in bed all day!
12 He is .... amazing musician!

13 **Rephrase the sentences in as many ways as possible, as in the example.**

1 What delicious food!
  ...*How delicious this food is! This is such delicious food!*
  This food is so delicious! Isn't this food delicious!...
2 This is such an interesting story!
3 How young he looks!
4 He's so handsome!
5 Don't they have a lovely house!
6 Doesn't she look happy!

Clauses of Contrast

*He prefers to make things by hand **although/even though** he could use a machine.*

Clauses of contrast are used to express a contrast. They are introduced with the following words/phrases:

> *but - although/even though/though - in spite of/despite - however - while/whereas - yet - nevertheless - on the other hand*

- ◆ **but** *e.g. It was cold, **but** she wasn't wearing a coat.*

- ◆ **although/even though/though + clause**
  ***Even though** is more emphatic than **although**. **Though** is informal and is often used in everyday speech. It can also be put at the end of a sentence.*
  *e.g. **Although/Even though/Though** it was summer, it was chilly.*
  *It was chilly **although/even though/though** it was summer.*
  *It was summer. It was chilly, **though**.*

- ◆ **in spite of/despite + noun/-ing form**
  *e.g. **In spite of/Despite his qualifications**, he couldn't get a job.*
  *He couldn't get a job **in spite of/despite (his) being** qualified.*

  in spite of/despite the fact that + clause
  *e.g. **In spite of/Despite the fact that he was qualified**, he couldn't get a job.*

- ◆ **however/nevertheless** A comma is always used after **however/nevertheless**.
  *e.g. The man fell off the ladder. **However/Nevertheless**, he wasn't hurt.*

- ◆ **while/whereas**
  *e.g. She is tall, **while/whereas** her brother is rather short.*

- ◆ **yet (formal)/still**
  *e.g. The fire was widespread, **yet** no property was damaged.*
  *My car is old. **Still**, it is in very good condition.*

- ◆ **on the other hand**
  e.g. Cars aren't environmentally friendly.
  ***On the other hand**, bicycles are./Bicycles, **on the other hand**, are.*

14 **Choose the correct answer.**

1 ...A... the heavy snow, we managed to get to the office.
   A In spite of   B However   C While
2 .... needing a rest, the team continued to work.
   A In spite   B Despite   C Although
3 I like peaches. I don't like bananas, ...
   A whereas   B on the other hand   C though
4 The film was good, ... it was also very frightening.
   A despite   B but   C in spite
5 Paul drives a car, ... Charles rides a motorbike.
   A whereas   B even though   C despite
6 .... she isn't fond of classical music, she went to the concert.
   A However   B Even though   C While
7 .... being hungry, Sally didn't eat anything.
   A However   B Yet   C In spite of
8 The alarm went off, ... he didn't wake up.
   A whereas   B yet   C while
9 .... we left the house early, we still missed the bus.
   A Although   B Despite   C In spite of
10 He wasn't wearing a coat, ... it was very cold.
   A whereas   B even though   C despite

15 **Complete the sentences.**

1 In spite of the rain, the football match took place.
  Although *...it was raining, the football match took place...*
2 Even though we were late, we stopped to have something to eat.
  Despite ....
3 Even though they are good friends, they argue a lot.
  In spite ....
4 In spite of having a lot of money, they are very mean.
  Although ....
5 In spite of winning the competition, he wasn't satisfied.
  Even though ....
6 Even though he woke up early, he was late for his appointment.
  Despite ....

16 **Rewrite the sentences using the word(s) in brackets.**

1 I live in London. Sarah lives in Manchester. **(while)**
  ...I live in London while Sarah lives in Manchester....
2 We went to the party. We were very tired. **(though)**
  ....
3 She doesn't earn much money. She works very hard. **(in spite of)**
  ....

4 He was ill. He went to work. **(despite)**
....

5 This appliance is very expensive. It is impractical. **(yet)**
....

6 The teacher explained the question in detail. I didn't understand it. **(still)**
....

7 I drank a bottle of water. I was still thirsty. **(even though)**
....

8 The film was boring. We continued to watch it. **(in spite of)**
....

9 David can't play football. He is good at basketball. **(on the other hand)**
....

10 It was very late. The guests didn't leave. **(nevertheless)**
....

11 Lisa went shopping. She didn't buy anything. **(but)**
....

12 The boy fell off his bicycle. He wasn't hurt. **(however)**
....

13 He was tired. He couldn't sleep. **(although)**
....

14 Brian is good at Maths. His sister is good at Science. **(whereas)**
....

15 Janet is clever. She finds some subjects difficult. **(still)**
....

16 He is rich. He is not happy. **(despite)**
....

17 **Rephrase the sentences using the words in brackets, as in the example.**

1 Dennis is tired. He doesn't want to go to bed. **(although, despite)**
   a) *Although Dennis is tired, he doesn't want to go to bed.*
   b) *Despite (his) being tired, Dennis doesn't want to go to bed.*

2 It was a lovely day. They stayed inside. **(however, in spite of)**

3 Martin is a good cook. He rarely cooks for his friends. **(still, though)**

4 The house is in bad condition. They paid a lot of money for it. **(even though, nevertheless)**

5 The lecture was very important. Few students attended. **(despite, yet)**

6 There wasn't much food in the fridge. We managed to make a meal. **(although, however)**

7 She hadn't slept well. She looked fresh and lively. **(still, in spite of)**

8 His parents are very rich. He never asks them for money. **(nevertheless, yet)**

9 I had seen the film before. I enjoyed watching it again. **(though, despite)**

10 Celine Dion is my favourite singer. I haven't been to any of her concerts. **(even though, however)**

Clauses of Manner

*They look **as if/as though** they are in a hurry.*

Clauses of manner are introduced with *as if/as though* and are used to express the way in which something is done/said, etc.

◆ We use *as if/as though* after verbs such as *act, appear, be, behave, feel, look, seem, smell, sound, taste* to say how somebody or something looks, behaves, etc.
   e.g. He *is acting as if/as though* he's had bad news.

   We also use *as if/as though* with other verbs to say how somebody does something.
   e.g. She *talks as if/as though* she knows everything.

◆ We use *as if/as though* + past tense when we are talking about an unreal present situation. *Were* can be used instead of *was* in all persons.
   e.g. He spends his money *as if/as though* he *was/were* a millionaire. (But he isn't.)
   He behaves *as if/as though* he *owned* the place. (But he doesn't.)

Note: We can use *like* instead of *as if/as though* in spoken English.
e.g. She looks *like* she's going to faint. (informal spoken English)

18 **Put the verbs in brackets into the correct tense.**

1 She was wandering up and down the street. She looked as though she ...*was*... (be) lost.

2 Although he had a degree in French, it sounded as though he .... (not/speak) it well.

3 The sky is dark. It looks as if it .... (rain).

4 There is a strange smell in the kitchen. It smells as though something .... (burn).

5 Tom is twenty-five years old, but he sometimes acts as though he .... (be) a child.

6 Colin was out of breath. He sounded as though he .... (run).

7 Jim has only just learned this game, but he plays it as if he .... (play) it for years.

8 We had never met before, but she greeted me as if we .... (know) each other all our lives.

Relative Clauses

A camel is an animal **which/that** lives in hot countries.
A computer is something **which/ that** we use for storing information.
A firefighter is someone **who/that** puts out fires and **whose** job is very risky.

Relative clauses are introduced with a) relative pronouns (who(m), which, whose, that) and b) relative adverbs (when, where, why).

We use:

◆ who/that to refer to people.

◆ which/that to refer to objects or animals.
Who/which/that can be omitted when it is the object of the relative clause; that is, when there is a noun or subject pronoun between the relative pronoun and the verb. It cannot be omitted when it is the subject of the relative clause. We can use whom instead of *who* when it is the object of the relative clause. **Whom** is not often used in everyday English.
e.g. a) I saw a friend. I hadn't seen |him| for years.

   I saw a friend **(who/whom/that)** I hadn't seen for years. (Who/whom/that is the object, therefore it can be omitted.)

   b) I met a woman. |She| was from Japan.

   I met a woman **who/that** was from Japan. (Who/that is the subject, therefore it cannot be omitted.)

◆ whose instead of possessive adjectives (my, your, his, etc.) with people, objects and animals in order to show possession.
e.g. a) That's the boy – | his | bicycle was stolen yesterday.
   That's the boy **whose** bicycle was stolen yesterday.

   b) That's the building – | its | windows were smashed.
   That's the building **whose** windows were smashed.

◆ We usually avoid using prepositions before relative pronouns.
e.g. a) The person **to whom** the money will be entrusted must be reliable. (formal English — unusual structure)

   b) The chair **that** you are sitting **on** is an antique. (usual structure)

   c) The chair you are sitting **on** is an antique. (everyday English)

◆ Which can refer back to a whole clause.
e.g. He helped me do the washing-up. That was kind of him.
   He helped me do the washing-up, **which** was kind of him. (Which refers back to the whole clause. That is, it refers to the fact that he helped the speaker do the washing-up.)

◆ We can use the structure **all/most/some/a few/half/ none/two, etc. + of + whom/which.**
e.g. a) He invited a lot of people. All of them were his friends.
   He invited a lot of people, **all of whom** were his friends.

   b) He has a number of watches. Three of them are solid gold.
   He has a number of watches, **three of which** are solid gold.

◆ That is never used after a comma or preposition.
e.g. a) The Chinese vase, which is on the coffee table, is very expensive.
   (NOT: ...~~that~~ is on the coffee table ...)

   b) The bank in which the money was deposited is across the street.
   (NOT: The bank in ~~that~~ the money ...)

◆ We use that with words such as *all, every(thing), some(thing), any(thing), no(thing), none, few, little, much, only* and with the *superlative form.*
e.g. Is this **all that** you can do for me? (more natural than ... **all which** you can do ...)
   The **only** thing **that** is important to me is my family.
   It's **the best** song **that** I've ever heard.

who/that (people)	subject — cannot be omitted
who/whom/that (people)	object — can be omitted
which/that (objects, animals)	subject — cannot be omitted object — can be omitted
whose (people, objects, animals)	possession — cannot be omitted

Relative Adverbs

We use:

◆ **where** to refer to place, usually after nouns such as *place, house, street, town, country,* etc.

It can be replaced by *which/that + preposition* and, in this case, *which/that* can be omitted.

e.g. The house **where** he was born has been demolished.
The house *(which/that)* he was born **in** has been demolished.

◆ **when** to refer to time, usually after nouns such as *time, period, moment, day, year, summer,* etc. It can either be replaced by *that* or can be omitted.

e.g. That was the year **when** she graduated.
That was the year *(that)* she graduated.

◆ **why** to give reason, usually after the word *reason*. It can either be replaced by *that* or can be omitted.

e.g. The reason **why** she left her job was that she didn't get on with her boss.
The reason *(that)* she left her job was that she didn't get on with her boss.

19 *How much do you know about films?* **Fill in the gaps with *who, which, whose, where* or *when*, then answer the questions.**

1 Name the actor ...*who*... plays Mr Bean.
   (A) Rowan Atkinson   **B** Rolph Harris

2 Name the US president .... was first an actor.
   A James Carter   **B** Ronald Reagan

3 Name the US city .... Hollywood can be found.
   A Los Angeles   **B** Las Vegas

4 Name the film .... tells the story of a strong mythical character.
   A Aladdin   **B** Hercules

5 Name the character .... nose grows when he tells lies.
   A Pinocchio   **B** Peter Pan

6 Name the year .... the first studio was built in Hollywood.
   A 1991   **B** 1911

7 Name the year .... *Titanic* was released.
   A 1998   **B** 1988

8 Name the superhero .... lives in Gotham City.
   A Superman   **B** Batman

9 Name the place .... *The Lion King* is set.
   A Africa   **B** America

10 Name the city .... the Hunchback of Notre Dame lived.
   A Paris   **B** Prague

20 **Complete the sentences with *who, which* or *where*.**

• The Coca-Cola Company, **1)** ...*which*... was founded in 1892, is famous all over the world.
• The company, **2)** .... produces many soft drinks, is based in Atlanta.
• John S. Pemberton, **3)** .... invented Coca-Cola, intended the drink to be used as a cure for common illnesses.
• Frank Robinson, **4)** .... worked for John Pemberton, chose the name Coca-Cola.
• Fanta, **5)** .... was originally produced in Germany, was bought by the Coca-Cola Company.
• Sprite, **6)** .... was introduced in 1961, is also made by the Coca-Cola Company.
• The US Patent Office, **7)** .... the trademark 'Coca-Cola' was registered, has also registered the trademark 'Coke' and the glass Coca-Cola bottle.
• In America, **8)** .... Coca-Cola was first produced, there is a large soft drink industry, but the Coca-Cola Company is the most successful.

21 **Fill in the correct relative pronoun/adverb. If it can be omitted, put it in brackets.**

1 When did you buy the jacket ...*(which/that)*... you are wearing?
2 Is that the girl .... sent you a Valentine's card?
3 The reason .... John is successful is that he works very hard.
4 What did you do with the money .... I gave you?
5 Sam is mending the chair .... he broke yesterday.
6 Is this the place .... you lost your jacket?
7 Have you met the people .... live next door to you?
8 I'll never forget the day .... my daughter was born.
9 Claire is reading the book .... she bought yesterday.
10 I've been running. That's .... I'm out of breath.
11 This is the town .... my favourite singer lives.
12 What is the name of the woman .... works in the chemist's?
13 Is this the boy .... parents own the factory?
14 I'll never forget the time .... she fell into the swimming pool.
15 Where are the children .... ball broke our window?

153

UNIT 10
Clauses - Linking Words

22 Fill in *who*, *which*, *whose*, *where* or *why*.

One of the most famous buildings in the world is the White House, **1)** ...*which*... is the official home of the US president. The White House is in Washington DC, **2)** .... there are many other important buildings and monuments. The city, **3)** .... was founded in 1790, was deliberately planned as a national capital. George Washington, **4)** .... was the first US president and **5)** .... name was given to the city, wanted it to be the place **6)** .... the nation's government would permanently reside.

The White House, **7)** .... was originally named Executive Mansion, was built in pale grey sandstone. The colour of the stone, **8)** .... was so different from the surrounding red brick buildings, was the reason **9)** .... the mansion became known as the White House. The main building, **10)** .... many presidents have lived, is part of a large complex **11)** .... consists of over 130 rooms.

People find the White House fascinating and that is the reason **12)** .... the parts of the complex **13)** .... are open to the public are toured every year by one and a half million people **14)** .... want to see the place **15)** .... their president lives and works.

23 Complete the pairs of sentences, as in the examples.

1 Tom is playing football with a boy. The boy is his cousin.
  A The boy ...*who/whom Tom is playing football with is his cousin*....
  B The boy ...*Tom is playing football with is his cousin*....
2 Sam has gone to a party. The party is at his friend's house.
  A The party ....
  B The party ....
3 I was talking to a woman. The woman is my boss.
  A The woman ....
  B The woman ....
4 She works for a writer. The writer is very famous.
  A The writer ....
  B The writer ....
5 I lent my jacket to Pam. The jacket is made of leather.
  A The jacket ....
  B The jacket ....

24 Join the sentences, as in the example.

1 My brother has lots of friends. Many of them are in his class.
  ...*My brother has lots of friends, many of whom are in his class*....
2 My father has a large collection of coins. Many of them are foreign.
  ....
3 I baked lots of biscuits yesterday. Very few of them are left now.
  ....
4 She knows lots of people at work. A few of them are from New Zealand.
  ....
5 I have four aunts. None of them are married.
  ....
6 There are thousands of trees in the forest. Some of them are very old.
  ....

25 Link the sentences in order to produce one sentence. The beginning is given.

1 The coach was packed with tourists. The coach was driving around London. The tourists had gone there to see the sights.
  The coach, ...*which was driving around London, was packed with tourists who had gone there to see the sights*....
2 I went to the dentist's. He is a friend of mine. I met him at university.
  The dentist ....
  ....
  ....
3 A song won the competition. It was written by a schoolboy. He was thirteen years old.
  The song ....
  ....
  ....
4 I helped someone with his homework. His name is Alec and he's a classmate of mine.
  I helped ....
  ....
  ....
5 Elaine's house is going to be pulled down. She is looking for a new flat.
  Elaine, ...
  ....
  ....
6 The book is a bestseller. It's written by Nathan Davis. He has written ten novels.
  The book, ...
  ....
  ....

154

Identifying / Non-identifying Clauses

There are two types of relative clause: *identifying relative clauses* and *non-identifying relative clauses*. An *identifying relative clause* gives necessary information and is essential to the meaning of the main sentence. It is not put in commas. A *non-identifying relative clause* gives extra information and is not essential to the meaning of the main sentence. It is put in commas.

> **Identifying relative clauses are introduced with:**

◆ **who, which, that. They can be omitted if they are the object of the relative clause.**

e.g. a) *People are prosecuted. (Which people? We don't know. The meaning of the sentence is not clear.)*
*People **who/that lie in court** are prosecuted. (Which people? Those who lie in court. The meaning of the sentence is clear.)*

b) *The papers are missing. (Which papers? We don't know. The meaning of the sentence is not clear.)*
*The papers **(which/that) you gave me to check** are missing. (Which papers? The ones you gave me to check. The meaning of the sentence is clear.)*

◆ **whose, where, when, (the reason) why. Whose cannot be omitted. Where can be omitted when there is a preposition. When and why can either be replaced by *that* or can be omitted.**

e.g. a) *The man was angry. (Which man? We don't know. The meaning of the sentence is not clear.)*
*The man **whose car was damaged** was angry. (Which man? The one whose car was damaged. The meaning of the sentence is clear.)*

b) *The shop is near my house. (Which shop? We don't know.)*
*The shop **where I bought this shirt** is near my house. OR The shop I bought this shirt **from** is near my house. (Which shop? The one I bought this shirt from.)*

c) *The day was the happiest day of my life. (Which day? We don't know.)*
*The day **(when/that) I got married** was the happiest day of my life. (Which day? The day I got married.)*

d) *I was upset. This is the reason. (The reason for what? We don't know.)*
*I was upset. This is the reason **(why/that) I didn't call you**. (The reason I didn't call you.)*

> **Non-identifying relative clauses are introduced with:**

◆ **who, whom, which. They cannot be omitted or replaced by *that*.**

e.g. a) *Jenny Ladd is my favourite author. (The meaning of the sentence is clear.)*
*Jenny Ladd, **who has written a lot of successful books**, is my favourite author. (The relative clause gives extra information.)*

b) *My cousin Peter is a doctor. (The meaning of the sentence is clear.)*
*My cousin Peter, **who(m) you have just met**, is a doctor. (The relative clause gives extra information.)*

c) *His flat is modern and spacious.*
*His flat, **which he bought two years ago**, is modern and spacious.*

◆ **whose, where, when. They cannot be omitted.**

e.g. a) *The bride looked stunning. (The meaning of the sentence is clear.)*
*The bride, **whose wedding dress was designed by Valentino**, looked stunning. (The relative clause gives extra information.)*

b) *Stratford-upon-Avon is visited by thousands of tourists every year.*
*Stratford-upon-Avon, **where Shakespeare was born**, is visited by thousands of tourists every year.*

c) *The best time to visit the island is in May.*
*The best time to visit the island is in May, **when it isn't too crowded**.*

 26 **Fill in the relative pronoun or adverb. Put commas where necessary. Write I for identifying, NI for non-identifying and say whether the relative can be omitted or not.**

1 Paul, ...*whose*... birthday is on Friday, is having a party tonight. *(NI, cannot be omitted)*
2 My office .... is very big is on the first floor.
3 Martin .... works in the library writes poetry in his spare time.
4 That's the woman .... house was burgled last week.
5 The day .... I left school was hot and sunny.
6 Sarah Jones .... I knew at university is a doctor now.
7 This is the girl .... letter was printed in the newspaper.
8 This CD .... I bought yesterday is awful.
9 Tina .... lives next door is a wonderful cook.
10 People .... play musical instruments are called musicians.
11 The café .... we had lunch served delicious food.
12 This is the reason .... I haven't finished.

13 My friend Peter .... has just moved to Wales sent me a long letter.

14 My boss .... office is next to mine is on holiday at the moment.

15 London .... the Houses of Parliament are is the capital of England.

16 My favourite time of the year is summer .... the weather is hot.

17 The woman .... won the lottery gave an interview to the newspaper.

27 **Complete each sentence with two to five words, including the word in bold.**

1 This is Mark. His sister is a famous author.
   whose   This is Mark ...*whose sister is a*... famous author.

2 This is the motorbike. I repaired it myself.
   that   This is the motorbike ....
   ....myself.

3 Mr Smith owns the company. He is a wealthy businessman.
   who   Mr Smith, ...
   ...., is a wealthy businessman.

4 I'm afraid of water. That's why I never swim in the sea.
   which   I'm afraid of water, ...
   .... swim in the sea.

5 You were talking to a girl. She is my niece.
   whom   The girl ....
   .... is my niece.

6 The boy broke the window. He said he was sorry.
   who   The boy ....
   .... said he was sorry.

7 Bath is the city he lived in when he was young.
   where   Bath is the city ....
   .... he was young.

8 People should be punished if they commit crimes.
   who   People ....
   .... should be punished.

9 The best time to go shopping is in the morning. The shops are not very busy then.
   when   The best time to go shopping is in the morning, ...
   .... are not very busy.

10 He lent me some money. That was very kind of him.
   which   He lent me some money, ...
   .... of him.

11 Michael lives next door to me. He is an architect.
   who   Michael, ...
   .... to me, is an architect.

12 This is the suit. I bought it last week. It doesn't fit me.
   which   This suit, ...
   ...., doesn't fit me.

13 She interviewed a man. He is my father.
   whom   The man ....
   .... is my father.

Linking Words

Linking words show the logical relationship between sentences or parts of a sentence.

Positive Addition

and, both ... and, too, besides (this/that), moreover, what is more, in addition (to), also, as well as (this/that), furthermore etc.
*She is **both** intelligent **and** beautiful.*

Negative Addition

neither ... nor, nor, neither, either
***Neither** John **nor** David goes to university.*

Contrast

but, although, in spite of, despite, while, whereas, even though, on the other hand, however, yet, still etc.
*Sarah is kind **but** not very reliable.*

Giving Examples

such as, like, for example, for instance, especially, in particular etc.
*All the food was delicious, but the steak **in particular** was excellent.*

Cause/Reason

as, because, because of, since, for this reason, due to, so, as a result (of) etc.
*I stayed in bed **because** I felt ill.*

Condition

if, whether, only if, in case of, in case, provided (that), providing (that), unless, as/so long as, otherwise, or (else), on condition (that) etc.
*We took an umbrella with us **in case** it rained.*

Purpose

to, so that, so as (not) to, in order (not) to, in order that, in case etc.
*I took some paper and a pen **so that** I could make notes.*

Effect/Result

such/so ... that, so, consequently, as a result, therefore, for this reason etc.
*It was **so** cold **that** we decided to light a fire.*

Time

when, whenever, as, as soon as, while, before, until/till, after, since etc.
*We did not leave **until/till** the babysitter arrived.*

Place

where, wherever
*We can't decide **where** to go on holiday this year.*

Exception

except (for), apart from
*The party was good fun, **apart from** the problem with the stereo.*

Relatives

who, whom, whose, which, what, that
*That's the horse **which/that** won the Grand National.*

Listing Points/Events

To begin: initially, first, at first, firstly, to start/begin with, first of all etc.
***First of all,** we greeted the guests.*

To continue: secondly, after this/that, second, afterwards, then, next etc.
***Then,** we offered them drinks.*

To conclude: finally, lastly, in the end, at last, eventually etc.
***Finally,** we served them the meal.*

Summarising

in conclusion, in summary, to sum up, on the whole, all in all, altogether, in short etc.
***To sum up,** I firmly believe that animals have the right to a happy life.*

 28 Read the sentences and underline the correct *linking word/phrase.*

1 I've never been here before **as/but** my friend has.
2 You can have some friends over, **apart from/as long as** you play quietly.
3 ***Afterwards/In conclusion***, I think that Mark is the best person for the job.
4 I went to the bank **in case/in order to** get some money.
5 We took a taxi **in short/because** we were late.
6 This house is beautiful. ***In addition to/However***, it is in poor condition.
7 I was tired, **so/for example** I went to bed early.
8 ***All in all/Although*** she felt ill, she didn't call a doctor.
9 We laughed ***then/when*** we heard the funny story.
10 Some foods, ***moreover/such as*** chocolate, are very fattening.
11 Everyone attended the meeting ***whereas/apart from*** Steve, who was on holiday.
12 I typed the reports ***despite/while*** Joanne interviewed a client.

29 Join the sentences using the word(s) in brackets.

1 He was hungry. He bought a sandwich. **(so)**
   ...He was hungry, so he bought a sandwich....
2 Claire is very tall. She is very thin. **(what is more)**
   ....

3 I was tired. I watched the late film. **(despite)**
   ....
4 John did his homework. His brother tidied the kitchen. **(while)**
   ....
5 Tom likes football. Stuart likes basketball. **(whereas)**
   ....
6 He fell asleep. The phone rang. **(as soon as)**
   ....
7 She brushed her teeth. She went to bed. **(then)**
   ....
8 We went to the shops. We had lunch. **(after that)**
   ....
9 I enjoy reading books. I enjoy watching TV. **(as well as)**
   ....
10 Jason doesn't like tomatoes. Paul doesn't like tomatoes. **(neither)**
   ....

 30 Join the sentences using a suitable word or phrase from the list.

neither ... nor, as well as, after, provided (that), in order to, which, as a result, so ... that, even though, where

1 I enjoyed the party. I didn't know anyone there.
   ...I enjoyed the party, even though I didn't know anyone there....
2 She invested some of her money in bonds. She wanted to increase her income.
   ....
3 He is a good sportsman. He is a talented writer.
   ....
4 Sandra can't cook. Louise can't cook.
   ....
5 I will drive you to school. You are ready on time.
   ....
6 That's the house. My uncle built it.
   ....
7 She left the taps running. The bathroom flooded.
   ....
8 They did the washing-up. They had eaten lunch.
   ....
9 It was very hot. We decided to go for a swim.
   ....
10 This is the restaurant. We had lunch here.
   ....

 31 Join the sentences using the correct word(s) in brackets.

1 Computers are very useful. You can use them to store information. **(for example/whereas)**
   ...Computers are very useful. For example, you can use them to store information....

2 Simon is often invited to parties. He is a popular person. **(for example/since)**

....

3 I had a great holiday. It rained all the time. **(and/even though)**

....

4 Paul is a builder. Robin is a plumber. **(whereas/too)**

....

5 We had salad for lunch. We both want to lose weight. **(in addition/because)**

....

6 My teacher is very kind. She can be strict at times. **(then/on the other hand)**

....

32 Fill in the correct word/phrase from the lists.

a *on the whole, finally, firstly, furthermore, wherever, so*

There are many advantages to owning a mobile phone. **1)** ...*Firstly*,... people can reach you immediately with important news, **2)** .... you happen to be. **3)** ...., you can call for help in an emergency, **4)** .... a mobile phone is important for personal safety. **5)** ...., if you are late for an appointment, you can use a mobile phone to call and explain. **6)** ...., I think everyone should have a mobile phone.

b *to sum up, to begin with, however, because, so as not to, as a result, whenever*

I have been playing the guitar for ten years. **1)** ...., I found it very difficult **2)** .... I wasn't used to playing a musical instrument. **3)** ...., I soon became quite good and, **4)** ...., I was asked to play in a local restaurant. I practised all the time **5)** .... make a mistake in public. **6)** .... I performed, people would always applaud. **7)** ...., I became a very popular musician.

33 Underline the correct word/phrase.

The party was a disaster. **1)** *Although/To begin with*, there were hardly any people there. **2)** *All in all/As a result*, there wasn't a very exciting atmosphere. **3)** *After that/In addition*, the stereo had broken, **4)** *because/so* there was no music to dance to. **5)** *On the whole/In the end*, we all watched a film on television. I left **6)** *before/as soon as* I could. **7)** *In short/Next*, it was a terrible evening.

34 Replace the words in bold with appropriate synonyms from the list.

while, at last, until, in short, in order that, so long as, for instance, apart from, provided that, due to the fact that, what is more, that

1 Don't make the announcement **before** I arrive.
...Don't make the announcement until I arrive....

2 Everyone passed the exam **except for** Paul, who hadn't revised.

....

3 **In summary**, we had a wonderful time at the concert.

....

4 That's the dress **which** I got for my birthday.

....

5 **Finally**, the group was ready to leave.

....

6 I'll give you a lift, **providing** you are ready on time.

....

7 Steve is very clever. **For example**, he got top marks in all his exams.

....

8 I bought some stamps **so that** I could post some letters.

....

9 She was hungry **because** she hadn't eaten all day.

....

10 Jane likes classical music, **whereas** Susan doesn't.

....

11 You'll be on time, **as long as** you hurry.

....

12 **Moreover**, the problem affects our customers.

....

35 Choose the correct answer.

There are many reasons for visiting the city of Rome. **1)** ...C..., it is a city with an interesting history. **2)** ...., it was the capital of the Roman Empire. **3)** ...., Rome is very beautiful, **4)** .... its many palaces, churches and squares. **5)** ...., many of the city's classical monuments have been preserved, **6)** .... it is possible to see how the city used to be. **7)** ...., many people travel to Rome every year. **8)** ...., I believe that, **9)** .... a trip to Rome may be expensive, it is well worth visiting such a wonderful city.

1	**A** Since	**B** On the whole	**C** Firstly
2	**A** Secondly	**B** Finally	**C** Therefore
3	**A** In order to	**B** Moreover	**C** All in all
4	**A** due to	**B** because	**C** so
5	**A** Apart from	**B** However	**C** In addition
6	**A** because	**B** so	**C** and
7	**A** Because	**B** But	**C** For this reason
8	**A** To sum up	**B** Although	**C** For example
9	**A** moreover	**B** although	**C** due to

IN OTHER WORDS

Study these examples. The second sentence has a similar meaning to the first sentence.

1   The man waving at me is my cousin Stewart.
    who   The man **who is waving at me** is my cousin Stewart.

2   She got up early because she wanted to do some shopping before she went to work.
    so   She got up early **so as to do** some shopping before she went to work.
    that   She got up early **so that she could do** some shopping before she went to work.

3   The jewellery kept in that safe belongs to my mother.
    which   The jewellery **which is kept** in that safe belongs to my mother.

4   The party was a success, so we all stayed very late.
    such   The party was **such a success that** we all stayed very late.

5   Having missed the last bus, Laura had to walk all the way home.
    because Laura had to walk all the way home **because she had missed** the last bus.

6   Although he is hardworking, he is not paid well.
    spite   In **spite of his being** hardworking, he is not paid well.

7   Children growing up in cities often get very little exercise.
    who   Children **who grow up** in cities often get very little exercise.

8   That's the café where we used to go when we were students.
    to   That's the café **we used to go to** when we were students.

---

36 **Complete each sentence with two to five words, including the word in bold.**

1   He didn't say anything because he didn't want to spoil the surprise.
    so   He didn't say anything ...*so as not to spoil*... the surprise.

2   That's the theatre where he gave his first performance.
    in   That's the theatre .... his first performance.

3   Her room was in a mess, so she had to spend hours tidying it up.
    such   Her room was in .... she had to spend hours tidying it up.

4   Drivers parking in this area will be fined.
    who   Drivers .... will be fined.

5   The woman driving that car is a famous journalist.
    who   The woman .... is a famous journalist.

6   Having forgotten her birthday, Tom apologised.
    because Tom apologised .... her birthday.

7   The photograph published in that magazine was not genuine.
    which   The photograph .... in that magazine was not genuine.

8   Although she was hurt, she didn't say anything.
    spite   In ...., she didn't say anything.

9   He has decided to give up his job and there's nothing you can do to stop him.
    prevent You can't .... his job.

10 Her feet hurt because her shoes were too tight.
    so   Her shoes were .... her feet hurt.

11 It was snowing heavily, so the village was cut off.
    due   The village was cut off .... it was snowing heavily.

12 She looked like she was going to explode when she heard his remarks.
    if   She looked .... to explode when she heard his remarks.

13 The hotel was rather expensive, so we decided to look for accommodation elsewhere.
    such   It was .... we decided to look for accommodation elsewhere.

14 Have a spare key cut; you may lose the original.
    case   Have a spare key cut .... the original.

15 Always make a shopping list if you don't want to forget anything important.
    avoid   Always make a shopping list .... anything important.

16 She invited a lot of people to her party. She knew most of them from work.
    whom   She invited a lot of people to her party, ... she knew from work.

17 He missed his flight, so he was the only one who didn't attend the conference.
    consequently He missed his flight .... the only one who didn't attend the conference.

18 Someone must have put too much sugar in my coffee.
    if   My coffee tastes ....too much sugar in it.

19 She introduced me to all her friends. This was very polite of her.
    which   She introduced me to all her friends, ... of her.

20 This is John Daniels. His novel became a bestseller.
    whose   This is John Daniels, ...a bestseller.

21 People living abroad often miss their friends and family.
    who   People .... often miss their friends and family.

Common mistakes

- This is the wallet **which I bought it** yesterday. ✗
  This is the wallet **which I bought** yesterday. ✓

- Is he the man **who he stole** your bag? ✗
  Is he the man **who stole** your bag? ✓

- My car, **that** cost me a fortune, was badly damaged in the accident. ✗
  My car, **which** cost me a fortune, was badly damaged in the accident. ✓

- Carol found a job last week. She had started looking for one a month **ago**. ✗
  Carol found a job last week. She had started looking for one a month **before**. ✓

- When he**'ll call**, I'll give him the message. ✗
  When he **calls**, I'll give him the message. ✓

- He gave me **so helpful advice** that I was able to solve the problem. ✗
  He gave me **such helpful advice** that I was able to solve the problem. ✓

- He took a taxi **not to be** late. ✗
  He took a taxi **so as not to/in order not to be** late. ✓

- You'd better book a table **in case the restaurant will be** busy. ✗
  You'd better book a table **in case the restaurant is** busy. ✓

- **Despite of her wealth**, she is still unhappy. ✗
  Despite her wealth, she is still unhappy. ✓

- He often speaks **as if he is** an expert on every subject. ✗
  He often speaks **as if he was/were** an expert on every subject. ✓

- This is the man **who's** dog attacked me. ✗
  This is the man **whose** dog attacked me. ✓

- The hotel **where we stayed at** was very luxurious. ✗
  The hotel **where we stayed** was very luxurious. ✓
  The hotel **(which) we stayed at** was very luxurious. ✓

37 Correct the mistakes.

1 He ran down the road not to miss the bus.
2 Despite of his talents, he is very shy.
3 This is the girl who's parents own the hotel.
4 She often acts as if she is better than everyone else.
5 She makes so delicious food, she ought to be a chef.
6 When I'll see her, I'll invite her to the party.
7 His house, that is very old, is opposite the post office.
8 This is the book which I borrowed it from the library.
9 Jane finished writing the letter at 8 o'clock. She had started writing it an hour ago.

10 Is she the woman who she lives next door to you?
11 You'd better take a jumper in case it will be cold.
12 The town where I grew up in has changed a lot.

38 Cross out the unnecessary word.

1 Take your credit card with you in case you will want to do some shopping.
2 They held a sponsored parachute jump in order that to raise money for the disabled people.
3 It was such an awful weather that it ruined our holiday.
4 Andrew, who he is my friend, has been promoted.
5 She has always wanted to visit the place where her parents were born there.
6 Despite of the traffic, I got to the station on time.
7 That's the boy whose his father is a surgeon.
8 When you will finish your work, we can go out.
9 She called Marie for to invite her to her birthday party.
10 What an expensive furniture you've got here!
11 You can go out after you will have finished cleaning your room.
12 He went to the bank so to withdraw some money.

39 Add the correct prefixes to the beginning of the words to form the opposites.

1 It was very ...*un*kind of you to laugh at Emily's haircut.
2 Many people ....approve of violent films and television programmes.
3 We became ....patient with the slow service.
4 It is ....legal to leave school before the age of 16 in many countries.
5 He was sacked due to his ....professional behaviour.
6 The nurse who treated me was gentle but ....personal.
7 Some frozen food does not have to be ....frosted before cooking.
8 My homework was wrong because I ....understood the instructions.
9 Dave was ....successful in his attempt to climb Mount Houghton.
10 You can't trust him to do anything. He is very ....responsible.

40 Fill in the correct form of the words in brackets.

Running a business involves many 1) ...*difficulties*... (difficult). It's 2) .... (benefit) to have some 3) .... (know) of management, but you could employ a 4) .... (manage) instead. Of course, you must make a 5) .... (commit) to the business and that will mean working for very long hours at the beginning. You may need to get some 6) .... (finance) support to start your business, and you must be able to make the 7) .... (repay) regularly. It is 8) .... (essence) to have loyal 9) .... (employ) to work for you. Eventually, your business could be a great 10) .... (succeed).

Phrasal Verbs

run across:	(tr) meet sb/find sth by chance
run away:	(int) escape (from home, duty, etc); **run off**
run away with:	(tr) steal sth and leave with it
run down:	1) (tr) knock down and damage or wound (with a vehicle), 2) (tr) speak badly of sb/sth, 3) (int) (of a clock/batteries) stop working
run into:	(tr) 1) meet sb unexpectedly, 2) collide with sth in a vehicle, 3) experience (difficulties)
run out (of):	(tr) no longer have a supply of sth
run over:	1) (tr) knock down and damage or wound (with a vehicle); **run down**, 2) (int) overflow
run through:	(tr) repeat; practise
run up:	(tr) allow (debts, bills, etc.) to increase
run up against:	(tr) face, (difficulties, problems, etc.)
see about:	(tr) make enquiries about or arrangements about sth
see off:	(tr) 1) accompany a traveller to his/her plane, train, etc., 2) make sure that sb leaves (one's property, etc.)
see out:	(tr) last until the end of (a period of time)
see through:	(tr) 1) not be deceived by sb/sth, 2) support sb in difficulties
see to:	(tr) care for sb

41 Fill in the correct particle.

1 I ran ...*into*... an old teacher of mine last weekend at the supermarket.
2 Be careful crossing that road. I don't want you to get run ....
3 The bath water ran .... because Dean forgot to turn off the taps.
4 'The baby's crying again.' 'Don't worry. I'll see .... him this time.'
5 Henry ran .... a huge telephone bill and then he couldn't afford to pay it.
6 You'll never guess what I ran .... at a car boot sale yesterday.
7 The garage roof is leaking. I must see .... getting it fixed.
8 The actor ran .... his lines once more on the night of the opening performance.
9 One of the employees ran .... the money from the till.
10 The alarm clock isn't working. I think the batteries must have run ....

11 The politician ran .... great opposition in his election campaign, but he still managed to win.
12 He's going to see the rest of his contract ...., and then leave the company.
13 They ran .... some difficulties when the jeep got a flat tyre while they were on safari.
14 We saw Linda .... at the airport, and then went home.
15 Neil ran .... from home when he was 17, but regretted it when he saw how hard life could be.
16 We've run .... milk again. I'll go and buy some more.
17 It isn't nice to run people .... all the time. You ought to be more tolerant.
18 Lucy saw .... the man's tricks immediately.
19 He lost control of the car and ran .... a tree.
20 The farmer saw the boys .... his land, and told them not to come back.
21 His parents saw him .... the difficult year, and gave him all the support they could.

42 Fill in the gaps with the correct preposition from the list. Some prepositions can be used more than once.

at, by, for, in, on, out of, off, under, from, without

1 That style of skirt went .... fashion years ago.
2 We heard about the earthquake .... the news.
3 This must be finished by five o'clock .... fail.
4 Paul and I arrived at the party .... the same time.
5 We were .... the impression that they were moving to France.
6 Crime is .... the increase in many cities.
7 The knock at the door took me .... surprise.
8 He erased his project from the computer and had to start .... scratch.
9 .... my opinion, he is the greatest musician of our time.
10 I don't know .... certain, but I think she's gone on holiday.
11 You're looking a bit .... colour — are you feeling alright?
12 The ceremony is being held .... honour of the Pope's visit.
13 He put salt in his tea .... mistake, thinking it was sugar.
14 I can't stop and talk. I'm .... a hurry.
15 She waved until the car was .... sight.
16 We always stay in. Why don't we go out .... a change?
17 He told us the plan .... brief and didn't go into detail.
18 I mustn't eat any chocolate. I'm .... a diet.
19 Peter has gone to London .... business.
20 She selected a CD .... random and put it in the CD player.

Revision Box

43 Put the verbs in brackets into the correct tense.

1 A: You had better ...*get up*... (get up) early tomorrow.
 B: I know. I have to be at the audition by eight o'clock.
2 A: The teacher shouted at me today.
 B: Well, if you .... (do) your homework, she wouldn't have shouted at you.
3 A: Stop making that noise, or else I .... (send) you to your room.
 B: I'm sorry, Mum. I'll be quiet.
4 A: I wish Sam .... (help) more around the house.
 B: Why don't you ask him?
5 A: Did you enjoy your steak?
 B: Not really. I'd rather .... (eat) pizza.
6 A: I wish I .... (not/forget) my purse.
 B: It doesn't matter. I'll lend you some money.
7 A: I don't think Louise liked the film.
 B: Well, she looked as though she .... (enjoy) it.
8 A: I'd rather you .... (not/play) your music so loudly.
 B: Sorry. I'll turn it down.
9 A: Supposing you were rich, what .... (you/buy)?
 B: A big house and a sports car.
10 A: I would have worn an evening dress if I .... (know) it was a formal occasion.
 B: It doesn't matter. You look lovely.

44 Complete each sentence with two to five words, including the word in bold.

1 I've never travelled by aeroplane before.
 first It's ...*the first time*... I've travelled by aeroplane.
2 Is this the fastest you can type?
 faster Can't .... than this?
3 We will probably have a dinner party next weekend.
 likely It .... have a dinner party next weekend.
4 'Alright, I'll help you with your research,' he said to me.
 agreed He .... my research.
5 Someone stole my bag while I was shopping.
 had I .... while I was shopping.
6 I've never heard such a wonderful song.
 the It's .... I've ever heard.

7 They let me go to the rock concert last Saturday.
 allowed I .... to the rock concert last Saturday.
8 He began to play the guitar when he was seventeen.
 since He has .... he was seventeen.
9 He was annoyed by her behaviour and left the party.
 found He .... and left the party.
10 Someone should tell David about the changes we've made.
 be David .... the changes we've made.
11 It wasn't necessary for her to do the washing-up, but she did.
 have She .... the washing-up.
12 'Why are you so angry?' Anne said to Michael.
 was Anne wanted to know .... so angry.
13 The question was so difficult that I couldn't answer it.
 too The question .... to answer.
14 Martin is repairing the car.
 by The car .... Martin.
15 We had no idea the car was stolen.
 know Little.................................. the car was stolen.
16 He can't carry that box. He is too weak.
 enough He .... to carry that box.
17 Someone sent us a large parcel.
 were We .... a large parcel.
18 You had better phone your parents.
 ought You .... your parents.

45 Fill in the gaps with the word which best fits each space. Use only one word in each space.

One of **1)** ...*the*... greatest tennis players **2)** .... the 20th century was Frenchman René Lacoste, **3)** .... success in the sport reached its peak in the 1920s.

He **4)** .... several tennis championships, both in Europe and in America, and **5)** .... nicknamed 'The Crocodile' due **6)** .... his method of playing the game. He never attacked at the start of a match. Instead he would wait **7)** .... his opponent had a moment of weakness and he would win the match.

In 1929, Lacoste retired from tennis. Some years later, he brought **8)** .... a range of sports and leisure clothing with his own 'crocodile' emblem. These designs quickly became popular **9)** .... people all over the world and today 'Lacoste' is still **10)** .... of the favourite labels on the market.

Revision Box

46 **Put the verbs in brackets into the *present simple* or the *present continuous*.**

1 A: That suitcase looks heavy!
   B: It is! It ...*weighs*... (weigh) nearly thirty kilos!
2 A: My feet .... (ache).
   B: Sit down and put them up, then.
3 A: This tea .... (taste) awful.
   B: Oh dear. I think the milk has gone off.
4 A: What are you doing?
   B: I .... (weigh) the ingredients for a cake.
5 A: Have you been to Peter's house before?
   B: Yes, but I .... (not/remember) how to get there.
6 A: Who is that woman?
   B: I .... (think) she works in the bookshop.
7 A: I love this music!
   B: I .... (not/see) how you can like it. It's awful!
8 A: Why .... (you/taste) the soup?
   B: To see if it needs more salt.
9 A: Are you busy this evening?
   B: Yes. I .... (see) some friends at eight o'clock.
10 A: You look happy.
   B: I am. I .... (think) about my holiday.

47 **There are ten unnecessary words in the text below. Cross them out.**

What's in a Name?

1 Many everyday objects are being given their names for
2 a reason. The Biro (a ballpoint pen) was invented by
3 Georg and Josef Biro, so that it was named after them.
4 The sandwich, on the other hand, it was named after the
5 4th Earl of Sandwich in 1762. Despite of the fact that the
6 idea of eating slices of meat between slices of bread was
7 not a new one, the Earl of Sandwich made it popular. He
8 would ask to be served this dish at his card table so that
9 he could play the all day. Morse code (the use of long
10 and short sounds to send the messages along a wire) was
11 been invented by Samuel Morse in 1844 and Bermuda
12 shorts were so named because they at first became popular
13 in Bermuda. So, next time you will use an everyday
14 object, why not to stop and think about where its name
15 came from? You might be surprised!

ORAL
Activity

Mr Blythe is a teacher at a secondary school. His class want to put on a play in order to raise money for charity. Look at the prompts below and make sentences using relative pronouns and adverbs, as in the example.

e.g. The school hall is the place where we hope to stage the play.

Help the RSPCA

- school hall/place/hope to stage/play
- 15th June/day/wish to perform/play
- 'Macbeth'/play/want to put on
- David Lee/boy/play Macbeth
- Sophie Jenkins/girl/mother/offer to make/costumes
- Mark Taylor/boy/father/agree to advertise/play
- £250/amount/hope to raise for charity
- RSPCA/charity/wish to donate money to

WRITING
Activity

Mr Blythe is now writing a letter to the headmaster to ask for permission to put on the play. Look at the Oral Activity again and use your notes to complete the letter below.

Dear Mr Johnson,

I am writing to request permission for my class to put on a play in order to raise money for charity. The school hall is the place where we hope to stage the play. 15th June is ....
..
..
..
..
... I hope you will allow us to put on the play, as it would be both educational and enjoyable for the class, as well as beneficial to our chosen charity.

Yours sincerely,
Mr Blythe

Pronouns

*This is Mr Branson's class. **He** is writing an example on the board. The students are reading **it**. **He** will ask **them** some questions later.*

Personal Pronouns

> **subject pronouns:** I , you, he, she, it, we, you, they
> **object pronouns:** me, you, him, her, it, us, you, them

Subject pronouns go before verbs as subjects and object pronouns go after verbs or prepositions as objects. *e.g. I like **him** a lot.*

◆ **We do not use a noun and a personal pronoun together.** *e.g. **Jim** is at work. (NOT: ~~Jim he is~~ ...)*

◆ **We use there + be to mention something for the first time or to say that something or someone exists. We use it + be to give more details about something or someone that has already been mentioned. We also use *it* to refer to a person when we are identifying him or her.**
> *e.g. **There is** a message for you. **It is** from your boss.*
> *'Who's on the phone?' '**It's** Mr Fox.'*
> *(NOT: ~~He's~~ Mr Fox.)*

◆ **We can use it as the subject to talk about weather, distance, temperature and time and also with: *It seems/appears that/It is said that, It doesn't matter, It looks like,* etc.**
> *e.g. **It's a ten-minute drive** to the station. **It's 23˚C** outside.*
> *__It seems that there are__ some problems with the new management. **OR There seem to be** some problems with the new management.*

◆ **We use it to talk about something that has already been made clear. We use one when it is not clear which thing in particular we are talking about.**
> *e.g. I can't find **my wallet**. Have you seen **it**? (The speaker is talking about a specific wallet.)*
> *I haven't got **any nice jumpers**; I need to buy **one**. (The speaker is not talking about a specific jumper.)*

◆ **In *short answers* and after *as* and *than* we use an *object pronoun* (informal) or a *subject pronoun + auxiliary verb* (formal).**
> *e.g. 'I hate jazz.' '**Me** too.'/'**I do** too.'*
> *She spends more money **than me/than I do**.*

  Fill in the blanks with the correct *subject* or *object* pronoun.

1 Joe's late. Has ...*he*... called? It's not like .... to be late.
2 Nick is lucky. .... has a good job and .... earns much more than .... do.
3 Marie works hard, because .... wants the boss to give .... a pay rise.
4 'Where is Sarah?' 'Isn't that .... over there?'
5 She's older than .... am, but I'm taller than ....
6 'I'm sick and tired of this job.' '.......... too.'
7 'John gave .... a great idea.' '.......... is so inventive, isn't ....?'

  Fill in the gaps with *there*, *it* or *one*.

1 A: Did you enjoy the party?
   B: No. ...*There*... weren't many people there. .... was boring.
2 A: .... is someone on the phone for you. I think .... is David.
   B: Hold on. I'll be there in a minute.
3 A: Was that a Ferrari going past?
   B: I didn't see ....
4 A: Look! .... is your friend!
   B: Oh yes! .... 's Ian.
5 A: When did you last see a film?
   B: I haven't seen .... for months.
6 A: Have you got your umbrella with you?
   B: No. .... wasn't raining this morning, so I left .... at home.
7 A: Did you sleep late yesterday?
   B: Yes. By the time I woke up, ... was lunch time.
8 A: Have you got a computer?
   B: No. I had .... , but I sold ....
9 A: Look at this mess! .... are toys everywhere.
   B: Sorry. I'll tidy up.
10 A: Did you visit the Acropolis?
   B: No. .... wasn't enough time.
11 A: Could I have the bill, please?
   B: Certainly. I'll bring .... at once.
12 A: .... seems to be a mistake in this report.
   B: Oh, sorry. I'll type .... again.
13 A: Josie is very pretty.
   B: Yes. .... doesn't matter what she wears, she always looks good.

Possessive Adjectives/Pronouns

*This is Melanie. She is sitting at **her** desk. She is giving a file to **her** colleague, Samantha. The files behind her are **hers**. Melanie's boss asks her to update them every week.*

Possessive Adjectives		Possessive Pronouns	
my	our	mine	ours
your	your	yours	yours
his		his	
her	their	hers	theirs
its		—	

◆ Both possessive adjectives and possessive pronouns can be used to talk about ownership or the relationship between people. Possessive adjectives are followed by nouns, whereas possessive pronouns are not.
  e.g. This is **her** bag. It's **hers**.

◆ We normally use *possessive adjectives* with parts of the body and clothes.
  e.g. Lucy twisted **her ankle**.
      He put on **his jacket** and **his hat** and left.

We use the and not possessive adjectives with prepositional phrases mostly when we are talking about things that happen to parts of people's bodies, for example blows, pains, etc. Verbs usually used in this pattern are: **hit, punch, slap, bite, touch, pat, sting,** etc.
  e.g. She patted him **on the shoulder**.
      He's got a pain **in the chest**.

◆ We use the word own in the following structures to emphasise the fact that something belongs to someone.
  noun + of + my/your, etc. + own
  my/your, etc. + own + noun
  e.g. I wish I had a **room of my own**.
  OR I wish I had **my own room**.

Note: its = possessive adjective
      e.g. The cat is licking **its** paw.
      it's = it is or it has
      e.g. **It's** (it is) raining. **It's** (it has) got one room.

Possessive case

The possessive case can be used to talk about ownership or the relationship between people. It is formed in two ways:

1. with 's/' for people or animals

● **singular nouns + 's** e.g. Bob's dog
● **plural nouns ending in -s + '** e.g. my parents' car
● **plural nouns not ending in -s + 's** e.g. the men's department
● **compound nouns + 's** e.g. my sister-in-law's family
● We use 's after the last of two or more names to show common possession.
  e.g. **Jackie** and **George's** camera. (The camera belongs to both of them.)
● We use 's after each name to show individual possession. e.g. **Peter's** and **Mike's** cameras. (Each boy has his own camera.)

2. with of for inanimate things

● **of + inanimate thing or abstract noun**
  e.g. the wheels **of** the car, the price **of** fame
● **a/the/this/that + noun + of + possessive**
  e.g. She's **a colleague of mine. That friend of Pamela's** is a doctor.

Note: When we refer to a certain place or time, the possessive case is formed as follows:
● phrase of place (shop/home/business, etc.) + 's
  e.g. at the **chemist's** (we mean the shop),
      at **Susan's** (house)
● phrase showing length of time/specific moment or event + 's/'
  e.g. a **year's** savings/two **hours'** drive/**today's** news
● We can use either 's or of when we talk about places or organisations.
  e.g. Rome's population OR the population of Rome

 3 **Connect the nouns using -'s, -' or ...of... .**

1 husband/Sarah ...*Sarah's husband*...
2 teacher/the children ....
3 coats/Sally and Jane ....
4 the Prime Minister/England ....
5 CDs/my sisters ....

6 the end/the road ....
7 books/the students ....
8 the owner/the building ....

4 **Fill in the correct *possessive adjective* or *pronoun*.**

1 A: Why did you lend Alf ...*your*... jacket?
   B: Because he forgot .... and it was cold.
2 A: Chloe looks upset. .... eyes are very red.
   B: Yes. She had an argument with .... best friend.
3 A: Tom looks nice. .... new clothes suit him.
   B: Yes. I like .... new shirt.
4 A: Have you met .... new boss yet?
   B: No, but I have met .... secretary.
5 A: Mr and Mrs Ford must be rich. .... car is very expensive.
   B: Yes, and it's much faster than ....
6 A: I like .... dress.
   B: Oh, it's not .... My sister lent it to me.
7 A: Celia enjoys .... job.
   B: Yes, and she gets on very well with .... colleagues.
8 A: Have you seen .... keys?
   B: Yes. They're on the table beside ....

5 **Fill in a *possessive adjective* or *the*.**

1 We always wash ...*our*... hands before eating anything.
2 Wipe .... feet before you come in.
3 She looked him in .... eye and told him the truth.
4 I trapped .... finger in the door.
5 He lost .... jacket at the party.
6 Julia says that Mike pulled .... hair.
7 He hit .... knee on the table.
8 She felt something tap her on .... shoulder.
9 The branch snapped back and hit him in .... face.
10 I like .... shoes. I wonder where she bought them.

6 **Fill in the gaps with *of* where necessary, and *my*, *your*, etc, *own*.**

1 If they had a garden ...*of their own*..., they could grow flowers.
2 John is lucky. He has got a computer ....
3 Don't treat me like a child! I've got a mind ....
4 I don't need a lift to work. I've got .... car.
5 They hope to set up .... business one day.
6 Haven't you got .... book? You're always taking mine.
7 Their new house is big, so Harry can have a room ....
8 We're saving up to buy a flat ....
9 You can't eat my sweets. Buy some ....

7 **Fill in *its* or *it's*.**

1 My new bike is great. ...*It's*... got lots of gears on it.
2 The house next door has got a fence around .... garden.
3 Let's go home. .... getting late.
4 I love this shop. .... got lots of lovely things in it.
5 .... the most beautiful house I've ever seen.
6 That dog has got a white patch over .... eye.

8 **Rewrite the sentences using the correct *possessive form*.**

1 He put his briefcase on **the car – the roof**.
   ...*He put his briefcase on the roof of the car*....
2 The **walk** to school takes **ten minutes**.
   ....
3 We are going on holiday **two weeks from now**.
   ....
4 She received the parcel in **the post – this morning**.
   ....
5 Paul never pays attention to **his parents – the advice**.
   ....
6 That girl on the stage is **a friend – my**.
   ....
7 **Sarah – David – bicycles** are being repaired.
   ....
8 Simon lost **a week of pay** when he was ill.
   ....
9 The girl shook **the man – the hand**.
   ....
10 Can I see **the menu – for today**, please?
   ....
11 We had a barbecue in **Bob-Marie-garden**.
   ....
12 The inspector looked at **the passengers – the tickets**.
   ....

9 **Fill in the correct *pronouns* or *possessives*.**

Dear Carol,

   Thank you for 1) ...*your*... last letter. I really enjoyed reading 2) .... Have 3) .... children started 4) .... new school yet? I'm sure 5) .... will enjoy 6) .... very much once they settle in and make new friends. Mary and John asked me for 7) .... new address, so I gave 8) .... to 9) .... I hope 10) .... don't mind. I saw Anne last week. She said 11) .... would phone you this week to invite you to 12) .... birthday party. Well, I'm going to 13) .... aerobics class now. Please write to 14) .... soon.

                                          Love,
                                          Rachel

Pronouns - Possessives - Demonstratives - Quantifiers

Reflexive Pronouns

Subject pronouns		Reflexive pronouns	Subject pronouns		Reflexive pronouns
I	→	myself	it	→	itself
you	→	yourself	we	→	ourselves
he	→	himself	you	→	yourselves
she	→	herself	they	→	themselves

We use reflexive pronouns:

◆ with verbs such as *behave, burn, cut, enjoy, hurt, introduce, kill, look at, teach*, etc., or with prepositions when the subject and the object of the verb are the same person. We do not use reflexive pronouns after *prepositions of place*.

e.g. **Sara** (subject) **has taught herself** how to play the guitar.
You look pleased **with yourself**.
BUT: She looked **behind her** because she heard footsteps. (NOT: She looked behind ~~herself~~ ...)

◆ with the preposition by when we mean alone =
1) without company = *on one's own*,
2) without help

e.g. Dad fixed the roof **by himself**.
(= Nobody helped Dad fix the roof.)
He hates travelling **by himself/on his own**.
(= He hates travelling alone, without company.)

◆ in the following expressions: *enjoy yourself* (have a good time), *behave yourself* (be good), *help yourself* (you are welcome to take something if you want).

◆ to emphasise the subject or the object of a sentence.

e.g. I spoke to the **manager himself**. (I spoke to the manager, not somebody else.)

Note: 1) We do not use reflexive pronouns with the verbs *concentrate, feel, meet* and *relax*.

e.g. I feel nervous. (NOT: I feel ~~myself~~ nervous.)

2) The verbs *dress, wash* and *shave* are not normally followed by a reflexive pronoun. However, we can use a reflexive pronoun with these verbs when we want to show that someone did something with a lot of effort.

e.g. She **washed, dressed** and then had breakfast.
He had a broken arm, but he managed to **shave himself**.

But we always say dry myself.

◆ **Each other** means *one another*. Study the following examples:

They are feeding **themselves**.   *They are feeding* **each other**.

10 Complete the sentences using verbs from the list below and a *reflexive pronoun*, as in the example.

fix, make, organise, teach, paint, decorate, dress, grow

1 Annie didn't buy her wedding dress. She ...*made it herself*....
2 Do you like these flowers? I ....
3 Look at this picture. My son ....
4 What a beautiful room! Did you ....?
5 I didn't call the plumber to fix the pipe. I ....
....
6 He didn't have piano lessons. He ....
7 My son is only three, but I don't dress him. He ....
....
8 Nobody helped Julie with the party. She ....
....

11 Fill in the appropriate *reflexive pronoun* or *each other/one another*.

1 A: Who built your shed for you?
   B: No one. We built it ...*ourselves*....
2 A: Will you keep in touch with Lucy when she moves?
   B: Oh, yes. We will write to ....
3 A: Paul and Sue don't get on very well.
   B: No. They're always arguing with ....
4 A: Did Mum help Jane to cook dinner?
   B: No. She did it all by ....
5 A: Why are you and Marie going into town?
   B: We are going to buy .... some new clothes.
6 A: Did you switch the heating on?
   B: No. It switches .... on every morning.
7 A: Help .... to coffee and biscuits.
   B: Thank you. I will.
8 A: How is Sarah?
   B: I don't know. We haven't seen .... for months.
9 A: What's the matter with Steve?
   B: I think he wants to be by .... for a while.
10 A: Do Mark and Ellen work well together?
   B: Oh, yes. They often help .... with their work.

Demonstratives
(This - That / These - Those)

This, these, that and **those** are used as *demonstrative adjectives* when they are followed by a noun and as *pronouns* when they are not followed by a noun.

e.g. **This vase** is made of crystal. *(demonstrative adjective)*
That is made of glass. *(pronoun)*

this/these are used:

◆ **for people or things which are near us.**
e.g. **This** is my favourite painting.

◆ **for present or future situations.**
e.g. My cousin is staying with me **this** week.

◆ **to refer to an idea we are about to mention.**
e.g. Listen to **this**. It's really funny.

◆ **to introduce oneself on the phone or to introduce people.**
e.g. 'Hello? **This** is Helen.' 'Mum, **this** is Kate.'

◆ **when the speaker is in or near the place he/she is referring to.** e.g. **This** room hasn't got enough light.

that/those are used:

◆ **for people or things which are not near us.**
e.g. **That** man over there is waving at you.

◆ **for past situations.** e.g. **That** was a great party. We enjoyed ourselves.

◆ **to refer back to something mentioned before.**
e.g. 'She lost her job.' '**That**'s awful.'

◆ **when speaking on the phone to ask who the other person is.** e.g. 'Who's **that** speaking?'

12 **Fill in the gaps with** *this, that, these* **or** *those*.

1   ...*That*... car over there belongs to the mayor.
2   .... people over there are waiting for the bus.
3   We're moving house .... month.
4   .... diamond earrings here are priceless.
5   'I've got a new job.' '....................'s wonderful news.'
6   'Mum, ... is my teacher, Miss Jones.'
7   .... are my holiday photographs. Would you like to look at them?
8   'Hello, ... is Jane Black speaking.'
9   .... house here was built in 1500.
10 The day I got married was wonderful. I will remember .... day for ever.
11 I had a wonderful childhood. We did things differently in .... days.
12 'Hello, this is Alan. Who's ...., please?'

Some/Any/No

The children are **somewhere** *outside the building. There aren't* **any** *chairs. The teacher is writing* **something** *on the board.* **Everybody** *is looking at the board.*

	Affirmative	Interrogative	Negative
Countable/ Uncountable	some	any	not any/no
People	someone/ somebody	anyone/ anybody	no one/not anyone nobody/not anybody
Things	something	anything	nothing/ not anything
Places	somewhere	anywhere	nowhere/not anywhere

◆ **Some, any and no are used with uncountable nouns (***rice, tea***, etc.) and plural countable nouns (***toys, books***, etc.).**
e.g. **some rice, some toys**

◆ **Some and its compounds (someone/somebody, something, somewhere) are normally used in affirmative sentences.**
e.g. I need **some** advice. He's got **something** in his pocket.

◆ **Any and its compounds are also used in interrogative sentences. Not any is used in negative sentences.**
e.g. Are there **any** vegetables in the fridge? There **isn't anybody** in the office.

Any and its compounds are also used with negative words such as *without, never, seldom, rarely, hardly*, etc.
e.g. I can do this without **any** help.
I have never seen **anything** like that.

◆ **No and its compounds are used instead of not any in negative sentences.**
e.g. She hasn't got **any** money./She's got **no** money.
He didn't give me **anything**. He gave me **nothing**.

◆ **We use a singular verb with compounds of *some, any* and *no*.**
e.g. There **is something** wrong with the computer.

Pronouns - Possessives - Demonstratives - Quantifiers

◆ *Some* and its compounds are also used in interrogative sentences when we expect a positive answer, for example when we make an offer or request.

e.g. a) *This place is crowded. Shall we go **somewhere** else? (We expect the answer **yes**.)*

b) *'Would you like **something** to drink?' (offer)*
*'Yes, please. Can I have **some** lemonade?' (request)*

◆ When *any* and its compounds are used in affirmative sentences, there is a difference in meaning. Study the following examples:

a) *You can come **any** day you want.*
(It doesn't matter which.)

b) ***Anyone/Anybody** can take part in the quiz show.*
(It doesn't matter who.)

c) *You can find **anything** you want in this shop.*
(It doesn't matter what.)

d) *I'll find you **anywhere** you go.*
(It doesn't matter where.)

◆ **Every** is used with singular countable nouns.
e.g. **Every** employee must clock in and out.

◆ The pronouns everyone/everybody, everything and the adverb everywhere are used in affirmative, interrogative and negative sentences and are followed by a singular verb.
e.g. ***Everybody/Everyone** has a right to a fair trial.*
(NOT: ...~~have a right~~.)

13 Bill has lost his keys. **Read the dialogue and underline the correct item.**

A: There is **1)** *nothing/**something*** more annoying than losing **2)** *something/**anything***.
B: What have you lost?
A: My keys. They must be **3)** *anywhere/**somewhere*** in the house, but I've got **4)** *no/**any*** idea where. I can't find them **5)** *nowhere/**anywhere***.
B: Are you sure you haven't left them **6)** *somewhere/**nowhere*** by mistake?
A: Of course not. They can't be **7)** *somewhere/**anywhere*** else but here. **8)** *No one/**Someone*** must have hidden them.
B: Why would **9)** *no one/**anyone*** hide your keys? There is **10)** *any/**no*** reason for **11)** *anyone/**no one*** to do **12)** *nothing/**something*** so silly.
A: Well, I need **13)** *some/**any*** help to find them. I have to go **14)** *anywhere/**somewhere*** important this afternoon.
B: Calm down. It's **15)** *some/**no*** use getting angry about **16)** *anything/**something*** like this. Look! There are **17)** *no/**some*** keys on that chair.
A: They're mine! Oh, I feel so silly!

14 Fill in the gaps with *everyone/everybody, everything* or *everywhere*, **and the correct form of the verbs in brackets.**

1 The meeting was a success. ...*Everything went*... (go) well.
2 .... (learn) a foreign language at this school.
3 The film is a box-office hit. .... (talk) about it.
4 We are going on holiday next week. .... (be) arranged.
5 On Friday afternoon, ... (leave) the office early.
6 Mark is a very popular boy. .... (like) him.
7 After the snow had fallen, ... (be) white.
8 I'm glad we came to the beach. .... (have) a wonderful time.
9 We wanted to go to a restaurant, but .... (be) full.
10 I dropped my bag and .... (fall) out.
11 We can't make the announcement until .... (arrive).

15 Fill in the gaps with *some, any, no* or one of their compounds.

1 A: Is there ...*anything*... good on television tonight?
   B: I don't know. Look in the newspaper.
2 A: Would you like .... to eat?
   B: No, I don't want ...., thank you.
3 A: There is .... here to see you.
   B: Who is it?
4 A: I went to Jane's house, but there was .... at home.
   B: Perhaps she has gone .... nice for the weekend.
5 A: I have .... time to do all this work.
   B: Is there .... I can do to help?
6 A: Was the party good last night?
   B: Not really. There were hardly .... people there.
7 A: I have to go shopping, but I don't have .... money.
   B: I'll lend you .... if you like.
8 A: Have you seen Michael ....?
   B: No, I haven't seen him.
9 A: The town was very busy today. There was .... to park.
   B: They should build .... new parking facilities.
10 A: What would you do if you were lost?
   B: I would ask .... for directions.
11 A: Is there .... you would like to go this weekend?
   B: I'd like to go .... nice and quiet.
12 A: Is .... wrong with Paul?
   B: No, there's .... wrong with him. He's just tired.

Else

◆ The adverb *else* means 'other, different', or 'more'. It is used after *somebody, anybody, nothing, everywhere*, etc. and *who, what, why, when, where* and *how*. It is followed by a singular verb.

e.g. a) Can I get you **anything else**?
b) Kim hasn't arrived yet but **everybody else** is here.
c) 'I've been to Lisbon twice this year.' 'Really? **Where else** have you been?'
d) 'I bought a lovely rug from the market.' 'What **else** did you buy?'

Anything (else) and **nothing (else)** can be used with but.
e.g. I haven't got **anything (else)** to offer **but** my advice.

◆ The possessive of else is else's.
e.g. I have taken somebody **else's** book by mistake.

◆ Or else means 'otherwise', 'if not'.
e.g. Hurry up **or else** we'll miss our flight.

◆ Elsewhere is formal and means 'somewhere else'.
e.g. If you are not satisfied with the service in this restaurant, you can go **elsewhere**.

16 Fill in the gaps with *else, else's, or else* or *elsewhere*.

1 He is ill. Why ...*else*... would he go to the doctor's?
2 The postman has delivered someone .... mail to our house.
3 She must be at work. Where .... could she be?
4 I love it here. I wouldn't want to live anywhere ....
5 This hotel is full. We will have to stay....................... .
6 Don't shout .... you will wake the baby.
7 What .... do we need to take with us?
8 This jacket isn't mine. It's somebody ....

17 Complete the sentences using *else* as in the example.

1 Hurry up, James, ...*everybody else*... (all the other people) has left.
2 If you can't help me, I'll ask .... (another person).
3 The manager isn't in his office. He must be .... (another place).
4 Have you invited .... (one more person) to the party?
5 If you've finished your work, I can give you .... (a different thing) to do.
6 I only have the ironing to do now. I've done .... (all the other things).

Every - Each

◆ Every and each are used with singular countable nouns. We normally use *each* when we talk about two people or things. We use *every* when we talk about three or more people or things.

e.g. He was holding an ice cream in **each** hand.
(NOT: ...in every hand.)
Every part of my body hurt after the fall.
(NOT: Each part of my body ...)

◆ Every one and each (one) can be followed by of.
e.g. It was the twins' birthday yesterday. I gave a present to **each (one) of** them.
I've seen all of Mel Gibson's films and I liked **every one of** them.

◆ We use every when we are thinking of people or things together, in a group to mean 'all', 'everybody/everything'.
e.g. **Every** employee is entitled to twenty days off. (all employees)

We use each when we are thinking of people or things separately, one at a time.
e.g. **Each** employee in turn will tell the manager when he wishes to take his holiday.

◆ We use every to show how often something happens.
e.g. There is a train **every twenty minutes**.
I have to attend a meeting **every two months**.

◆ We use *every* but not *each* with words and expressions such as *almost, nearly, practically* and *without exception*.
e.g. She has invited **every** person she knows, **without exception**. (NOT: ...each person she knows ...)

18 Fill in the gaps with *each* or *every*.

1 We have two cars and ...*each*... of them is blue.
2 There were lots of sweets and she ate .... one of them.
3 .... of the two boxes has bottles inside.
4 The teacher gave one book to .... student.
5 She gave .... of the children an ice cream.
6 He is wearing a different colour sock on .... foot.
7 I've got .... book that author's ever written.
8 I have seen almost .... episode of this programme.
9 Almost .... T-shirt she owns is a designer label.
10 The Olympic Games are held .... four years.
11 I eat an apple .... day.
12 She bought .... of her friends a souvenir from Paris.

A lot of - Much - Many

There aren't **many cherries**, but there are **a lot of strawberries**.
Is there **much pasta**? Yes, there is **a lot**.

◆ A lot of/lots of are used with both plural countable and uncountable nouns. They are normally used in affirmative sentences. Of is omitted when a lot/lots are not followed by a noun.
e.g. There were **a lot of/lots of people** at the concert.
There is **a lot of/lots of yoghurt** in the fridge.
Have you got many books? Yes, I've got **a lot**.

◆ *Much* and *many* are normally used in interrogative and negative sentences. Much is used with uncountable nouns and many with plural countable nouns.
e.g. Is there **much sugar** in the cupboard?
There **isn't much sugar** in this cake.
Have you got **many CDs**? I **haven't got many CDs**.

◆ *How much* and *how many* are used in questions and negations.
How much + uncountable noun → amount
How many + countable noun → number
e.g. '**How much money** have you got?' 'Not much.'
'**How many** stamps do you need?' '**Six**.'

◆ Too many is used with plural countable nouns. It has a negative meaning and shows that there is more of something than is wanted or needed.
e.g. You eat **too many sweets**. Your teeth will rot.

◆ Too much is used with uncountable nouns. It has the same negative meaning as *too many*.
e.g. I've got **too much work** to do. I can't go out.

◆ We use *most/some/any/many/much/(a) few/(a) little/several/one, two, etc.* + of when a noun follows, preceded by *this, that, these, those, a, the* or *possessives*.
e.g. **Most of the people** at the party were from work.
but: Most people like parties.

A few/Few - A little/Little

Laura has got **a few peaches.** She can make some jam.

Lucy has got **(very) few peaches.** She can't make any jam.

Simon has got **a little paint**. He can paint the door.

Rick has got **(very) little paint**. He can't paint the door.

◆ A few/few are used with plural countable nouns (*flowers, letters*, etc.).

A few means **not many, but enough.**

e.g. There are **a few hotels** in this town. You'll probably find a room to spend the night.

Few means **hardly any, almost none** and can be used with very for emphasis.

e.g. There are **(very) few cupboards** in the kitchen. There's not enough room to store my plates and glasses.

◆ A little/little are used with uncountable nouns (*milk, time*, etc.).

A little means **not much, but enough.**

e.g. There is **a little petrol** in the tank. It will get us to the next town.

Little means **hardly any, almost none** and can be used with very for emphasis.

e.g. There's **(very) little coffee** left. We need to buy some more.

19 Fill in *many, much, how many, how much* or *a lot (of)*.

1 A: Shall we go out tonight?
   B: I can't. I don't have ...*much*... money, I'm afraid.
2 A: Can you help me, please?
   B: I'm sorry. I haven't got .... time at the moment.
3 A: .... potatoes are in that bag?
   B: Seven, I think. Why?
4 A: What did you do on your holiday?
   B: Well, I read .... and I relaxed on the beach.
5 A: There isn't .... milk left.
   B: Well, I'll buy some later this afternoon.
6 A: .... homework have you got?
   B: Quite .... I'd better start now.
7 A: Did you enjoy your dinner?
   B: Yes. I ate .... and I'm very full.
8 A: Mark is a wonderful athlete.
   B: Yes. He has won .... competitions.
9 A: Are there .... flowers in the garden?
   B: Yes, and they are beautiful too.
10 A: Are you very busy?
   B: No. I haven't got .... to do today.
11 A: She has got .... clothes.
   B: I know. She wears something different every day.
12 A: .... times have you seen this film?
   B: Three times, but I always cry at the end.
13 A: .... food should we take on the picnic?
   B: Oh, enough for all four of us.
14 A: Have you travelled to .... places?
   B: Yes, I go to a different country every year.

20 Fill in the gaps with *too much* or *too many*.

1 A: Would you like to spend the weekend with us?
   B: I can't. I have ...*too many*... things to do.
2 A: Shall we go to London tomorrow?
   B: No. It takes .... time to get there.
3 A: I had a terrible nightmare last night.
   B: That's because you watch .... horror films.
4 A: .... red meat is bad for your health.
   B: I know. I rarely eat red meat.
5 A: There are .... people on this train.
   B: I know. It's very crowded.
6 A: I have spent .... money this month.
   B: You should have been more sensible.
7 A: This sauce tastes awful.
   B: I think I put .... salt in it.
8 A: I made .... food for the party.
   B: I know. There is a lot left over.
9 A: There are .... books in this bag.
   B: I know. It's very heavy, isn't it?
10 A: You are making .... noise. I can't concentrate.
   B: I'm sorry. I'll try to be quiet.

21 Underline the correct item.

1 I have a lot of records, but **very few/little/very little** CDs.
2 We have **very little/very few/few** spaghetti, so I can't make Spaghetti Bolognese.
3 I'm tired. I didn't get **many/much/few** sleep last night.
4 I've made **many/much/a lot of** notes, but I haven't written my essay yet.
5 This coffee is bitter. It needs **a few/a little/little** more sugar.
6 I have invited **a few/a lot of/much** people to the party. I hope there will be room for them all.
7 I don't have **many/much/few** time at the moment. I'll talk to you later.
8 I have had **a few/very few/very little** success in my search for a job.
9 There are **much/a lot of/a little** reasons why he should go to university.
10 I'd love to come to the beach. I just need **a few/a little/many** minutes to get ready.
11 There are **much/little/few** people who are as hard-working as James.
12 I have **little/a little/a few** work to do before I can leave.
13 I made **a lot/a little/a few** biscuits this morning. Would you like to try one?
14 There weren't **few/much/many** people in town today. It was very quiet.
15 There is **a little/little/a few** chance of his getting the job. He has no experience.

22 Fill in *many, few, much* or *little*.

Claire pushed the door open a 1) ...*little*... and looked inside. The house was small and there was not 2) .... furniture. There were a 3) .... chairs and a table, but there were very 4) .... signs of comfort. There was not 5) .... light, but Claire could see that there were not 6) .... pictures or ornaments. It was as though the owner of the house spent very 7) .... time there. After a 8) .... more moments, she quietly closed the door and walked away.

23 Add *of* where necessary.

1 A lot ...*of*... people have mobile phones these days.
2 Many .... her books are very old.
3 Most .... children enjoy watching cartoons.
4 I've met several .... his colleagues.
5 A few .... birds were singing in the tree.
6 Have you ever seen any .... Bruce Willis films?
7 Some .... my friends live abroad.
8 One .... her books has won an award.
9 I have hardly any .... free time at the moment.
10 A few .... the guests arrived early.

Both/Neither - All/None - Either

Both the motorcycle and the bicycle have got handlebars.
Both of these have two wheels.
Neither of these has/have room for luggage.
Neither the motorcycle nor the bicycle
is convenient in winter.

All of these are means of transport.
None of these can travel across water.
All of these can carry passengers.

◆ **Both** refers to two people, things or groups. It has a positive meaning and is followed by a plural verb.
  e.g. **Both** men **work** at the bank.
       Both of them cost a lot of money.

◆ **Neither** refers to two people, things or groups and has a negative meaning. Neither of + plural noun phrase can be followed by either a singular or plural verb in the affirmative.
  e.g. **Neither of the films has/have** won an award.
       Neither of them is/are working at the moment.
  But: **Neither dress is** long enough.

◆ **All** refers to more than two people, things or groups. It has a positive meaning and is followed by a plural verb.
  e.g. **All the actors were** brilliant.
       All of them are well-qualified.

◆ **Both/All** can go: a) after the verb to be, b) after the auxiliary verb, but before the main verb.
  e.g. They **are both/all** excited. They **have both/all signed** the contract.

◆ **Whole** is used with singular countable nouns. We use a/the/this/my etc. + whole + noun.
  e.g. He was hungry, so he ate **the whole pie**.
  Also: He was hungry, so he ate **all the pie**.
  We don't use **whole** with uncountable nouns.
  e.g. She spent **all the money** you gave her.
       (NOT: ...~~the whole money~~...)
  All + day/morning/week/ year = the whole + day/ morning/week/year
  e.g. He's been making phone calls **all morning/the whole morning**.

◆ **None of** refers to more than two people, things or groups and has a negative meaning. It is used with nouns or object pronouns and is followed by either a singular or plural verb.
  e.g. **None of my friends has/have travelled** abroad.
  But: 'How many books did you buy?' '**None.**'

◆ **Either** refers to two people, things or groups and is followed by a singular countable noun.
  e.g. You can paint the walls blue or green.
       Either colour is fine with me.

  Either of + plural noun phrase can be followed by either a singular or plural verb.
  e.g. **Either of these two dresses suits/suit** you.
  But: **Either dress suits** you.
  We can use not ... either (of) instead of neither (of).
  Either can also be used at the end of a negative sentence.
  e.g. I saw two plays, but I did**n't** like **either of** them.
       My sister can't drive, and I can't **either**.

◆ **Both ... and** is followed by a plural verb.
  e.g. **Both** Mark **and** Sam **work** here.

  Neither ... nor/Either ... or take either a singular or plural verb, depending on the subject which follows **nor** or **or**.
  e.g. **Either Mum or Dad is** going to pick me up.

24 **Underline the correct items.**

Oliver has got two jobs, but **1)** *neither/neither of* them pay very well. He has had more jobs already than **2)** *most/most of* people have in their whole lives, but **3)** *none/none of* them really suited him. It is a shame, because he spent **4)** *several/several of* years at college and has got **5)** *some/any* good qualifications. **6)** *Either of/Both* his parents are very proud of him for getting a good education, but **7)** *each of/neither of* them can understand why he can't find a suitable job. He buys **8)** *several/most* newspapers every week and looks carefully through **9)** *each of/every one of* them to see if **10)** *any/no* good jobs are being advertised. He applies for **11)** *every one of/every* available position, but often receives **12)** *some/no* reply. He still believes that he will find his ideal job one day.

25 **Choose the correct answer.**

1 'How many brothers do you have?'
  'Two, and ...C... of them are older than me.'
  A either   **B** all   **C** both

2 'There were a lot of people at the party.'
  'I know. But .... of them were strangers to me.'
  A all   **B** neither   **C** either

3 'Mum, did you wash my blue shirt?'
  'Well, I washed two shirts, but .... of them was blue.'
  A both   **B** neither   **C** either

4 'You can't be lonely. You have lots of friends.'
  'Yes, but .... of them can come to visit today.'
  A none   **B** all   **C** both

5 'Have you seen any *James Bond* films?'
  'I've seen two. .... of them were very good.'
  A Either   **B** Both   **C** All

6 'Why didn't you buy anything?'
  'Because .... of those clothes were very nice.'
  A both   **B** either   **C** none

7 'Both of those dresses are beautiful.'
  'Yes, but I don't think .... of them will fit me.'
  A either   **B** neither   **C** all

8 'You have lots of CDs, don't you?'
  'Yes, and .... of them are in my room.'
  A none   **B** all   **C** both

9 'Did you read both of those books?'
  'Yes, but I didn't enjoy .... of them.'
  A neither   **B** all   **C** either

10 'Did you watch a comedy last night?'
   'No. We watched two films, but .... of them were comedies.'
   A either   **B** neither   **C** both

11 'Do you have many pen-friends?'
   'Yes, and .... of them live abroad.'
   A all   **B** either   **C** none

26 **Rewrite the sentences using** *both...and,* *neither...nor* **or** *either...or.*

1 Beth hasn't got a car. Lucy hasn't got a car, either.
  ...Neither Beth nor Lucy has got a car....

2 Harold wears glasses. Helen wears glasses, too.
  ....

3 Kerry is cleaning the house, or maybe Joe is.
  ....

4 Clive can't speak French. Bill can't speak French, either.
  ....

5 Kim loves chocolate. Laura loves chocolate, too.
  ....

6 Simon needs a haircut. Mike needs one, too.
  ....

7 Daphne doesn't eat meat. Jayne doesn't, either.
  ....

8 Scott is washing the car, or maybe Jim is.
  ....

9 Debbie goes to school. Hannah goes to school, too.
  ....

10 Henry repaired the fence, or maybe Todd did.
   ....

11 Beth can't play the piano. Doug can't, either.
   ....

12 Pam will water the plants, or else Carl will.
   ....

27 **Fill in the gaps with the correct missing word(s).**

A: Can you give me **1)** ...*some*... advice, please?
B: Of course. Is **2)** .... worrying you?
A: Well, yes. I've had **3)** .... problems at university recently.
B: Maybe there's **4)** .... I can do to help you. Tell me what's wrong and I'll see if there's **5)** .... I can do.
A: Well, the main problem is that I have **6)** .... work to do for my exams and I don't have **7)** .... time left to study. I've left it very late and so far I haven't done **8)** .... revision.
B: I see. How **9)** .... time do you have until the exams?
A: Three weeks. I should be studying **10)** .... day, but I don't know where to start. I have so **11)** .... subjects to study. Also, I don't really have **12)** .... to sit in peace and quiet. Our house is always noisy.
B: Well, if you want **13)** .... quiet to work, why don't you go to the library? It's always quiet there and there are **14)** .... useful books there which you could use in your revision.
A: That's a great idea. Thank you very much. You've been very helpful.

Other and its forms

◆ **another** = additional, an extra one. It is used with singular countable nouns.
*e.g. Would you like **another cup** of tea?*
*These apples are delicious. Can I have **another** (one)?*

◆ **another** + few/two, three etc. + noun
*e.g. We're going to stay for **another few days**/**another four days**.*

◆ **other/another** = different, besides this/these
*e.g. Have you got any **other blouses** in black?*
*I don't like this tie. Can you show me **another** one?*

◆ **other/others** When *other* is used with a noun, it has no plural form.
*e.g. Where are **the other files**? (NOT: ... others files?)*
***But:** I've got some files here. Where are **the others**?*

Note: ***Others** can also be used to mean (the) other people. e.g. Some people enjoy playing golf, **others** hate it.*

◆ **each other** = one another
*e.g. We don't visit **each other** very often.*

◆ **every other** = every second
*e.g. We go to the supermarket **every other** Friday.*

◆ **the other day** = a few days ago
*e.g. Jack called me **the other day**; he said he was coming home the following week.*

Note: We can use they/them/ their to refer to a person whose sex is unknown.
*e.g. Suppose **a friend** of yours asked you to lend **them** some money, what would you do?*
*(**Also:** ... to lend **him** or **her** some money ... - less usual)*
Compare:
*My grandmother celebrated **her** 70th birthday last week.*

We also use they/them/their after words such as **somebody, anybody, nobody, whoever, no, each, every, a person**.
*e.g. If **anybody** calls while I'm out, ask **them** to leave a message.*
*'**Whoever** told you that? **They** must have been lying.'*

---

29 **Fill in the gaps with the correct pronoun or possessive adjective.**

1 Someone called for you today, but ...*they*... didn't leave .... name.
2 If you saw a person in trouble, would you help ....?
3 Somebody has parked .... car across the drive. I can't get out.
4 My aunt left .... bag here when she visited us this morning.
5 If a colleague of mine got promoted, I'd be happy for ....
6 Everyone brings .... own lunch to work with ....
7 My brother has crashed .... car. It is at the garage now.
8 He told each person to order whatever .... wanted.
9 The police inspector asked everybody in the room to give .... names.

---

28 **Fill in *another, (the) other(s), each other* or *every other*.**

1 Can I have ...*another*... cup of coffee, please?
2 This book is mine and .... are Dave's.
3 Frank and Barbara have had an argument. They aren't talking to .... today.
4 This magazine comes out .... week.
5 That watch is gold; .... are silver.
6 You have .... two days to register for the course.
7 Some people work during the day, ... work at night.
8 We usually help .... with our homework.
9 I have my hair cut .... month.
10 Would you like .... biscuit?
11 Brothers and sisters look after ....
12 Jack works the night shift .... week.
13 I saw Mark .... day. He looked well.
14 That cake was lovely. Can I have .... piece?
15 'Where are .... children?' 'Outside.'
16 Are there any .... questions before we go?

---

30 **Underline the correct item.**

1 He ate the ***whole*/*all*** cake by himself.
2 ***Is*/*Are*** everyone ready to begin the exam?
3 You must sign ***every*/*each one*** of these letters.
4 I've never met ***no one*/*anyone*** I like more than Jonathan.
5 I've been working hard ***all*/*every*** day and now I'm exhausted.
6 ***Either*/*Neither*** Sam or John will give you a lift.
7 ***No*/*None*** of those books is interesting.
8 I've been to Paris twice and I went to the Eiffel Tower ***both*/*all*** times.
9 ***Neither*/*Either*** Mary nor Sue went to the beach last Saturday.
10 He was so thirsty that he drank ***the whole*/*all the*** water in one go.

Common mistakes

- There's somebody on the phone. **He** must be Sam. ✗
  There's somebody on the phone . **It** must be Sam. ✓

- She earns a lot more **than I**. ✗
  She earns a lot more **than me**. ✓
  She earns a lot more **than I do**. ✓

- The ball **hit** him on **his head**. ✗
  The ball **hit** him on **the head**. ✓

- Don't sit on that chair. One of **it's** legs is broken. ✗
  Don't sit on that chair. One of **its** legs is broken. ✓

- This car is my **brother's-in-law**. ✗
  This car is my **brother-in-law's**. ✓

- Those are **Ben and Tim's bicycles**. ✗
  Those are **Ben's and Tim's bicycles**. ✓

- **Relax yourself** and put your feet up. ✗
  Relax and put your feet up. ✓

- I have **rarely** met **someone** as polite as Greg. ✗
  I have **rarely** met **anyone** as polite as Greg. ✓

- The girl was wearing a bracelet on **every wrist**. ✗
  The girl was wearing a bracelet on **each wrist**. ✓

- I've seen **nearly each** film he has directed. ✗
  I've seen **nearly every** film he has directed. ✓

- They **all have been** to France before. ✗
  They **have all been** to France before. ✓

- We spent **the all week** lying on the beach. ✗
  We spent **all week** lying on the beach. ✓
  We spent **the whole week** lying on the beach. ✓

- She seems to be talking on the telephone **the whole time**. ✗
  She seems to be talking on the telephone **all the time**. ✓

- There **isn't nothing** in the fridge. It's empty. ✗
  There **isn't anything** in the fridge. It's empty. ✓
  There **is nothing** in the fridge. It's empty. ✓

- The **womens' department** is on the second floor. ✗
  The **women's department** is on the second floor. ✓

- All **my friends bicycles** are better than mine. ✗
  All **my friends' bicycles** are better than mine. ✓

- The phone book is right **in front of yourself**. ✗
  The phone book is right **in front of you**. ✓

- We have **very few milk** left. We need to buy some. ✗
  We have **very little milk** left. We need to buy some. ✓

- You can buy a sports car or a jeep. **Either cars are** fine with me. ✗
  You can buy a sports car or a jeep. **Either car is** fine with me. ✓

- Where have you put **the others bags**? ✗
  Where have you put **the other bags**? ✓

31 Correct the mistakes.

1 We can watch the comedy or the thriller. Either films is fine with me.
2 I have very few time. You'd better make it quick.
3 The childrens' area is run by experienced staff.
4 There isn't nothing good on television this evening.
5 The boy had a cut on every knee.
6 We have rarely been somewhere as beautiful as this.
7 He works a lot harder than I.
8 What have you told the others staff?
9 The cupboard was right next to himself.
10 Don't drink the whole lemonade by yourself. Offer some to your friends.
11 She spent all the day talking to customers.
12 We all have been invited to Samantha's party.
13 The teacher patted her on her head.
14 That dog is hurt. One of it's paws is bleeding.
15 These are Jane and Claire's school bags.
16 All my clients files are on the desk.
17 I've visited nearly each house on this list.
18 This jacket is my father's-in-law.
19 There's someone here to see you. She must be your sister.
20 Feel yourself free to ask any question you like.

32 Cross out the unnecessary word.

1 The teacher wants all of students to participate in the concert at the end of term.
2 She concentrated herself on the exam questions.
3 Neither of the coach nor the players were happy with their performance in the game.
4 They spent the all morning looking for a place to put up their tent.
5 Please, don't hesitate to call any one time you want.
6 There it seems to be something wrong with the alarm system.
7 Every one citizen has to pay taxes.
8 John's sister she got engaged to a young doctor last week.
9 There she is a woman at the door. It's our new neighbour.
10 These jumpers are quite expensive, but the others ones are cheap.
11 Some people enjoy playing golf, while others people find it very boring.
12 She bought a lots of decorations for the party.
13 The meeting was attended by a very few people, and as a result no important decisions were made.
14 If anyone person reveals anything to the press, they will be fired.

Pronouns - Possessives - Demonstratives - Quantifiers

33 Complete each sentence with two to five words, including the word in bold.

1 The only person he didn't send an invitation to was Margaret.
 everyone He sent ...*an invitation to everyone*... except Margaret.

2 He didn't pay any attention to her complaints.
 no He ....
 .... to her complaints.

3 I asked Emily about the missing ring and I asked her brother too.
 both I asked ....
 .... about the missing ring.

4 He's got little patience with young children.
 much He ....
 .... patience with young children.

5 Helen wasn't happy with my idea and Peter wasn't, either.
 nor Neither Helen ....
 .... happy with my idea.

6 When he first saw her, she was sitting alone on a bench.
 by When he first saw her, she ....
 .... on a bench.

7 There are only a few people who can speak Hungarian.
 many There ....
 .... can speak Hungarian.

8 She spent all day watching soap operas.
 whole She spent ....
 .... watching soap operas.

9 He took another person's briefcase by mistake.
 someone He took ....
 .... by mistake.

10 She was able to put her clothes on although her arm was bandaged.
 dress She was able to ....
 .... although her arm was bandaged.

11 People don't understand me when I speak Arabic.
 myself I can't ....
 .... when I speak Arabic.

12 I hope you have a good time at the party.
 yourself I hope ....
 .... at the party.

13 It takes me an hour to drive from my house to the airport.
 drive It is ....
 .... from my house to the airport.

14 He said that I could borrow whatever I wanted as long as I returned it.
 anything He said that I ....
 .... as long as I returned it.

15 It was clear that the three boys knew nothing about the theft.
 of It was clear that ....
 .... knew anything about the theft.

16 I enjoy spending time alone sometimes.
 on I enjoy spending ....
 .... sometimes.

17 John will help you, or else Martin will.
 or Either .... will help you.

34 Fill in the gaps with the correct form of the words in brackets.

1 It is ...*encouraging*... to see so many young people reaching a high level of .... in school. **(encourage, achieve)**

2 Brian has a very .... mind, and all his work shows great .... **(create, original)**

3 The high .... of children at the .... came as a .... surprise. **(attend, perform, please)**

4 The .... have invested in an .... campaign aiming at .... young people from smoking. **(govern, advertise, discourage)**

5 Her .... from the office this week has caused a great deal of .... **(absent, inconvenient)**

6 He could barely contain his .... at the .... of moving to London. **(excite, think)**

7 The .... stood behind a .... screen during the experiment, in case there was an unexpected .... **(invent, protect, explode)**

8 James is the .... of an .... art .... which includes some very .... paintings. **(own, extend, collect, value)**

35 Fill in the gaps with the correct preposition from the list. Some of the prepositions can be used more than once.

at, by, for, in, on, out of, off, under, within, before, from

1 We met Alice ...*by*... chance when we were shopping in town.

2 I hadn't seen Mark for years, but I recognised him .... sight.

3 You should never take your friends .... granted.

4 In her jeans and T-shirt, Kate felt .... place in the expensive restaurant.

5 This room is .... limits to students.

6 We called the police and they arrived .... minutes.

7 Policemen usually wear uniforms when they are .... duty.

8 She wants to be by herself .... the time being.

9 She put her jewellery in a locked drawer .... safe keeping.

10 We walked up the stairs, as the lift was .... order.

11 He used to live in the city centre but now he lives .... the suburbs.

12 The teacher gave us our exam results .... the beginning of the lesson.

13 I can see smoke in the sky. Something must be .... fire.

14 I lent Adam my car .... condition that he drove carefully.

15 Stuart never feels .... ease when his boss is in the room.

16 I promise to be more careful .... now on.

17 It's getting late. We will have to leave .... long.

18 He didn't have any cash with him, so he paid .... cheque.

19 This product has only been .... the market for a few months.

20 John is in bed. He is feeling .... the weather.

Phrasal Verbs

set aside:	(tr) save for a special purpose; **set by**
set in:	(int) (of weather) start and seem likely to continue
set off:	(int) start a journey
set out:	1) (int) begin a journey, 2) intend (to do sth)
set up:	(tr) start a business
stand by:	(tr) support sb esp in difficulties
stand for:	(tr) be an abbreviation for
stand in for:	(tr) replace sb temporarily
stand out:	(int) be noticeable
stand up:	fail to meet (sb)
stand up for:	(tr) support sb or sth
stand up to:	(tr) resist; defend oneself against (sb) without fear
take after:	(tr) look or act like a relative; resemble
take away:	(tr) 1) remove, 2) seize from people
take back:	(tr) admit saying sth wrong
take down:	(tr) separate into pieces so as to repair or remove
take in:	(tr) make clothes narrower (opp: **let out**)
take off:	1) (tr) remove clothes (opp: **put on**), 2) (int) (of planes) leave the ground, 3) (int) start to improve
take time off:	be allowed not to go to work for a short period of time
take on:	(tr) employ
take out:	(tr) remove; extract
take sb out:	(tr) take sb to a restaurant, etc.
take over:	(tr) gain control of sth
take to:	(tr) like
take up:	(tr) 1) begin a hobby, sport, job, 2) fill (time, space)
take up on:	(tr) accept sb's offer or invitation
be taken aback:	be strongly surprised
be taken in:	be deceived

36 Fill in the correct particle.

1 The dentist took ...*out*... one of my teeth last month.

2 Tom set .... on his voyage, full of excitement.

3 Michael takes .... his mother. They've both got brown hair and green eyes.

4 Ian's wife stood .... him when he lost his job two months ago.

5 Once the cold weather sets ...., we'll be glad of the fire in the living room.

6 Lesley's business is really taking .... She's had lots of orders.

7 The chef set .... some strawberries to put on top of the cake.

8 The letters UN stand .... United Nations.

9 I have decided to take .... aerobics because I want to get fit.

10 I'm sorry. I take .... everything I said about this restaurant. The meal was delicious.

11 The group set .... on their journey, wondering what adventures lay ahead.

12 Of all the essays, that one stands .... because it is very well-written.

13 The teacher took .... the boy's football and put it in the cupboard.

14 No one was taken .... by her clever lies.

15 He stood me .... last night, so I'm very angry with him.

16 By the end of the day, Jack had done everything he set .... to do.

17 You ought to stand .... your boss. I'm sure he will respect you for it.

18 I took him .... his dinner invitation, and we went to a lovely restaurant.

19 When their camping trip was over, the girls took .... their tent and put it away carefully.

20 The factory is taking .... more employees at the moment.

21 Work takes .... most of my time these days.

22 Amanda has recently set .... her own accountancy business.

23 I bought this skirt but it's too wide. Could you take it .... a little bit, please?

24 My husband took me .... for a meal last night to celebrate our anniversary.

25 I took .... my jacket and hung it in the wardrobe.

26 You ought to stand .... yourself. Don't let anyone intimidate you.

27 The company is being taken .... by a very large firm.

28 I'm taking some time .... next month. I need a holiday.

29 Jenny hasn't really taken .... her new school. She's not at all happy.

30 Alex was taken .... when he heard the news.

31 I offered to stand .... Emily yesterday, because she was ill.

32 If you've finished lunch, I'll take your plate ....

33 The plane sped along the runway and took ....

Revision Box

37 **Join the sentences using the word(s) in brackets.**

1 Liz gave Tom a map. Then Tom could find her house. **(so that)**

...*Liz gave Tom a map so that he could find her house.*...

2 I always lock the doors and windows. I don't want to be burgled. **(avoid)**

....

3 I went to the bank. I wanted to withdraw some money. **(to)**

....

4 Let's take an umbrella. It may rain. **(in case)**

....

5 The bus was late. They had to take a taxi. **(so ... that)**

....

6 It was an expensive dress. She couldn't afford it. **(such ... that)**

....

7 I went to a party. I stayed up very late. **(and as a result)**

....

8 Stuart has no money. He can't go to the concert. **(since)**

....

9 They are rich people. They don't have to work. **(such ... that)**

....

10 Pauline doesn't wear a watch. She is often late. **(consequently)**

....

11 She felt lonely. She was surrounded by lots of people. **(although)**

....

38 **Fill in *where, why, who, which* or *whose.***

Lionel Robson, **1)** ...*who*... is 50, loves his job. He works at a centre **2)** .... people learn how to do parachute jumps. The centre, **3)** .... opened ten years ago, is very popular with people of all ages **4)** .... want to take up an exciting hobby. Lionel first became interested in parachute jumps while he was at university. His wife, **5)** .... hobby is flying planes, is the person **6)** .... owns the centre. 'The sky is the place **7)** .... I like to be most of all,' she says. 'That's **8)** .... I started the centre — so that I can do my hobby for a living.'

A restaurant critic is comparing two Italian restaurants — 'The Capri' and 'Marco's'. Make sentences from the prompts below, using *Both* or *Neither*, as in the example.

e.g. Both 'The Capri' and 'Marco's' serve a variety of dishes. Neither ...

- serve a variety of dishes ✓
- serve much vegetarian food ✗
- have a lot of regular customers ✓
- receive very few complaints ✓
- employ many people ✗
- need a little redecorating ✓
- charge much for a meal ✗
- have several special offers every month ✓

WRITING
Activity

The restaurant critic is writing an article for a local newspaper. Look at the Oral Activity again and complete the article.

I recently dined at 'The Capri' and also at 'Marco's', both of which are popular Italian restaurants in the city centre. Both 'The Capri' and 'Marco's' serve a variety of dishes, although neither ....

....

....

To conclude, I strongly recommend both these restaurants for an enjoyable and affordable meal.

Questions and Answers - Words often Confused

Questions with Yes/No Answers

'*Is she* a scientist?'
'*Yes, she is.*'
'*Does she* work hard?'
'*Yes, she does.*'

◆ Questions with Yes/No answers begin with an auxiliary or modal verb (*is, are, do, does, can*, etc.) which is followed by the subject. We usually answer these questions with Yes or No.
e.g. '*Are you* upset?' '*Yes, I am.*'
'*Need I* say more?' '*No, you needn't.*'

◆ When the main verb of the sentence is in the present simple, we form the question with do or does. When the main verb is in the past simple, we form the question with did.
e.g. '*Does Peter* go out often?' '*No, he doesn't.*'
'*Did you talk* to John?' '*Yes, I did.*'

◆ We use short answers to avoid repetition of the question asked before. Positive short answers are formed with Yes + personal pronoun + auxiliary verb. Negative short answers are formed with No + personal pronoun + negative auxiliary verb.
e.g. '*Have you* finished?' '*Yes, I have.*'
'*Did you* see that film?' '*No, I didn't.*'

1 Write *questions and answers* for the following statements, as in the example.

1 Sam was hungry when he reached the restaurant.
...*Was Sam hungry when he reached the restaurant? Yes, he was.*...

2 They should concentrate in class.
....

3 She can't speak any foreign languages.
....

4 They have to work overtime.
....

5 The boss was angry when Stuart arrived late.
....

6 The children didn't enjoy the film.
....

7 She wanted to go to the supermarket.
....

8 The train leaves at half past six.
....

Wh- Questions

'*How many people* are there in the picture?'
'*Five.*'
'*Where* are they?' '*In the kitchen.*'
'*What* are they doing?' '*They're having lunch.*'

Wh- questions begin with a question word such as who, what, where, when, etc. We put the auxiliary or modal verb before the subject.

(question word + auxiliary/modal + subject)

● **Who** is used without a noun to ask about people.
e.g. '*Who* called while I was out?' '*Your mother.*'
● **Whose** is used to ask about possession.
e.g. '*Whose* is this car/car is this?' '*It's Ted's.*'
● **What** is used alone or before a noun to ask about things.
e.g. '*What* caused the fire?' '*Faulty wiring.*'
'*What size* shoes do you wear?'
What is also used to ask about people, animals or things when there is an unlimited choice of answers.
e.g. '*What* music do you prefer listening to?' (There are many kinds of music to choose from. — unlimited choice)
● **Which** is used alone, or before nouns, **one**/**ones** or **of**, to ask about people, animals or things.
e.g. **Which** is your house?/**Which house** is yours?
'*Which one* do you want to buy?' '*The red one.*'
Which of those boys is your son?
Which is normally used when there is only a limited choice of answers.
e.g. '*Which* hotel are you going to stay at — the 'Park Hotel' or the 'King's Hotel'? (There are only two hotels to choose from. — limited choice.)
Which is also used with comparative and superlative forms.
e.g. **Which** is **faster**, a cheetah or an ostrich?
Which is **the best** thing to do?
● **Where**
e.g. '*Where* have you put my shoes?' '*Under your bed.*'
● **When**
e.g. '*When* will you be back?' '*Next week.*'
● **Why**
e.g. '*Why* did you throw away the milk?' '*Because it had gone off.*'

Questions and Answers - Words often Confused

- **How is used alone or before an adjective/adverb.**
  e.g. a) '**How** was the party?' 'Excellent.'
  b) '**How old** is your daughter?' 'She's three.'
  c) '**How far** can a kangaroo jump?' 'A long way.'
- **How long**
  e.g. '**How long** does it take you to get to work?'
  'Twenty minutes.'
- **How long ago**
  e.g. '**How long ago** did he graduate?'
  'Six years ago.'
- **How often**
  e.g. '**How often** do you exercise?' 'Every day.'
- **How much is used with uncountable nouns.**
  e.g. '**How much money** did he spend?' 'A lot.'
- **How many is used with countable nouns.**
  e.g. '**How many biscuits** did you eat?' 'A whole packet.'

> **Note**
> We use what + be ... like to ask for a description of somebody's character.
> e.g. '**What is Emily like**?' 'She's pleasant and friendly.'
> We use what + do ... look like to ask for a description of somebody's physical appearance.
> e.g. '**What does Emily look like**?' 'She's tall, with blonde hair and blue eyes.'

 2 Fill in *who, whose, what, which, where, when, how long, how often, what time, why, how much, how many* **or** *how long ago*.

1 '...*How often*... do you play football?' 'Twice a week.'
2 '...................... does the train leave?' 'Nine o'clock.'
3 '.......................... is Martin?' 'In the garden.'
4 '................................... is it?' 'Half past ten.'
5 '........................... does he earn?' '£1,000 a month.'
6 '.................................. sisters have you got?' 'Two.'
7 '...................................... is this book?' '£5.'
8 '........................... did he call?' 'To invite me out to dinner.'
9 '................................. is the new driver like?' 'He's very friendly.'
10 '......................... shall we do this evening?' 'Let's go out.'
11 '........................... is the office party?' 'On Saturday.'
12 '.............................. have you been waiting?' 'About half an hour.'
13 '........................ is that briefcase?' 'I think it's Tom's.'
14 '.................................. of these rings do you prefer?' 'The gold one.'
15 '..................... spilt coffee on the desk?' 'I did. Sorry.'
16 '................................. did you get your exam results?' 'Last Friday.'
17 '.................... did you meet Jessie?' 'Two years ago.'
18 '................................. is the easiest way to get to the cinema?' 'Go through the city centre.'

 3 Write *questions* to which the words in bold are the answers.

1 They live **near the beach**.
...*Where do they live?*...
2 It takes **ten minutes** to drive to the supermarket.
....
3 George is **selfish**.
....
4 Mary is **tall, with dark hair and green eyes**.
....
5 I go swimming **twice a week**.
....
6 **The joke** made them laugh.
....
7 They are **Miss Drake's** books.
....
8 The shoes cost **twenty pounds**.
....
9 The film starts **at 7 pm**.
....
10 **Mr Samson** wants to open a shop.
....
11 Todd has been **to Spain**.
....
12 She is happy **because she has won the competition**.
....
13 Alan is a **very serious** person.
....
14 They moved here **six months ago**.
....

4 Write *questions* to which the words in bold are the answers.

Louise is **eight years old**. She lives **in Brighton, England**, and she has lived there **since she was two years old**. Louise goes to school every day and her favourite subjects are **English and History**. She has **two** brothers. Their names are **Steven and James**. Louise has several hobbies, such as **collecting wild flowers and playing the violin**. She practises the violin **every evening**. Her mother enjoys this, **because she likes listening to music**.

e.g. **1** ...*How old is Louise?*.......................................
....
....
....
....
....
....
....
....
....
....
....
....

Subject / Object Questions

◆ Subject questions are questions we ask when we want to know the subject of the sentence. These questions usually begin with the words who, whose, what or which. The verb is in the affirmative form.

e.g. **Who told** you the news?
(NOT: ~~Who did tell you the news?~~)
Whose house **was broken** into last night?
What made that noise?
Which costs more - the package holiday or the cruise?

subject	verb	object
►Emma	called	Peter.
└►Who	called	Peter?

◆ Object questions are questions we ask when we want to know the object of the sentence. These questions usually begin with the words who, whose, what or which. The verb is in the interrogative form.

e.g. **Who did you ask** for information?
Whose is this jacket?
What are you going to buy?
Which magazine **are you reading**?

subject	verb	object
Emma	called	►Peter.
Who ◄		did Emma call?

Note: In object questions if a verb is followed by a preposition, the preposition usually comes at the end of the question.

e.g. Where does Kevin come **from**?
What are you most interested **in**?

5 **Write questions to which the words in bold are the answers.**

1 Mark is decorating **the living room**.
...*What is Mark decorating?*...

2 She found **Steven's** wallet.
....

3 **Mum** made these cakes.
....

4 **Fiona's** dress was ruined at the party.
....

5 Melissa is wearing **a blue dress**.
....

6 **Bob** is the older of the two brothers.
....

7 Stacey has bought **a new bag**.
....

8 I like **the blue** jumper best.
....

9 **The roof** was blown off in the storm.
....

10 I ran into **Jason** the other day.
....

11 I spoke to the **manager's** secretary about my complaint.
....

12 **The Ethiopian runner** won the 1500m race.
....

6 **Complete the questions.**

1 Ryan won two races.
a 'Who ...*won two races*...?' 'Ryan.'
b 'How many ...*races did Ryan win*...?' 'Two.'

2 Stanley goes swimming three times a week.
a 'Who ....?' 'Stanley.'
b 'How often ....?' 'Three times a week.'

3 There are two shirts. The yellow one is mine.
a 'Which ....?' 'The yellow one.'
b 'Whose ....?' 'Mine.'

4 Steven has broken Jim's mug.
a 'Whose ....?' 'Jim's.'
b 'Who ....?' 'Steven.'

5 Linda is going to the theatre this evening.
a 'Who ....?' 'Linda.'
b 'Where ....?' 'To the theatre.'

6 Anne bought Ralph a present yesterday.
a 'Who ....?' 'Anne.'
b 'Who ....?' 'Ralph.'

7 There are two bags. The one on the chair is Fay's.
a 'Whose ....?' 'Fay's.'
b 'Which ....?' 'The one on the chair.'

7 **Use the prepositions in brackets to write questions to match the statements.**

1 She bought some flowers. Who ...*did she buy them for?*... (for)

2 I got an invitation this morning. Who ....? (from)

3 Pedro comes from Spain. Where exactly ....? (from)

4 I read an interesting article yesterday. What ....? (about)

5 Lisa is excited. What ....? (about)

6 Linda played tennis. Who ....? (with)

7 Sam wrote a letter. Who ....? (to)

8 I went to a restaurant last night. Who ....? (with)

Questions and Answers - Words often Confused

Negative Questions

◆ Negative questions are formed with not, but there is a difference in the word order between the full form and the short form.

Full form: auxiliary + subject + not + verb
e.g. **Did I not tell** you not to talk to strangers?

Short form: auxiliary + n't + subject + verb
e.g. **Didn't I tell** you not to talk to strangers?

◆ We use negative questions in speech
a) to ask for confirmation e.g. **Isn't Tom going** on holiday this week? and **b)** to express:

- surprise. e.g. **Don't you know** where Nick is?
- admiration. e.g. **Isn't she** a great hostess!
- annoyance. e.g. **Can't you be** on time just for once!

8 Write the short form of the following *negative questions*.

1 Has she not replied to your letter yet?
   ...Hasn't she replied to your letter yet?...
2 Do they not live here any more?
   ....
3 Can she not drive a car?
   ....
4 Does he not understand what he has to do?
   ....
5 Do you not know the answer to this question?
   ....
6 Did he not offer you anything to drink?
   ....
7 Have we not got any milk left?
   ....
8 Could you not do anything to help him?
   ....

9 Make *negative questions* using the words given, as in the example.

1 A: I'm really tired today.
   B: Why? ...*Didn't you go*... (go) to bed early last night?
2 A: .... (know) what time the film starts?
   B: No, but I'll phone the cinema and ask now.
3 A: Let's go to see the new Brad Pitt film tonight.
   B: .... (already/see) it?
4 A: .... (help) me make dinner?
   B: No, sorry. I'm very busy at the moment.
5 A: .... (type) the reports yet?
   B: No, sir. I'll finish them before I go home, though.
6 A: .... (cold)?
   B: No. Actually I think it's quite warm in here.

Indirect Questions

We use indirect questions when we ask for information politely. The word order in indirect questions is the same as in statements (subject + verb). Indirect questions are introduced with question words (who, what, where, etc.) or with **if/whether**.

e.g. a) **Direct question:** *Where is the post office?*
     Indirect question: *Could you tell me **where the post office is**?*
   b) **Direct question:** *Has John been invited?*
     Indirect question: *Do you know **if/whether John has been invited**?*

Indirect questions are usually used after the following expressions: **I don't know .../I'd like to know .../I wonder .../We need to find out .../I'd like to find out ...** as well as: **Do you know ...?/Can you tell me ...?/Could you tell me ...?/Could you explain ...?/Have you any idea...?**

If the indirect question is part of a question, we put a question mark at the end of the sentence. If it is part of a statement, we put a full stop.

e.g. a) **Direct question:** *How does this machine work?*
     Indirect question: **Could you explain how this machine works?**
   b) **Direct question:** *Should I call a lawyer?*
     Indirect question: **I wonder if/whether I should call a lawyer.**

10 Turn the following into *indirect questions*.

1 Who left this bag here?
   Do you know ...*who left this bag here?*...
2 Who is that woman?
   We need to find out ....
3 What time does the next train leave?
   Can you tell me ....
4 How much does this dress cost?
   Could you tell me ....
5 Where does Mary live?
   I don't know ....
6 Are the police investigating the robbery?
   Have you any idea ....
7 Did the caller leave a message?
   I'd like to find out ....
8 Is he the manager?
   I'd like to know ....
9 Who reported the crime?
   Do you know ....
10 How did they find the missing jewellery?
   Have you any idea ....

Questions and Answers - Words often Confused

So - Neither/Nor

We use:

◆ **so + auxiliary verb + personal pronoun/noun** to show that we agree with a positive statement.

  e.g. *'They're painting their house this week.' 'So are we.'* (We are painting our house too.)
  'Janet passed her exams.' 'So did Diana.' (Diana passed her exams, too.)

◆ **neither/nor + auxiliary verb + personal pronoun/ noun** to show that we agree with a negative statement.

  e.g. *'Kate doesn't like red meat.' 'Neither/Nor do I.'*
  (I don't like red meat either.)
  'Paul can't play the guitar.' 'Neither/Nor can Tim.'
  (Tim can't play the guitar either.)

11 Decide if the statement after each exchange is true (T) or false (F).

1 Mark: I love playing football.
   Paul: So do I.
   ...T...   Paul loves playing football.
2 Lucy: I don't enjoy watching horror films.
   Jessica: Neither do I.
   ....   Jessica enjoys watching horror films.
3 Simon: I have never been to America before.
   Steven: Neither have I.
   ....   Steven has never been to America before.
4 Richard: I have got a lot of pen-friends.
   Julia: So have I.
   ....   Julia hasn't got a lot of pen-friends.
5 Belinda: I am going to take the bus to school.
   Lucy: So am I.
   ....   Lucy is going to take the bus to school.

12 Fill in the gaps with appropriate responses.

1 A: I didn't go to the party last night.
   B: *...Neither/Nor did I....* I wish I had, though.
2 A: I enjoyed that film.
   B: .... It was brilliant.
3 A: I don't like omelettes.
   B: .... I think they're horrible.
4 A: I'm not looking forward to this exam.
   B: .... I'm sure it will be very difficult.
5 A: I'm going to York next weekend.
   B: ....! Perhaps I'll see you there.
6 A: I've just bought a new car.
   B: .... Mine is a Rover.
7 A: I haven't got any pets.
   B: .... I used to have a dog, though.
8 A: I was quite ill last week.
   B: .... I had the flu.

I think so / I'm afraid so, etc.

◆ We can use *so* to avoid repeating a clause after the following verbs: *be afraid, believe, expect, guess, hope, imagine, suppose, think, it seems/appears,* etc.
  e.g. *'Is he going to be late?' 'I'm afraid so.'*
  (= I'm afraid he is going to be late.)

◆ We can form negations in two ways:

  a) **negative verb + so** *(I don't expect so)*
  b) **positive verb + not** *(I guess not)*

● The negative of the verbs *appear, believe, seem* and *suppose* is formed in either way.
  e.g. *'Is he leaving tonight?' 'I don't suppose so.'* OR
  'I suppose not.'

● The negative of the verbs *expect, imagine* and *think* is usually formed with **negative verb + so.**
  e.g. *'Is Helen working upstairs?' 'I don't think so.'*

● The negative of the verbs *be afraid, guess* and *hope* is formed with **positive verb + not.**
  e.g. *'Are you going on holiday this year?'*
  'I'm afraid not.'

13 Fill in the blanks with phrases using the verbs given and *so* or *not.*

1 A: Are they going on holiday this year?
   B: *...I don't imagine so...* (imagine). They haven't saved any money.
2 A: Is Debbie ill?
   B: .... (think). I saw her in town this morning.
3 A: Did John fail his exams?
   B: .... (afraid). He'll have to take them again.
4 A: Will you be finished soon?
   B: .... (expect). I haven't got much left to do.
5 A: Can you come to the meeting after work?
   B: .... (think). I haven't got any other plans.
6 A: Have they sold their house?
   B: .... (appear). There's a 'sold' sign up outside.
7 A: Has he got a new car?
   B: .... (believe). I saw him driving a different one last week.
8 A: Could you lend me some money, please?
   B: .... (afraid). I haven't got any.
9 A: Are you going anywhere nice this weekend?
   B: .... (suppose). My boss wants me to work.

Questions and Answers - Words often Confused

Question Tags

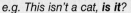

It isn't a gorilla, **is it**?   They are rabbits, **aren't they**?

◆ Question tags are short questions at the end of statements. They are mainly used in speech when we want to confirm something or when we want to find out if something is true or not.

◆ Question tags are formed with the auxiliary or modal verb from the main sentence and the appropriate subject pronoun. When the verb of the sentence is in the present or past simple, we form the question tag with do, does or did and the subject pronoun.
   e.g. a) **Mike lives** in California, **doesn't he**?
        b) **They sold** their house, **didn't they**?

◆ A positive statement is followed by a negative question tag, and a negative statement is followed by a positive question tag.
   e.g. **She looks** beautiful, **doesn't she**?
        You don't eat meat, **do you**?

   When the sentence contains a word with a negative meaning like never, hardly, seldom or rarely, the question tag is positive.
   e.g. She **never** goes anywhere alone, **does she**?

◆ Some verbs/expressions form question tags differently. Study the following examples:

I am → aren't I?	I am younger than you, **aren't I**?
Imperative → will/won't you?	Close the door, **will/won't you**?
Don't → will you?	Don't move, **will you**?
Let's → shall we?	Let's dance, **shall we**?
I have (got) → haven't I?	He has got his own business, **hasn't he**?
I have → don't I?	You have a lot on your mind, **don't you**?
There is/are → isn't/ aren't there?	There are many shops in the area, **aren't there**?
This/That is → isn't it?	That's your wife over there, **isn't it**?
Everyone/Someone/ Anyone/No one → they?	Everyone enjoyed the party, didn't **they**?

Intonation

◆ When we are sure of the answer and expect agreement, the voice goes down in the question tag.
   e.g. This isn't a cat, **is it**?

◆ When we aren't sure of the answer and want to check information, the voice goes up in the question tag.
   e.g. This is a donkey, **isn't it**?

14 Fill in the correct *question tags* and *short answers*.

1 A: You've seen that film, ...*haven't you*...?
   B: Yes, ...*I have*....
2 A: They want to go skiing this year, ...?
   B: No, ... They want to go on an adventure holiday.
3 A: He'll probably be hungry when he comes in, ...
   ....?
   B: Yes, ... I'll make him some sandwiches.
4 A: She likes going to the cinema, ...?
   B: No, ... She prefers going to the theatre.
5 A: You've been to university, ...?
   B: Yes, ...
6 A: I'm a bit younger than Sally, ...?
   B: Yes, ...
7 A: They aren't moving, ...?
   B: Yes, ...
8 A: You won't forget to call me, ...?
   B: No, ... Don't worry.
9 A: You took some photographs at the ceremony, ...
   ....?
   B: Yes, ... They're in this album.
10 A: He knows I'm planning a party for him, ...?
   B: No, ... He doesn't suspect a thing.
11 A: They have bought a new car, ...?
   B: Yes, ... It's a Volvo.
12 A: He works for his father, ...?
   B: Yes, ... His father owns a large company.
13 A: I'm not late, ...?
   B: No, ... You're just on time.
14 A: They'll be here in a minute, ...?
   B: Yes, ... We'd better tidy up.
15 A: You did the washing-up, ...?
   B: Yes, ..., and I cleaned the kitchen.

15 Underline the correct answer.

1 A: You're new here, ***are you/aren't you***?
   B: Yes. I started work here yesterday.
   A: Ah. Well, you've met everyone in the office, ***hadn't you/haven't you***?
   B: Yes. There are a lot of people working here, ***aren't they/aren't there***?

2 A: You will remember to lock all the doors when you leave, ***will you/won't you***?
   B: Of course. I'm not stupid, ***am I/aren't I***?
   A: No. But you forgot to lock the doors last week, ***didn't you/did you***?
   B: You're not going to let me forget that, ***aren't you/are you***?

3 A: You haven't seen Linda lately, ***have you/haven't you***?
   B: I saw her today. I told you, ***did I/didn't I***?
   A: Oh, yes! She didn't mention the party, ***did she/didn't she***?
   B: No, she didn't. It's tomorrow night, ***is it/isn't it***?

16 Fill in the question tags, then read the sentences aloud with the correct intonation.

sure	not sure		
	✓	1	You haven't got any money, ...*have you*...?
✓		2	There's some water in the jug, ...?
	✓	3	She will be here on time, ...?
	✓	4	Mum can give me a lift, ...?
✓		5	You know my brother, ...?
✓		6	They live together, ...?
	✓	7	We have plenty of time, ...?
✓		8	That boy is very clever, ...?
	✓	9	You have a car, ...?
✓		10	The train will arrive soon, ...?
✓		11	He has finished his homework, ...?
	✓	12	That's my wallet, ...?

Common mistakes

- I'm really helpful, **am I not**? ✗
  I'm really helpful, **aren't I**? ✓

- Bob is keen on sports, **isn't Bob**? ✗
  Bob is keen on sports, **isn't he**? ✓

- Everybody is coming to the party, **isn't they**? ✗
  Everybody is coming to the party, **aren't they**? ✓

- Stay here, **don't you**? ✗
  Stay here, **won't you**? ✓

- He **rarely** visits you, **doesn't he**? ✗
  He **rarely** visits you, **does he**? ✓

- **Who did win** the competition? ✗
  Who won the competition? ✓

- Could you tell me **where is the bank**? ✗
  Could you tell me **where the bank is**? ✓

- 'Jack is leaving soon.' **'So I am.'** ✗
  'Jack is leaving soon.' **'So am I.'** ✓

- 'Helen doesn't like rock music.' **'Neither I don't.'** ✗
  'Helen doesn't like rock music.' **'Neither do I.'** ✓

17 Correct the mistakes.

1 'Paul doesn't like going to the theatre.' 'Neither I don't.'
2 Sally is good at Maths, isn't Sally?
3 She never writes to you, doesn't she?
4 'Mark is going to the supermarket.' 'So I am.'
5 Who did make all this mess?
6 Could you tell me when does the bus leave?
7 Come back soon, don't you?
8 She seldom receives visitors, doesn't she?
9 Everybody is here now, isn't they?

18 Cross out the unnecessary word.

1 Who did gave you this wonderful ring?
2 That was Martha's sister, wasn't it she?
3 How far is it the sports centre?
4 You don't really mean that, do you mean?
5 Didn't they not pay for the damage?
6 Don't forget to give him a call, will you not?
7 How long ago have you been studying Japanese?
8 Have you any idea what time does the train leaves?
9 They haven't got a green car, do have they?
10 'Is Tom going away this weekend?' 'I'm not afraid so.'
11 Didn't we tell you to not watch that film?
12 We need to find out where does Bob lives.
13 Who did travelled to Portugal last month?
14 'What is Rod look like?' 'He's generous and kind.'

Questions and Answers - Words often Confused

Phrasal Verbs	
turn away:	(tr) not allow sb to enter a place
turn down:	1) (tr) refuse an offer; reject, 2) (tr) reduce volume etc (opp: **turn up**)
turn sb in:	(tr) give sb to the police
turn into:	(tr) change into, become
turn off:	(tr) switch off (opp: **turn on**)
turn on:	switch on
turn out:	1) (tr) produce, 2) (int) prove to be in the end; result, 3) (tr) force sb to leave 4) (tr) empty (one's pockets, handbag, etc)
turn over:	turn to a new page; change TV channel
turn sb over to sb:	(tr) deliver sb (to the police, authorities)
turn to:	(tr) go to sb for help, advice
turn up:	1) (int) arrive or appear (unexpectedly), 2) (tr) increase (volume, pressure)
wear sb down:	(tr) make sb gradually weaker
wear off:	(of feelings) disappear gradually
wear out:	1) (tr) use until no longer serviceable, 2) (tr) exhaust
work on:	(tr) have an effect on
work out:	1) (tr) find the solution to a problem by reasoning or calculation, 2) (int) develop successfully
work up:	(tr) develop, increase

19 **Fill in the correct particle.**

1 I'm worn ...*out*...! I've been working hard all day long.
2 We turned .... the heater because the room was cold.
3 The policeman asked him to turn .... his pockets so he could examine the contents.
4 The effects of the anaesthetic the dentist gave me are gradually wearing ....
5 He had to work .... his courage before asking for a pay rise.
6 They turned .... the burglar to the police when they caught him in their house.
7 I've got a problem and I don't know who to turn .... for help.
8 Anna was offered the job, but she turned it ....
9 It turned .... to be the wrong road, so we had no idea where we were.
10 The class was silently trying to work .... the solution to the maths problem.
11 I can't hear the news. Please turn .... the volume on the TV.
12 Our neighbours have turned their garage .... a study.

13 That washing powder doesn't work .... grass stains. You'll have to use something stronger.
14 Sam turned .... on the doorstep at midnight in the pouring rain.
15 The old lady turned .... the thief she had caught .... the police.
16 We turn .... about ten thousand of these cars every month.
17 The family were turned .... of their flat by the landlord when they couldn't pay the rent.
18 The tennis player gradually wore .... his opponent, until he finally won the match.
19 That music is very loud. Could you turn the volume ...., please?
20 The children were turned .... from the cinema because there were no tickets left.
21 This arrangement has worked .... very well for everyone.
22 Turn .... the page and look at exercise ten.
23 If you're no longer watching TV, why don't you turn it ....?
24 The vacuum cleaner is worn .... We need to buy a new one.

20 **Fill in the gaps with the correct preposition from the list. Some of the prepositions can be used more than once.**

at, by, for, in, on, out of, off, under, against, from

1 They tried to get closer to the stage at the concert, but there were too many people ...*in*... the way.
2 I try to keep fit. .... instance, I go jogging every morning.
3 The secretary signed the letters .... behalf of the manager.
4 Colin has been .... work for a week with flu.
5 He has had no training. He has learnt .... experience.
6 The proposed changes to the company are .... discussion at the moment.
7 Sarah's calendar was .... date, so she bought a new one.
8 The soldier was .... leave for a week, so he visited his family.
9 .... the time I got home, it was already dark.
10 I gave him my jacket .... exchange for his walkman.
11 I like Martin, but he can be very annoying .... times.
12 We waited .... the queue to get into the theatre.
13 He buys old furniture, then sells it .... a profit.
14 .... the whole, I am very satisfied with my life.
15 The rescue team arrived .... the nick of time.
16 It is .... the law to drive a car without insurance.
17 He is six years old. He should be able to read .... now.
18 Many young people find themselves .... work when they leave university.
19 He tore his shirt .... purpose, but he said it was an accident.

21 **Fill in the blanks with the correct form of the words in brackets.**

1 The ...*artist*... got .... reviews from the critics. (art, impress)

2 The police placed great .... on the .... they discovered. (important, evident)

3 His .... was proved thanks to the .... of an eye-witness who testified that he had not been party to the act of .... (innocent, present, violent)

4 You must be very .... as this substance can be .... (care, harm)

5 Lots of .... find .... in this .... part of the town. (tour, accommodate, peace)

6 She is .... that her .... investments were.................., as she is now a very .... woman and owns .... properties throughout the country. (luck, finance, success, wealth, number)

22 **Fill in the blanks with the correct form of the words in brackets.**

Ian Fleming is famous for writing the extremely **1)** ...*successful*... (success) James Bond novels, which are packed with **2)** .... (act) and adventure. But Fleming himself had quite an **3)** .... (adventure) life which has been recorded in several biographies.

He tried a career in banking but did not find it **4)** .... (interest) enough. In May, 1939, he joined the intelligence service and carried out several **5)** .... (danger) missions during the war. He planned clever **6)** .... (operate) and lived a life not unlike that of his famous hero, James Bond.

In 1952, he began to write a novel. *Casino Royale* was the first of the James Bond novels, all of which became **7)** .... (incredible) popular. They reflected his **8)** .... (usual) life and love of adventure. Fleming died in 1964 at the age of 56.

Revision Box

23 **Complete each sentence with two to five words, including the word in bold.**

1 If you leave the cake in the oven too long, it will burn.
  else   Don't leave the cake in the oven too long ...*or else it will*... burn.

2 You can't leave. You have to tidy your desk first.
  until   You can't .... your desk.

3 I don't think it's a good idea to wear that dress.
  were   If ...., I wouldn't wear that dress.

4 I want to buy a car, but I haven't got enough money.
  wish   I .... enough money to buy a car.

5 Although he is poor, he likes giving people presents.
  spite   He likes giving people presents .... poor.

6 The lesson was cancelled. The teacher was ill.
  as   The lesson was cancelled .... ill.

7 You shouldn't go outside without a coat; you might catch a cold.
  better   You .... outside without a coat; you might catch a cold.

8 She took some money. She thought she might want to buy something.
  case   She took some money .... to buy something.

9 The match was cancelled. The weather was very bad.
  of   The match was cancelled .... bad weather.

10 Carol would prefer to make a cake herself rather than buy one.
  rather   Carol .... a cake herself than buy one.

24 **Rewrite the sentences in the *passive*.**

1 David will wash the dishes.
  ...*The dishes will be washed by David*....

2 When did the postman deliver the parcel?
  ....

3 Emily is telling them a joke.
  ....

4 Did they announce the results on the radio?
  ....

5 Tina can't stand people interrupting her.
  ....

6 He expects his father to give him a lift.
  ....

Questions and Answers - Words often Confused

Revision Box

25 **Choose the correct answer.**

1 'This is a nice room.'
'Yes. It's the one ....B.... we've just redecorated.'
A who   **B** which   **C** when

2 'Did you know that Ted is getting married?'
'Yes. He .... me last week.'
A tell   **B** said   **C** told

3 'Have you seen your brother recently?'
'Yes. I saw .... yesterday.'
A it   **B** her   **C** him

4 'There is someone here to see you, sir.'
'Good. Send .... in.'
A they   **B** them   **C** their

5 'I'm afraid I can't come to your party.'
'Oh no! You .... to come ages ago!'
A promised   **B** refused   **C** denied

6 'What a beautiful day!'
'Yes, it is, but it's .... colder than yesterday.'
A little   **B** a few   **C** a little

7 'Did you ask Harry about the missing money?'
'Yes. He .... to having taken it.'
A agreed   **B** accused   **C** admitted

8 'This cake tastes very sweet.'
'I think I put .... sugar in it.'
A too much   **B** too many   **C** a lot

9 'Do you know that man?'
'Yes. He's the man .... sister lives next door to me.'
A who   **B** whose   **C** which

10 'Shall I take my coat with me?'
'Yes. Take it .... it gets cold later.'
A in case   **B** in spite   **C** whereas

11 'What did the doctor tell you?'
'He .... me to go on a diet.'
A suggested   **B** advised   **C** explained

12 'The sun is very bright today.'
'I know. That's .... I'm wearing sunglasses.'
A where   **B** why   **C** when

13 '............ is your house?'
'It's the one with the red door.'
A Where   **B** Who   **C** Which

14 'Laura is getting engaged next week.'
'Then, that must be the reason .... she looks so happy.'
A which   **B** why   **C** who

It is Charlotte's first day at school and Ian is showing her around. Use question words from the list and the prompts below to ask and answer questions, as in the example.

how, how long, how much, how many, where, when, why, which/what

e.g. Charlotte: How long have you been at this school?
Ian: Since I was seven years old.

1 you / be / at this school ? since / I / be / seven years old
2 I / put my coat ? in / cloakroom
3 children / be / in my class ? twenty
4 we / have exams ? once a year
5 homework / the teachers give us ? not too much
6 we / have lunch ? at twelve o'clock
7 the teacher / take register ? make sure / everyone / be / here
8 I / get to my classroom? I / take / you there

Charlotte also asked Ian some other questions. Look at the prompts and write out her questions and suggest suitable replies.

- play / during / break?
- eat / in classrooms?
- eat lunch?
- your favourite subject?
- class / you / be in?
- your / favourite teacher?
- the / headmaster's / name?
- school / finish?

UNIT 12
Words often Confused

ago · before	
ago (adv)	before now *e.g. Sandra left school six months* **ago**.
before (adv)	before a past time *e.g. She washed her hair* **before** *she went to the party.*

 1 **Fill in *ago* or *before*.**

1 They moved to this neighbourhood two years ....
2 I have seen this film ....
3 In 1996 she finished the degree which she had started four years ....
4 He took up cycling ten years ....

beside · besides	
beside (prep)	next to *e.g. The sofa is* **beside** *the fireplace in my house.*
besides (prep)	also, in addition to *e.g.* **Besides** *buying us dinner last night, he paid for the theatre tickets.*

 2 **Fill in *beside* or *besides*.**

1 Put the book on the table .... the vase.
2 My house is .... a big park.
3 .... a tent, you'll need a sleeping bag.
4 He's taken seven other tests .... this one.

after · afterwards	
after (prep)	following in time *e.g. He called me* **after** *I had finished work.*
afterwards (adv)	at a later time *e.g. They went to the cinema and* **afterwards** *they went home.*

 3 **Fill in *after* or *afterwards*.**

1 Let's go out .... work this evening.
2 She ironed the clothes and .... she put them away.
3 They went to the meeting and .... they drove home.
4 .... they had eaten, they did the washing-up.

good · well	
good (adj)	well-behaved, not naughty *e.g. Their children are always* **good** *when they go out.*
well (adv)	in a skilful or good way *e.g. He speaks Russian very* **well**.
well (adj)	healthy *e.g. I don't feel* **well** *today.*

 4 **Fill in *good* or *well*.**

1 If you're .... at school today, we'll go to the park later.
2 They sing very .... together, don't they?
3 Be a .... girl at school today.
4 After eating four hamburgers, he didn't feel ....
5 Did Adam do .... in the test?

hard · hardly	
hard (adj)	difficult, vigorous *e.g. Tom found the exam very* **hard**, *and that's why he failed it.*
hardly (adv)	barely *e.g. It was so hot last night that I* **hardly** *slept at all.*

 5 **Fill in *hard* or *hardly*.**

1 Eric always works ....
2 I have .... any free time these days.
3 They could .... hear each other because the music was so loud.
4 If you train ...., you'll win the race on Saturday.

it's · its	
it's	it is **or** it has (short form) *e.g.* **It's** *time to go to bed!* **It's** *been two months since I last saw him.*
its (poss adj)	of a thing/animal *e.g. The cat curled up in* **its** *basket and went to sleep.*

 6 **Fill in *it's* or *its*.**

1 .... eight o'clock already! We're going to be late!
2 Their house is huge. .... got fifteen rooms.
3 The dog buried .... bone in the garden.
4 The plane lowered .... wheels just before landing.

quite - enough	
quite (adv)	fairly, but not very e.g. The party we went to was **quite** good.
enough (adv)	sufficient, satisfactory e.g. The sofa was big **enough** for four people.

7 **Fill in** *quite* **or** *enough*.

1 I enjoyed the meal. It was .... tasty.
2 She wasn't tall .... to become a model.
3 The test was .... difficult. I hope I did well.
4 Is the room warm .... for you?

used to - be used to	
used to	refers to past habits and states e.g. I **used to** exercise every day, but I don't any more.
be used to	refers to an action which has been done so often that is very familiar to the person involved e.g. Joan **is used to** getting up early in the mornings.

8 **Fill in** *used to* **or** *be used to* **in the correct form.**

1 They .... live by the sea, but now they live in the city.
2 We .... meet for lunch every day, but we don't any more.
3 They .... being on their own.
4 Tom .... working night shifts now, although he found it hard at the beginning.

affect - effect	
affect (v)	to influence sth/sb e.g. The closing down of the factory **affected** many families in the town.
effect (n)	result; change produced by an action or a cause. e.g. The **effects** of pollution can be seen all over the world.

9 **Fill in** *affect* **or** *effect*.

1 You shouldn't let her comments .... you.
2 The advertising campaign had a good .... on the sales figures.

3 Famous people can .... the lives of young people.
4 The polluted water had a serious .... on the fish in the river.

besides - except - but - except for - apart from	
besides (adv)	in addition, moreover, including, as well e.g. It's too late to go out now. **Besides**, it's going to rain.
except (prep)	not including, apart from (in the middle of a sentence) e.g. Everyone in the company got a pay rise **except** James.
but (conj)	not including, apart from (never at the beginning of a sentence) e.g. I cleaned every room **but** the kitchen.
except for (prep)	not including, apart from (usually followed by a noun or -ing form) e.g. **Except for** the security guard, the building was empty.
apart from (prep)	not including (usually followed by a noun or -ing form) e.g. **Apart from** washing the car, what else have you done today?

10 **Fill in** *besides*, *except*, *but* **or** *apart*.

1 We got cards from everyone .... for Alec.
2 .... from the singing of the birds, everything was quiet.
3 I didn't like the idea of working for that company; .... the salary wasn't good enough.
4 She locked every door .... the fire exit.
5 .... from Pauline, everyone at the meeting agreed with the plan.
6 Let's get a taxi since it's raining. ...., we've already missed the last bus.
7 Every guest came on time .... Claire.
8 .... going shopping, what else shall we do on Saturday?
9 I'm going to bed because I'm tired. ...., it's very late.

bring - take	
bring (v)	move sth towards sb/sth else e.g. **Bring** me those files, please.
take (v)	move sth away from sb e.g. Will you **take** the rubbish out when you leave, please?

UNIT 12
Words often Confused

11 Fill in *bring* or *take* in the correct form.

1 Please .... this box outside to the garden.
2 .... me a chair from the kitchen, please.
3 He .... the children to play in the park yesterday evening.
4 Will you .... me the dishes from the dining room, please?

until - by	
until (prep)	before the time when something happens and not after it *e.g. He worked for this company **until** he retired.*
by (prep)	no later than a specified time *e.g. You must finish the report **by** Friday afternoon.*

12 Fill in *until* or *by*.

1 We waited at the station .... the train came.
2 I'll be in the office .... 6 o'clock. Call me before then.
3 You must return the library books .... Wednesday.
4 Sam will know his exam results .... the end of July.
5 We can't announce anything to the public .... we get the Prime Minister's consent.

since - for	
since (prep)	from a specified time in the past until a later past time or until the present *e.g. He's been on holiday **since** last Friday.*
for (prep)	indicating a length of time *e.g. They've been working here **for** ten years.*

13 Fill in *since* or *for*.

1 They have known each other .... many years.
2 He hasn't heard from Alice .... last summer.
3 Janet hasn't written to John .... January.
4 I have been waiting for the train .... an hour.
5 I have been good friends with James .... we were at school together.

listen - hear	
listen to (v)	to hear intentionally *e.g. They **listened** to the news broadcast on the radio.*
hear (v)	to perceive sounds with the ears *e.g. Susan **heard** someone calling for help.*

14 Fill in *listen* or *hear* in the correct form.

1 You must .... carefully or you won't know what to do.
2 I think I .... a noise outside.
3 Please speak louder, I can't .... you.
4 Tom .... to music every evening to help him relax.

on time - in time	
on time	neither late nor early, at the correct time *e.g. I always make sure I get to work **on time**.*
in time	not late *e.g. I hope I'll get to the airport **in time** to watch the plane land.*

15 Fill in *on time* or *in time*.

1 Bill is always late. He's never .... for work.
2 I woke up just .... to see the sunrise this morning.
3 We're having guests tonight so make sure you're home .... to welcome them.
4 If we hurry, we'll get to the station .... to catch the train.

Expressions with *Do*

one's best/worst, business with sb, a crossword, damage to, one's duty, an exercise, a test, an experiment, good, one's hair, harm, one's homework, the housework, a job, sth for a living, research, right/wrong, the shopping, a translation, the washing-up, work, etc.

Expressions with *Make*

an appointment, an arrangement, the beds, a cake, changes, coffee, a decision, a discovery, an effort, an excuse, a fortune, an impression, a joke, a mess, a mistake, money, a noise, an offer, peace, preparations, progress, sure, trouble, war, up one's mind, etc.

16 Fill in *do* or *make* in the correct form.

1 James .... an exercise in his book when his pen ran out.
2 She .... lots of mistakes in her homework.
3 We could .... a fortune if we sold all this jewellery.
4 I like .... the washing-up straight after dinner.
5 Sam .... the shopping for me on his way home yesterday.
6 She .... a joke but nobody laughed.
7 They .... progress with the building.
8 Just a small slice of cake won't .... any harm.
9 John is going to .... an appointment to have his hair cut.
10 If you're going to .... a job you should do it properly.
11 Mum is busy .... preparations for the party.
12 Will you .... your beds now, please?
13 Could you .... a translation of this article for me, please?
14 I don't mind if you fail the test, so long as you .... your best.
15 Yesterday we .... an offer on the house we want to buy.

at the beginning · in the beginning · at the end · in the end	
at the beginning	at the place or time at which sth starts *e.g. There is a contents page **at the beginning** of the book.*
in the beginning	initially. This suggests further change. *e.g. He thought German was hard **in the beginning**, but now he finds it easy.*
at the end	at the furthest or last part of sth *e.g. **At the end** of the day I like to relax in front of the TV.*
in the end	at last, finally, when everything is taken into consideration *e.g. I was going to take the bus home, but **in the end** I got a taxi.*

17 Fill in *at the beginning, in the beginning, at the end* or *in the end.*

1 She didn't feel very confident .... of her career, but she has changed a lot since then.

2 ...., the work was interesting, but now I find it boring.
3 It was a difficult situation, but .... everything worked out nicely.
4 There is a revision chapter .... of the book.
5 She didn't know anyone ...., but then she made lots of friends.
6 .... of the week, the weather was awful, but then it improved.
7 The big new supermarket is .... of the street.
8 The story has a tragic beginning, but fortunately everything turns out well ....
9 ...., nothing grew on the land, but it is covered with trees now.

any way · anyway	
any way	in any manner *e.g. They couldn't find **any way** to get out of the building.*
anyway (adv)	anyhow, in any case *e.g. The coat was expensive, but I bought it **anyway**.*

18 Fill in *any way* or *anyway.*

1 Is there .... I can help you?
2 You can do this .... you think best.
3 I wasn't keen on the idea of going to the party, but I went ....
4 It wasn't raining, but I took my umbrella with me ....
5 You can't treat people .... you want; you must always take their feelings into consideration.

all ready · already	
all ready	everyone prepared *e.g. The children are **all ready** to go.*
already (adv)	by this time *e.g. By the time I got there, the train had **already** left.*

19 Fill in *all ready* or *already.*

1 The teams are ...., so the competition can begin.
2 When you are .... we can leave.
3 They've .... finished all the work.
4 I've .... done the shopping this week.
5 The children had put on their costumes and they were .... to go on stage.

Revision 4 (Units 1 - 12)

 1   **Choose the correct answer.**

1   ...C... time have we got before the train leaves?
A How   B How many   C How much

2   He cut his finger while he .... some wood.
A chopped   B is chopping   C was chopping

3   She was very tired, ... she couldn't sleep.
A although   B despite   C yet

4   .... is that letter I wrote? Have you seen it?
A Where   B Who   C What

5   When we lived by the sea, we .... to swim every morning.
A were used   B got used   C used

6   I love roses, ... my sister loves carnations.
A when   B whereas   C wherever

7   She .... get a job as a teacher. She loves children.
A ought   B can   C might

8   We waved goodbye .... the car was out of sight.
A while   B until   C by the time

9   He slept for eight hours, ... he was still tired.
A in spite   B but   C although

10 'I love going to the beach.' '............'.
A Neither do I B So do I   C So I do

11 I've made .... biscuits. Would you like one?
A some   B any   C no

12 We .... go out to dinner, if you like.
A should   B could   C might

13 I think .... has been reading my diary.
A no one   B someone   C anyone

14 They .... haven't finished building the new supermarket.
A still   B yet   C just

15 By the time the rain stopped, we .... two pots of coffee.
A have drunk   B had drunk
C had been drinking

16 .... we have a barbecue this evening?
A Shall   B Will   C Mustn't

17 We're going to the theatre .... a play.
A see   B to see   C seeing

18 That is the right answer, ...?
A isn't it   B wasn't it   C is it

19 .... painted this beautiful picture?
A Who   B What   C Where

20 If you had studied more, you .... the exam.
A would pass   B will pass
C would have passed

21 He can't decide who .... to his birthday party.
A to invite   B invite   C inviting

22 I tried on two pairs of trousers, but .... of them fitted me.
A both   B neither   C either

23 'I don't like bananas.' '............'.
A Neither I do   B Neither do I   C So do I

24 He's tired. He .... properly for days.
A hasn't slept   B didn't sleep   C doesn't sleep

25 They own a motorboat, ...?
A do they   B they don't   C don't they

26 If I had a bigger flat, I .... a party.
A have   B will have   C would have

27 He .... be famous. I've never heard of him.
A must   B can't   C mustn't

28 I have .... received a letter from my pen-friend.
A just   B yet   C still

29 When I opened the door, there wasn't .... there.
A someone   B no one   C anyone

30 Chris is the .... person I have ever met.
A patient   B more patient C most patient

31 I live in the city, so I .... to busy traffic.
A am used   B get used   C used

32 I'm hungry. I haven't had .... to eat all day.
A something   B nothing   C anything

33 When I buy a new house, I .... every room myself.
A paint   B will paint   C would paint

34 We must run to the cinema. The film .... in five minutes.
A starts   B is starting C will start

35 It's no use .... about the exam results. You'll know soon enough.
A worry   B to worry   C worrying

36 We are thinking about .... a new car.
  A buy   **B** to buy   **C** buying

37 He was dirty because he .... in the garden.
  A had been working   **B** had worked
  C has been working

38 She has lots of T-shirts, but .... of them are in the wash.
  A both   **B** all   **C** either

39 Tom is three years .... than his brother.
  A old   **B** older   **C** oldest

40 We live in .... large block of flats.
  A a   **B** one   **C** the

2 **Rewrite the following sentences in the passive.**

1 People say that she owns several companies.
  ...It is said that she owns several companies/She is said to own several companies....

2 Dad is cleaning the floor at the moment.
  ....

3 The phone company cut off our telephone yesterday.
  ....

4 You must do the washing-up after dinner.
  ....

5 She will have typed all the letters by five o'clock.
  ....

6 They are interviewing two candidates at the moment.
  ....

7 He has torn his shirt again.
  ....

8 Mark feeds the dogs every morning.
  ....

9 We shouldn't reveal anything to the press.
  ....

10 Where have they sent those parcels to?
  ....

11 People think that he will win the race.
  ....

12 I object to her taking my books without permission.
  ....

13 They had sold all the tickets by the time we arrived.
  ....

14 People make wine from grapes.
  ....

15 They saw him talking to the manager.
  ....

16 Who took that beautiful photo?
  ....

17 When did they open their shop?
  ....

3 **Write questions to which the words in bold are the answers.**

1 Andrew has been **to New York**.
  ...Where has Andrew been?...

2 He is sad **because his bicycle is broken**.
  ....

3 Sarah is **tall with blonde curly hair**.
  ....

4 Barry is **very generous**.
  ....

5 Claire is **in her office**.
  ....

6 The play starts **at eight o'clock**.
  ....

7 He bought that car **two months ago**.
  ....

8 **Jonathan** wants to go on holiday.
  ....

9 We got to the island **by boat**.
  ....

10 That is **Joanne's** book.
  ....

4 **Rewrite the following sentences using *have something done*.**

1 The gardener cuts their grass once a week.
  ...They have their grass cut once a week....

2 They will ask the porter to carry their bags for them.
  ....

3 I must get someone to clean the windows.
  ....

4 His fence was built by a carpenter.
  ....

5 The hairdresser is styling Lucy's hair.
  ....

6 The doctor has bandaged his arm for him.
  ....

7 The dentist was checking Tom's teeth.
  ....

8 The cleaner had washed the floor for me.
  ....

9 It's worth asking someone to repair the roof.
  ....

10 The builders will be building the wall for him.
  ....

5 **Complete the sentences.**

1 He is very ill. He can't go to work.
  He is ...*too ill to go to work....*

2 She has got a lot of time. She can have a cup of tea.
  She has got ....

3 This meat is very tough. I can't cut it.
  This meat is ....

Revision 4 (Units 1 - 12)

4 These bags are very heavy. He can't carry them.
These bags are ....

5 We have got a lot of money. We can go out to dinner.
We have got ....

6 I have made a lot of food. I can feed all the guests.
I have made ....

7 Sarah is beautiful. She could be a model.
Sarah is ....

8 Adam is very young. He can't drive a car.
Adam is ....

9 It's very cold outside. You can't wear shorts.
It's ....

10 Peter is very clever. He can pass his exams.
Peter is ....

6 Rewrite the sentences using the words/ phrases given.

1 She had barely woken up when the telephone rang.
Barely ...*had she woken up when the telephone rang*....

2 I haven't seen such beautiful mountains anywhere else.
Nowhere else ....

3 If I were you, I would get a cat.
Were ....

4 The policeman didn't realise that the thief had already escaped.
Little ....

5 He hasn't had an ice cream since last summer.
Not since ....

6 She not only broke the glass, but she cut her hand.
Not only ....

7 We have seldom seen such a well-kept garden.
Seldom ....

8 They have never stayed in such a wonderful hotel before.
Never before ....

9 He has not once apologised for his appalling behaviour.
Not once ....

10 I only noticed the broken window after the children had left.
Only after ....

7 Rewrite the following sentences in reported speech.

1 'Be quiet, or I'll send you to bed', she said to them.
...*She threatened to send them to bed if they were not quiet*....

2 'He always makes too much noise', she said.
....

3 'Yes, I'll lend you the money', I said to her.
....

4 'That was a delicious meal!' said Julia.
....

5 He said, 'Shall we go shopping?'
....

6 'I didn't break your stereo', he said to me.
....

7 He said to her, 'Please, please don't go without me.'
....

8 'I'm the prettiest girl at the party', said Emma.
....

9 She said to him, 'Open the window, please.'
....

10 'Don't forget to set the alarm', Mary said to Liz.
....

11 'You ruined my dress', she said to her sister.
....

12 Karen said, 'You should do some revision.'
....

13 'It was me who crashed the car', Sophie said.
....

14 'Children, stand up!' said the headmistress.
....

15 'Don't touch this button', the scientist said to them.
....

8 Underline the correct form of the infinitive.

1 It is considered **to be**/**be**/**being** unlucky **to walk**/**walk**/**walking** under ladders.
2 I hate **go**/**to go**/**going** out in the rain.
3 She went for a walk **get**/**to get**/**getting** some fresh air.
4 I don't want **watch**/**to watch**/**watching** this film.
5 He was happy **be**/**to be**/**being** home at last.
6 My father made me **tidy**/**to tidy**/**tidying** my bedroom.
7 Sam agreed **help**/**to help**/**helping** me with my homework.
8 The man confessed **steal**/**to steal**/**to stealing** the documents.
9 My boss expects me **finish**/**to finish**/**finishing** this work before six o'clock.
10 He warned them about **swim**/**to swim**/**swimming** in that river, but they took no notice.
11 The children complained about **miss**/**to miss**/**missing** the party.
12 Carl denied **break**/**to break**/**breaking** the computer.
13 We could hear the choir **sing**/**to sing**/**singing** as we passed the church.
14 I don't know what **do**/**to do**/**doing** about this problem.
15 **Ski**/**To ski**/**Skiing** is a very exciting sport.

9 Rewrite the sentences using participles.

1 The woman who is serving the tea is my aunt.
...*The woman serving the tea is my aunt*....

2 Because we were tired, we stayed at home.
....

3 After the boss had explained the problem, he asked the employee to solve it.
....

4 Katie locked the doors before she went to the shop.
....

5 Because he felt ill, Stuart went to the doctor's.
....

6 The boy who is wearing a hat is Nicholas.
....

196

7 The files which were stored on that disk were very important.

....

8 After Caroline had made the beds, she went to work.

....

9 Because he had overslept, he had to take a taxi to the office.

....

10 Robin got oil on his shirt while he was fixing his bike.

....

11 Rachel picked up a book and started to read.

....

12 Oliver was sitting on a bench and he was watching the football match.

....

 10 **Put the verbs in brackets into the correct tense.**

1 If only I ...*had done* ... (do) some of this work yesterday.
2 I wish I .... (afford) to buy some new clothes.
3 If only he .... (talk) so much.
4 I wish she .... (not/leave) so early last night.
5 I wish they .... (visit) more often.
6 If only we .... (not/miss) the train.
7 If only you .... (ask) me to help you before.
8 I wish I .... (have) more free time.
9 If only we .... (not/have) to go to work today.
10 I wish she .... (tell) me what is wrong.

11 **Put the verbs in brackets into the correct tense.**

1 I ...*am going*... (go) to the beach tomorrow. Would you like to come?
2 We .... (think) about moving to the city recently.
3 Hurry up! The lesson .... (start) in five minutes.
4 I'm starving! I .... (not/eat) a thing all day.
5 I'm afraid you .... (not/get) the job unless you look smart.
6 Don't make too much noise when you come in. We ....
.... (sleep).
7 I saw David as I .... (do) the shopping. He looked well.
8 He said he .... (help) me with my homework if he has time.
9 'How long .... (you/work) as a waiter?' 'Since I was sixteen.'
10 We can't leave until the taxi .... (arrive).
11 Mum .... (make) a cake this morning. Would you like some?
12 .... (you/go) to the library today? I need to return some books.

 12 **Fill in the gaps with *some, any, no* or one of their compounds.**

1 A: Are you doing ...*anything* ... at the weekend?
 B: No, I haven't made any plans yet.
2 A: I think there's .... else in this envelope.
 B: Take it out and see what it is.
3 A: Are you off work next week?
 B: Yes, but I'm not going .... I'm going to stay at home.
4 A: The meal was a great success last night.
 B: I know. There was .... food left over, either.
5 A: Where's David?
 B: He's gone .... with his brother.
6 A: Did you enjoy your visit to the museum?
 B: Yes, but there was .... to tell us about the exhibits.
7 A: There's .... at the door for you.
 B: Who is it?
8 A: Is .... wrong?
 B: Not really. I'm just very tired.
9 A: The bus was really crowded today. There was ....
.... to sit.
 B: I know. I wish I had my own car.
10 A: Can I borrow .... sugar from you, please?
 B: Yes, of course. How much do you need?

13 **Underline the correct answer.**

1 ***There*/It/One** were lots of people at the opening ceremony last night.
2 He's faster than I am, but I'm cleverer than **he/*him*/his**.
3 They always take off **they/them/*their*** shoes before going upstairs.
4 The ball bounced up and hit her on **the/her/–** head.
5 Our neighbours designed their house **themselves/ ourselves/they**.
6 **This/*That*/These** man over there is my teacher.
7 Your room is a mess! Put **everywhere/everyone/ *everything*** away immediately!
8 I haven't got **many/little/*much*** money, so I won't go out tonight.

14 **Underline the correct preposition.**

1 This flat is small, but it will do **from/by/*for*** the time being.
2 He gave a speech **in/*on*/for** behalf of the class.
3 ***At*/In/By** the end of the concert, the orchestra took a bow.
4 I will give you the job **on/*in*/under** condition that you work hard.
5 Your assignments must be given in tomorrow **at/under/ *without*** fail.
6 This calendar is **out/*out of*/of** date. I need a new one.
7 The policeman wasn't **at/in/*on*** duty, but he still helped us.
8 It's too late to go to the cinema. The film will have started **by/for/from** now.

9 He has been **out of/of/out** work for six months now.

10 It is **against/for/by** the law to leave school before the age of 16.

11 I found this book **off/by/with** chance when I was tidying the attic.

12 She takes her parents **for/off/by** granted.

13 It was raining and the sun was shining **in/at/for** the same time.

14 I don't know **by/in/for** certain, but I think the boss is on holiday.

15 He deleted the file from the computer **on/at/by** mistake.

 15 **Fill in the gaps with the correct particle from the list.**

> up, in, down, off, out, for, on

1 When the plane eventually took ...*off*..., the passengers cheered.

2 I hear your company are taking .... new staff.

3 My watch had run .... so I was late for work.

4 HRH stands .... Her Royal Highness.

5 Can you turn .... the television? I can't hear it.

6 The children worked .... a great deal of excitement before the party.

7 We saw the happy couple .... on their honeymoon, then went home.

8 She had to take .... her skirts and trousers after her diet.

9 Leaving all the lights on is a sure way to run .... a huge electricity bill.

10 I've been working hard all day and I'm worn ....

11 Clive has taken .... jogging in order to keep fit.

12 He was whistling as he set .... on his journey.

13 Can you turn .... the lamp? It's getting dark.

14 The dark clouds gathered and the rain set ....

15 The man in the dark suit turned .... to be our new boss.

 16 **Complete each sentence with two to five words, including the word in bold.**

1 I hope you will behave well at the party.
yourself I hope ...*you will behave yourself*... at the party.

2 I saw Louise walking alone in the park.
by I saw Louise .... in the park.

3 He looked like he hadn't eaten for days.
if He looked .... eaten for days.

4 It takes half an hour to walk from my house to the office.
walk It is .... from my house to the office.

5 That's the hospital where I was born.
in That's the hospital .... I was born.

6 I invited Sam to the party. I also invited Andrew.
both I invited .... to the party.

7 Take some money with you. You might want to buy something.
case Take some money with you .... to buy something.

8 She stayed up late because she wanted to finish some work.
so She stayed up late .... some work.

9 There were many people at the meeting. Some of them were important clients.
whom There were many people at the meeting, ... were important clients.

10 This is Andrea. Her parents live in Spain.
whose This is Andrea .... in Spain.

11 The river had flooded because of the heavy rain.
due The river had flooded .... heavy rain.

12 He has little time in which to relax.
much He .... in which to relax.

13 He went to the theatre alone in the end.
on He went to the theatre .... in the end.

14 There are only a few people waiting for the train.
many There .... waiting for the train.

15 Having run to school, Steven was out of breath.
because Steven was out of breath .... to school.

16 We spent all afternoon printing those files.
whole We spent .... printing those files.

17 The film was so funny that we laughed all the way through.
such It .... that we laughed all the way through.

18 I find people dropping litter disgusting.
that I find .... disgusting.

19 No one understood me when I tried to explain the problem.
myself I couldn't .... when I tried to explain the problem.

20 It seemed that the two women knew nothing about the incident.
of It seemed that .... knew anything about the incident.

 17 **Fill in the correct form of the word in brackets.**

1 Being a doctor is a very demanding ...*occupation*... (occupy).

2 It is very .... of you to mind the baby for me. (help)

3 We were woken up by a .... in the street. (disturb)

4 Seeing his best friends at the party increased his .... of the evening. (enjoy)

5 Eating more fresh fruit would be .... to your health. (benefit)

6 My father is a very .... businessman. (succeed)

7 I am running out of .... with you! (patient)

8 The .... of the block of flats took less than a week. (destroy)

9 He is in hospital having a minor .... (operate)

10 It was very .... of you to visit me in hospital. (thought)

11 The manager has reached a .... about which candidate to employ. (decide)

12 Winning the competition was quite an .... for him. (achieve)

13 She has to wear .... clothing when she is working. (protect)

14 Despite his firm ...., I still think he is guilty. (deny)

15 It would be .... to be more careful in future. (advise)

16 Michael won second prize in the school art .... (compete)

18 Cross out the unnecessary word.

1 Despite of being hungry, I didn't eat anything.
2 Didn't he not help you make dinner?
3 She spent the all night worrying about the exam.
4 That was Mark you were talking to, wasn't it he?
5 Every one employee must report to the manager.
6 That's the girl whose her mother is an actress.
7 I phoned Mum for to ask her for some advice.
8 Don't forget to feed the cat, will you not?
9 There it seems to be a problem with the computer.
10 Who did sent this parcel?
11 Where is it my watch?
12 The children are making a lots of noise.
13 These glasses are pretty, but the others ones are awful.
14 When I will finish my homework, I will tidy my room.
15 There she is a woman on the phone for you.

19 Choose the correct answer.

1 'Did you speak to Carol before she left?'
'No, but I ...B... leave a message with her secretary.'
A couldn't   **B** was able to   **C** would

2 'What shall I do with this application form?'
'You .... fill it in and return it to the office by Friday.'
A must   **B** would   **C** needn't

3 '............ we invite Liz and Tony for dinner tomorrow?'
'Yes. Let's ask Keith and Lesley, too.'
A Would   **B** Will   **C** Shall

4 'That man is my biology teacher.'
'He .... be a teacher. He looks much too young.'
A needn't   **B** can't   **C** mustn't

5 'I think this plant is dying and I don't know what to do.'
'You .... water it more often, I think.'
A would   **B** might   **C** should

6 'Would you like to come to the cinema tonight?'
'Sorry, I can't. My boss says I .... work late tonight.'
A have to   **B** mustn't   **C** might

7 '............ I help you, madam?'
'Yes. I'm looking for the customer service department.'
A Should   **B** Must   **C** May

8 '............ I see you in my office, please?'
'Certainly, Mrs Simpson.'
A Must   **B** Could   **C** Would

9 'Shall I get some more salt at the supermarket?'
'No, you .... There's plenty.'
A needn't   **B** mustn't   **C** couldn't

10 'Did you post that card to Matthew?'
'No, I .... He came to see me so I gave it to him then!'
A mustn't   **B** didn't need to   **C** needn't

11 'I'm leaving now. I .... take this parcel to the post office.'
'I know. The boss told me he'd asked you take it.'
A have got to   **B** don't need to   **C** mustn't

12 '............ I borrow your calculator, please?'
'Of course. It's on my desk.'
A Would   **B** Must   **C** Can

13 'Can you still speak Russian?'
'No. I .... when I was young, but I've forgotten it now!'
A can   **B** couldn't   **C** could

14 'I've lost my passport.'
'You .... report it to the police.'
A oughtn't to   **B** ought to   **C** might

15 '............ you pick me up from work today, please?'
'Yes. I'll be there at 5 o'clock.'
A Will   **B** Shall   **C** May

Irregular Verbs

Infinitive	Past	Past Participle	Infinitive	Past	Past Participle
be	was	been	let	let	let
bear	bore	born(e)	lie	lay	lain
beat	beat	beaten	light	lit	lit
become	became	become	lose	lost	lost
begin	began	begun	make	made	made
bite	bit	bitten	mean	meant	meant
blow	blew	blown	meet	met	met
break	broke	broken	pay	paid	paid
bring	brought	brought	put	put	put
build	built	built	read	read	read
burn	burnt (burned)	burnt (burned)	ride	rode	ridden
burst	burst	burst	ring	rang	rung
buy	bought	bought	rise	rose	risen
can	could	(been able to)	run	ran	run
catch	caught	caught	say	said	said
choose	chose	chosen	see	saw	seen
come	came	come	seek	sought	sought
cost	cost	cost	sell	sold	sold
cut	cut	cut	send	sent	sent
deal	dealt	dealt	set	set	set
dig	dug	dug	sew	sewed	sewn
do	did	done	shake	shook	shaken
draw	drew	drawn	shine	shone	shone
dream	dreamt (dreamed)	dreamt (dreamed)	shoot	shot	shot
drink	drank	drunk	show	showed	shown
drive	drove	driven	shut	shut	shut
eat	ate	eaten	sing	sang	sung
fall	fell	fallen	sit	sat	sat
feed	fed	fed	sleep	slept	slept
feel	felt	felt	smell	smelt (smelled)	smelt (smelled)
fight	fought	fought	speak	spoke	spoken
find	found	found	spell	spelt (spelled)	spelt (spelled)
fly	flew	flown	spend	spent	spent
forbid	forbade	forbidden	spill	spilt	spilt
forget	forgot	forgotten	split	split	split
forgive	forgave	forgiven	spoil	spoilt (spoiled)	spoilt (spoiled)
freeze	froze	frozen	spread	spread	spread
get	got	got	spring	sprang	sprung
give	gave	given	stand	stood	stood
go	went	gone	steal	stole	stolen
grow	grew	grown	stick	stuck	stuck
hang	hung (hanged)	hung (hanged)	sting	stung	stung
have	had	had	strike	struck	struck
hear	heard	heard	swear	swore	sworn
hide	hid	hidden	sweep	swept	swept
hit	hit	hit	swim	swam	swum
hold	held	held	take	took	taken
hurt	hurt	hurt	teach	taught	taught
keep	kept	kept	tear	tore	torn
know	knew	known	tell	told	told
lay	laid	laid	think	thought	thought
lead	led	led	throw	threw	thrown
learn	learnt (learned)	learnt (learned)	understand	understood	understood
leave	left	left	wake	woke	woken
lend	lent	lent	wear	wore	worn
			win	won	won
			write	wrote	written

APPENDICES

Appendix 1

Present Simple

1) **Most verbs take -s in the third person singular.**
   I run - he runs
2) **Verbs ending in -ss, -sh, -ch, -x and -o, take -es.**
   I kiss - he kisses, I brush - he brushes, I teach - he teaches, I fix - he fixes, I go - he goes
3) **Verbs ending in a consonant + y, drop the -y and take -ies.**
   I fry - he fries
4) **Verbs ending in a vowel + y, take -s.**
   I play - he plays

Present Continuous

1) **Verbs ending in -e, drop the -e and take the -ing suffix.**
   *starve - starving **but** see - seeing*
2) **Verbs ending in one stressed vowel between two consonants, double the last consonant and take the -ing suffix.**
   *rub - rubbing **but** open - opening*

3) **Verbs ending in -l, double the -l and take the -ing suffix.**
   quarel - quarelling
4) **Verbs ending in -ie, drop the -ie and take -y + ing.**
   lie - lying

Past Simple

1) **Verbs ending in -e, take only -d.**
   improve - improved
2) **Verbs ending in a consonant + y, drop the -y and take -ied.**
   try - tried
3) **Verbs ending in a vowel + y, take -ed.**
   pray - prayed
4) **Verbs ending in one stressed vowel between two consonants, double the last consonant and take -ed.**
   *rub - rubbed **but** open - opened*
5) **Verbs ending in -l, double the -l and take -ed.**
   travel - travelled

Appendix 2

Present Simple

Affirmative	Negative
I clean	I **don't** clean
You clean	You don't clean
He cleans	He **doesn't** clean etc.
She cleans	**Interrogative**
It cleans	
We clean	**Do** I clean?
You clean	Do you clean?
They clean	**Does** he clean? etc.

Present Continuous

Affirmative	Negative
I **am** clean**ing**	I'm not cleaning
You are cleaning	You aren't cleaning
He is cleaning	He isn't cleaning etc.
She is cleaning	**Interrogative**
It is cleaning	
We are cleaning	Am I cleaning?
You are cleaning	Are you cleaning?
They are cleaning	Is he cleaning? etc.

Future Simple

Affirmative	Negative
I **will** clean	I **won't** clean
You will clean	You won't clean
He will clean	He won't clean etc.
She will clean	**Interrogative**
It will clean	
We will clean	**Will** I clean?
You will clean	Will you clean?
They will clean	Will he clean? etc.

Future Continuous

Affirmative	Negative
I **will be** clean**ing**	I **won't** be cleaning
You will be cleaning	You won't be cleaning
He will be cleaning	He won't be cleaning etc.
She will be cleaning	**Interrogative**
It will be cleaning	
We will be cleaning	Will I be cleaning?
You will be cleaning	Will you be cleaning?
They will be cleaning	Will he be cleaning? etc.

Future Perfect

Affirmative	Negative
I **will have** clean**ed**	I **won't** have cleaned
You will have cleaned	You won't have cleaned
He will have cleaned	He won't have cleaned etc.
She will have cleaned	**Interrogative**
It will have cleaned	
We will have cleaned	Will I have cleaned?
You will have cleaned	Will you have cleaned?
They will have cleaned	Will he have cleaned? etc.

Future Perfect Continuous

Affirmative

I **will have been** clean**ing**
You will have been cleaning
He will have been cleaning
She will have been cleaning
It will have been cleaning
We will have been cleaning
You will have been cleaning
They will have been cleaning

Negative

I won't have been cleaning
You won't have been cleaning
He won't have been cleaning etc.

Interrogative

Will I have been cleaning?
Will you have been cleaning?
Will he have been cleaning? etc.

Present Perfect

Affirmative

I **have** clean**ed**
You have cleaned
He **has** clean**ed**
She has cleaned
It has cleaned
We have cleaned
You have cleaned
They have cleaned

Negative

I haven't cleaned
You haven't cleaned
He hasn't cleaned etc.

Interrogative

Have I cleaned?
Have you cleaned?
Has he cleaned? etc.

Present Perfect Continuous

Affirmative

I **have been** clean**ing**
You have been cleaning
He has been cleaning
She **has been** clean**ing**
It has been cleaning
We have been cleaning
You have been cleaning
They have been cleaning

Negative

I haven't been cleaning
You haven't been cleaning
He hasn't been cleaning etc.

Interrogative

Have I been cleaning?
Have you been cleaning?
Has he been cleaning? etc.

Past Simple

Affirmative

I clean**ed**
You cleaned
He cleaned
She cleaned
It cleaned
We cleaned
You cleaned
They cleaned

Negative

I **didn't** clean
You didn't clean
He didn't clean etc.

Interrogative

Did I clean?
Did you clean?
Did he clean? etc.

Past Continuous

Affirmative

I **was** clean**ing**
You **were** cleaning
He was cleaning
She was cleaning
It was cleaning
We were cleaning
You were cleaning
They were cleaning

Negative

I wasn't cleaning
You weren't cleaning
He wasn't cleaning etc.

Interrogative

Was I cleaning?
Were you cleaning?
Was he cleaning? etc.

Past Perfect

Affirmative

I **had** clean**ed**
You had cleaned
He had cleaned
She had cleaned
It had cleaned
We had cleaned
You had cleaned
They had cleaned

Negative

I hadn't cleaned
You hadn't cleaned
He hadn't cleaned etc.

Interrogative

Had I cleaned?
Had you cleaned?
Had he cleaned? etc.

Past Perfect Continuous

Affirmative

I **had been** clean**ing**
You had been cleaning
He had been cleaning
She had been cleaning
It had been cleaning
We had been cleaning
You had been cleaning
They had been cleaning

Negative

I hadn't been cleaning
You hadn't been cleaning
He hadn't been cleaning etc.

Interrogative

Had I been cleaning?
Had you been cleaning?
Had he been cleaning? etc.

Appendix 3

Verbs, Adjectives, Nouns with Prepositions

A

absent from (adj)
accompanied by (adj)
according to (prep)
account for (v)
accuse sb of (v)
accustomed to (adj)
addicted to (adj)
advantage of (n)
(but: there's an **advantage in** - (have) an **advantage over** sb)
advice on (n)
afraid of (adj)
agree to/on sth (v)
agree with sb (v)

ahead of (prep)
aim at (v)
allergic to (adj)
amazed at/by (adj)
amused by (adj)
angry at what sb does (adj)
angry with sb about sth (adj)
angry with sb for doing sth (adj)
annoyed with sb about sth (adj)
(in) answer to (n)
anxious about sth (adj)
(be) anxious for sth to happen (adj)
apologise to sb for sth (v)
(make an) appeal to sb for sth (n)
appeal to/against (v)

apply to sb for sth (v)
approve of (v)
argue with sb about sth (v)
arrest sb for sth (v)
arrive at (a small place) (v)
arrive in (a town) (v)
ashamed of (adj)
ask for (v) (but: ask sb a question)
assure (sb) of (v)
astonished at/by (adj)
attached to (adj)
attack on (n)
attend to (v)
(un) aware of (adj)

B

bad at (adj) (but: He was very **bad to** me.)
base on (v)
basis for (n)
beg for (v)
begin with (v)
believe in (v)

benefit from (v)
bet on (v)
beware of (v)
(put the) blame on sb (n)
blame sb for sth (v)
blame sth on sb (v)
boast about/of (v)

bored with/of (adj)
borrow sth from sb (v)
brilliant at (adj)
bump into (v)
busy with (adj)

C

call at/on (phr v)
call for (= demand) (phr v)
campaign against/for (v)
capable of (adj)
care about (v)
care for sb (v) (= like)
(take) care of (n)
care for sth (v) (= like to do sth)
careful of (adj)
careless about sth (adj)
cause of (n)
certain of (adj)
change into (v)
characteristic of (n/adj)
charge for (v)
charge sb with (v)
cheque for (n)
choice between/of (n)
clever at (adj) (but: It was very **clever of** you to buy it.)
close to (adj)
collaborate with (v)

collide with (v)
comment on (v)
communicate with (v)
compare with (v) (how people and things are alike and how they are different)
compare to (v) (show the likeness between sb/sth and sb/sth else)
comparison between (n)
complain of (v) (= suffer from)
complain to sb about sth (v) (= be annoyed at)
compliment sb on (v)
comply with (v)
conceal sth from sb (v)
concentrate on (v)
(have) confidence in sb (n)
confusion over (n)
congratulate sb on sth (v)
connect to/with (v)
connection between (n) (but: **in connection with**)
conscious of (adj)
consist of (v)

contact between (n) (but: **in contact with**)
content with (adj)
contrary to (prep)
contrast with (v)
contribute to (v)
convert to/into (v)
cope with (v)
correspond to/with (v)
count against (v)
count on sb (phr v)
cover in/with (v)
covered in/with (adj)
crash into (v)
(have) a craving for sth (n)
crazy about (adj)
crowded with (adj)
cruel to (adj)
cruelty towards/to (n)
cure for (n)
curious about (adj)
cut in (phr v) (= interrupt sb/a conversation)

Verbs, Adjectives, Nouns with Prepositions

D

damage to (n)
date back to (v)
date from (v)
deal with (v)
dear to (adj)
decide on/against (v)
decrease in (n)
dedicate to (v)
definition of (n)
delight in (v)
delighted with (adj)
demand for (n)
demand from (v)
depart from (v)
departure from (n)
depend on/upon (v)

dependent on (adj)
describe sb/sth to sb else (v)
description of (n)
die of/from (v)
die in an accident (v)
differ from (v)
(have) difference between/of (n)
different from (adj)
difficulty in/with (n)
disadvantage of (n) (but: there's a
disadvantage in doing sth)
disagree with (v)
disappointed with/about (adj)
disapprove of (v)
discharge sb from (v)
discouraged from (adj)

discussion about/on (n)
disgusted by/at (adj)
dismiss from (v)
dispose of (v)
disqualified from (adj)
dissatisfied with (adj)
distinguish between (v)
divide between/among (v)
divide into/by (v)
do sth about (v)
doubtful about (adj)
dream about (v)
dream of (v) (= imagine)
dressed in (adj)

E

eager for (adj)
efficient at (adj)
(put) effort into sth (n)
emphasis on (n)
engaged to sb/in sth (adj)
engagement to sb (n)
enter into (= start) (v)
enthusiastic about (adj)
envious of (adj)
equal to (adj)

escape from/to (v)
example of (n)
excellent at (adj)
exception to (n)
exchange sth for sth else (v)
excited about (adj)
exclaim at (v)
excuse for (n)
excuse sb for (v)
expel from (v)

experienced in (adj)
experiment on/with (v)
expert at/in (sth/doing sth) (n)
(= person good at sth)
expert at/in (sth/doing sth) (adj)
(= done with skill or involving great
knowledge)
expert with sth (n) (= good at using sth)
expert on (n) (= person knowledgeable
about a subject)

F

face up to (phr v)
fail in an attempt (v)
fail to do sth (v)
failure in (an exam) (n)
failure to (do sth) (n)
faithful to (adj)
fall in (n)
familiar to sb (= known to sb) (adj)

familiar with (= have knowledge of) (adj)
famous for (adj)
fed up with (adj)
fill sth with sth else (v)
finish with (v)
fire at (v)
fond of (adj)
forget about (v)

forgive sb for (v)
fortunate in (adj)
friendly with/to/towards (adj)
frightened of (adj)
full of (adj)
furious with sb about/at sth (adj)

G

generosity to/towards (n)
genius at (n)
glance at (v)
glare at (v)

good at (adj) (but: He was very
good to me.)
grateful to sb for sth (adj)
guess at (v)

guilty of (adj) (but: he felt **guilty
about** his crime)

H

happen to (v)
happy about/with (adj)
harmful to (adj)
hear about (v) (= be told)

hear from (v) (= receive a letter)
hear of (v) (= learn that sth or sb exists)
heir to (n)
hint to sb about sth (v) (but: **hint at** sth)

hope for (v)
hope to do sth (v)
(no) hope of (n)
hopeless at (adj)

Verbs, Adjectives, Nouns with Prepositions

I

idea of (n)
identical to (adj)
ignorant of/about (adj)
ill with (adj)
impact on (n)
impressed by/with (adj)
(make an) impression on sb (n)
improvement in/on (n)
incapable of (adj)
include ln (v)

increase in (n)
independent of (adj)
indifferent to (adj)
inferior to (adj)
information about/on (n)
(be) informed about (adj)
insist on (v)
insure against (v)
intent on (adj)
(have no) intention of (n)

interest in (n)
interested in (adj)
interfere with/in (v)
invasion of (n)
invest in (v)
invitation to (n)
invite sb to (v)
involve in (v)
irritated by (adj)

J

jealous of (adj)

join in (v)

joke about (v)

K

knock at/on (v)
know about/of (v)
keen on sth (adj)

keen to do sth (adj)
kind to (adj)

key to (n)
knowledge of (n)

L

lack in (v)
lack of (n)
laugh at (v)
lean on/against (v)

leave for (v) (= head for)
lend sth to sb (v)
listen to (v)
live on (v)

long for (v)
look after (phr v) (= take care of)
look at (v)
look for (= search for) (v)

M

married to (adj)
mean to (adj)

mention to (v)
mistake sb for (v)

mix with (v)

N

name after (v)
necessary for (adj)
need for (n)
neglect of (n)

nervous about (adj)
new to (adj)
nice to (adj)

nominate sb (for/as sth) (v)
(take) (no) notice of (n)
notorious for doing sth (adj)

O

obedient to (adj)
object to (v)
objection to (n)
obliged to sb for sth (adj)

obvious to (adj)
occur to (v)
offence against (n)
operate on (v)

opinion of/on (n)
opposite of/to (n)

P

part with (v)
patient with (adj)
pay by (cheque) (v)
pay for (v) (but: **pay a bill**)
pay in (cash) (v)
peculiar to (adj)
persist in (v)
(but: **insist on**)
(take a) photograph of (n)
picture of (n)
pity for (n)
take pity on sb (exp)
pleasant to (adj)

pleased with (adj)
(take) pleasure in (n)
(have the) pleasure of (n)
point at/to (v)
(im)polite to (adj)
popular with (adj)
praise sb for (v)
pray for sth/sb (v)
prefer sth to sth else (v)
(have a) preference for (n)
prepare for (v)
present sb with (v)
prevent sb from (v)

(take) pride in (n)
pride oneself on sth/on doing (v)
prohibit sb from doing sth (v)
prone to (adj)
protect against/from (v)
protection from/against (n)
protest about/at (v)
proud of (adj)
provide sb with (v)
punish sb for (v)
puzzled about/by (adj)

Q

quarrel about sth/with sb (v/n)

qualified for (adj)

quick at (adj)

Verbs, Adjectives, Nouns with Prepositions

R

react to (v)
reaction to (n)
ready for (adj)
reason for (n)
reason with (v)
rebel against (v)
receive from (v)
(keep) a record of (n)
recover from (v)
reduction in (n)
refer to (v)
(in/with) reference to (n)
regard as (v)
regardless of (prep)

related to (adj)
relationship between (n) (but: a good
relationship with sb)
relevant to (adj)
rely on (v)
remind sb of/about (v)
remove from (v)
replace sth with sth else (v)
reply to (n/v)
report on (n/v)
reputation for (n)
research on/into (n)
respect for (n)
respected for (adj)

respond to (v)
responsiblity for (n)
responsible for (adj)
result from (v) (= be the
consequence of)
result in (v) (= cause)
result of (n)
resulting from (adj)
rich in (adj)
(get) rid of (phr)
rise in (n)
(make) room for (n)
rude to (adj)
run into (phr v)

S

safe from (adj)
same as (adj)
satisfied with (adj)
save sb from (v)
scared of (adj)
search for (v/n)
(be) in search of (n)
sensible of sb (adj)
sensitive to (adj) (= aware of
sth)
sentence sb to (v)
separate from (v)
serious about (adj)
share in/of sth (n)
shelter from (v)
shocked at/by (adj)
shoot at (v)
short of (adj)
shout at (v)

shy of (adj)
sick of (adj)
silly to do sth (adj) (but: it was **silly of**
him)
similar to (adj)
skilful/skilled at (adj)
slow in/about doing sth/to sth (adj)
smell of (n/v)
smile at (v)
solution to (n)
sorry about (adj) (= feel sorry for sb)
(but: I'm **sorry for** doing sth)
speak to/with sb about (v)
specialise in (v)
specialist in (n)
spend money on sth (v)
spend time in (a place)/doing sth (v)
split into/in (v)
spy on (v)

stand for (phr v)
stare at (v)
strain on (n)
subject to (adj/v)
submit to (v) (but: **submit for** publication)
subscribe to (v)
succeed in (v)
suffer from (v)
(in)sufficient for sth/sb (adj)
superior to (adj)
sure of/about (adj)
surprised at/by (adj)
surrender to (v)
surrounded by (adj)
suspect sb of (v)
suspicious of (adj)
(un)sympathetic to/towards (adj)
sympathise with (v)

T

take sth to sb/sth (v)
talent for sth (n)
talk to sb about sth (v)
(have good/bad) taste in (n)
taste of (v)
terrible at (adj)
terrified of (adj)

thank sb for (v)
thankful for (adj)
think about/of (v)
threat to sb/sth of sth (n)
threaten sb with sth (v)
throw sth at (v) (in order to hit)
throw sth to (v) (in order to catch)

tired from (adj)
tired of (adj) (= fed up with)
translate from ... into (v)
tread on (v)
trip over (v)
trouble with (n)
typical of (adj)

U

unaware of (adj)
understanding of (n)

uneasy about (adj)
upset about/over sth (adj)

(make) use of (n)
used to (adj)

V

valid for (length of time) (adj)
valid in (places) (adj)

value sth at (v)
vote against/for (v)

W

wait for (v)
warn sb against/about/of (v)
waste (time/money) on (v)

wonder about (v)
worry about (v)
worthy of (adj)

write to sb (v)
wrong about (adj)

Prepositional Phrases

At

at the age of
at the airport
at the beginning of (when
sth started) (but: **in the
beginning** = originally)
at breakfast/lunch etc
at the bottom of
at the bus stop
at the corner/on the corner
at all costs
at the crossroads
at dawn
at one's desk
at the door
at the end (= when sth is
finished) (but: **in the end**
= finally at all events)
at fault
at first
at first hand
at first sight

at a glance
at a guess
at hand
at heart
at home
at/in a hotel
at ... km per hour
at last
at the latest
at least
at liberty
at a loss
at the match
at midnight
at the moment
at most
at night (but:**in the** night)
at noon
at once
at peace/war
at present

at a profit
at the prospect
at random
at any rate
at one's request
at the same time
at school
at sea
at the seaside
at short notice
at/in the station
at sunset
at the table
at the time
at times
at the top of (but: **on top of**)
at university
at the weekend
at work
at 4, Rose St.

By

by accident
by all accounts
by appointment
by the arm/hand
by birth
by bus/train/plane/
helicopter/taxi/ coach/
ship/boat/sea/air/car etc
(but: **on a/the** bus/plane/
train/coach/ship/boat
in a taxi/car/helicopter/plane)
by chance
by cheque
by correspondence

by day/night
by degrees
by the dozen
by far
by force
by hand
by heart
by invitation
by land/sea/air
by law
by luck
by marriage
by means of
by mistake

by nature
by now
by oneself
by phone
by post/airmail
by profession
by request
by (the/one's) side
by sight
by surprise
by the time
by the way
by one's watch

For

for ages
for breakfast/lunch/dinner
for certain
for a change
for ever
for fear (of)
for fun (= for amusement)
for good
for granted

for hire
for instance
for life
for love
for luck
for nothing
for once
for the rest of
for safe keeping

for one's sake
for the sake of
for sale
for short
for the time being
for a visit/holiday
for a walk
for a while

209

Prepositional Phrases

In

in action
in addition to (+ -ing form)
in advance (of)
in agreement (with)
in aid of
in all (all in all)
in answer to
in an armchair
in a good/bad temper
in bed
in the beginning
(= originally)
in a book
in brief
in any case
in cash
in the centre of
in charge (of)
in code
in colour
in comfort
in common
in comparison with
in conclusion (to)
in (good/bad) condition
in confidence
in control (of)
in the country
in danger
in the dark
in debt
in demand
in detail
(be) in difficulty
in the direction of
in doubt
in a ... dress
in the end (= finally)
in exchange for
in existence
in fact
in fashion
in favour of
in flames
in the flesh
in one's free time
in fun
in (the) future

in general
in good time
in half
in hand
in haste
in good/bad health
in honour of
in the hope of
in hospital
in a hotel
in a hurry
in ink/pencil/pen
in sb's interest
in length/width etc
in all sb's life
in a line
in the long run
in love (with)
in luxury
in the meantime
in a mess
in the middle of
in a mirror
in a moment
in a good/bad mood
in the mood
in the morning
in name only (= not in reality)
in need of
in the news
in a newspaper
in the name of (= on behalf of)
in the nick of time
in the north/south
in a nutshell
in oils
in the open
in one's opinion
in orbit
in order of/to
in other words
in pain
in pairs
in the park
in particular
in the past
in person
in pieces

in place of
in politics
in pounds
in practice
in principle
in prison
in private/public
in all probability
in progress
in a queue
in reality
in return
in the right/wrong
in a row/rows
in ruins
in safety
in season
in secret
in self-defence
in short
in sight (of)
in the sky
in some respects
in stock
in the streets
in succession
in the suburbs
in the sun/shade
in good/bad taste
in tears
in theory
in a tick
in time
in no time
in touch
in town
in tune (with)
in turn
in two/half
in uniform
in use
in vain
in view of
in a loud/low voice
in a way (= in a manner)
in the way
in writing
in a word

Prepositional Phrases

On

on account of
on a ... afternoon/evening
on the agenda
on the air
on approval
on arrival
on average
on bail
on balance
on the beach
on behalf of
on one's birthday
on board
on the border
on business
on call
on a campsite (at a campsite)
on the coast
on condition
on the contrary
on credit
on a(n) cruise/excursion/trip/tour
on (a ...) day
on demand
on a diet
on duty

on earth
on edge
on an expedition
on a farm (but: **in a field**)
on fire
on the (4th) floor (of)
on the floor
on foot
on the one hand
on the other hand
on holiday
on horseback
on impulse
on the increase
on an island (but: **in the mountains**)
on a journey
on one's knees
on leave
on the left/right
on loan
on the market (= available to the public)
on one's mind
on that morning
on the move
on New Year's Day
on the news
on order
on the outskirts

on one's own
on page ...
on parade
on the pavement
on the phone
on a platform
on principle
on purpose
on the radio/TV
on the River Seine
on sale
on schedule
on (the) screen
on second thoughts
on sight
on the sofa
on this street/on the street(s)
on strike
on good/bad terms
on time
on top (of)
on the trail of
on a trip
on the way (to) (= as I was going)
on the whole

Out of

out of breath
out of character
out of condition
out of control
out of danger
out of date
out of debt
out of doors
out of fashion

out of focus
out of hand
out of luck
out of order
out of the ordinary
out of place
out of practice
out of print
out of the question

out of reach
out of season
out of sight
out of step
out of stock
out of tune
out of turn
out of use
out of work

Off

off air
off colour
off duty

off limits
off the map
off the point

off the record
off the road
off school/work

Under

under age
under arrest
under one's breath
under control

under discussion
under the impression
under orders

under pressure
under repair
under the weather

211

Prepositional Phrases

Against	against the law
Ahead	ahead of schedule/time
Before	before long
Behind	behind schedule, behind the times
From	from time to time, from now on, from experience, from memory, from scratch
Into	into pieces
To	to one's astonishment, to one's surprise, to this day, to some extent
With	with regard to, with a view to (+ -ing form)
Within	within minutes/seconds/hours
Without	without delay, without fail, without success, without warning

Prepositions of Time

AT	IN	ON
at 10.30	in the morning/evening/afternoon/night	on Monday
at Christmas/Easter	in the Easter/Christmas holiday(s)	on Easter Sunday etc.
at noon/night/midnight	in January (months)	on Christmas Day
at lunch/dinner/breakfast (time)	in (the) winter (seasons)	on Friday night
at that time	in 1992 (years)	on July 30th
at the moment	in the 19th century	on a summer afternoon
at the weekend (on the weekend: Am. English)	in two hours (two hours from now)	on that day

We never use **at**, **in** or **on** before **yesterday**, **tomorrow**, **next**, **this**, **last**, **every**. *She's leaving **next** Sunday.*

PROGRESS TESTS

Progress Test 1 (Units 1-2)

1 Choose the correct answer.

1 'Kate .... hard recently.'
'Yes. She is taking her exams next month.'
A has been studying   **B** has studied
C studied

2 'I must go to the library.'
'I .... there this afternoon. I'll give you a lift.'
A have been   **B** am going   **C** go

3 '............ is very good for you.'
'Yes. It's my favourite form of exercise.'
A Swim   **B** Swimming   **C** To swim

4 'We'd better run to the stadium.'
'I know. The game .... in five minutes.'
A is starting   **B** has started   **C** starts

5 'I'm very hungry.'
'I'm not surprised. You .... all day.'
A haven't been eating   **B** haven't eaten
C don't eat

6 'I can't decide what .... for lunch.'
'Why don't you buy a sandwich?'
A have   **B** having   **C** to have

7 'Why did you go to the shop this morning?'
'............ some bread. We had run out.'
A Get   **B** Getting   **C** To get

8 'How did you hurt your hand?'
'I cut it as I .... some vegetables.'
A chopped   **B** am chopping   **C** was chopping

9 'The journey here was very tiring.'
'Yes. I'm very glad .... here at last.'
A being   **B** to be   **C** be

10 'Let's go for a walk.'
'We can't go out until the rain ....'
A stopped   **B** will stop   **C** stops

11 'I want to call Simon.'
'Well, don't call him before eight o'clock. He ....'
A will sleep   **B** will be sleeping   **C** is sleeping

12 'Would you like to watch the film with me?'
'No thanks. I'd rather .... my book.'
A read   **B** reading   **C** to read

13 'He .... a famous writer one day.'
'Yes, I think you're right.'
A was   **B** will be   **C** is being

14 'What are you doing on Saturday?'
'Well, Paul suggested .... to the cinema.'
A go   **B** going   **C** to go

2 Complete each sentence with two to five words, including the word in bold.

15 This soup is too cold for me to eat.
enough   This soup .... for me to eat.

16 We haven't been to the theatre for months.
time   The ....
to the theatre was months ago.

17 The car was so expensive that he couldn't afford it.
too   The car ....
to afford.

18 I haven't written to Paul yet.
still   I .... to Paul.

19 Someone saw him leave the building.
was   He .... the building.

20 Food is not allowed to be eaten in the library.
eat   People ....
food in the library.

21 He was bored by the film and fell asleep.
found   He ....
and fell asleep.

22 She began playing the piano when she was eight.
since   She has ....
she was eight.

23 Telling lies is very bad.
to   It .... lies.

24 She didn't go to bed until she had finished her homework.
before   She finished .... to bed.

3 Put the verbs in brackets into the correct *infinitive form* or the *-ing form*.

25 She was unwilling .... (help).
26 Tom had difficulty .... (unscrew) the lid.
27 I would rather .... (eat) Chinese food tonight.
28 Mary stopped .... (buy) a newspaper
on her way to work.
29 He admitted to .... (lie) to the police.
30 They called the theatre box office only ....
(find) that there were no tickets left.
31 She is too old .... (take up) windsurfing.
32 After .... (take) his degree, he looked for a job.
33 They tried .... (locate) the company
president, but he was on holiday.
34 Did he mention anything about .... (leave)?
35 I'm sorry .... (have to) ask you to do
this, but could you possibly work late tonight?
36 It was kind of you .... (send) me flowers.
37 In addition to .... (miss) the bus, she also
lost her umbrella.
38 Did you remember .... (thank) Aunt Hilary
for her present?
39 You shouldn't .... (believe) everything he says.
40 He wasted valuable time .... (talk) on the phone.

Progress Test 2 (Units 3-4)

 1 Put the adjectives in brackets into the *comparative* or *superlative form*, adding any necessary words.

1 A: David is .... (old) Steve, isn't he?

B: Yes. David is 14 and Steve is 12.

2 A: Do you like being at university?

B: Yes. It's .... (interesting) being at school.

3 A: Did you enjoy the meal?

B: Yes. It was .... (delicious) meal I've ever eaten.

4 A: Laura is a lovely person.

B: Yes. She's .... (nice) person I know.

5 A: Did you get a good grade in the exam?

B: Yes. It was much .... (good) I had expected.

6 A: Did you buy that jacket?

B: No. It was far .... (expensive) I had thought.

7 A: Do you like my new dress?

B: I love it! It's .... (beautiful) dress I've ever seen.

8 A: It was a great party, wasn't it?

B: Oh yes! It was .... (good) party I've ever been to.

9 A: Why are you so tired?

B: The meeting finished much .... (late) than I had expected.

10 A: Mark is very clever.

B: Yes. He's .... (intelligent) boy in the school.

 2 Complete each sentence using the noun in brackets in the *singular* or *plural form* and *a/an* where necessary.

11 The wind blew all the important .... off my desk. (paper)

12 I can't talk now. I haven't got much .... (time)

13 Travelling around the world was .... I will never forget. (experience)

14 There is not much .... in this office. (room)

15 These .... are delicious. Would you like one? (chocolate)

16 I have seen this film several .... before. (time)

17 We had booked .... in a hotel before we arrived. (room)

18 He has plenty of .... in this kind of work. (experience)

 3 Underline the correct item.

19 We had **hard/hardly** left the house when the storm broke.

20 I haven't got much free **times/time** these days, because I'm taking French lessons.

21 Maths **was/were** George's least favourite subject when he was at school.

22 His ambition is to swim across **the English Channel/ English Channel.**

23 **The Queen/Queen** is going to address the nation this evening.

24 **Most/The most** people enjoy spending their holidays on the beach.

25 Henry is looking for **a/one** bigger flat, as his wife is expecting their new baby.

26 I've been working very hard **lately/late** so I'm planning to take some time off.

27 These tomatoes cost £1.20 **a/the** kilo.

28 The plane landed at **the JFK/JFK** Airport.

29 **Bears/The bears** love honey.

30 Mrs Houston went to **college/the college** to pick up her husband.

31 The secretary has **near/nearly** finished typing the report so you can have it in a few minutes.

32 The cattle **was/were** grazing in the field.

33 Three years **are/is** a long time to be out of work.

 4 Complete each sentence with two to five words, including the word in bold.

34 I've never had such a bad day.

the It's .... I've ever had.

35 Meg is the fastest typist of all.

than Meg .... anyone else.

36 Tim is more imaginative than Alan.

less Alan .... Tim.

37 Lucy spent the same amount of money on clothes as Laura.

much Lucy spent .... on clothes as Laura.

38 Can't you do any better than that?

best Is that .... you can do?

39 As he gets older, he becomes less tolerant.

the The older he gets, ... he becomes.

40 Rita is prettier than Sheila.

as Sheila .... Rita.

Progress Test 3 (Units 5-6)

1 Choose the correct answer.

1 You .... tell the police about the burglary.
   A would   B shall   C must

2 This room .... last week.
   A was decorated   B will be decorated
   C decorated

3 .... we go for a picnic tomorrow?
   A Shall   B Should   C Would

4 The Marathon .... by a famous athlete.
   A has been won   B was won   C won

5 You .... wear jeans to the interview.
   A must   B mustn't   C couldn't

6 I .... swim until I was five years old.
   A couldn't   B could   C can't

7 I took the bus to work because my car .... at the moment.
   A was being serviced   B is being serviced
   C is serviced

8 Mum .... have gone shopping.
   A might   B will   C ought

9 I .... my hair cut yesterday.
   A had   B have had   C have

10 .... I help you, sir?
   A Should   B Must   C May

11 Bob .... be on holiday. I saw him yesterday.
   A would   B could   C can't

12 John .... his car stolen last night.
   A has   B has had   C had

13 You .... have eaten so many sweets.
   A shouldn't   B should   C might

14 I .... water the garden. It rained this morning.
   A didn't need to   B needn't   C have to

15 He .... solve the problem, although it was difficult.
   A was able to   B could   C couldn't

16 The new bridge .... next week.
   A was opened   B will be opened
   C is opened

17 Laura .... her tonsils taken out last week.
   A has had   B has   C had

18 .... you do me a favour, please?
   A Should   B Could   C Need

19 Janice .... her house painted at the moment.
   A is having   B has   C will have

2 Rewrite the sentences in the *passive*.

20 Someone broke into their flat last night.
   ....

21 Steve hasn't opened the mail yet.
   ....

22 Are they inviting many people to the party?
   ....

23 Jake painted the house last week.
   ....

24 Paul hates people interrupting him.
   ....

25 People consider him to be the greatest composer of our time.
   ....

26 The reporter asked the candidate several questions.
   ....

27 No one said anything about the matter.
   ....

28 Do they allow you to receive phone calls at work?
   ....

29 They are organising a protest march.
   ....

30 They say she will take part in the negotiations.
   ....

3 Complete each sentence with two to five words, including the word in bold.

31 We will probably go to Spain this summer.
   likely   It ....
                 go to Spain this summer.

32 I advise you to take notes during the lecture.
   ought   You ....
                 during the lecture.

33 I'm certain Martin doesn't work in York.
   can't   Martin ....
                 in York.

34 Perhaps David has missed the train.
   could   David .... the train.

35 It is possible that she has forgotten the arrangements.
   may   She ....
                 .... the arrangements.

36 I advise you to study for the exam.
   should   You ....
                 for the exam.

37 It isn't necessary for you to work late tonight.
   have   You ....
                 late tonight.

38 I broke my glasses when I fell down the steps.
   got   My glasses ....
                 down the steps.

39 Let's talk about this later.
   can   We .... later.

40 I'm sure Susan has already left.
   must   Susan .... left.

217

Progress Test 4 (Units 7-8)

1 **Complete each sentence with two to five words, including the word in bold.**

1 'I haven't got any money', he said.
complained   He ....
any money.

2 You'll be able to go on holiday if you save some money.
will   Only if you ....
be able to go on holiday.

3 'You should be more careful', she told him.
advised   She ....
more careful.

4 'Why don't we buy Mark a present?' said Paul.
should   Paul ....
buy Mark a present.

5 As soon as I reached the station the train arrived.
sooner   No ....
the station than the train arrived.

6 If I were you, I would apologise.
you   Were .... apologise.

7 'Sit down!' the teacher told the children.
ordered   The teacher ....
sit down.

8 It was only when I arrived at work that I realised I had forgotten my briefcase.
did   Only when I arrived at work ....
....
that I had forgotten my briefcase.

9 'Don't forget to lock the door', Mum said to me.
reminded   Mum .... the door.

10 'You took my favourite CD', Jane said to Oliver.
of   Jane ....
her favourite CD.

11 He's a wonderful musician and a great artist as well.
only   Not ....
musician, but he's also a great artist.

12 Don't leave this room until I call you.
should   On no account ....
.... this room until I call you.

13 'Why are you baking a cake?' Dave asked Lisa.
was   Dave wanted to know ....
.... a cake.

14 If I had been asked, I would have helped.
asked   Had ....
I would have helped.

15 'I'm sorry I was late', he said.
for   He .... late.

16 'You must tidy your room before you go out', he said to Sally.
on   He ....
her room before she went out.

17 We had no idea she was a famous actress.
know   Little ....
she was a famous actress.

18 I had never eaten such delicious food before.
before   Never ....
such delicious food.

19 'I don't suppose you can help me with my homework?' Jim said to me.
whether   Jim wanted to know ....
.... with his homework.

20 I rarely have time to watch television.
have   Hardly ever ....
.... to watch television.

2 **Turn the following from direct into reported speech, using an appropriate introductory verb.**

21 'I promise I won't forget to call', Julie said to Tim.
....

22 'No, I didn't break the dish', Martin said.
....

23 'No, you may not watch the late film', Dad said to us.
....

24 'That's the best cake I've ever tasted!' said Joanne.
....

25 'You should go to the doctor's', Mum said to Peter.
....

26 'Let's go for a walk', he said.
....

27 'Please, please, take me with you!' he said to her.
....

28 'Everyone be quiet!' the teacher said to the class.
....

29 'Yes, I'll give you a lift into town', she said to him.
....

30 'I'll send you to your room if you misbehave', Dad said to Jamie.
....

31 'Could I have a cup of tea, please?' Pam said to me.
....

32 'It was me who spilt the coffee,' he said.
....

33 'Don't forget to do the shopping', she said to him.
....

34 'Put your hands up!' the policeman said to the thieves.
....

35 'You must stay for dinner', we said to them.
....

3 **Rewrite the sentences using emphatic constructions starting with the words given.**

36 Colin left the door open.
It was ....

37 She needs a new house.
What ....

38 Be quiet!
Do ....

39 When did you move to London?
When was ....

40 He promised to write to me.
He ....

1 **Choose the correct answer.**

1 If you had got up earlier, you .... the bus.
A wouldn't miss   B wouldn't have missed
C won't miss

2 Yesterday I went to the cinema and .... I had dinner with a friend.
A all in all   B as a result   C after that

3 If she .... her umbrella, she wouldn't have got wet.
A take   B had taken   C would take

4 Carol, ... parents own this shop, is very clever.
A who   B whom   C whose

5 .... you study hard, you will pass your exams.
A Supposing   B Providing   C Unless

6 Mark is kind .... funny.
A as a result   B as well as   C all in all

7 This computer game, ... I bought yesterday, is really boring.
A which   B that   C who

8 .... you wear warm clothes, you will catch a cold.
A Unless   B Providing   C If

9 If I finish work early tomorrow, I .... go to the cinema.
A would   B might   C should

10 I like to go out, ... Steve likes to stay in.
A due to   B whereas   C whenever

11 If I won the lottery, I .... whatever I liked.
A will buy   B can buy   C could buy

12 You can take the car ..... you promise to drive carefully.
A as long as   B as soon as   C such as

13 If he were more polite, he .... more popular.
A will be   B would be   C can be

14 This is the jacket .... I got for my birthday.
A which   B who   C when

15 Our new boss is very friendly, but .... he can be quite strict.
A moreover   B on the other hand   C also

16 If Jessica calls, ... her I'm out.
A will tell   B would tell   C tell

17 Jack is saving money .... buy a new car.
A in order that   B so that   C in order to

18 If I were you, I .... professional advice.
A would seek   B will seek   C can seek

19 Bob didn't attend the meeting, and .... the boss was angry with him.
A all in all   B because   C as a result

20 .... the car broke down, what would we do?
A Supposing   B Providing   C When

2 **Complete each sentence with two to five words, including the word in bold.**

21 Why don't you listen to me?
would   I wish .... to me.

22 It was Sunday, so the shops were closed.
due   The shops were closed, ...
.... it was Sunday.

23 I think it would be a good idea to get a mobile phone.
were   If .... get a mobile phone.

24 This is Mark. His mother is a teacher.
whose   This is Mark, ... a teacher.

25 If you go too near the river you will fall in.
else   Don't go too near the river ....
.... fall in.

26 There were a lot of people at the meeting. I had never met some of them before.
whom   There were a lot of people at the meeting
.... I had never met before.

27 I missed the train, so I was late.
result   I missed the train .... was late.

28 The weather was bad so it wasn't the perfect holiday.
for   But ....
would have been the perfect holiday.

29 If you don't work hard, you won't get promoted.
unless   You won't .... you work hard.

30 He forgot to lock the door. This was very careless of him.
which   He forgot to lock the door, ...
.... of him.

31 Sue would prefer to eat chocolate rather than eat salad.
rather   Sue ....
.... eat salad.

32 I was having fun. I stayed longer than I should have done.
such   I was having ....
longer than I should have done.

33 She looked like she was going to cry.
if   She looked .... to cry.

34 Although it was cold, we sat outside.
spite   In ...., we sat outside.

35 If Martin buys a car, he will be able to drive to work.
provided   Martin will be able to drive to work ....
.... a car.

36 I regret arguing with my best friend.
wish   I .... with my best friend.

37 He went to the bank to get some money.
so   He went to the bank .... money.

38 You should lock all the doors before you leave.
better   You ....
.... all the doors before you leave.

39 Take a torch. You might need it.
case   Take a torch .... it.

40 I was upset, that's why I didn't say anything.
would   If I hadn't been upset, ... something.

Progress Test 6 (Units 11-12)

1 Choose the correct answer.

1 She's really bossy, ...?
 A is she B was she C isn't she

2 Robert hurt .... while he was climbing up the tree.
 A him B himself C oneself

3 'Would you like .... ice cream?' 'Yes, please.'
 A some B any C no

4 She has been to nearly .... European capital.
 A each B every one C every

5 Let's call it a day, ...?
 A shall we B will we C won't we

6 We didn't go to the shops because .... wasn't enough time.
 A there B it C we

7 Sharon says she would do .... for her children.
 A nothing B something C anything

8 Penny and I call .... almost every day.
 A ourselves B each other C us

9 There's very .... time left. We need to hurry up.
 A a little B few C little

10 The ball hit Paul in .... eye.
 A one B the C his

11 .... would you rather be, an actor or an author?
 A Which B What C Who

12 There are .... people in this room. We can hardly move.
 A too much B too many C a lot

13 Everyone .... that the sun rises in the east.
 A knows B know C have known

14 Come and sit beside ....; there's plenty of room.
 A me B myself C my

15 'Did .... leave a message for me?' 'Yes. Here it is.'
 A anyone B someone C everyone

16 Jill and Emma are my friends, but .... of them lives near me.
 A both B neither C none

17 Some people are not upset by violence, but .... are.
 A another B the others C others

18 'Is Sue coming with us?' 'I .... She's pretty busy these days.'
 A imagine so B don't think so
 C suppose so

19 'Eva is Swedish.' '............ is Ingrid.'
 A So B Neither C Nor

20 Mary goes to the library .... Monday.
 A every other B each other C the other

2 Write questions to which the words in bold are the answers.

21 Susie is wearing **a dress**.
 ....

22 **Daniel** is washing the car.
 ....

23 Peter goes to college **every Wednesday**.
 ....

24 She is sending a parcel **to her sister**.
 ....

25 I am going shopping **because I want some new clothes**.
 ....

26 She has been living here **for two years**.
 ....

27 They went to work **by bus**.
 ....

28 Simon is going **to the cinema**.
 ....

29 **Claire** is watching television.
 ....

30 This suit cost **£80**.
 ....

3 Complete each sentence with two to five words, including the word in bold.

31 The only thing she hasn't eaten is the cabbage.
 everything She ....
 the cabbage.

32 He really had a good time at school today.
 himself He really .... today.

33 She is going on holiday alone this year.
 by She is going on holiday ....
 .... this year.

34 We could see that the two girls were very happy.
 of We could see that ....
 .... were very happy.

35 She didn't give any explanation for her absence.
 no She .... her absence.

36 There are only a few seats left on the bus.
 many There are .... on the bus.

37 Mum said that I could go wherever I liked as long as I was home before dark.
 anywhere Mum said that I .... as
 long as I was home before dark.

38 I visited Paul today. I visited Stuart, too.
 both I visited .... today.

39 Helen doesn't like loud music. Chris doesn't either.
 nor Neither ....
 likes loud music.

40 The shop sent me another person's order by mistake.
 someone The shop sent me ....
 by mistake.

Word List

A

abandon
absorbed
accountancy
accurately
advance
affect
aim at
alarm system
anniversary
announcement
annual
answering machine
appalling
applaud
appliance
assignment
asthma attack
at top speed
at the sight of
attempt
attend
attic
auction
available

B

bandage
bather
be bound to
be fast asleep
be in a good mood
be made redundant
be party to
beans
beforehand
bid
bid for
bin
bleed
blind
blunt
boarding school
bonds
bonfire
bounce
box-office hit
branch
bravery
breeze
brick wall
bridesmaid
bring to life
brooch
burst its banks

C

calculator
calendar
cancel
candidate
candlestick
carnation
cater for
ceremony
chairman
chalet
championship
charity
cheer
cheer sb on
chest
childminder
chimney
choir
chop
cinnamon
cloakroom
close down
clue
clumsy
coal
collective
collide
come face to face with sb
commit
committee
company
competitor
complex
complicated
condition
conduct
conference
confess
con man
consent
contact
contact lens
contain
contestant
contract
convenient
country lane
creep
cruise
cry
cultivate
culture
currency
current

custom
cutlery

D

dash
deal with
debts
decoration
degree
delay
delete
deliberately
demanding
demonstration
densely populated
deposit
developing countries
discharge
discourage
disgusting
display
distress signals
disturbing
documents
donate
doorframe
double glazing
doubt
dozens of
drama group
dreadful
dressmaking
dripping
drive

E

Earl
earn a reputation
edge
efficient
elect
election campaign
embarrassed
emblem
emergency
encouraging
engagement
ensure
equipment
erase
essay
estimate
evidence
exceed
exhaust fumes
exhibit

Word List

exhibition
expand
expedition
experiment
explode
extension
eye-witness

F

facilities
fasten one's seatbelt
fiancé
fibres
fierce
filling
fine
fireworks
firm
fishing line
fizzy drink
flat tyre
flexible hours
flock
flooding
flourish
for the time being
formula
fortune
found
fraud
fuel

G

gas plant
gasp
genuine
gesture
give sb a fright
glittering
global warming
govern
graceful
greet
grind
grounds
gust

H

hang out
hardships
have access
hay fever
heatwave
hesitate
honour

hopefully
hydrofoil

I

identical
identity
immature
impractical
impress
in advance
in one go
in public
income
independent
individual
infection
inhabitant
innocent
inspect
inspector
install
instant coffee powder
insult
intelligence service
interior decoration
intimidate
inventive
invest
investigation
investment
irritated

J

jury

L

label
laboratory
lace
lay the foundations
lead-free petrol
leak
lecture
licence
linen
literature
loan
locker
locket
lose one's temper
loss

M

maiden voyage

make a fuss
make it quick
malaria
manners
manual
mat
mature
mayfly
mean
measles
medication
mild
miner
moat
modernise
motion picture
mould
mumble

N

nasty
naughty
navy
needle
negotiations
nickname
nightmare
nomination

O

oak
objection
off duty
offence
office block
official
open
open-air
operate
operation
opponent
opposition
optician
originate from
ornament
out of breath
outfit
outing
overtake
overtime
oyster

P

pale
paperwork

parachute jump
particularly
passenger liner
patch
patent office
patience
paw
peaceful
pebble
performance
permanently
personal
pipe
platform
policy
power cut
premiere
presentation
preserve
press
press conference
priceless
privileged
process
profits
properly
property
propose
protest
prove
provide
prune
put up

Q

qualifications
quarrel
question
quit

R

radiator
radio operator
range
rattle
reach its peak
react
receipt book
recharge
reconsider
recover
recycle
reflect
refreshments

region
register
rehearse
reliable
remark
research
reside
resident
respected
reveal
review
riot
roast
route
row
ruby
runway
rusty

S

sack
safety regulations
sandstone
scented
scratch
seafront
seashell
seed
self-assured
sell out
sensible
sentence
set
settle
settle in
settlement
severe
sharp
shed
shelter
shift
shoot
shortcrust pastry
show off
shriek
shrink
shrub
sigh
skid
skill
sleep soundly
slightly
slippery
smash
smelling salts
snap

soak
soaking wet
soft drink
solid gold
sore throat
sour
specially
species
spectacular
spoil
spokesperson
sponsor
stain
stall
stamina
steep
stew
stiff
stone
stop dead
stop off
storey
stray
stressful
strike
study
suburbs
subway
sunscreen
supernatural
superstition
supervise
supplies
surgeon
surroundings
survey
suspect
sweep

T

tablecloth
take a bow
take a short cut
take action
take out a loan
take register
tap
tax
tear
tenant
testify
thoroughly
thread
throw a party
till
time off

Word List

tolerant
tournament
trademark
traffic warden
transport
treatment
trim
trophy
tropics
tutor

U

unique
unwilling
utterly

V

vacuum
valley
valuable

value
velvet
venue
verdict
viewer
vital
voting
voucher

W

wander
weapon
wear oneself out
well-kept
well-off
will
wire
withdraw
workforce
workings